Palgrave Studies in African and Development Economics

Series Editor
Arkebe Oqubay
British Academy Global Professor
SOAS University of London
London, UK

This series provides a wide-ranging analysis of African economics, development economics, and global transformation. Combing theoretical and empirical evidence, it offers thoughtful and policy relevant insight to the economic challenges and opportunities seen within the developing world. It engages with emerging and topical debates, including issues relating to sustainable development, food security, and the green transition, to make sure countries in Africa and the developing world are included in these important discussions.

Sean Gossel

The Promise and Peril of FDI in Sub-Saharan Africa

Overcoming Resource Dependence, Underdevelopment and Dysfunctional Capitalism

palgrave
macmillan

Sean Gossel
Graduate School of Business
University of Cape Town
Cape Town, South Africa

ISSN 3004-9601 ISSN 3004-961X (electronic)
Palgrave Studies in African and Development Economics
ISBN 978-3-032-01319-4 ISBN 978-3-032-01320-0 (eBook)
https://doi.org/10.1007/978-3-032-01320-0

This Palgrave Macmillan imprint is published by the registered company Springer Nature Switzerland AG.
The registered company address is: Gewerbestrasse 11, 6330 Cham, Switzerland

FOR YOLANDA AND SAM

Preface

Sub-Saharan Africa (SSA) is a region of immense potential but suffers from complex challenges and significant capital constraints. Despite experiencing robust economic growth since the 1990s, the region remains chronically poor and undeveloped. Foreign direct investment (FDI) has been touted as a means to directly support development by complementing domestic savings, strengthening financial systems, increasing liquidity, promoting global integration, and improving financial stability. FDI can also indirectly improve socio-economic development by enhancing knowledge transfers, technological advancements, and improved production and organisational systems. However, FDI may pose risks for an emerging country because the repatriation of capital could strain balance of payments, and the anticipated benefits may not spill over into the wider economy or could displace domestic investment. In addition, weak institutions, governance, and rule of law in host countries could attract FDI that contributes to environmental degradation, abuse of human and labour rights, and tax evasion.

To date, SSA has not attracted significant FDI and has consequently not reaped the envisaged benefits. Compared to other regions in the world, SSA remains at the low end of FDI recipients, receiving only 1.5% of cumulative world FDI. This book uses academic literature from the areas of development studies, institutional theory, political economics, and macroeconomics; along with indicative econometric and statistical analyses of long-run data, to explore the developmental prospects, risks, limitations, and implications of FDI to SSA.

The book argues that colonial legacies along with endogenous and exogenous policy choices have bequeathed SSA with a range of institutional weaknesses and socio-economic outcomes that create a vicious cycle by discouraging diversified FDI and instead entrenching resource extractive FDI. Unfortunately, this form of capital negates industrialization, beneficiation, and manufacturing; and locks much of SSA into neocolonial resource dependence, under-development, and dysfunctional capitalism instead. The book further argues that breaking this cycle will require considerable institutional and political reforms, which will need to be undertaken in a geopolitical environment fraught with competitive and transactional capitalism. The evidence thus shows that FDI to SSA is not an early-stage source of developmental capital and instead can significantly hinder socio-economic and political development. Hence, although FDI is found to be integrated into the region's trade, financial sector, and economic growth dynamics—suggesting that heightened FDI holds great promise for regional development—the benefits are only likely to be realised once SSA has progressed away from resource extraction to greater inter-African trade.

Cape Town, South Africa Sean Gossel

List of World Bank Country Codes

Country	*Code*
Angola	AGO
Benin	BEN
Botswana	BWA
Burkina Faso	BFA
Burundi	BDI
Cameroon	CMR
Central African Republic	CAF
Chad	TCD
Congo, Dem. Rep.	COD
Congo, Rep.	COG
Cote d'Ivoire	CIV
Equatorial Guinea	GNQ
Eritrea	ERI
Eswatini	SWZ
Ethiopia	ETH
Gabon	GAB
Gambia	GMB
Ghana	GHA
Guinea	GIN
Guinea-Bissau	GNB
Kenya	KEN
Lesotho	LSO
Liberia	LBR
Madagascar	MDG
Malawi	MWI
Mali	MLI
Mozambique	MOZ

Country	*Code*
Namibia	NAM
Niger	NER
Nigeria	NGA
Rwanda	RWA
Senegal	SEN
Sierra Leone	SLE
Somalia	SOM
South Africa	ZAF
South Sudan	SSD
Sudan	SDN
Tanzania	TZA
Togo	TGO
Uganda	UGA
Zambia	ZMB
Zimbabwe	ZWE

Map 1 Sub-Saharan Africa, All maps in this book were created using map. chart.net

Competing Interests The author has no competing interests to declare that are relevant to the content of this manuscript.

The World Stands on Three Things: Justice, Truth, and Peace
(R'Shimon ben Gamliel, Pirkey Avot, 1, 18).

Contents

1	**Introduction**	1
	1.1 Overview of FDI to SSA	6
	1.2 Overview of Key Theories of FDI	9
	1.3 Chapter Overview	12
	References	16
2	**The Colonial Legacies Hampering FDI to Sub-Saharan Africa**	23
	2.1 Border Design	25
	2.2 Political Geography	30
	2.3 Slavery	38
	2.4 Institutional Legacies	42
	References	54
3	**The Economic Policy Legacies Hampering FDI to Sub-Saharan Africa**	63
	3.1 The Rise and Fall of African Socialism	65
	3.2 The Rise and Fall of Neoliberalism	70
	3.3 From OAU to AU Agenda 2063	75
	3.4 From ODA to FDI in SSA	81
	References	88

4 The Relationship Between Democracy and FDI in Sub-Saharan Africa 97
4.1 Democracy and Capitalism 103
4.2 Democracy and Economic Growth 104
4.3 'Political Resource Curse' 107
4.4 Democratisation and FDI 111
4.5 Elections and FDI 116
References 122

5 The Relationship Between Corruption and FDI in Sub-Saharan Africa 135
5.1 Gatekeeper States and Dysfunctional Capitalism 140
5.2 Corruption and Democratisation 147
5.3 Political Corruption 151
5.4 Illicit Financial Flows and Capital Flight 154
5.5 Corruption and FDI 159
Appendices 166
References 167

6 The Effects of China, India, and Russia's Competing Strategies on FDI to Sub-Saharan Africa 183
6.1 China 194
6.2 India 202
6.3 Russia 209
Appendix 216
References 217

7 The Relationship Between Financial Sector Development and FDI in Sub-Saharan Africa 229
7.1 Bank-Led versus Market-Led Financial Sector Development 235
7.2 Sovereign Credit Ratings 240
7.3 Financial Sector Development and Democracy 244
7.4 The Financial Resource Curse 247
7.5 Financial Sector Development and FDI 253
Appendix 257
References 258

8 FDI and Sub-Saharan Africa's Economic Growth Cycle 275
8.1 Trade-Led Growth 278
8.2 FDI-Led Growth 283
8.3 Financial Sector Development and Economic Growth 289
8.4 Interlinkages 292
Appendices: TYDL Summary 297
References 303

Index 319

Abbreviations

AfCFTA	African Continental Free Trade Agreement
ANC	African National Congress
AOR	Association and organisational rights
APRM	African Peer Review Mechanism
AU	African Union
BRI	China's Belt and Road Initiative
CDF	Comprehensive Development Framework
CEO	Chief executive officer
CIT	Company income taxation
CL	Civil liberties
CPI	Corruption Perception Index
DD	'Dutch Disease'
DGI	Dan Gertler International
DoJ	US Department of Justice
ECOWAS	Economic Community of West African States
ELG	Export-led growth
EP	Electoral processes
EU	European Union
EUR	Euro
FDI	Foreign direct investment
FEB	Freedom of expression and beliefs
FG	Functioning of government
FOCAC	Forum on China-Africa Cooperation
FSD	Financial sector development
G8	Group of Eight
GDP	Gross domestic product
GLE	Growth-led exports

GNI	Gross national income
HDI	Human Development Index
ICT	Information and Communication Technology
IFF	Illicit financial flows
ILG	Import-led growth
IMF	International Monetary Fund
IQI	Institutional Quality Index
ISI	Import substitution industrialisation
IT	Information technology
JSE	Johannesburg Stock Exchange
KGB	Committee for State Security (USSR)
LOF	Liability of foreignness (Glaister et al., 2020)
M&A	Mergers and acquisitions
MENA	Middle East and North Africa
MFI	Microfinance institution
MPLA	Movimento Popular de Libertação de Angola
MTEF	Medium term expenditure framework
NELB	New Eurasian Lan Bridge (BRI)
NELDA	National Elections Across Democracy and Autocracy
NEPAD	New Partnership for Africa's Development
NGO	non-governmental organisation
NPA	National Prosecuting Authority of South Africa
NPM	New public management
OAU	Organisation of African Unity
ODA	Official development assistance
OECD	Organisation for Economic Cooperation and Development
OLI	Ownership Location Internalisation theory of Dunning (1977)
PAB	Pan African bank
PAIR	Personal autonomy and individual rights
PPP	Pluralism and participation
PR	Political rights
PR	Public relations
R&D	Research and development
REC	African Regional Economic Communities
REER	Real effective exchange rate
RL	Rule of law
SADC	Southern African Development Community
SADCC	Southern African Development Coordination Conference
SAP	Structural adjustment program
SCR	Sovereign credit rating
SIC	Schwartz information criterion
SOE	State owned enterprise

SSA	Sub-Saharan Africa
TYDL	Toda and Yamamoto (1995) and Dolado and Lutkepohl (1996)
UK	United Kingdom
UN	United Nations
UNCTAD	United Nations Conference on Trade and Development
UNDP	United Nations Development Program
UNICEF	United Nations International Children's Emergency Fund
USA	United States of America
USD	United States Dollar
USSR	Union of Soviet Socialist Republics
VAR	Vector autoregression
WHO	World Health Organisation
WTO	World Trade Organisation

List of Figures

Fig. 1.1	Net FDI inflows. (Data source: World Development Indicators)	7
Fig. 1.2	Regional net FDI inflows. (Data source: World Development Indicators)	7
Fig. 2.1	Herbst (2000) categorisation and socio-economic performance. (Data sources: World Development Indicators, World Goverenance)	33
Fig. 3.1	GDP and per capita growth in SSA. (Data source: World Development Indicators)	80
Fig. 3.2	ODA, foreign debt, and FDI to SSA. (Data source: World Development Indicators)	82
Fig. 4.1	Polity V democracy ratings. (Data source: ourworldindata.org, Polity V)	98
Fig. 4.2	FDI and democracy. (Data sources: Polity V, Freedom House, World Development Indicators)	115
Fig. 4.3	Elections and FDI in SSA. (Data sources: NELDA, World Development Indicators)	121
Fig. 5.1	Emerging country corruption perceptions indices. (Data source: Transparency International)	138
Fig. 5.2	Scatterplot of corruption and democracy in SSA. (Sources: Transparency International, Polity V)	150
Fig. 5.3	Scatterplots of net FDI inflows and corruption perceptions index. (Data sources: World Bank, Transparency International)	161
Fig. 5.4	Scatterplots of net FDI outflows and corruption perceptions index. (Data sources: World Bank, Transparency International)	162
Fig. 5.5	Net FDI inflows and illicit financial flows. (Source: World Development Indicators, Global Financial Integrity)	164

Fig. 5.6 Net FDI outflows and illicit financial flows. (Source: World Development Indicators, Global Financial Integrity) 165
Fig. 6.1 China's FDI to SSA. (Data source: SAIS-CARI) 198
Fig. 6.2 Total Chinese FDI to SSA. (Data source: SAIS-CARI, 2003–2020, * indicates natural resource dependent) 199
Fig. 6.3 Chinese FDI composition to SSA (Figure 6.3 excludes the two sectors of leasing and commercial services, and scientific research and technological services due to paucity of the data.). (Data source: SAIS-CARI, 2013–2020) 201
Fig. 6.4 Scatterplot of Chinese FDI flows and SSA's institutional quality. (Data sources: SAIS-CARI, World Bank) 203
Fig. 6.5 India's regional FDI strategies. (Source: Author's compilation based on Chaudhry et al. (2018) and Reserve Bank of India data) 206
Fig. 6.6 Indian FDI outflows. (Data source: Reserve Bank of India) 207
Fig. 6.7 Indian Sectoral FDI. (Data source: Reserve Bank of India) 208
Fig. 6.8 Indian FDI to SSA (excluding Mauritius). (Data source: Reserve Bank of India) 209
Fig. 7.1 Regional FSD. (Data source: IMF) 230
Fig. 7.2 Average SCRs in SSA. (Data sources: S&P, Fitch, Freedom House) 232
Fig. 7.3 Scatterplot of FSD and democracy. (Data sources: Polity V, IMF) 248
Fig. 7.4 Scatterplots of FSD and institutional quality. (Data sources: World Governance Indicators, IMF) 252
Fig. 7.5 Scatterplot of FSD and FDI inflows. (Data sources: World Development Indicators, IMF) 255
Fig. 7.6 Scatterplot of FSD and FDI inflows excluding outliers. (Data sources: World Development Indicators, IMF) 256
Fig. 8.1 Economic growth cycle 277
Fig. 8.2 Economic growth and trade. (Data source: World Development Indicators) 282
Fig. 8.3 Selected commodity prices and FDI inflows to SSA. (Data sources: Federal Reserve Economic Data and World Development Indicators) 287
Fig. 8.4 Economic growth and FDI. (Data source: World Development Indicators) 288
Fig. 8.5 FSD and economic growth. (Data source: World Development Indicators) 291
Fig. 8.6 Economic growth cycle in Sub-Saharan Africa. (Data sources: World Development Indicators. Exports are exports of goods and services (% of GDP), FDI is net FDI inflows (% of GDP), Imports are imports of goods and services (% of GDP), FSD is domestic credit to private sector (% of GDP), and GDPG is GDP growth (annual %)) 296

List of Maps

Map 1	Sub-Saharan Africa, All maps in this book were created using map.chart.net	xi
Map 1.1	Oil rents	4
Map 1.2	Ores and metals exports	5
Map 1.3	Agricultural raw materials exports	6
Map 2.1	Cultural provinces in pre-colonial Africa. Source: Michalopoulos and Papaioannou (2013)	27
Map 2.2	Herbst political geography. Source: Author's compilation based on Herbst (2000)	32
Map 2.3	Incidence of Trypanosomiasis in sub-Saharan Africa. Source: Masocha and Kristensson (2019)	36
Map 2.4	Incidence of malaria in sub-Saharan Africa. Data source: World Development Indicators averaged over 2000–2020	37
Map 2.5	Number of slaves exported during the slave trades. Source: Nunn (2017, p. 43)	41
Map 5.1	Average corruption perceptions index (2012–2020). (Source: Author's compilation from Transparency International data, categorised from Warf (2017))	139
Map 5.2	Illicit financial flows as a percentage of total trade. (Source: Author's compilation from Global Financial Integrity data)	156
Map 6.1	Russia's military involvement in Africa. (Source: Author's compilation from Scorpio (2019))	213

List of Tables

Table 1.1	Regional indicators	2
Table 2.1	Economic performance in landlocked and non-landlocked SSA countries	29
Table 2.2	Economic performance by malaria incidence	38
Table 2.3	Indicators by slavery incidence	42
Table 2.4	Quality of institutions in SSA by colonial power	45
Table 2.5	FDI to SSA by former colonial power	48
Table 2.6	SSA country-specific colonial disadvantage exposure	51
Table 3.1	Regional net FDI inflows	85
Table 3.2	Net FDI inflows to SSA	86
Table 4.1	SSA Polity V categories	99
Table 4.2	SSA regimes	102
Table 4.3	Natural resource-related democracy and economic performance	114
Table 4.4	Post-liberalisation democracy and economic performance	116
Table 4.5	Adverse election events	117
Table 5.1	Granger causality results of net FDI and the corruption perceptions index	162
Table 5.2	Granger causality results between net FDI and illicit financial flows	166
Table 6.1	Regional Economic Communities	185
Table 6.2	Economic performance of the Regional Economic and Monetary Communities	187
Table 6.3	Granger causality results between Chinese FDI flows and SSA's IQI	204
Table 7.1	Regional domestic credit	239
Table 7.2	SCR changes in SSA	242

Table 7.3 FSD and democracy 249
Table 7.4 FSD and the institutional quality 253
Table 7.5 FSD and FDI 257
Table 8.1 Trade and economic growth 283
Table 8.2 FDI and economic growth 288
Table 8.3 FSD and economic growth 292

CHAPTER 1

Introduction

Sub-Saharan Africa (SSA) is a region of immense opportunities and complex challenges. Home to over 1.1 billion people (15% of the world's population), SSA comprises 49 countries spanning four time zones, covering more than 15% of the world's land surface (AfDB, 2023). Yet, as shown in Table 1.1(a), despite having the fastest population growth, SSA has the lowest life expectancy, literacy rates, urban population, and the worst infant and child mortality rates. SSA is however renowned for having the highest natural resource endowments in the world, including the largest arable landmass, the second largest tropical forest, 30% of global mineral reserves (including abundant asbestos, chromite, coal, cobalt, columbite tantalum, copper, and uranium), 8% of the world's oil reserves, 7% of the world's natural gas reserves, the highest reserves of platinum and diamonds, and 40% of the world's gold deposits (Taylor, 2012, pp. 99–100; AfDB, 2016). Table 1.1(b) further shows that SSA's contribution to world trade has remained stubbornly low at around 3% (IMF, 2022) even though total trade comprises 47.4% of SSA's gross domestic product (GDP). While average merchandise trade from SSA is an impressive 40.4% of GDP, which is higher than from Latin America and Caribbean (30.1%), East Asia and Pacific (38.1%), and North America (24.9%), a significant portion of this merchandise trade is in natural resources. SSA's agricultural and ores and metals raw materials exports comprise the highest component of merchandise exports of any region in the world (at 5.1% and 12.5%

S. Gossel, *The Promise and Peril of FDI in Sub-Saharan Africa*, Palgrave Studies in African and Development Economics, https://doi.org/10.1007/978-3-032-01320-0_1

Table 1.1 Regional indicators

Average (1970–2020)	*Unit*	*Sub-Saharan Africa*	*East Asia & Pacific*	*Latin America & Caribbean*	*Middle East & North Africa*	*North America*	*Europe & Central Asia*	*World*
(a) Human capital:								
Life expectancy at birth	Years	51.7	69.4	68.7	65.5	76.0	73.0	66.3
Literacy rate of youth	% of people ages 15–24	69.4	95.0	93.6	79.7	99.6	99.2	85.4
Mortality rate under-5	Per 1000 live births	126.9	32.1	29.8	38.3	8.0	17.6	64.6
Population growth	Annual %	2.8	1.2	1.7	2.5	1.0	0.5	1.5
Urban population	% of total population	29.4	39.6	71.7	55.9	77.5	67.8	45.4
Gross domestic savings	% of GDP	25.4	33.8	21.0	33.2	20.1	23.5	25.1
(b) Trade:								
Trade	% of GDP	47.4	45.4	36.2	72.0	24.9	61.4	44.1
Merchandise trade	% of GDP	40.4	38.1	30.1	54.7	19.6	48.0	35.4
Agricultural raw materials	% of merchandise exports	5.1	1.9	3.5	0.3	4.3	2.1	3.0
Oil rents	% of GDP	4.7	0.8	2.9	22.9	0.7	0.6	1.7
Ores and metals	% of merchandise exports	12.5	2.8	11.0	4.9	4.2	3.3	4.1

Data source: World Development Indicators

respectively compared to the world averages of 3.0% and 4.1%), while oil exports from SSA were second behind the Middle East and North Africa (MENA) (4.7% and 22.9% respectively).

In theory, the extraction and export of natural resources could fund economic growth and development in SSA by overcoming the human capital and infrastructure deficits that hamper sustainable and inclusive socio-economic progress (Deaton, 1999; Lundgren et al., 2013). Yet, although SSA has experienced robust economic growth since the 1990s, it remains the most chronically poor and undeveloped region in the world (World Bank, 2019). The contradiction between Africa's resource exports and ongoing poverty is commonly ascribed to the Resource Curse, Political Resource Curse, and Dutch Disease (Auty, 1993; Sachs & Warner, 1995) whereby resource rents are used to maintain patron-client relationships among a predatory elite, entrenching weak institutions, rule of law, and endemic corruption (Van der Ploeg, 2011), and thus negatively affecting socio-economic development and stability (UNDP, 2016). Hence, rather than driving economic growth and development, SSA's natural resources have entrenched multifaceted political and institutional problems (Bresser-Pereira, 2020).

One of the reasons for this contradiction between resource wealth and poor developmental outcomes relates to SSA's high degree of natural resource export concentration. Studies show that the less diversified an economy's export mix, the more likely it is to suffer from the Resource Curse (Sachs & Warner, 1995). In many SSA countries, exports of just two or three primary commodities commonly account for over 80% of merchandise exports (UNCTAD, 2019). Maps 1.1, 1.2, 1.3 show that over the last fifty years,[1] 43% of SSA (18 out of 42 SSA countries) can be classified as significantly resource export dependent.[2] Among the most oil export-dependent SSA countries are South Sudan (31.9% of GDP), the Congo (28.9%), Angola (27.6%), and Equatorial Guinea (27.1%) while the most ore and mineral export-dependent countries are Zambia (79.5% of merchandise exports), Liberia (69.9%), the Democratic Republic of the Congo (66.1%), Guinea (55.5%), Niger (46.3%), Mozambique (34.9%), Togo (30.5%), and Rwanda (29.5%). Lastly, the most agricultural export-dependent SSA countries are Chad (67.8% of merchandise exports), Benin

[1] Data sourced from the World Development Indicators covering the period of 1970–2020.

[2] A country is categorised as resource dependent if natural resource exports exceed 25% of total exports (IMF, 2012).

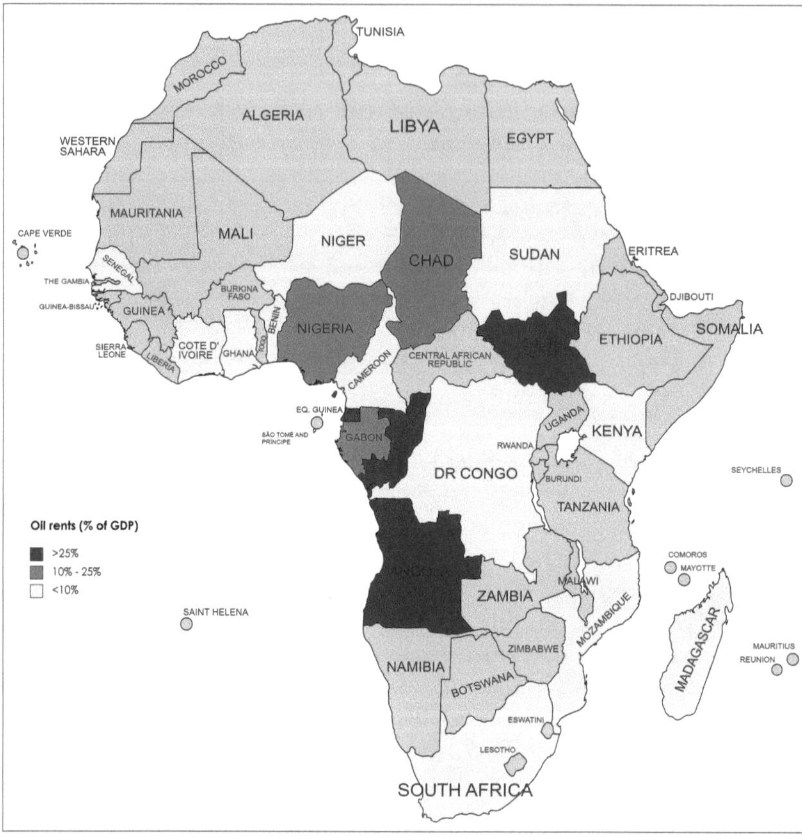

Map 1.1 Oil rents

(46.6%), Burkina Faso (38.7%), Mali (35.8%), Central African Republic (33.9%), and Sudan (31.5%).

It has thus been argued that foreign direct investment (FDI) can alleviate SSA's developmental impediments and increase economic growth (Reisen, 1998; Mody & Murshid, 2005) by supplementing domestic savings, driving financial sector development, improving liquidity, deepening international integration, and enhancing financial stability (World Bank, 1999; Henry, 2000), as well as fostering knowledge, technological, production, and organisational spillover effects (de Mello, 1997, 1999; Borensztein et al., 1998). However, many studies also show that FDI may

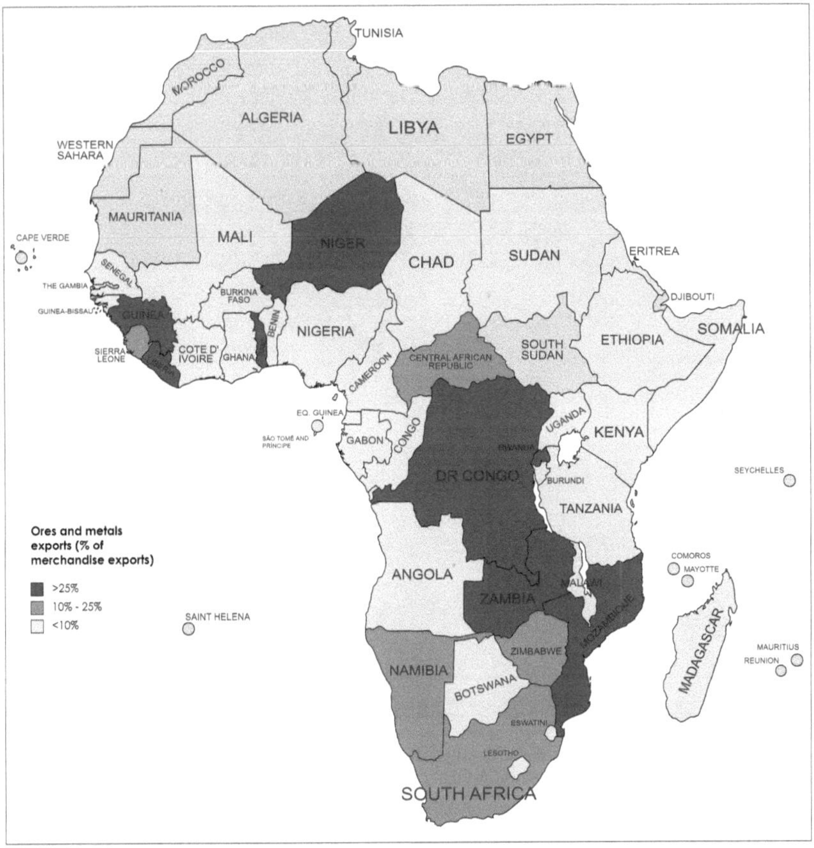

Map 1.2 Ores and metals exports

pose risks for an emerging country because capital flight and the repatriation of capital could weaken balance of payments, and the spillover effects may not feed through into the rest of the host economy or crowd out domestic investment (Markusen & Venables, 1999; OECD, 2002). In addition, weak institutions and rule of law in host countries may attract FDI prone to environmental degradation, human and labour rights abuses, and tax evasion (Resnick, 2001; Busse, 2004; Gehlbach & Keefer, 2011).

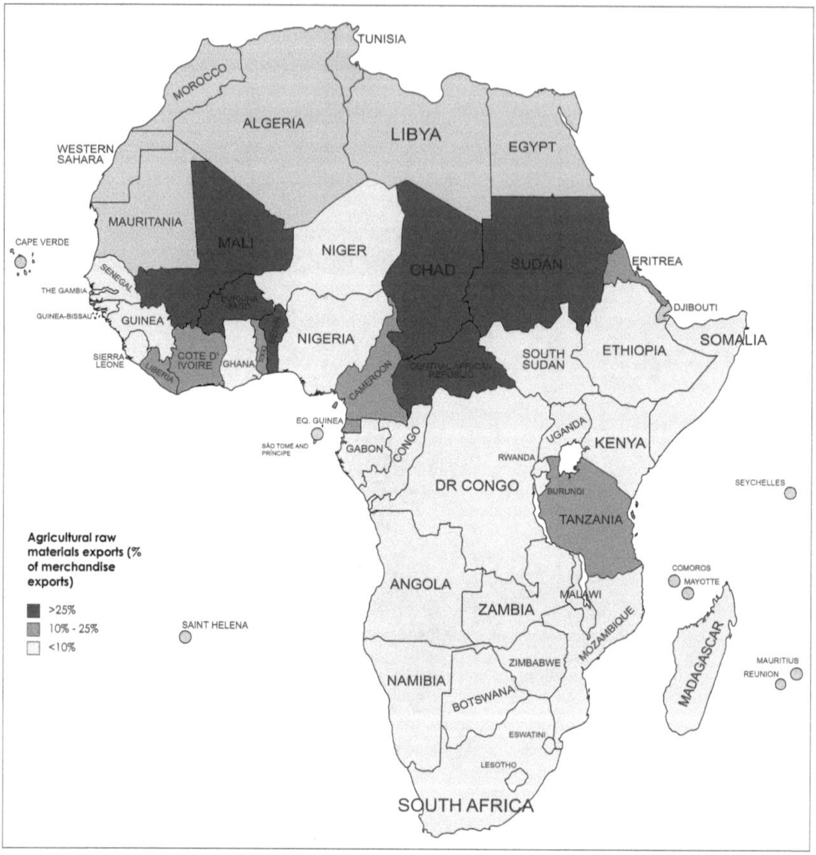

Map 1.3 Agricultural raw materials exports

1.1 Overview of FDI to SSA

Over the last few decades, FDI has been a significant source of developmental capital and thus emerging countries actively compete to attract FDI (Farole & Winkler, 2014, p. 9; Ayenew, 2022). Despite the optimism, SSA has not as yet attracted significant FDI and has consequently not reaped the envisaged benefits (Taylor, 2012, pp. 100–101). As can be seen from Fig. 1.1, over the last fifty years, world net FDI inflows rose dramatically from just USD 12.4 billion in 1970, peaking at USD 3.2 trillion in 2007, before falling back to USD 1.2 trillion in 2020 (after a

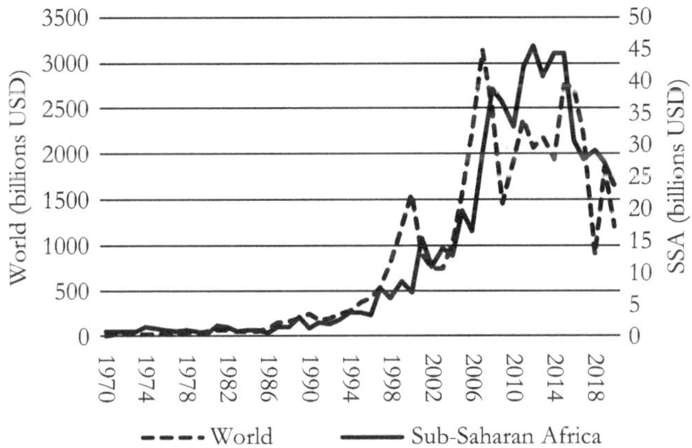

Fig. 1.1 Net FDI inflows. (Data source: World Development Indicators)

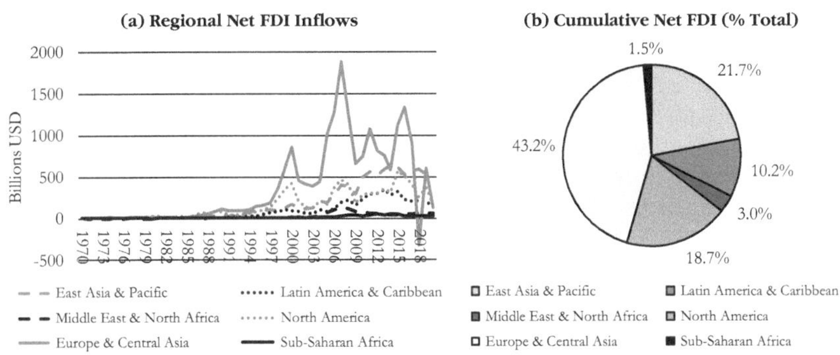

Fig. 1.2 Regional net FDI inflows. (Data source: World Development Indicators)

resurgence to USD 2.7 trillion in 2015 and 2016). Over the same period, FDI to SSA similarly increased dramatically, from just USD 800 million in 1970 to a high of USD 45.5 billion in 2012, before declining to USD 23.6 billion in 2020.

Figure 1.2 however shows that compared to other regions in the world, SSA remains at the low end of FDI recipients, receiving only 1.5% of cumulative world FDI. The bulk of world FDI therefore flows to the four regions of Europe and Central Asia (43.2%), East Asia and Pacific (21.7%), North America (18.7%), Latin America and the Caribbean (10.2%), and the Middle East and North Africa (3.0%). According to UNCTAD (2024), the top four FDI investing countries in SSA are the Netherlands (USD 109 billion), France (USD 58 billion), the USA (46 billion), and the UK (USD 46 billion).

Despite the generalised terminology, there are three forms of FDI. The first is equity-based FDI, which occurs when a company in one country invests directly in a company in another country, typically via mergers and acquisitions (M&A). In recent years, 15% of FDI to Africa consisted of cross-border M&A (UNCTAD, 2024). Equity-based FDI differs from indirect investment such as portfolio investment because the investment is not made in equities listed in a country's stock exchange. Instead, the investing company seeks to acquire "a lasting interest" and "an effective voice" in the management and/or control of the foreign company (IMF, 1993). Hence, portfolio investment tends to be more passive, focusing on returns, while FDI is more active, focusing on control, management, and ownership of a particular company or group of related companies (Marandu & Ditshweu, 2018).

The second is greenfield FDI, which occurs when a multinational parent company sets up a new subsidiary or expands their business operations in another country. Greenfield FDI thus uses less M&A than equity-based FDI, although there is evidence that M&A drives greenfield investment (Calderón et al., 2004). Moses' (2023) review of energy projects in Africa finds that over the period of 2012–2021, greenfield FDI totalled USD 103.8 billion while M&A totalled USD 44.8 billion. Empirically however, it has been found that although greenfield FDI has a positive effect on poverty reduction, it does not significantly affect economic growth in SSA (Anetor, 2025).

The third type of FDI is brownfield FDI, which is when a company invests in an existing production facility or infrastructure needed to commence operating in a foreign country. Unlike greenfield FDI, brownfield FDI can entail the use of M&A or leasing. Although aggregate data for SSA are scant, it is logical to presume that as a result of SSA's significant infrastructure gaps (Calderon et al., 2018), natural resource dependence (UNCTAD, 2019), and limited financial sector development (IMF, 2016), the majority of FDI to SSA is in the form of greenfield rather than brownfield or equity-based FDI.[3]

[3]The discussion in the rest of this book does not differentiate between these three forms of FDI because of a lack of suitable data and because most of the academic theories and empirical literature only consider FDI broadly.

1.2 Overview of Key Theories of FDI

Beyond the typology of FDI, there is a vast theoretical and empirical literature on the motivations of FDI, and the brief discussion below thus focusses on the seven most predominant theories that have emerged since the 1960s.

(a) Industrial Organisation Theory

Industrial Organisation Theory (Hymer, 1960; Calvet, 1981) posits that companies operating in a country will have to compete with domestic companies in that country. These domestic companies have a range of advantages, including a knowledge of consumer preferences, languages, cultures, and legal and political systems. Foreign companies therefore use FDI to take advantage of market imperfections arising from economies of scale, technological and human capital disparities, patent-protected products, brand recognition, management skills, distribution networks, product diversification, and credit access (Lall, 1976; Kindleberger, 1969).

(b) Production Cycle Theory

Production Cycle Theory (Vernon, 1966) argues that there are four stages in the production cycle: innovation, growth, maturity, and decline. In the first stage, companies develop new products for domestic consumption and any surplus is then exported internationally thereafter. In the second stage, demand in the export markets is sufficient to warrant manufacturing in the foreign market and thus exports from the domestic market decline, replaced by production in the foreign market. In the third stage, the use of innovative technologies and low-skilled cheap labour in the foreign country allows the company to compete with companies in more developed economies. The final stage is when the foreign country becomes an import rather than an export market, and comparative advantage thus shifts to other countries. Production Cycle Theory therefore posits that FDI is primarily associated with the second and third stages (growth and maturity respectively).

(c) Internalisation Theory

Internalisation Theory (Buckley & Casson, 1976) states that companies that specialise in innovative knowledge-intensive industries and/or industries that make use of components and raw materials that are difficult to measure and control (Casson, 2015) will take advantage of imperfections in the intermediate product markets. This is achieved by controlling the knowledge flows from research and development (R&D) to production using proprietary knowledge, patents, or trademarks (Dunning & Lundan, 2008); or by controlling flows of components and raw materials from upstream production facilities to downstream facilities (Rugman, 1981). In effect, the theory posits that companies use FDI to "internalize the market in knowledge within the firm" (Casson, 2015), particularly in environments of high market risks, transaction costs, and uncertainty. It has been claimed that Internalisation stimulates a company to become a multinational because the internalised knowledge that is centralised in the home country company is diffused to the company's subsidiaries in other countries via greenfield FDI (ibid.).

(d) Differential Rates of Return Theory

The Differential Rates of Return Theory (Calvet, 1981) hypothesises that capital will flow from rich countries to poor countries in order to benefit from the higher rates of return (interest rates) in poor countries (Okafor et al., 2015). This theory therefore considers capital as a commodity, and consequently, the price determines supply, demand, and allocation (Abdulai, 2007). However, since this theory focusses on the sourcing and allocation of capital, it does not consider the purpose of the investment and thus does not consider any of the motivations associated with Industrial Organisation Theory. In addition, studies show that despite the potential returns, significant capital does not flow from developed to developing countries (the Lucas Paradox), mainly because of the associated risk and uncertainty (Lucas, 1990). Consequently, the differential rates of return theory is more applicable to portfolio investment than to FDI.

(e) Eclectic Paradigm Theory

The Eclectic Paradigm Theory (OLI) of Dunning (1977) combines Industrial Organisation and Internalisation theories and argues that companies will take advantage of ownership (O), location (L), and internalisation (I) competitive advantages when expanding abroad (Dunning, 1980, 1998). OLI thus seeks "to offer a holistic framework by which it is possible to identify and evaluate the significance of the factors influencing both the initial act of foreign production by enterprises and the growth of such production" (Dunning, 1988, p. 1). OLI is widely regarded as the most comprehensive framework for examining the motives for international business (Verbeke, 2009).

The ownership advantages (O) refer to the activities of the company that underlie the ability to generate profits and growth (da Silva Lopez, 2010). The location (L) benefits arise from the geographic positioning of the tangible and intangible assets that can generate future profits or by taking advantage of location-specific benefits such as low tax rates, production costs, transport costs, access to large and growing markets, markets with few competitors, or lower risks (Dunning & Lundan, 2008). In the case of FDI, the location benefits arise from the immobility of beneficial factors such as low labour costs, specialised knowledge or highly skilled human capital, market dynamics, or natural resources (Okafor et al., 2015). Lastly, the Internalisation benefits arise from the advantageous application of ownership and location (OL) whereby the company can use its international location advantages to exploit its core competencies (da Silva Lopez, 2010). Ownership (O) is therefore the 'why', Location (L) is the 'where', and Internalisation (I) is the 'how' (Wilson & Baack, 2012).

(f) Advantage Seeking Theories

Advantage Seeking FDI theories arise from Dunning's Eclectic Paradigm and argue that FDI is motivated by market seeking, efficiency seeking, strategic asset seeking, and resource seeking opportunities (Dunning, 1977, 1993). Market seeking FDI takes advantage of growing demand in foreign markets by entering, expanding, or serving the product or production needs of the destination market (Asiedu, 2002). Efficiency seeking FDI is an outcome of the Location component of Dunning's Eclectic Paradigm whereby FDI is channelled to foreign countries that can provide macroeconomic, human capital, institutional, or social factors that will enable the investing company to benefit from heightened production efficiencies and thus compete internationally (Jovanovic & Rousseau, 2008). Strategic asset seeking FDI arises from a company's ability to direct its Internalisation advantages to gain a strategic advantage over its competitors through augmentation or internationalisation (Meyer, 2015). Resource seeking FDI is driven by the opportunity to extract natural resources or to gain from low-cost unskilled or semi-skilled labour in developing countries (Dunning, 1993).

(g) Push-Pull Theory

Push-Pull Theory posits that capital will flow out (pushed) from source countries in search of investment opportunities abroad and can be attracted (pulled) by domestic factors in destination countries (Koepke, 2019). Empirical studies have found that the most significant push factors are changes in international interest rates, economic growth, and investor risk appetite while the most significant pull factors are fiscal policies, trade openness, creditworthiness, private consumption, country risk premiums, and institutional quality (Gossel & Biekpe, 2017). Prior to the 1990s, it was assumed that if capital flows are driven primarily by push factors then policy makers in recipient countries would only have a marginal ability to formulate policies that would pull capital from source to destination countries (Fernandez-Arias & Montiel, 1996). However, after the 1990s, empirical evidence found that even if capital flows are driven by push factors, policy makers in recipient countries can still design policies to shape the inflows and outflows (Taylor & Sarno, 1997) or to shift the composition of capital flows in favour of FDI (Montiel & Reinhart, 1999; Kim, 2000). As the subsequent chapter of this book will show, the theories most applicable to SSA are Eclectic Paradigm (OLI), market and resource advantage seeking, and push-pull theory.

1.3 Chapter Overview

This book uses academic literature from the areas of development studies, institutional theory, political economy, and macroeconomics; along with econometric and statistical analyses of long-run data to explore the developmental prospects, risks, limitations, and implications of FDI to SSA. The chapters proceed as follows.

Centuries of colonial exploitation of SSA's natural resources and control of industrialisation, production, and consumption has limited the ability of post-independent SSA countries to transition from natural resource extraction to manufacturing (Acemoglu & Robinson, 2013, p. 115). Ongoing resource export dependence has also entrenched a range of socio-political, institutional, and developmental legacies. Chapter 2 thus explores how colonial border design, political geography, and slavery have affected SSA's institutional development, and hindered SSA's ability to attract FDI.

Following the end of colonialism, post-independent SSA states suffered from the colonially entrenched weak and fragile linkages between government institutions and society (Young, 1988), exacerbated by the international Cold War geopolitical dynamics and then by the developmental distortions arising from the World Bank and IMF's neoliberal reform agendas. Thus, post-independent SSA was significantly shaped by the conflicting pressures and tensions between domestic policy ideology and international realpolitik. Chapter 3 therefore explores how post-independent economic policies and global geopolitics shaped SSA's FDI flows. The discussion commences with a review of the three post-independent political economic waves. First, African Socialism and the Cold War. Second, Neoliberalism, the Washington Consensus, and Structural Adjustment Programs. Third, the African Union (AU), New Partnership for Africa's Development (NEPAD), Agenda 2063, and globalisation. Thereafter, the chapter explores the effects of these ideologies and policies on SSA's FDI inflows.

After examining how colonialism and domestic and international geopolitics have shaped SSA's post-independent FDI, the discussion next considers the effects of democracy. Africa has experienced three waves of democratisation (Guseh & Oritsejafor, 2005). The first was the long struggle for independence from colonial rule throughout the nineteenth and twentieth centuries. The second wave then covered the short period from independence in the 1960s to the end of the 1970s. The third wave started with the fall of the Union of Soviet Socialist Republics (USSR) in 1989, leading to the subsequent emergence of pro-democracy movements. Since the reforms of the 1990s, SSA, in common with many countries in Latin America and Asia, undertook democratic reforms while also liberalising their trade, capital, labour, and technology arrangements (Gossel, 2017). However, most SSA countries fall in the 'grey zone' between democracy and autocracy, characterised by populism, unaccountable leadership, and weak institutions (Dumludag, 2009). These systemic deficiencies are an outcome of both post-colonial institutional voids and the effects of post-Washington Consensus "partial reform syndrome" (van der Walle, 2001:16). In SSA's many resource export-dependent states this has given rise to rentier states (Beblawi & Luciani, 1987), which are characterised by dependence on resource rent-seeking opportunities and neopatrimonial clientelism (Pitcher, 2012, p. 8) Hence, rentier states do not rely on taxation revenues (McGuirk, 2013; Mlambo, 2022) and are accordingly unresponsive to the needs and demand of citizens (Desierto,

2018), and thus lack the impetus to develop sophisticated institutions and government (Mkandawire, 2001). These deficiencies in turn discourage manufacturing-based FDI in favour of resource-extractive FDI, which locks most of SSA into an extractive cycle of patronage, patron-clientelism, and democratic dysfunction. Chapter 4 thus explores the association between democracy and economic growth, and the effects of the political resource curse before focussing on the relationship between democratisation and FDI, and elections and FDI.

Although corruption in SSA is an intrinsic feature of the aforementioned weaknesses, it has its roots in the legacies of colonialism. Systemically, colonialism imposed domestically unaccountable administration that protected the interests of foreign powers while institutionalising corruption, entrenching 'might is right', and fragmenting ethnic identities and societies (Zalanga, 2018). In the first decades after independence, the elites used wealth and power for their financial benefit and to maintain their hold on power (*ibid*). In the wake of the neoliberal reforms however, formally centralised corruption devolved into decentralised bribery (Shah, 2006) while neoliberal privatisation of many public services and assets birthed a new round of patron-client corruption as many international companies were willing to pay bribes and engage in illegal activities to secure lucrative contracts (Jeffries, 1993; Carmody, 2016, p. 21). Corruption in SSA hinders socio-economic development and good governance and thus continues to hamper SSA's ability to reverse the region's significant poverty levels, widening inequality and fostering social instability as political leaders, public officials, and private sector companies and individuals encourage public programs and procurement for self-enrichment (Mbaku, 2010, p. 3). Hence, Chap. 5 first explores how SSA's post-independent political economic development entrenched corruption and then examines the relationship between democracy and corruption, before focussing more specifically on political corruption. The chapter then turns to the effects of capital flows, first by considering illicit financial flows and capital flight, and thereafter, the relationship between corruption and FDI.

As SSA's developmental challenges cascaded in the decades after independence, Western countries gradually lost interest in SSA, turning their attention to other developing regions in the world, particularly Asia (Signe, 2018). However, this void was soon filled by emerging countries such as China, India, and Russia who actively sought to entrench themselves as SSA's development partners, and thus as beneficiaries of SSA's potential and opportunities. It was only in the last two decades that the West returned its attention to SSA, after China, India, and Russia's economic and political activities threatened to usurp Western interests. Chapter 6 thus explores how China, India, and Russia have each adopted different strategies to engage with SSA politically and economically and considers the implications for SSA's FDI in the contestation between the West and East.

In accordance with the IMF and the World Bank's neoliberal reforms, many SSA countries liberalised their financial markets but despite these programs (and subsequent improved financial integration), financial sector development (FSD) in SSA still lags other regions in the world. Domestically, SSA's relatively undeveloped FSD may be a contributor to the region's instability by heightening economic growth volatility and lowering potential consumption and investment growth (Ibrahim & Alagidede, 2017). Among the most important gatekeepers for FSD are the international ratings agencies. Countries with low sovereign credit ratings (SCRs) have difficulty accessing international credit markets, have higher cost of capital and borrowing costs, and attract more "hot money" flows than FDI (Mensah et al., 2017). By their nature, natural resource-dependent states derive most of their revenues from the export taxes and resource extraction royalties of international resource companies rather than from the wealth, savings, and taxation of the citizenry (Mcferson, 2010). Hence, an SCR downgrade in a resource-dependent state will increase the cost of doing business for resource companies, thus leading to economic hardship, which in turn will raise the risk of socio-political instability, creating a vicious cycle (Leite & Weidmann, 1999; Isham et al., 2005). Consequently, resource-dependent states tend to have lower SCRs than more diversified countries and thus SSA's natural resource dependence may act as a channel between SCR changes and socio-economic and political risk. However, despite these challenges, in recent decades, SSA has experienced rapid expansion in pan-African banks, mobile money, online financial services, and microfinance. Thus, Chap. 7 commences with an exploration of SSA's bank- and market-led FSD, the effects of SCRs on SSA's FSD, the interaction between FSD and democracy, and SSA's financial resource curse. Thereafter, the chapter focusses more explicitly on the relationship between FDI and FSD.

Since the 1990s, it has been argued that the emergence of the "Asian Tigers" shows that developing countries can increase their economic growth rates via heightened trade, FDI inflows, and FSD. Evidence suggests that countries that successfully transition from reliance on comparative advantage to exports of increasingly complex manufactured goods tend to attract the FDI needed to support diversification of trade and FDI (Romer, 1992; Cui & Xu, 2019) while also aiding integration into the global economy via the heightened liquidity, depth, and mobilisation of FSD (McKinnon, 1973; Shaw, 1973). Chapter 8 therefore explores the relationships between trade, FDI, FSD, and economic growth in SSA with a focus on the export-led and import-led growth hypotheses, followed by the FDI-led and FSD-led growth hypotheses. The discussion then examines the interlinkages between these hypothesised channels in resource-dependent and non-dependent SSA countries.

Hence, this book seeks to answer the following key questions:

i. What legacies associated with colonial border design, political geography, slavery, and institutional development continue to impede FDI to SSA?
ii. What post-independence policy choices have hampered FDI to SSA?
iii. Is democracy a prerequisite for FDI to SSA?
iv. Does corruption hinder or facilitate FDI to SSA?
v. What do the competing strategies of China, India, and Russia mean for FDI to SSA?
vi. Does SSA's limited financial sector development (FSD) stifle FDI to SSA or does SSA's FDI stimulate FSD?
vii. Where does FDI fit in SSA's economic growth dynamics?

References

Abdulai, D. N. (2007). Attracting Foreign Direct Investment for Growth and Development in Sub-Saharan Africa: Policy Options and Strategic Alternatives. *African Development, 32*(2), 1–23.

Acemoglu, D., & Robinson, S. (2013). *Why Nations Fail: The Origins of Power, Prosperity and Poverty*. Profile Books.

AfDB. (2016). *African Economic Outlook, 2016*. African Development Bank. Retrieved November, 2023, from www.afdb.org

AfDB. (2023). *Human Development*. African Development Bank Group. Retrieved November, 2023, from https://www.afdb.org/en/knowledge/publications/tracking-africa%E2%80%99s-progress-in-figures/human-development

Anetor, F. O. (2025). Do Greenfield Foreign Direct Investments Contribute to Poverty Reduction and Economic Growth in Africa? *Journal of Policy Modeling*

(forthcoming). Retrieved November, 2023, from https://doi.org/10.1016/j.jpolmod.2025.03.001i
Asiedu, E. (2002). On the Determinants of Foreign Direct Investment to Developing Countries: Is Africa Different? *World Development, 30*(1), 107–119.
Auty, R. (1993). *Sustaining Development in Mineral Economies: The Resource Curse Thesis.* Routledge.
Ayenew, B. B. (2022). The Effect of Foreign Direct Investment on the Economic Growth of Sub-Saharan African Countries: An Empirical Approach. *Cogent Economics & Finance, 10*(1), 2038862.
Beblawi, H., & Luciani, G. (1987). *The Rentier State.* Croom Helm.
Borensztein, E., De Gregorio, J., & Lee, J. W. (1998). How Does Foreign Direct Investment Affect Economic Growth? *Journal of International Economics, 45*, 115–135.
Bresser-Pereira, L. C. (2020). Neutralizing the Dutch Disease. *Journal of Post Keynesian Economics, 43*(2), 298–316.
Buckley, P. J., & Casson, M. C. (1976). *The Future of the Multinational Enterprise.* Homes & Meier.
Busse, M. (2004). Transnational Corporations and Repression of Political Rights and Civil Liberties: An Empirical Analysis. *Kyklos, 57*(1), 45–66.
Calderón, C., Loayza, N., & Servén, L. (2004). Greenfield Foreign Direct Investment and Mergers and Acquisitions: Feedback and Macroeconomic Effects. *Policy Research Working Paper 3192.* World Bank.
Calderon, C. A., Cantu, C., & Chuhan-Pole, P. (2018). Infrastructure Development in Sub-Saharan Africa: A Scorecard. *World Bank Policy Research Working Paper No. 8425.* World Bank Group.
Calvet, A. L. (1981). A Synthesis of Foreign Direct Investment Theories and Theories of Multinational Firms. *Journal of International Business Studies, 12*, 43–59.
Carmody, P. (2016). *The New Scramble for Africa.* Polity Press.
Casson, M. (2015). Coase and International Business. *Managerial and Decision Economics, 36*(1) Special Issue: Coase and the Theory of the Firm, 55–66.
Cui, L., & Xu, Y. (2019). Outward FDI and Profitability of Emerging Economy Firms: Diversifying from Home Resource Dependence in Early-Stage Internationalization. *Journal of World Business, 54*, 372–386.
da Silva Lopez, T. (2010). Using History to Help Refine International Business Theory: Ownership Advantages and the Eclectic Paradigm. *Working Paper No. 54.* The York Management School, University of York.
de Mello, L. R. (1997). Foreign Direct Investment in Developing Countries and Growth: A Selective Survey. *Journal of Development Studies, 34*, 1–24.
de Mello, L. R. (1999). Foreign Direct Investment-Led Growth: Evidence from Time Series and Panel Data. *Oxford Economic Papers, 51*(1), 133–151.
Deaton, A. (1999). Commodity Prices and Growth in Africa. *Journal of Economic Perspectives, 13*(3), 23–40.

Desierto, D. A. (2018). Formal Models of the Political Resource Curse. *Economics of Governance, 19*, 225–259.

Dumludag, D. (2009). *Political Institutions and Foreign Direct Investment Flows into Developing Countries*. MPRA Paper No. 27327. Munich Personal RePEc Archive, University Library of Munich.

Dunning, J. H. (1977). Trade, Location of Economic Activity and the MNE: A Search for an Eclectic Approach. In B. Ohlin, P. O. Hesselborn, & P. M. Wijkman (Eds.), *The International Allocation of Economic Activity* (pp. 395–418). Macmillan.

Dunning, J. H. (1980). Toward an Eclectic Theory of International Production: Some Empirical Tests. *Journal of International Business Studies, 11*(1), 9–31.

Dunning, J. H. (1988). The Eclectic Paradigm of International Production: A Restatement and Some Possible Extensions. *Journal of International Business Studies, 19*(1), 1–31.

Dunning, J. H. (1993). *Multinational Enterprises and the Global Economy*. Addison-Wesley Publication Company.

Dunning, J. H. (1998). Location and the Multinational Enterprise: A Neglected Factor? *Journal of International Business Studies, 29*(1), 45–66.

Dunning, J. H., & Lundan, S. M. (2008). *Multinational Enterprises in the Global Economy*. Edward Elgar.

Farole, T., & Winkler, D. (Eds.). (2014). *Making Foreign Direct Investment Work for Sub-Saharan Africa: Local Spillovers and Competitiveness in Global Value Chains*. World Bank.

Fernandez-Arias, E., & Montiel, P. (1996). The Surge in Capital Inflows to Developing Countries: An Analytical Overview. *World Bank Economic Review, 10*(1), 51–77.

Gehlbach, S., & Keefer, P. (2011). Investment Without Democracy: Ruling-Party Institutionalization and Credible Commitment in Autocracies. *Journal of Comparative Economics, 39*(2), 123–139.

Gossel, S. J. (2017). Democratic Capital, Democratic Rights and FDI in Sub-Saharan Africa. *Journal of International Development, 29*(8), 1033–1061.

Gossel, S. J., & Biekpe, N. (2017). Push-Pull Effects on South Africa's Capital Inflows. *Journal of International Development, 29*, 751–767.

Guseh, J. S., & Oritsejafor, E. (2005). Democracy and Economic Growth in Africa: The Cases of Ghana and South Africa. *Journal of Third World Studies, XXII*(2), 121–137.

Henry, P. B. (2000). Do Stock Market Liberalizations Cause Investment Booms? *Journal of Financial Economics, 58*(1–2), 301–334.

Hymer, S. H. (1960). *The International Operation of National Firms: A Study of Direct Investment* (Ph.D. thesis). Published by M.I.T. Press in 1976, Massachusetts Institute of Technology.

Ibrahim, M., & Alagidede, P. (2017). Financial Sector Development, Economic Volatility and Shocks in Sub-Saharan Africa. *Physica A, 484*, 66–81.
IMF. (1993). *Balance of Payments Manual* (5th ed.). International Monetary Fund.
IMF. (2012). *The Liberalization and Management of Capital Flows: An Institutional View*. International Monetary Fund.
IMF. (2016). *Financial Development in Sub-Saharan Africa: Promoting Inclusive and Sustainable Growth*. International Monetary Fund.
IMF. (2022). Greater and More Diverse Participation in Global Trade is Key to Achieving Africa's Economic Transformation, says New World Bank Book. *Press Release No. 2022/040/AFW*. International Monetary Fund.
Isham, J., Woolcock, M., Pritchett, L., & Busby, G. (2005). The Varieties of Resource Experience: Natural Resource Export Structures and the Political Economy of Economic Growth. *World Bank Economic Review, 19*(2), 141–174.
Jeffries, R. (1993). The State, Structural Adjustment and Good Government in Africa. *The Journal of Commonwealth & Comparative Politics, 31*(1), 20–35.
Jovanovic, B., & Rousseau, P. L. (2008). Mergers as Reallocation. *The Review of Economics and Statistics, 90*(4), 765–776.
Kim, Y. (2000). Causes of Capital Flows in Developing Countries. *Journal of International Money and Finance, 19*, 235–253.
Kindleberger, C. P. (1969). *American Business Abroad: Six Lectures on Direct Investment*. Yale University Press.
Koepke, R. (2019). What Drives Capital Flows to Emerging Markets? A Survey of the Empirical Literature. *Journal of Economic Surveys, 33*, 516–540.
Lall, S. (1976). Financial and Profit Performance of MNCs in Developing Countries: Some Evidence from an Indian and Columbian Sample. *World Development, 4*, 713–724.
Leite, C. A., & Weidmann, J. (1999), Does Mother Nature Corrupt? Natural Resources, Corruption, and Economic Growth. *IMF Working Papers 1999/085*. International Monetary Fund.
Lucas, R. (1990). Why Doesn't Capital Flow from Rich to Poor Countries? *American Economic Review, 80*, 92–96.
Lundgren, C. J., Thomas, A. H., & York, R. C. (2013). *Boom, Bust, or Prosperity? Managing Sub-Saharan Africa's Natural Resource Wealth*. International Monetary Fund.
Marandu, E. E., & Ditshweu, T. (2018). An Overview of the Key Theories of Foreign Direct Investment: The Way Forward. *Advances in Social Sciences Research Journal, 5*(12), 30–39.
Markusen, J., & Venables, A. J. (1999). Foreign Direct Investment as a Catalyst for Industrial Development. *European Economic Review, 43*(2), 335–356.
Mbaku, J. M. (2010). *Corruption in Africa: Causes Consequences, and Cleanups*. Lexington Books.

McFerson, H. M. (2010). Extractive Industries and African Democracy: Can the 'Resource Curse' be Exorcised? *International Studies Perspectives, 11*, 335–353.
McGuirk, E. F. (2013). The Illusory Leader: Natural Resources, Taxation and Accountability. *Public Choice, 154*(3/4), 285–313.
McKinnon, R. (1973). *Money and Capital in Economic Development*. Brookings Institution.
Mensah, M. O., Agbloyor, E. K., Harvey, S. K., & Fiador, V. O. (2017). Sovereign Credit Ratings and Bank Funding Cost: Evidence from Africa. *Research in International Business and Finance, 42*, 887–899.
Meyer, K. (2015). What is 'Strategic Asset Seeking FDI'? *The Multinational Business Review, 23*(1), 57–66.
Mkandawire, T. (2001). Thinking about Developmental States in Africa. *Cambridge Journal of Economics, 25*(3), 289–313.
Mlambo, C. (2022). Politics and the Natural Resource Curse: Evidence from Selected African States. *Cogent Social Science, 8*, 1–17.
Mody, A., & Murshid, A. P. (2005). Growing Up with Capital Flows. *Journal of International Economics, 65*, 249–266.
Montiel, P., & Reinhart, C. M. (1999). Do Capital Controls and Macroeconomic Policies Influence the Volume and Composition of Capital Flows? Evidence from the 1990s. *Journal of International Money and Finance, 18*(4), 619–635.
Moses, O. (2023). "Who Finances Energy Projects in Africa?" Carnegie Endowment for International Peace. *Working Paper*. Retrieved November, 2023, from https://carnegieendowment.org/files/Moses_Energy_Finance_1.pdf
OECD. (2002). *Foreign Direct Investment for Development: Maximizing Benefits, Minimizing Costs*. Organisation for Economic Co-operation and Development. Retrieved November, 2023, from https://www.oecd.org/investment/investmentfordevelopment/1959815.pdf
Okafor, G., Piesse, J., & Webster, A. (2015). The Motives for Inward FDI into Sub-Saharan African Countries. *Journal of Policy Modeling, 37*, 875–890.
Pitcher, A. (2012). *Party Politics and Economic Reform in Africa's Democracies*. Cambridge University Press.
Reisen, H. (1998). Sustainable and Excessive Current Account Deficits. *Empirica, 25*(2), 111–131.
Resnick, A. L. (2001). Investors, Turbulence, and Transition: Democratic Transition and Foreign Direct Investment in Nineteen Developing Countries. *International Interactions, 27*, 381–398.
Romer, P. M. (1992). Two Strategies for Economic Development: Using Ideas and Producing Ideas. *The World Bank Economic Review, 6*(1), 63–91.
Rugman, A. M. (1981). *Inside the Multinationals*. Croom Helm.
Sachs, J. D., & Warner, A. M. (1995). Natural Resource Abundance and Economic Growth. *NBER Working Paper No. 5398*. National Bureau of Economic Research.

Shah, A. S. (2006). Corruption and Decentralized Public Governance. *Policy Research Working Paper No. 3824*. World Bank.
Shaw, E. (1973). *Financial Deepening in Economic Development*. Oxford University Press.
Signe, L. (2018, March 14). Capturing Africa's High Returns. *Brookings*. Retrieved November, 2023, from https://www.brookings.edu/opinions/capturing-africas-high-returns/
Taylor, M. P., & Sarno, L. (1997). Capital Flows to Developing Countries: Long- and Short-Term Determinants. *The World Bank Economic Review, 11*(3), 451–470.
Taylor, S. D. (2012). Chapter 4: Foreign Investment beyond Compradorism and Primary Commodities. In *Globalization and the Cultures of Business in Africa: From Patrimonialism to Profit*. Indiana University Press.
UNCTAD. (2019). *State of Commodity Dependence*. In *United Nations Conference on Trade and Development*.
UNCTAD. (2024). Chapter 1: International Investment Trends. *World Investment Report*. Retrieved April, 2025, from https://unctad.org/publication/world-investment-report-2024
UNDP. (2016). *Primary Commodity Booms and Busts: Emerging Lessons from Sub-Saharan Africa*. United Nations Development Programme, Regional Bureau for Africa.
van der Walle, N. (2001). *African Economies and the Politics of Permanent Crisis, 1979–1999*. Cambridge University Press.
Van Der Ploeg, F. (2011). Natural Resources: Curse or Blessing? *Journal of Economic Literature, 49*(2), 366–420.
Verbeke, A. (2009). *International Business Strategy*. Cambridge University Press.
Vernon, R. (1966). International Investment and International Trade in the Product Cycle. *Quarterly Journal of Economics, 80*(2), 190–207.
Wilson, R. T., & Baack, D. W. (2012). Attracting Foreign Direct Investment: Applying Dunning's Location Advantages Framework to FDI Advertising. *Journal of International Marketing, 20*(2), 96–115.
World Bank. (1999). *Global Economic Prospects and the Developing Countries*. Oxford University Press.
World Bank. (2019). Ending Poverty, Investing in Opportunity. *Annual Report*.
Young, C. (1988). The African Colonial State and its Political Legacy. In D. Rothchild & N. Chazan (Eds.), *The Precarious Balance: State and Society in Africa* (pp. 25–66). Westview Press.
Zalanga, S. (2018). The Political Economy of Corruption. In S. O. Oloruntoba & T. Falola (Eds.), *The Palgrave Handbook of African Politics, Governance and Development* (pp. 869–882). Palgrave Macmillan.

CHAPTER 2

The Colonial Legacies Hampering FDI to Sub-Saharan Africa

Colonialism can be broadly defined as the political, economic, and social domination of a country by a foreign state. The European colonialism of sub-Saharan Africa (SSA) principally occurred during the period from 1800 to the 1960s, and was predominately driven by the industrial revolution, which rapidly transformed the socio-economic strata and technological means of production in the European countries (Ocheni & Nwankwo, 2012). Because industrial production was faster than agricultural production, the European powers had to look elsewhere for agricultural and industrial raw materials, and SSA's abundant natural resources, arable land, cheap labour, and potential capital investment opportunities made the region an attractive prize (ibid.).

These motivations in turn drove imperialism because the European powers needed to maintain control of the economic and political administration that would ensure a steady flow of natural resources back to Europe while safeguarding the expansion of manufactured goods and capital into the colonial states (ibid.; Tatah, 2017, p. 135). Tragically, SSA still bears the structural economic effects of colonisation. Principally, the colonial extraction of natural resources and control of manufacturing production and technologies mean that SSA has not been able to adequately industrialise or to adopt the technologies and human capital needed to shift from competitive advantage natural resource extraction to manufacturing-based economies (Acemoglu & Robinson, 2013, p. 115).

S. Gossel, *The Promise and Peril of FDI in Sub-Saharan Africa*, Palgrave Studies in African and Development Economics, https://doi.org/10.1007/978-3-032-01320-0_2

In addition to the economic outcomes of colonialism, SSA also suffers from a range of socio-political, institutional, and developmental legacies that have arisen from the five characteristics of colonial administration (Ndlovu-Gatsheni, 2015). First, the use of violence as a means of conquest, control, domination, and repression. Second, the use of racial classifications to define the distinction between subjects and citizens, and colonised and coloniser. Third, colonial governments favoured the urban colonial settlers. Fourth, the misappropriation of African identities as wholly tribal, and thus outside of civilisation and bound by local custom. Finally, the commandeering of African subjectivity while ensuring the dispossession of the 'African personality' through assimilation policies, "forced particularism," and "ghettoisation."

Capitalism argues that private ownership of the means of production will maximise the efficiency, distribution, and well-being of the political, economic, and social structures of the state. Capitalism thus places faith in competitive markets to generate investment and equitable distribution, which implies that the participants in the capitalist system have competitive freedom of choice with respect to production, consumption, and investment. As a result, the main roles of government are to protect the rights of citizens and maintain the legal framework for the proper functioning of the markets (IMF, 2020). Although capitalist forms of ownership and exchange in Africa preceded Western colonialism (Moghalu, 2014; Jerven, 2014), the system of colonialism introduced an extractive form of capitalism that "primarily aimed to enhance the development of Europe at the expense and disadvantage of Africa" (Omeje, 2021, p. 10).

Capitalism and colonialism in SSA thus overlapped in a system of "Racial Capitalism" (Robinson, 2000), which entailed the division of labour, society, and capital along racial lines (Miapyen & Bozkurt, 2022). The racialisation of capital naturally feeds through all the capitalist social structures because "Capital can only be capital when it is accumulating, and it can only accumulate by producing and moving through relations of severe inequality among human groups - capitalists with the means of production/workers without the means of subsistence, creditors/debtors, conquerors of land made property/the dispossessed and removed. These antinomies of accumulation require loss, disposability, and the unequal differentiation of human value, and racism enshrines the inequalities that capitalism requires. Most obviously, it does this by displacing the uneven life chances that are inescapably part of capitalist social relations onto fictions of differing human capacities, historically race" (Melamed, 2015).

Thus, colonialism bequeathed SSA with the structural conditions for exploiting natural resources and people rather than land; and consequently, the foundations for establishing institutions and states were neglected (Robinson, 2002). The long-run distortionary effects of these colonial systems are still readily apparent in SSA's political instability and ethnic conflicts (Van Bavel, 2021), and economic and institutional weaknesses, fostered by the extraction and exploitation of capital. As summarised by Bertocci and Canova (2002), "Colonialism drained the wealth of SSA extracted by the metropolitan countries (in the form of interest payments on loans, repatriated profits, salaries and pensions) and this, by reducing the indigenous capital accumulation process, had a negative effect on the colonies' growth prospects. Direct exploitation also included taxes, tariffs, restrictions on trade and foreign investment, forced labour, and even enslavement of the indigenous population. These distortions furtherly hampered the colonies' growth potential. The impact of the latter two practices, combined with distorting educational policies, may also have created disincentives to human capital accumulation, therefore affecting growth also through this indirect channel. Finally, colonial domination may be responsible for generating societies with dysfunctional institutions, rent-seeking elites and ethnic conflict, features which characterize much of Africa's recent history."

Based on the preceding discussion, this chapter explores how colonialism, specifically colonial border design, political geography, and slavery[1] have each shaped SSA's institutional development, and how these hindrances and complexities have affected SSA's ability to attract FDI in turn.

2.1 Border Design

Among the most significant root causes of SSA's developmental deficits is the colonial imposition of ill-conceived borders during the 'Scramble for Africa', which arose primarily from the Berlin Conference of 1884–1885, hosted by the German Chancellor Otto von Bismarck. This conference

[1] Which of these three factors are most important is an area of ongoing research. According to the institutions hypothesis of Acemoglu et al. (2001), Easterly and Levine (2003) and Rodrik et al. (2004), the quality of legal and political institutions matters more than geography. In contrast, the geography hypothesis of Gallup et al. (1999), Sachs (2003), and Assenova and Regele (2017) posits that geography shaped colonisation and subsequent institutional development. Maseland (2018) however finds that the effect of colonisation on institutional development is becoming less important over time.

defined the rules that the colonial powers would use to balkanise Africa into revenue maximising coloniaable parts (Green, 2012; Omeje, 2021, p. 15); or as King Leopold II of Belgium called the continent, a "magnificent cake," before devouring large portions of the Belgium-Congo (now known as the Democratic Republic of Congo), leading to the death of millions of people (Cheeseman, 2015, p. 33). British Foreign Secretary and Prime Minister Lord Salisbury satirically described the process of SSA's border design as simply "drawing lines upon maps where no white man's feet have ever trod. We have been giving away mountains and rivers and lakes to each other, only hindered by the small impediment that we never knew exactly where the mountains and rivers and lakes were" (Michalopoulos & Papaioannou, 2017, p. 50). Over the course of only two decades, "ten thousand African tribal kingdoms were transformed into just forty states, of which thirty-six were under direct European control. Never in human history had there been such drastic redrawing of the map of a continent" (Ferguson, 2004, p. 222).

Prior to colonialism, SSA had a wide range of dynamic civilisations, kingdoms, trade routes, and cultures. Map 2.1 presents George Murdock's (1959, 1967) map of the spatial distribution of ethnic political centralisation where a zero score indicates stateless societies that had no centralised political organisation, a score of 1 indicates a small chiefdom, a score of 2 designates a large or dominant chiefdom, and 3 and 4 indicate ethnic groups that were part of large states. As can be seen, Murdock finds that most pre-colonial states consisted of relatively small ethnically defined regions.

The imposition of the illogical colonial borders[2] meant that African people of a wide variety of different ethnic and cultural backgrounds were forcibly contained in new colonial states, or peoples of the same ethnic and cultural backgrounds were separated and fragmented (Ndlovu-Gatsheni, 2015, p. 28). This traumatic social upheaval occurred over many decades, complicated by the political manoeuvrings between the colonial power, especially the United Kingdom (UK) and France (Zouache, 2018).

Michalopoulos and Papaioannou (2014) describe four consequences of the imposition of these artificial boundaries. First, the inclusion of various ethnic groups into a single area led to heightened ethnic conflict, repression, and discrimination. Second, the boundaries moulded the ethnicity of

[2] 44% are straight lines delineating African countries that are 2.4 times larger than European states (Green, 2012).

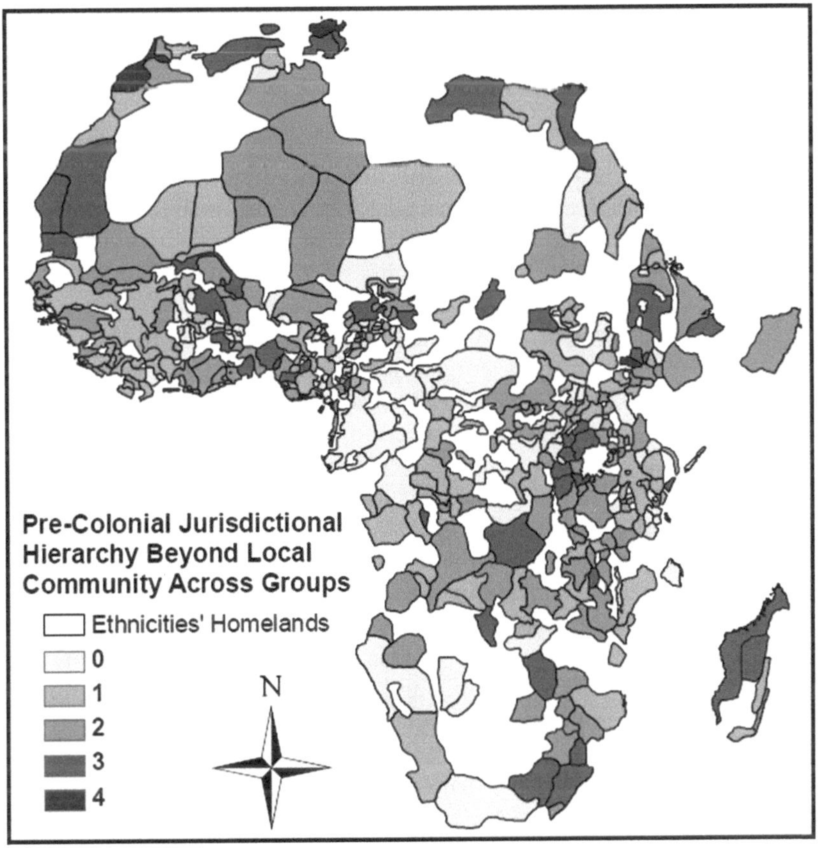

Map 2.1 Cultural provinces in pre-colonial Africa. Source: Michalopoulos and Papaioannou (2013)

the newly formulated colonial states, shaping the institutional and economic development thereafter. Third, the boundaries created a significant number of landlocked countries. Finally, the carving up of SSA by foreign states produced SSA countries that are either unusually small,[3] extremely large,[4] or have illogical shapes.[5]

[3] Such as Benin, Burundi, Djibouti, Equatorial Guinea, Gambia, Guinea-Bissau, Liberia, Rwanda, Sierra-Leone, and Togo.

[4] Such as Angola, the Democratic Republic of Congo, South Africa, and the Sudan.

[5] Such as Eritrea, Malawi, Namibia, Somalia, and Zambia.

Studies have found that these boundary conditions negatively affect a country's economic outcomes, such as GDP per capita (Alesina et al., 2005, 2011), economic growth (Alouini & Hubert, 2019), international competitiveness (Armstrong & Read, 2003), output and government consumption volatility (Crucini, 1997; Easterly & Kraay, 2000; Furceri et al., 2016), and trade volumes and diversification (Castello & Ozawa, 1999). Country size and shape has also been found to affect institutional factors such as the frequency and intensity of conflicts (Englebert et al., 2002; Raleigh & Hegre, 2009), quality of institutions, and rule of law (Olsson & Hansson, 2011).

Among the most detrimental developmental outcomes of the imposition of the colonial artificial boundaries on the pre-colonial regions were the resultant low population density levels (World Bank, 2009), which meant that the imperial powers needed to create urban centres where the 'thin white line' could exercise direct colonial administrative oversight (Richens, 2009) while also ensuring indirect rural control, achieved by bolstering the role of tribal leaders (Mamdani, 1996). However, because the colonial authorities lacked the infrastructure to govern the rural areas, African citizens living outside of the urban areas remained reliant on the pre-colonial ethnic structures rather than on the colonial government (Englebert, 2000). The legacy of this disparate direct-indirect power structure is that today, economic and political activities in SSA remain primarily a well-resourced urban phenomenon while the rural areas are still socio-economically and politically undeveloped (Herbst, 2014, p. 18). In addition, there is evidence that contemporary citizens in formerly centralised pre-colonial regions tend to have stronger national identities while citizens in formerly less centralised regions have stronger ethnic identities, mainly because descendants of more decentralised regions have less economic and institutional advantages (Adera, 2024).

Beyond the domestic colonial legacy effects, studies have also found that a country's economic development is affected by the prosperity, economic integration, and institutional quality of its neighbours (Easterly & Levine, 1998; Redding & Venables, 2004; Rodrik et al., 2004; Bosker & Garretsen, 2009), as well as by the number of landlocked countries (Collier, 2009; Sachs, 2008). Being landlocked is developmentally detrimental because the economy is typically far from major markets, is overly dependent on the coastal neighbours for ocean access, and has limited trade routes. In addition, landlocked countries are vulnerable to changes in the neighbouring countries' economic and infrastructure policy choices, political peace and stability, and administrative practices and effectiveness, much of which is beyond the direct control of the landlocked country (Collier, 2007; Lahiri & Masjidi, 2012; Faye et al., 2004).

The economic disparity between landlocked countries and other SSA countries can be seen from Table 2.1. Although economic growth in landlocked countries is generally higher than in non-landlocked countries (primarily driven by the high growth rates of Botswana, Ethiopia, Uganda, and Rwanda), average GDP per capita of non-landlocked countries is double that of landlocked SSA countries and export volumes in non-landlocked SSA countries are nearly six times larger than in landlocked SSA countries. In addition, while non-landlocked countries have higher oil rents, landlocked countries are more reliant on ore and metal commodity exports (particularly Zambia, Niger, Rwanda, Zimbabwe, and Central African Republic). Although landlocked and non-landlocked SSA countries are both positioned closer to autocracy than democracy, landlocked countries suffer from a greater democratic deficit than non-landlocked countries. With regards to FDI, non-landlocked countries received on average nearly twice as much inflows (as a percentage of GDP) compared to landlocked countries while on a total USD basis, non-landlocked countries received nearly five times as much FDI compared to landlocked

Table 2.1 Economic performance in landlocked and non-landlocked SSA countries

Average	*Measure*	*(a) Non-landlocked [27]*	*(b) Landlocked [15]*	*(a)/(b)*
GDP growth	Annual %	3.62	4.06	0.9
GDP per capita	Constant 2015 USD	1738.77	945.80	1.8
Exports of goods and services	Constant 2015 millions USD	8545.50	1620.67	5.3
Oil rents	% of GDP	10.74	4.77	2.3
Ores and metals exports	% of merchandise exports	12.19	17.05	0.7
Democracy	Polity2	−1.68	−1.78	0.9
FDI inflows	% of GDP	3.45	1.89	1.8
FDI inflows	Total billions USD	521.54	112.22	4.6

[#] indicates the number of SSA countries in the sample. SSA's landlocked countries comprise Botswana, Burkina Faso, Burundi, Central African Republic, Chad, Eswatini, Ethiopia, Lesotho, Malawi, Mali, Niger, Rwanda, South Sudan (excluded from Table 2.1), Uganda, Zambia, and Zimbabwe

Data sources: World Development Indicators (1970–2020), Polity V (1970–2018)

countries. Among the non-landlocked countries, the four countries that have received the most FDI inflows (in total billions of USD) are Nigeria (102.9), South Africa (98.1), Ghana (43.6), and Mozambique (44.7), collectively accounting for 55.5% of the FDI to non-landlocked SSA countries. Among the landlocked sub-sample, Ethiopia (27.3) received 24.5% of FDI followed by Zambia (20.2) with 18.0% and Uganda (15.8) at 14.1%.

2.2 Political Geography

In his ground-breaking book, Jared Diamond (1997) argues that physical geography and ecology affect institutional, political, and societal developmental trajectories. Of all the regions in the world, SSA has the highest proportions of land and population located in the tropics. Furthermore, the climate in tropical SSA is singularly inhospitable because of the size of the African landmass, which means that cool air from the sea does not reach the vast tropical interior, and as a result, SSA suffers from year-round rainfall near the equator but unpredictable rainfall and periodic drought north and south of the tropics (Bloom & Sachs, 1998). Studies find that the higher temperature close to the equator reduces economic growth in poor countries by 1.3% because of decreased agricultural and industrial output (Dell et al., 2012). In addition, the resultant high disease-related infant mortality rates mean that families tend to have many children, which in turn creates a bottom-heavy population demographic, stifles per capita incomes, and worsens inequality (Alesina et al., 2016).

Jeffrey Herbst (2000) further argues that Africa's ability to develop functional states has been negatively affected by the interaction between colonial institutional voids, population density, and geography. Herbst thus sorts African countries into four categories. The first are the "Difficult" countries, which are large, non-contiguous, and have high population densities. Countries that fall in the *Difficult* category tend to struggle to exert power and control, are unable to efficiently collect or administer taxation, have poor transportation networks, and are prone to complex ethnic structures. The second are the "Hinterland" countries, which are large countries where a significant portion of the population is concentrated into a small area with a sparse population density in the periphery. *Hinterland* North African countries tend to suffer from large swathes of land that are outside central government control, rendering these areas susceptible to developmental challengers such as rebel groups, separatists, and terrorist organisations. The high population density in the capital cities however means that there is the possibility to extract taxes and thus these states tend to have well-resourced and developed economic centres, surrounded by inhospitable and relatively uncontrolled peripheries. It is therefore unsurprising that Christensen and Laitin (2019) find that *Difficult* and *Hinterland* countries are more prone to violent civil wars.

The third category are the "Favourable" countries, which are smaller countries than the preceding two categories, and have populations that are concentrated in and near a capital city. *Favourable* countries tend to have sufficient control and authority from the capitals to the borders to collect and administer taxation and are of a size and geography that makes the establishment of transportation infrastructure more cost effective compared to doing so in the *Difficult* and *Hinterland* countries. The final category are the "Neutral" countries, which are those that do not fit the other categories. *Neutral* countries are similar to *Hinterland* countries, but the periphery is less inhospitable and more populated, and thus the density-geography mix is less detrimental to economic development. Based on these defining characteristics, the countries falling in the four categories are presented in Map 2.2.[6]

Figure 2.1a shows that the *Favourable* countries have consistently higher GDP per capita than the other categories. Figure 2.1b indicates that although *Favourable* countries had the highest levels of human development (HDI) from the 1990s to the mid-2000s, thereafter, the HDI of *Neutral* countries overtook *Favourable* countries while *Difficult* and *Hinterland* countries continue to trail. The government effectiveness index in all four of the categories presented in Fig. 2.1c is negative but the *Neutral* countries demonstrate relatively level performance whereas the other three categories deteriorated after the early 2000s. Nevertheless, the effectiveness of *Neutral* and *Favourable* countries is stronger than in the *Hinterland* and *Difficult* countries.

Total FDI inflows in USD are presented in Fig. 2.1d and show that cumulatively, *Difficult* countries, with a total of USD 271.6 billion, attracted the most FDI (43.0%) of the four categories. Over half of the inflows to the *Difficult* countries however went to Nigeria and Mozambique (USD 102.9 billion and USD 44.7 billion or 37.9% and 16.4% respectively). *Favourable* countries received 32.9% of the inflows (USD 208.0

[6] Herbst (2000) originally included 38 African countries, but Map 2.2 includes the additional countries of Djibouti, Malawi, South Africa, and Uganda.

Map 2.2 Herbst political geography. Source: Author's compilation based on Herbst (2000)

billion) of which 58.8% flowed to South Africa and the Congo (USD 98.1 billion and USD 24.1 billion or 47.2% and 11.6% respectively). In third place are the *Neutral* countries, which received USD 121.2 billion (19.2% of the total FDI) but a third (32.9%) of the *Neutral* sample FDI went to Ghana (USD 43.6 billion). In contrast, only a small proportion (4.8% or USD 30.6 billion) of total FDI flowed to *Hinterland* countries.

In addition to political geography, another commonly cited factor proposed to account for SSA's diverse economic development is exposure to tropical diseases, principally Tsetse fly-transmitted Trypanosomiasis

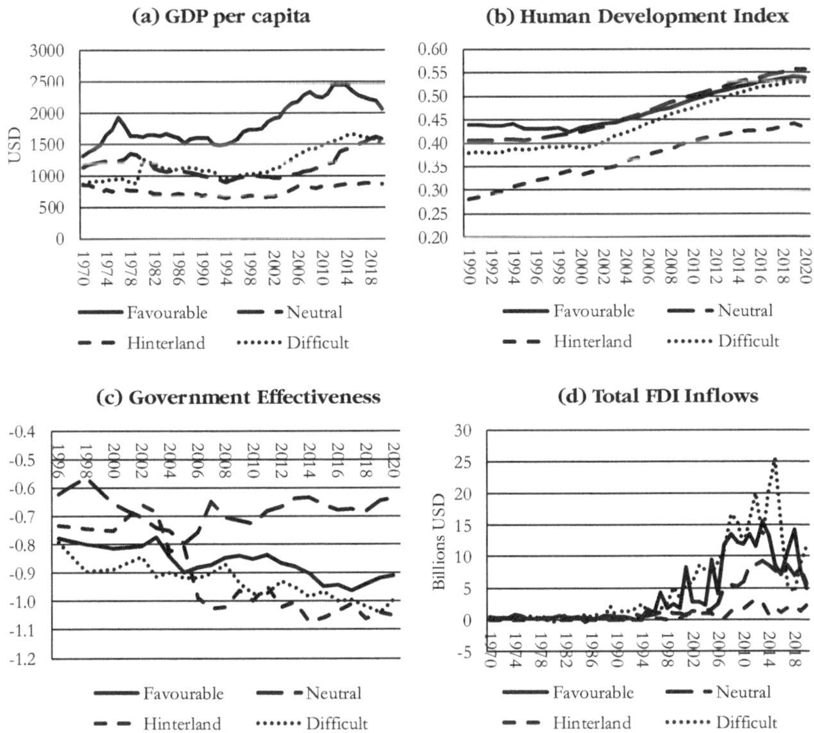

Fig. 2.1 Herbst (2000) categorisation and socio-economic performance. (Data sources: World Development Indicators, World Goverenance)

('sleeping sickness') and Anopheles mosquito-borne malaria. However, as argued by Acemoglu and Robinson (2013, p. 51), "Tropical diseases obviously cause much suffering and high rates of infant mortality in Africa, but they are not the reason Africa is poor. Disease is largely a consequence of poverty and of governments being unable or unwilling to undertake the public health measures necessary to eradicate them."

In SSA, colonial health provision embodied the ideological prejudices along both racial and economic lines. A core feature of colonialism was the belief that the 'superior races' of Europe had the role and responsibility to 'civilise, educate, improve, and develop' the 'inferior races' they ruled (Tilley, 2016; Zouache, 2018). This underscored the racialisation of medical thought, which theorised that Europeans would be at risk of tropical diseases until they acclimatised, and thus become immune to diseases over generations, whereas Africans would be more at risk to exogenous diseases (Coghe, 2020). Consequently, for most of the colonial period, healthcare formed a significant function of European administration and capital (Havinden & Meredith, 1993) but devoted greater attention and resources to "preserving the health of European soldiers, administrators, and settlers, who were deemed particularly vulnerable to tropical climate and its diseases" (Coghe, 2020) rather than on the health and well-being of the African population who were falsely assumed to have built up intergenerational immunity.

By the start of the twentieth century, colonial healthcare finally began to devote attention and resources to the health of the African population (Coghe, 2020) because the colonial export economies, reliant on African labour for mining, agriculture, and infrastructure, began to increasingly suffer from labour problems associated with injury and illness (Tilley, 2016). Acemoglu et al. (2003, p. 403) however posit that the long-run developmental effects of tropical diseases depend on the extent to which the disease incidence prevented the establishment of colonial settlements because "European colonists were much more likely to develop institutions of private property, encouraging economic and social development in places where they settled. In contrast, in places where they did not settle, they were more likely to opt for extractive institutions, designed to extract resources without investing in institutional development. In these places, institutions were highly centralized, with political power concentrated in the hands of a small elite and with almost no checks on this elite. The property rights and more general rights of the majority of the population were not protected." Hence, colonial healthcare was more prevalent in the urban centres than in the rural regions, worsening the urban-rural divide (Coghe, 2020). Studies have found that the direct long-run effects of diseases are lower productivity, life expectancy, and human capital investment (Acemoglu et al., 2003; Sachs & Malaney, 2002; Gallup et al., 2001).

Tsetse flies (Glossina palpalis) are endemic to Africa and feed exclusively on vertebrate blood. These insects transmit the Trypanosomiasis parasite, which causes nagana in domesticated animals and 'sleeping sickness' in humans (Leak, 1999). Unlike other livestock diseases, such as rinderpest and footrot, nagana infects all species of ungulates rather than preferring a particular species (Brown & Gilfoyle, 2010). Regions affected by Tsetse flies could thus only make limited use of domesticated animals and therefore had lower agricultural production and tended to be less administratively centralised because large-scale farming would have been difficult. Instead, the population would be reliant on subsistence farming, which in turn would discourage permanent settlements, heightening food insecurity, and making it difficult to support a non-agricultural workforce and establishing a tax base (Alsan, 2015).

The disparities between tropical areas affected by Tsetse flies and those that were not were worsened by the different treatment approaches used by colonial authorities. The British would cordon off affected populations, and force or coerce the inhabitants to leave their villages (Headrick, 2014) whereas French and German authorities would instead administer drugs (some of which contained arsenic and were nearly fatal in administered doses) (Tilley, 2011, 2016). Consequently, to this day, citizens in formerly British colonies tend to have higher levels of trust in medicines and higher vaccination rates (Lowes & Montero, 2021) (Map 2.3).

Despite the high mortality rate of 'sleeping sickness', with over 500,000 deaths during the Congo basin outbreak in 1896–1906 and around 300,000 deaths during the Ugandan epidemic of 1900–1920 (Dirk, 2021), these figures are dwarfed by SSA's malaria deaths. In 2021, 95% of world malaria cases and 96% of world malaria deaths were in SSA (WHO, 2022). Malaria kills 500,000 people in SSA each year, most of whom are children; worldwide, malaria has killed more people than all other diseases and wars combined (Weingartner, 2020).

Climatic conditions determine the mosquito breeding conditions and mix of species of mosquito and thus the severity of the disease (Depetris-Chauvin & Weil, 2013). During the 1800s, there was wide disparity between malaria mortality rates in the coastal cities (such as Lagos and Freetown) versus the interior with mortality rates of around 8% at the coast (Dumett, 1968) compared to 50% in the worse-affected interior (Curtin, 1989). The situation was eventually so dire that when the Gold Coast was declared a British colony in 1874, the three nominated candidates declined the position of Governor because of the associated health risks, which appears to have been well founded because the person to assume the role (James Maxwell) died of malaria within a month (Dumett, 1968 cited in Bump & Aniebo, 2022). Tropical Africa became so widely regarded as the most dangerous place on earth for Europeans that it was referred to as "the white man's grave" (Coghe, 2020), and in 1865, a British parliamentary committee recommended withdrawing from West Africa due to the risk of disease (Bump & Aniebo, 2022).

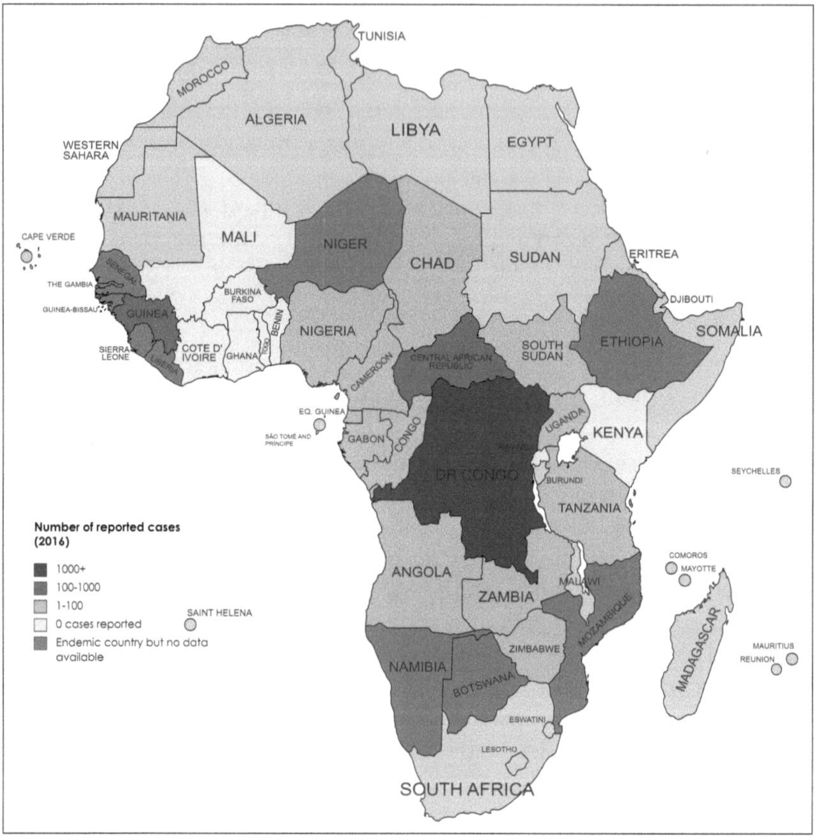

Map 2.3 Incidence of Trypanosomiasis in sub-Saharan Africa. Source: Masocha and Kristensson (2019)

Being a water-borne disease, malaria had a substantial effect on large-scale agriculture, worsened by the colonial practises of labour conscription and forced migration; and by the racist policies of segregation, which focussed on situating and building residential homes and administrative buildings in less affected areas while ignoring the health risks and needs of Africans (Packard, 2007). Consequently, "this led to a conflation of segregation and safety—safety defined with sole reference to European concerns—while deploying the benefits of malaria knowledge almost exclusively for Europeans" (Bump & Aniebo, 2022). In addition, the preventive use of quinine by the British substantially lowered the mortality rates among the colonial settler, soldiers, and civil servants, whereas the other European powers that did not use quinine were less able to entrench colonial control (Coghe, 2020) (Map 2.4).[7]

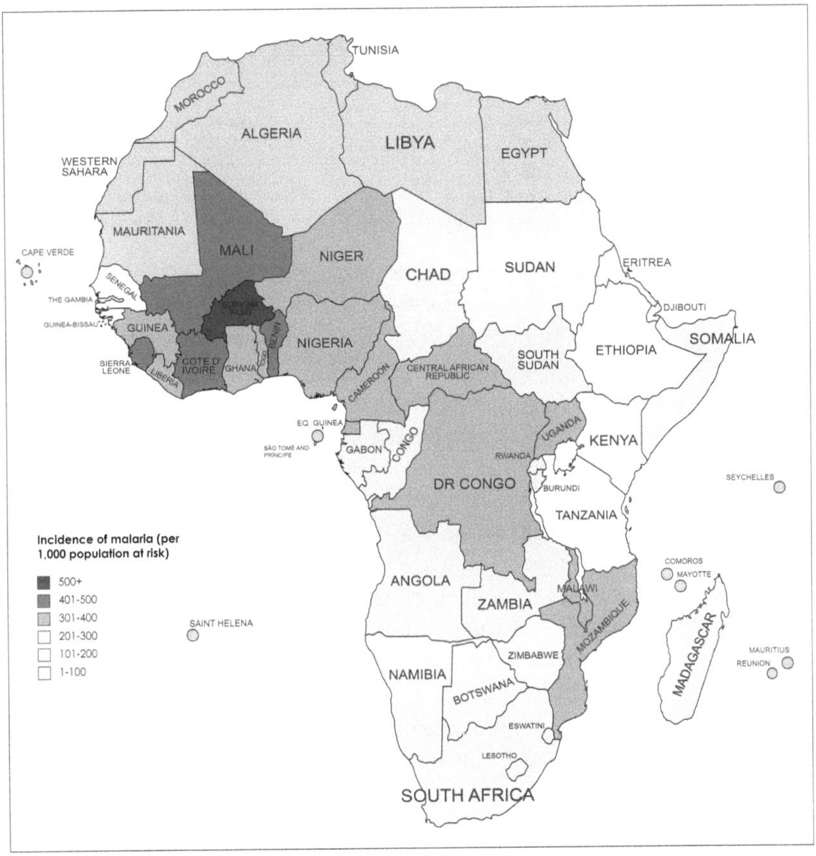

Map 2.4 Incidence of malaria in sub-Saharan Africa. Data source: World Development Indicators averaged over 2000–2020

[7] Philip Curtin and Daniel Headrick thus argue that gun technology, steamships, and quinine were each a "tool of empire" (Curtin, 1998; Headrick, 1994, pp. 3–14, 58–79).

Table 2.2 Economic performance by malaria incidence

Average	*Measure*	*(a) Low [24]*	*(b) High [18]*	*(a)/(b)*
GDP growth	Annual %	3.66	3.86	0.9
GDP per capita	Constant 2015 USD	1778.92	1075.84	1.7
Exports of goods and services	Constant 2015 millions USD	6115.70	4583.75	1.3
Human Development Index	Index	0.49	0.42	1.2
Life expectancy	Years	53.42	50.43	1.1
Literacy rate	% of people ages 15–24	72.89	59.36	1.2
Democracy	Polity2	−1.50	−2.09	0.7
FDI inflows	% of GDP	2.28	3.63	0.6
FDI inflows	Total billions USD	309.29	322.58	1.0

Low incidence refers to 1–300 persons at risk per 1000, while high incidence is 301–500+ per 1000. *[#]* indicates the number of countries

Data sources: World Development Indicators (1970–2020), Polity V (1970–2018), Human Development Index (1990–2020)

The variations in economic performance between SSA countries that experience high versus low incidence of malaria are presented in Table 2.2. Although malaria-prevalent SSA countries have higher average economic growth rates, they also have 70% lower average GDP per capita (with 12 out of 18 countries having an annual GDP per capita of less than USD 1000) and 30% lower export values. Socially, countries affected by malaria have lower human development, life expectancy, and literacy rates, as well as lower democracy levels than countries less affected by the disease. Despite these socio-economic disparities, SSA countries that have a higher prevalence of malaria have received greater FDI inflows, both as a percentage of GDP and in total USD. However, 59.3% of the FDI that flowed to malaria-prevalent countries went to the three countries of Nigeria (USD 102.9 billion), Mozambique (USD 44.7 billion), and Ghana (USD 43.6 billion) while 31.7% of the FDI that flowed to less malaria-affected countries went to South Africa (USD 98.1 billion). Thus, FDI to less malaria-prevalent countries is less concentrated than to malaria-affected countries.

2.3 Slavery

Slavery is commonly sub-categorised as indigenous slavery and export slavery, although both forms existed in tandem (Lovejoy, 1981, 1983, 2012) and used the same slave networks (Ewald, 1992). Indigenous slavery occurred before and during the centuries of export slavery, and primarily consisted of the use of African slaves for military or administrative positions, or for commercial value and production (Lovejoy, 2012, pp. 279–280).[8] Hence, although indigenous slavery was used to "secure political power, prestige, and wealth from nonelite subjects" (Stilwell, 2014, p. 91), this does not mean that slaves dominated the administration of all African states, nor that African politics always led to slavery (ibid., p. 109). Indigenous slavery was however common in most African countries, especially in West and West-Central African countries, which also had Atlantic slave trade markets (Bezemer et al., 2013).

Export slavery in contrast was the natural outcome of the colonial dehumanisation of Africans, which claimed that Africa was largely empty of inhabitants, and that the few peoples that lived on the continent were irrational, apolitical nomadic pastoralists who had no concept of private property (Blaut, 1993, p. 15). Hence, it was the "the white man's burden" (Kipling, 1899) to civilise, uplift, and develop the indigenous populations under colonial control (Maseland, 2018). As summarised by M'baye (2006), p. 614), "The political impact of the Atlantic trade is visible in the changes it wrought in African societies. It subverted the existing political balance in traditional African societies. Since slavery became a dominant source of revenue in the continent, personal wealth was thought to derive from one's ability to help capture and sell one's neighbours or criminals to strangers. As a consequence, the scenario Europeans created became a Darwinian universe in which the African turned into a wolf preying on other Africans."

According to Joseph Ki-Zerbo's (1978), p. 2189) calculations, over the period from the fifteenth through the nineteenth centuries, 100 million men and women were shipped from Africa during the four slave trades (the trans-Atlantic, the trans-Saharan, Red Sea, and Indian Ocean slave trades). However, considering that five times as many slaves died enroute or during capture, the realistic number of slaves exported from Africa is likely closer to 500 million (Martin, 2005). In addition to the sheer volume of slaves, slavery in Africa was also very different from the slave

[8] While the discussion below briefly discusses the economic ramifications for the system of slavery, it should be borne in mind that the rationale for slavery was not purely economic, as Stilwell (2014, p. 31) states, "Slavery in Africa often facilitated reproduction without being tied directly to production. That is, slaves were regularly acquired for noneconomic reasons, most often for their reproductive capacity."

systems of the Americas (Lovejoy, 2012, p. 276). First, American slavery was exclusively import slavery—there was no significant indigenous slavery—whereas slavery in Africa transformed from indigenous slavery to export slavery. Second, American slave markets were dependent on their European masters whereas African slavery was controlled by European immigrants. Third, in the American slave system, social control was based on race whereas African slave markets were based on regional and colonial domination (Map 2.5).

Manning (1990) estimates that by the turn of the nineteenth century, Africa's population was half of what it would have been in the absence of slavery while Inikori (1982, p. 37) argues that SSA's population should be 112 million higher. Nunn (2010) further shows that had Africa not been devastated by slavery, SSA would be at a similar level of socio-economic development as Latin America or Asia. Empirical studies report that the long-run effects of export slavery on SSA include significant ethno-linguistic fractionalisation (Whatley & Gillezeau, 2011; Green, 2012; Whatley, 2014), higher occurrences and intensity of civil, ethnic, and political conflicts (Nunn, 2008; Boxell et al., 2019; Anyanwu & Ani, 2020; Zhang et al., 2021), lower levels of trust (Nunn & Wantchekon, 2011), and weak legal and political institutions (Inikori, 2000, 2003; Heywood, 2009). Economically, these countries tend to have lower levels of credit access and capital investment (Pierce & Snyder, 2018) and suffer from concentrated firm ownership (Pierce & Snyder, 2020).

A socio-economic comparison between the SSA countries that experienced relatively low levels of slavery (below 213 slave exports per kilometre) versus those that endured high levels of slavery is summarised in Table 2.3. SSA countries that were less affected by slavery tend to have 10% higher average economic growth rates, and average per capita GDP that is more than double that of SSA countries that were more affected by slavery even though the trade value of both samples is relatively similar. The social factors further show that SSA countries that were less affected by slave exports have higher levels of human development, longer life expectancy, 30% better youth literacy, and better democracy levels.

With regards to FDI inflows, countries that endured high slave exports have received 40% less FDI as a percentage of GDP than low incidence countries. On a total USD basis, high incidence countries have received 30% more FDI than low incidence countries. The main recipients among the high incidence countries are Nigeria (28.4%), Mozambique (12.3%),

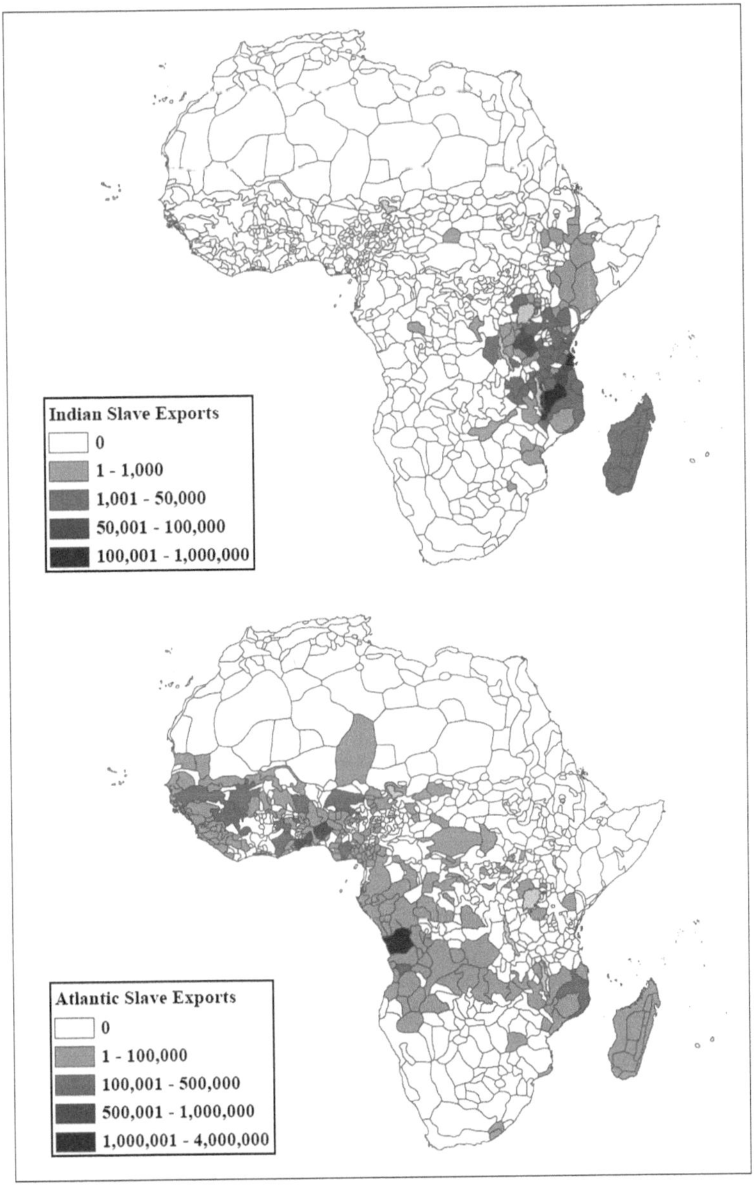

Map 2.5 Number of slaves exported during the slave trades. Source: Nunn (2017, p. 43)

Table 2.3 Indicators by slavery incidence

Average	*Measure*	*(a) Low [23]*	*(b) High [19]*	*(a)/ (b)*
GDP growth	Annual %	3.90	3.66	1.1
GDP per capita	Constant 2015 USD	1933.46	890.68	2.2
Exports of goods and services	Constant 2015 millions USD	5384.86	5246.97	1.0
Human Development Index	Index	0.48	0.43	1.1
Life expectancy	Years	53.51	51.08	1.0
Literacy rate	% of people ages 15–24	75.37	58.06	1.3
Democracy	Polity2	−1.51	−1.97	0.8
FDI inflows	% of GDP	3.29	2.35	1.4
FDI inflows	Total billions USD	271.33	362.43	0.7

[#] indicates the number of SSA countries in the sample. Slave exports per square km based on Pierce and Snyder (2020): Low = 0–213, High = 213+ The high slavery export countries comprise Angola, Benin, Burkina Faso, Chad, Congo Republic, Democratic Republic of Congo, Ethiopia, Ghana, Guinea, Guinea-Bissau, Malawi, Mali, Mozambique, Nigeria, Senegal, Sierra Leone, Sudan, Tanzania, Togo

Data sources: World Development Indicators (1970–2020), Polity V (1970–2018)

and Ghana (12.0%) with only South Africa (36.2%) as the main recipient among low incidence countries. Thus, FDI appears to be less concentrated among SSA countries that experienced lower levels of slave exports than the SSA countries that endured high incidence.

2.4 Institutional Legacies

Douglass North (1990, p. 3) defines institutions as "the rules of the game in a society or, more formally, are the humanly devised constraints that shape human interaction." Institutions shape development over the long run and thus colonialism continue to influence post-colonial institutional development (Jones, 2013; Spolaore & Wacziarg, 2013). Acemoglu and Robinson (2008, p. 6) differentiate between economic and political institutions whereby economic institutions affect the economic incentives and distribution of resources in society, and thus shape the organisation and investment in technology, and physical and human capital whereas political institutions determine the incentives, distribution, and constraints on *de jure* political power (Acemoglu & Robinson, 2006). While economic and political institutions evolve and interact slowly over the long run, they interact in feedback loops. Acemoglu and Robinson (2008) refer to this long-run effect as "institutional persistence". They argue that although political institutions allocate political power, the holders of this political power can shape the political institutions to maintain their power, thus developing a persistent elitist-insider political system.

In SSA, these economic and political institutional weaknesses have arisen in part because of the region's colonial experience. As Francis Fukuyama (2014, pp. 23–24) argues, SSA's post-colonial experience is largely a result of the uniquely harsh form of colonialism that the region endured compared to the variants that afflicted East Asia and Latin America. As he explains, prior to the arrival of the colonial powers, East Asian countries had complex bureaucracies and institutions, starting in China, and then spreading to neighbouring Japan, Korea, and Vietnam. Consequently, although colonialisation severely disrupted these endogenous systems, after colonial rule, efficient public institutions were restored, laying the foundation for post-colonial economic success. Latin America did not develop institutions of similar complexity, efficiency, or breadth, and the colonial powers destroyed the existing political systems, replacing them with authoritarian and mercantilist institutions mirrored on those found in Spain and Portugal but further distorted by race and ethnicity-based hierarchies. Consequently, Spanish colonialism left a legacy of stratified societies, predatory states, and dysfunctional markets (Lange et al., 2006). In contrast to the complex institutions of pre-colonial East Asia, and emerging institutions of pre-colonial Latin America, pre-colonial SSA did not have wide-ranging centralised institutions of state.[9] Thus, rather than introducing complex institutions, colonial powers were more comfortable to rule indirectly, and once colonial rule ended, there were very little institutional foundations upon which to build complex modern states.

Recent studies have further argued that SSA's institutional development should be considered in relation to the degree of political centralisation, shaped by the conflicts between colonial and pre-colonial systems (Englebert, 2000) and between *de jure* and *de facto* power (Acemoglu & Robinson, 2005). As summarised by Gennaioli and Rainer (2007, p. 186) "in areas inhabited by centralized ethnic groups, the existence of

[9] Studies have however described complex ethnic centralised institutions in Africa, for example in the Shongai Empire in Western Africa, the Luba kingdom in Central Africa, the kingdoms of Buganda and Ankole in Eastern Africa, and the Zulu and Swazi kingdoms in South Africa (Murdock, 1967).

pre-colonial chiefly hierarchy made local chiefs accountable to higher-level traditional authority. By bargaining with senior traditional leaders, colonial and postcolonial governments could foster policy coordination and implementation in those areas, leading to faster adoption of European policies and technologies. By contrast, in areas inhabited by politically fragmented groups the presence of too many traditional power holders rendered such bargaining very costly or infeasible. As a result, in those areas unrestrained local chiefs were often allowed to follow parochial and personalistic policies, leading to tyranny, disorder and ultimately halting modernization."

Consequently, the direct versus indirect form of colonisation is at the root of SSA's divergent post-colonial institutional development (Maseland, 2018). The direct (formal), institutional factors include regulatory, economic, and public administration while indirect (informal), institutions are the 'unwritten rules of engagement' encompassing the social, cultural, and ideological norms (Glaister et al., 2020). Tedeschi (2018) further reports that individuals belonging to ethnic groups that were controlled by a centralised pre-colonial state tend to have higher levels of trust in post-colonial institutions even among individuals who are living outside of their ethnic homeland, which implies that this is "an intergenerationally transmitted belief." Gennaioli and Rainer (2006, 2007) further show that countries that arose from regions where ethnic groups were ruled by centralised pre-colonial political institutions tend to have higher institutional quality whereas countries that arose from fragmented ethnic control have worse social outcomes, such as lower immunisation rates, educational outcomes, higher infant mortality rates, and ethnic conflict (Michalopoulos & Papaioannou, 2016).

In SSA, British imperial institutions, rule of law, and identity were more adaptable and decentralised compared to the more centralised, mercantilist, and statist Spanish and French colonies (Glaister et al., 2020), and consequently, the long-run effects on institutional development were less detrimental in British colonies than under the direct colonisation of the other European powers (Lange et al., 2006; North et al., 2009; Klerman et al., 2011; Lee & Schultz, 2012). This effect can be seen in Table 2.4, which presents the average of the World Bank's World Governance Indices of SSA countries over the period of 1996–2020 grouped by colonial control as at 1913 (ranging between −2.5 having the lowest institutional quality to 2.5 having the highest). Although all of the institutional metrics are below zero, highlighting SSA's institutional voids and weaknesses, the

Table 2.4 Quality of institutions in SSA by colonial power

Colonial power	*Countries*	*Control of corruption*	*Government effectiveness*	*Political stability and absence of violence/terrorism*	*Regulatory quality*	*Rule of law*	*Voice and accountability*	*Average*
Belgium *[2]*	Burundi, Democratic Republic of the Congo	−0.82	−1.06	−1.51	−1.00	−1.13	−1.30	−1.14
Germany *[5]*	Cameroon, Namibia, Rwanda, Tanzania, Togo	−0.56	−0.62	−0.22	−0.49	−0.53	−0.48	−0.49
France *[13]*	Benin, Burkina Faso, Central African Republic, Chad, Cote d'Ivoire, Djibouti, Gabon, Guinea, Madagascar, Mali, Niger, Republic of the Congo, Senegal	−0.76	−0.88	−0.67	−0.68	−0.82	−0.63	−0.74
Italy *[2]*	Eritrea, Somalia	−1.09	−1.74	−1.71	−2.10	−1.75	−1.95	−1.72
Portugal *[3]*	Angola, Guinea-Bissau, Mozambique	−1.06	−1.02	−0.53	−0.93	−1.14	−0.73	−0.90
Spain *[1]*	Equatorial-Guinea	−1.58	−1.48	−0.03	−1.43	−1.39	−1.81	−1.29
United Kingdom *[15]*	Botswana, Eswatini, Gambia, Ghana, Kenya, Lesotho, Malawi, Nigeria, Sierre Leone, South Africa, South Sudan, Sudan, Uganda, Zambia, Zimbabwe	−0.56	−0.62	−0.53	−0.55	−0.55	−0.49	−0.55

[#] indicates the number of SSA countries under colonial control. Ethiopia and Liberia were independent and are thus excluded

Data source: World Bank World Governance Indicators

scores are slightly better for the decentralised colonialism of the United Kingdom and Germany (−0.55 and −0.48 respectively) than for more centralised colonialism of the other European powers, which range between −0.74 (France) to −1.72 (Italy).

With the rise of institutional economics after the mid-1990s, there has been wide-ranging debate whether institutional development drives economic outcomes (Acemoglu et al., 2005; North, 1990) or whether economic performance drives institutional development (Chang, 2003, 2011; Reinert, 2007, 2008; Constantine, 2017). Until relatively recently, the former held sway and thus from the mid-1980s through the 1990s, organisations such as the World Bank and IMF, among others, conditioned financial assistance on institutional reforms (such as neoliberal "Structural Adjustment Programs"). Unfortunately, instead of improving governance and economic performance, these reforms resulted in socioeconomic distress and a collapse in economic growth in many countries in SSA and other developing regions (Heidhues & Obare, 2011). Consequently, in recent years, the possibility that economic performance drives institutional development has been gaining ground. Chang (2011) argues that economic development affects institutional development via three channels. First, rising wealth creation and accumulation will stimulate demand for strong institutions that can protect property rights and increase political accountability. Second, economic development will increase taxation and other revenues thus making the development of institutions more affordable. Third, economic development fosters social mobility, and the resultant beneficiaries will support institutional development that will favour and protect their interests.

According to Acemoglu et al. (2005) and Acemoglu and Robinson (2013), the economic outcome of institutional development depends on whether the institutional foundations are extractive or inclusive. Extractive institutions are characterised by non-democratic political institutions with weak rule of law and little private property rights. Inclusive institutions in contrast are characterised by democratic political institutions, and strong rule of law and private property protection. It is therefore argued that extractive economies tend to limit or exclude most of the population from participating in the political and economic activities of state while inclusive economies will facilitate and trust citizens to make individual decisions about their lives. Given SSA's colonial experiences, it is unsurprising that the majority of SSA countries tend to have stronger extractive than inclusive institutions.

Reinert (2007) and Constantine (2017) argue however that characterising institutions as either extractive or inclusive is incomplete because these definitions do not adequately consider that economic development can only occur if institutions of production are effectively administered. Hence, they posit that institutions should rather be characterised as institutions of production (such as economic, trade, and industrial policies) and institutions of exchange (such as property rights, rule of law, control of corruption). Consequently, they argue that the hypothesis that countries can develop by supporting inclusive institutions is unrealistic because most emerging countries commence their developmental trajectories without production capabilities or technologies and suffer from an inadequate allocation of resources. Consequently, poor countries cannot simply stimulate economic growth and development by 'downloading institutions' from developed countries. In addition, while many emerging countries have basic institutions of exchange, these cannot produce economic growth-enhancing structural transformations because these institutions exist on paper only, mainly because of insufficient capital as a result of the poor returns from the institutions of production. Furthermore, the lack of a well-developed private sector means that tax bases are narrow, private sector employment returns are low, and the population is rural rather than urban. Consequently, institutional development in SSA may suffer from shortcomings of extraction but are shaped by the political need to ensure continuity of state employment and benefits. Thus, institutions of production are limited by state control while institutions of exchange are hampered by structural rigidities and political elitism as they must ensure political power is unaffected by the emergence of private sector interests.

Beyond an emerging country's ability to develop institutions of production and exchange, Hidalgo et al. (2007) contend that the structure of an economy is also shaped by the position of its trade products in the global market space. Countries with production near the centre of the market space are better able to beneficiate production using complimentary technologies while countries located at the periphery must produce a range of products using different technologies. In addition, the economic costs of moving from the periphery to the centre are high as they include the introduction of sophisticated production processes and technologies. Unfortunately, most natural resource-dependent countries, including most of SSA, tend to be located at the periphery, which limits their trade opportunities to exporting unsophisticated primary products because beneficiation and diversification are too costly, which locks SSA countries into a path of resource dependence with weak institutions of production and extractive institutions of exchange.

With regards to FDI, Legal System theory argues that the colonial legal system will shape the structural ability of the post-colonial country to attract FDI (La Porta et al., 1999; Beck et al., 2001). Empirical evidence indicates that countries that endured statist, centralised colonial systems tend to have worse economic and political institutions than countries that had decentralised British common law systems (Asngar et al., 2022). This is because British systems typically have better shareholder and creditor protection, and enforcement of contract and property rights protection, and are thus more likely to become market economies (Ferguson, 2003), have better investment protection (La Porta et al., 1998), and develop smaller public sectors compared to former colonies that fell under French, Spanish, and Portuguese control (La Porta et al., 1999, 2008). This is borne out by Table 2.5 which shows that SSA countries that are former colonies of the United Kingdom and Germany have together received nearly three times as much FDI compared to the SSA countries that experienced the more centralised colonisation of the other European colonial powers (USD 398.3 billion versus USD 135.6 billion).

Endowment theory argues that, in accordance with Herbst (2000), geographic conditions at the time of colonisation shape subsequent institutional development to a greater extent than the adopted legal system (Acemoglu et al., 2001). The defining character of colonialism was that "Europeans settled and established institutions that protected their

Table 2.5 FDI to SSA by former colonial power

Colonial power	*Average % GDP*	*Average millions USD*	*Total billions USD*	*Ratio % total*
Belgium *[2]*	1.09	234.13	23.65	3.93%
France *[13]*	2.31	178.50	118.35	19.65%
Germany *[5]*	1.94	189.50	50.03	8.31%
Italy *[2]*	2.23	45.71	4.66	0.77%
Portugal *[3]*	4.72	276.42	42.02	6.98%
Spain *[1]*	17.04	299.72	15.29	2.54%
United Kingdom *[15]*	2.06	455.28	348.29	57.83%

[#] indicates the number of SSA countries under colonial control

Data sources: World Development Indicators (1970–2020)

property rights against the indigenous peoples, as well as efficient political and economic institutions that mirrored those of their home countries" (Asngar et al., 2022). Hence, regions with low levels of settler mortality could provide the conducive conditions needed to develop centralised administration and institutions that would attract FDI whereas regions that had inhospitable geography and had high settler mortality and poor institutional quality during colonisation tend to suffer from poor socio-economic progress and institutional development after colonialism (Asngar et al., 2022), and thus suffer from lower levels of FDI, savings, investment, and productivity (Levine, 1999; Sachs & Malaney, 2002).

In addition to the colonial legal system and geographic settler mortality effects, FDI in SSA can also be shaped by the historical ties between the former colonial power and post-colonial country, which Glaister et al. (2020) define as the "liability of foreignness" (LOF). When the two countries share historical ties, the LOF can be reduced by shared institutional and legal foundations, and common language and culture, which increases the trust between the investing parties, leading to higher FDI inflows (Chowdhury & Maung, 2018; Guiso et al., 2009; Glaister et al., 2020). In contrast, when there is a high LOF as a result of dissimilar institutions, limited historical interaction, or high levels of distrust, the company investing in the foreign market will face a range of hindrances that include higher risks and uncertainty, a competitive disadvantage, difficulties in working with domestic suppliers and companies, building trust, and establishing legitimacy (Kostova & Zaheer, 1999) and attracting customers (Zaheer & Mosakowski, 1997; Salomon & Wu, 2012).

LOF could therefore significantly affect the magnitude and type of FDI a former colonial country attracts because vertical and resource-seeking FDI tends to be more affected by institutional risk compared to horizontal or market-seeking FDI (Slangen & Beugelsdijk, 2010; Luo & Mezias, 2002). This is because natural resource investment usually needs permits and regulatory approval from the host country's government, and thus multinationals with high LOF will be less likely to be granted permission and may have to pay higher transaction costs compared to multinationals that have low LOF (Glaister et al., 2020). Market-seeking FDI however can also be affected by high LOF because greater production, operation, and marketing costs will be required to adapt to a new unfamiliar market (Zhou & Guillen, 2016). Furthermore, if the LOF is too high, then it is possible that the costs will exceed the potential benefits, thus discouraging the investment. This tends to occur when the destination market has a negative perception of its former colonial overseer, especially if decolonisation was a violent process (Glaister et al., 2020).

The country-specific exposures to these colonial legacies are summarised in Table 2.6. Out of the 42 SSA countries assessed, only three countries (South Africa, Kenya, and Gambia) have no exposure to these colonial factors, while 16 countries (38.1% of the sample) are exposed to one of the factors, 9 countries (21.4%) are exposed to two factors, and 14 countries (33.3%) are exposed to three or more of the factors. Thus, over half (54.8%) of the SSA countries in Table 2.6 are potentially disadvantaged by at least two of the colonial legacy factors.

Table 2.6 SSA country-specific colonial disadvantage exposure

Country	*Ranked FDI (billions USD)*	*% total FDI*	*Border design*	*Herbst geography*[a]	*Malaria*[b] *(per 1000)*	*Slavery incidence*[c]	*Legal origin*
Nigeria	102.94	16.05%	–	**Difficult**	**358**	**5**	UK
South Africa	98.17	15.31%	–	Favourable	2	1	UK
Ghana	43.62	6.80%	–	Neutral	**316**	**5**	UK
Mozambique*	43.49	6.78%	–	**Difficult**	**388**	3	**Portugal**
Congo*	34.85	5.44%	–	Favourable	241	2	**France**
Sudan*	29.42	4.59%	–	**Difficult**	53	2	UK
Ethiopia	27.28	4.25%	**Landlocked**	**Difficult**	143	**4**	–
Democratic Republic of Congo*	23.34	3.64%	–	**Difficult**	**393**	2	**Belgium**
Tanzania	22.24	3.47%	–	**Difficult**	187	2	Germany
Zambia*	19.78	3.08%	**Landlocked**	Neutral	238	1	UK
Uganda	15.47	2.41%	**Landlocked**	Neutral	**380**	1	UK
Equatorial Guinea*	15.29	2.38%	–	Favourable	**341**	1	**Spain**
Gabon	15.02	2.34%	–	Favourable	209	1	**France**
Liberia*	14.09	2.20%	–	Favourable	**379**	1	–
Kenya	13.61	2.12%	–	Neutral	106	1	UK
Cote d'Ivoire	12.29	1.92%	–	Neutral	**404**	1	**France**

(continued)

Table 2.6 (continued)

Country	*Ranked FDI (billions USD)*	*% total FDI*	*Border design*	*Herbst geography*[a]	*Malaria*[b] *(per 1000)*	*Slavery incidence*[c]	*Legal origin*
Cameroon	11.37	1.77%	–	Neutral	**326**	1	Germany
Madagascar	10.39	1.62%	–	–	58	1	**France**
Namibia	9.95	1.55%	–	**Difficult**	26	1	Germany
Senegal	9.31	1.45%	–	**Difficult**	103	**4**	**France**
Niger*	8.46	1.32%	**Landlocked**	**Hinterland**	**359**	1	**France**
Chad*	7.05	1.10%	**Landlocked**	**Hinterland**	218	2	**France**
Botswana	6.86	1.07%	**Landlocked**	Favourable	2	1	UK
Mali*	6.60	1.03%	**Landlocked**	**Hinterland**	**401**	3	**France**
Guinea*	5.87	0.92%	–	Favourable	**381**	**4**	**France**
Zimbabwe	5.30	0.83%	**Landlocked**	Favourable	98	1	UK
Sierra Leone	5.00	0.78%	–	Favourable	**413**	**4**	UK
Malawi	3.69	0.58%	**Landlocked**	Neutral	**328**	**4**	UK
Somalia	3.62	0.56%	–	**Difficult**	76	1	**Italy**
Togo*	3.24	0.51%	–	Favourable	**364**	**5**	Germany
Rwanda*	3.22	0.50%	**Landlocked**	Favourable	222	1	Germany
Burkina Faso*	3.01	0.47%	**Landlocked**	Favourable	**503**	3	**France**
Benin*	2.43	0.38%	–	Favourable	**425**	**5**	**France**
Eswatini	2.11	0.33%	**Landlocked**	Favourable	1	1	UK
Gambia	1.46	0.23%	–	Favourable	245	1	UK
Lesotho	1.42	0.22%	**Landlocked**	Favourable	–	1	UK
Eritrea	1.05	0.16%	–	Favourable	21	1	**Italy**
Central African Republic*	0.67	0.11%	**Landlocked**	Favourable	**392**	1	**France**

Guinea-Bissau	0.39	0.06%	–	Favourable	131	**5**	**Portugal**
Burundi	0.31	0.05%	**Landlocked**	Favourable	269	1	**Belgium**
South Sudan*	−0.56	−0.09%	**Landlocked**	Neutral	298	1	UK
Angola*	−1.86	−0.29%	–	**Difficult**	238	**5**	**Portugal**

Note: * indicates resource export dependent. FDI measured as the sum over 1970–2020 using World Development Indicators data

[a]Herbst (2000)

[b]Malaria incidence measured as the average over the period of 2000–2020 using World Development Indicators data

[c]Pierce and Snyder (2020) where 1 = 0–213.3, 2 = 213.3–565.8, 3 = 565.8–780.3, 4 = 780.3–1923, 5 = 1923–6756.3

References

Acemoglu, D., Robinson, J., & Johnson, S. (2001). The Colonial Origins of Comparative Development: An Empirical Investigation. *American Economic Review, 91*(5), 1369–1401.

Acemoglu, D., Robinson, J., & Johnson, S. (2003). Disease and Development in Historical Perspective. *Journal of the European Economic Association, 1*(2–3), 397–405.

Acemoglu, D., Robinson, J., & Johnson, S. (2005). The Rise of Europe: Atlantic Trade, Institutional Change and Economic Growth. *American Economic Review, 95*, 546–579.

Acemoglu, D., & Robinson, S. (2005). Unbundling Institutions. *Journal of Political Economy, 113*(5), 949–995.

Acemoglu, D., & Robinson, S. (2006). *Economic Origins of Dictatorship and Democracy*. Cambridge University Press.

Acemoglu, D., & Robinson, S. (2008). The Role of Institutions in Growth and Development. *Commission of Growth and Development Working Paper No. 10*. The World Bank.

Acemoglu, D., & Robinson, S. (2013). *Why Nations Fail: The Origins of Power, Prosperity and Poverty*. Profile Books.

Adera, A. (2024). Ancestral Institutions and the Salience of African Ethnicity: Theory and Evidence. *Journal of Institutional Economics, 20*(e11), 1–18.

Alesina, A., Easterly, W., & Matuszeski, J. (2011). Artificial States. *Journal of the European Economic Association, 9*(2), 246.

Alesina, A., Michalopoulos, S., & Papaioannou, E. (2016). Ethnic Inequality. *Journal of Political Economy, 124*(2), 428–488.

Alesina, A., Spolaore, E., & Wacziarg, R. (2005). Trade, Growth and the Size of Countries. *Handbook of Economic Growth, 1*(23), 1499–1542.

Alouini, O., & Hubert, P. (2019). Country Size, Economic Performance and Volatility. *Revue de l'OFCE, 164*(4), 139–163.

Alsan, M. (2015). The Effect of the TseTse Fly on African Development. *The American Economic Review, 105*(1), 382–410.

Anyanwu, T. C., & Ani, K. J. (2020). Slavery and Colonialism: The Roots of Post-Colonial Conflicts in Africa. *World Affairs: The Journal of International Issues, 24*(1), 132–141.

Armstrong, H., & Read, R. (2003). The Determinants of Economic Growth in Small States. *The Round Table, 92*(368), 99–124.

Assenova, V.A. & Regele, M. (2017). "Revisiting the Effect of Colonial Institutions on Comparative Economic Development, *PLoS ONE*, 12(5), e0177100.

Asngar, T. M., Nkoa, B. E. O., & Zambo, C. C. A. (2022). Does Colonisation Explain the Low Level of Growth in African Financial Markets? *Economic Systems, 46*, 101013.

Beck, T., Demirguc-Kunt, A., & Levine, R. (2001). "Law and Finance: Why Does Legal origin Matter?" *Journal of Comparative Economics*, 31(4), 653–676.

Bertocchi, G. & Canova, F. (2002). "Did Colonization Matter for Growth? An Empirical Exploration into the Historical Causes of Africa's Underdevelopment," *European Economic Review*, 46, 1851–1871.

Bezemer, D., Bolt, J., & Lensink, R. (2013). Slavery, Statehood, and Economic Development in Sub-Saharan Africa. *World Development, 57*, 148–163.

Blaut, J. M. (1993). *The Colonizers Model of the World: Geographic Diffusionism and Eurocentric History*. Guilford Press.

Bloom, D., & Sachs, J. (1998). *Geography, Demography, and Economic Growth in Africa*. Harvard Institute for International Development, Harvard University.

Bosker, M., & Garretsen, H. (2009). Economic Development and the Geography of Institutions. *Journal of Economic Geography, 9*(3), 295–328.

Boxell, L., Dalton, J. T., & Leung, T. C. (2019). The Slave Trade and Conflict in Africa, 1400–2000. *MPRA Paper No. 94468*. Munich Personal RePEc Archive

Brown, K., & Gilfoyle, D. (Eds.). (2010). *Healing the Herds: Disease, Livestock Economies, and the Globalization of Veterinary Medicine*. Ohio University Press.

Bump, J. B., & Aniebo, I. (2022). Colonialism, Malaria, and the Decolonization of Global Health. *PLOS Global Public Health, 2*(9), e0000936.

Castello, S., & Ozawa, T. (1999). *Globalization of Small Economies as a Strategic Behavior in International Business. Routledge.*

Chang, J. H. (2003). *Kicking Away the Ladder: Development Strategy in Historical Perspective*. Anthem Press.

Chang, J. H. (2011). Institutions and Economic Development. *Journal of Institutional Economics, 7*(4), 473–498.

Cheeseman, N. (2015). *Democracy in Africa: Successes, Failures, and the Struggle for Political Reform*. Cambridge University Press.

Chowdhury, R. H., & Maung, M. (2018). Historical Ties Between Nations: How Do They Matter in Cross-Border Mergers and Acquisitions? *International Review of Economics and Finance, 58*, 30–48.

Christensen, D., & Laitin, D. D. (2019). *African States since Independence: Order, Development, and Democracy*. Yale University Press.

Coghe, S. (2020). Disease Control and Public Health in Colonial Africa. In *Oxford Research Encyclopaedias, African History* (pp. 1–44). Oxford University Press.

Collier, P. (2007). *The Bottom Billion: Why the Poorest Countries Are Failing and What Can Be Done About It*. Oxford University Press.

Collier, P. (2009). *Wars, Guns, and Votes: Democracy in Dangerous Places.* Harper Books.

Constantine, C. (2017). Economic Structures, Institutions and Economic Performance. *Economic Structures, 6*(2), 1–18.

Crucini, M. J. (1997). Country Size and Economic Fluctuations. *Review of International Economics, 5*(2), 204–220.

Curtin, P. D. (1989). *Death by Migration: Europe's Encounter with the Tropical World in the Nineteenth Century*. Cambridge University Press.
Curtin, P. D. (1998). *Disease and Empire: The Health of European Troops in the Conquest of Africa*. Cambridge University Press.
Dell, M., Jones, M. F., & Olken, B. A. (2012). Temperature Shocks and Economic Growth: Evidence from the Last Half Century. *American Economic Journal: Macroeconomics, 4*(3), 66–95.
Depetris-Chauvin, E., & Weil, D. N. (2013). Malaria and Early African Development: Evidence from the Sickle Cell Trait. *NBER Working Paper No. 19603*. National Bureau of Economic Research.
Diamond, J. (1997). *Guns, Germs, and Steel. The Fates of Human Societies*. W.W. Norton and Company.
Dirk, K. (2021). On the Socio-Economic Impact of Pandemics in Africa: Lessons Learned from COVID-19, Trypanosomiasis, HIV, Yellow Fever and Cholera. *MPRA Paper No. 107591*. Munich Personal RePEc Archive.
Dumett, R. E. (1968). The Campaign Against Malaria and the Expansion of Scientific, Medical and Sanitary Services in British West Africa, 1898–1910. *African Historical Studies, 1*, 153–197.
Easterly, W., & Kraay, A. (2000). Small States, Small Problems? Income, Growth, and Volatility in Small States. *World Development, 28*(11), 2013–2027.
Easterly, W., & Levine, R. (1998). Troubles with the Neighbours: Africa's Problem, Africa's Opportunity. *Journal of African Economics, 7*(1), 120–142.
Easterly, W., & Levine, R. (2003). Tropics, Germs, and Crops: How Endowments Influence Economic Development. *Journal of Monetary Economics, 50*, 3–40.
Englebert, P. (2000). Pre-Colonial Institutions, Post-Colonial States, and Economic Development in Tropical Africa. *Political Research Quarterly, 53*(1), 7–36.
Englebert, P., Tarango, S., & Carter, M. (2002). Dismemberment and Suffocation: A Contribution the Debate on African Boundaries. *Comparative Political Studies, 35*(10), 1093–1118.
Ewald, J. (1992). Slavery in Africa and the Slave Trade from Africa. *American Historical Review, 97*(2), 465–485.
Faye, M. L., Macarthur, J. W., Sachs, J. D., & Snow, T. (2004). The Challenges Facing Landlocked Developing Countries. *Journal of Human Development, 5*(1), 31–68.
Ferguson, N. (2003). *Empire: The Rise and Demise of the British World Order and the Lessons for Global Power*. Basic Books.
Ferguson, N. (2004). *Empire: How Britain Made the Modern World*. Penguin Books.
Fukuyama, F. (2014). *Political Order and Political Decay*. Profile Books.
Furceri, D., Çelik, S. K., & Poplawski-Ribeiro, M. (2016). Government Consumption Volatility and the Size of Nations. *FinanzArchiv/Public Finance Analysis, 72*(2), 211–228.

Gallup, J. L., Luke, J., & Sachs, J. D. (2001). The Economic Burden of Malaria. *Supplement to the American Journal of Tropical Medicine & Hygiene, 64*(1–2), 85–96.

Gallup, J. L., Sachs, J. D., & Mellinger, A. D. (1999). Geography and Economic Development. *International Regional Science Review, 22*(2), 179–232.

Gennaioli, N., & Rainer, I. (2006). Precolonial Centralization and Institutional Quality in Africa. In M. Gradstein & K. Konrad (Eds.), *Institutions and Norms in Economic Development.* MIT Press.

Gennaioli, N., & Rainer, I. (2007). The Modern Impact of Precolonial Centralization in Africa. *Journal of Economic Growth, 12*(3), 185–234.

Glaister, K. W., Driffield, N., & Lin, Y. (2020). Foreign Direct Investment to Africa: Is There a Colonial Legacy? *Management International Review, 60*, 315–349.

Green, E. (2012). Explaining African Ethnic Diversity. *International Political Science Review, 34*, 235–253.

Guiso, L., Sapienza, P., & Zingales, L. (2009). Cultural Biases in Economic Exchange. *Quarterly Journal of Economics, 124*(3), 1095–1131.

Havinden, M., & Meredith, D. (1993). *Colonialism and Development: Britain and its Tropical Colonies, 1850–1960.* Routledge.

Headrick, D. (2014). Sleeping Sickness Epidemics and Colonial Responses in East and Central Africa, 1900–1940. *PLoS Neglected Tropical Diseases, 8*(4), e2772.

Headrick, R. (1994). *Colonialism, Health, and Illness in French Equatorial Africa, 1885–1935.* African Studies Association Press.

Heidhues, F., & Obare, G. (2011). Lessons from Structural Adjustment Programmes and their Effects in Africa. *Quarterly Journal of International Agriculture, 50*(1), 55–64.

Herbst, J. (2000). *States and Power in Africa.* Princeton University Press.

Herbst, J. (2014). *States and Power in Africa: A Comparative Lessons in Authority and Control.* Princeton University Press.

Heywood, L. (2009). Slavery and its Transformation in the Kingdom of Kongo: 1491–1800. *The Journal of African History, 50*, 1–22.

Hidalgo, C., Klinger, B., Barabasi, A., & Hausmann, R. (2007). The Product Space Conditions the Development of Nations. *Science, 317*(5837), 482–487.

IMF. (2020). What is Capitalism. *Back to Basics Series.* International Monetary Fund. Retrieved April, 2024, from https://www.imf.org/external/pubs/ft/fandd/basics/2_capitalism.htm

Inikori, J. E. (1982). *Forced Migration: The Impact of the Export Slave Trade on West African Societies.* Africana Publishing.

Inikori, J. E. (2000). Africa and the Trans-Atlantic Slave Trade. In T. Falola (Ed.), *Africa Volume I: African History before 1885.* Carolina Academic Press.

Inikori, J. E. (2003). The Struggle against the Trans-Atlantic Slave Trade. In A. Diouf (Ed.), *Fighting the Slave Trade: West African Strategies.* Ohio University Press.

Jerven, M. (2014). The Emergence of Capitalism in Africa. In L. Neal (Ed.), *Cambridge History of Capitalism.* Cambridge University Press.

Jones, P. (2013). History Matters: New Evidence on the Long-Run Impact of Colonial Rule on Institutions. *Journal of Comparative Economics, 41*(1), 181–200.

Kipling, R. (1899). *The White Man's Burden.* Retrieved May, 2024, from https://www.kiplingsociety.co.uk/poem/poems_burden.htm

Ki-Zerbo, J. (1978). *Histoire de l'Afrique Noire, d'Hier à Demain.* Hatier.

Klerman, D. M., Mahoney, P. G., Spamann, H., & Weinstein, M. I. (2011). Legal Origin or Colonial History? *Journal of Legal Analysis, 3*(2), 379–409.

Kostova, T., & Zaheer, S. (1999). Organizational Legitimacy Under Conditions of Complexity: The Case of the Multi-National Enterprise. *Academy of Management Review, 24*(1), 64–81.

La Porta, R., Lopez-de Silanes, F., & Shleifer, A. (2008). The Economic Consequences of Legal Origins. *Journal of Economic Literature, 46*(2), 285–332.

La Porta, R., Lopez-de-Silanes, F., Shleifer, A., & Vishny, R. W. (1998). Law and Finance. *The Journal of Political Economy, 106*(6), 1113–1155.

La Porta, R., Lopez-de-Silanes, F., Shleifer, A., & Vishny, R. W. (1999). The Quality of Government. *Journal of Law, Economics, and Organization, 15*, 222–279.

Lahiri, B., & Masjidi, F. K. (2012). Landlocked Countries: A Way to Integrate with Coastal Economies. *Journal of Economic Integration, 27*(4), 505–519.

Lange, M., Mahoney, J., & vom Hau, M. (2006). Colonialism and Development: A Comparative Analysis of Spanish and British Colonies. *American Journal of Sociology, 111*(5), 1412–1462.

Leak, S. G. A. (1999). *Tsetse Biology and Ecology: Their Role in the Epidemiology and Control of Trypanosomosis.* CABI Publishing.

Lee, A., & Schultz, K. A. (2012). Comparing British and French Colonial Legacies: A Discontinuity Analysis of Cameroon. *Quarterly Journal of Political Science, 7*, 1–46.

Levine, R. (1999). Financial Development and Economic Growth: Views and Agenda. *Policy Research Working Papers.* World Bank.

Lovejoy, P. (Ed.). (1981). *The Ideology of Slavery in Africa.* Sage Books.

Lovejoy, P. (1983). Transformations in Slavery. *African Studies Series No. 36.* Cambridge University Press.

Lovejoy, P. E. (2012). *Transformations in Slavery: A History of Slavery in Africa.* Cambridge University Press.

Lowes, S., & Montero, E. (2021). The Legacy of Colonial Medicine in Central Africa. *American Economic Review, 111*(4), 1284–1314.

Luo, Y., & Mezias, J. M. (2002). Liabilities of Foreignness: Concepts, Constructs, and Consequences. *Journal of International Management, 8*(3), 217–221.
M'baye, B. (2006). The Economic, Political, and Social Impact of the Atlantic Slave Trade on Africa. *The European Legacy, 11*(6), 607–622.
Mamdani, M. (1996). *Citizen and Subject: Contemporary Africa and the Legacy of Late Colonialism*. Princeton University Press.
Manning, P. (1990). *Slavery and African Life: Occidental, Oriental, and African Slave Trades*. Cambridge University Press.
Martin, G. (2005). The West, Natural Resources and Population Control Policies in Africa in Historical Perspective. *Journal of Third World Studies, 22*(1), 69–107.
Maseland, R. (2018). Is Colonialism History? The Declining Impact of Colonial Legacies on African Institutional and Economic Development. *Journal of Institutional Economics, 14*(2), 259–287.
Masocha, W., & Kristensson, K. (2019). Human African trypanosomiasis: How do the parasites enter and cause dysfunctions of the nervous system in murine models? *Brain Research Bulletin, 145*, 19–29.
Melamed, J. (2015). Racial Capitalism. *Critical Ethnic Studies, 1*(1), 76–85.
Miapyen, B. S., & Bozkurt, U. (2022). Racial Capitalism and Capitalism in Africa: The Utility and Limits of Cedric Robinson's Perspective. *Review of African Political Economy*. Retrieved May, 2024, from https://doi.org/10.1080/03056244.2022.2075722
Michalopoulos, S., & Papaioannou, E. (2013). Pre-Colonial Ethnic Institutions and Contemporary African Development. *Econometrica, 81*(1), 113–152.
Michalopoulos, S., & Papaioannou, E. (2014). National Institutions and Subnational Development in Africa. *Quarterly Journal of Economics, 129*(1), 151–213.
Michalopoulos, S., & Papaioannou, E. (2016). The Long-Run Effects of the Scramble for Africa. *American Economic Review, 106*(7), 1802–1848.
Michalopoulos, S., & Papaioannou, E. (Eds.). (2017). *The Long Economic and Political Shadow of History Volume II. Africa and Asia*. Vox e-Book, CEPR Press, Centre for Economic Policy Research.
Moghalu, C. K. (2014). *Emerging Africa: How the Global Economy's 'Last Frontier' can Prosper and Matter*. Penguin Book.
Murdock, G. P. (1959). *Africa: Its Peoples and Their Culture History*. McGraw-Hill Book Company.
Murdock, G. P. (1967). *Ethnographic Atlas*. University of Pittsburgh Press; Pittsburgh.
Ndlovu-Gatsheni, S. J. (2015). Genealogies of Coloniality and Implications for Africa's Development. *African Development, 40*(3), 13–40.
North, D. C. (1990). *Institutions, Institutional Change, and Economic Performance*. Cambridge University Press.

North, D. C., Wallis, J. J., & Weingast, B. R. (2009). *Violence and Social Orders: A Conceptual Framework for Interpreting Recorded Human History*. Cambridge University Press.

Nunn, N. (2008). The Long-Term Effects of Africa's Slave Trades. *Quarterly Journal of Economics, 123*(1), 139–176.

Nunn, N. (2010). "Shackled to the Past: The Causes and Consequences of Africa's Slave Trades," in *Natural Experiments of History* (eds. Diamond, J. and Robinson, J.A.), 142-184, Harvard University Press, Harvard, USA.

Nunn, N. (2017). Understanding the Long-Run Effects of Africa's Slave Trades. In S. Michalopoulos & E. Papaioannou (Eds.), *The Long Economic and Political Shadow of History Volume II. Africa and Asia* (pp. 37–50). Vox e-Book, CEPR Press, Centre for Economic Policy Research.

Nunn, N., & Wantchekon, K. (2011). The Slave Trade and the Origins of Mistrust in Africa. *American Economic Review, 101*(7), 3221–3252.

Ocheni, S., & Nwankwo, B. C. (2012). Analysis of Colonialism and Its Impact in Africa. *Cross-Cultural Communication, 8*(3), 46–54.

Olsson, O., & Hansson, G. (2011). Country Size and the Rule of Law: Resuscitating Montesquieu. *European Economic Review, 55*(5), 613–629.

Omeje, K. (2021). *The Failure and Feasibility of Capitalism in Africa*. Palgrave Macmillan.

Packard, R. M. (2007). *The Making of a Tropical Disease: A Short History of Malaria*. JHU Press.

Pierce, L., & Snyder, J. A. (2018). The Historical Slave Trade and Firm Access to Finance in Africa. *The Review of Financial Studies, 31*(1), 142–174.

Pierce, L., & Snyder, J. A. (2020). Historical Origins of Firm Ownership Structure: The Persistent Effects of the African Slave Trade. *Academy of Management Journal, 63*(6), 1687–1713.

Raleigh, C., & Hegre, H. (2009). Population Size, Concentration and Civil War: A Geographically Disaggregated Analysis. *Political Geography, 28*(4), 224.

Redding, S., & Venables, A. J. (2004). Economic Geography and International Inequality. *Journal of International Economics, 62*(1), 53–82.

Reinert, E. (2007). Institutionalism, Ancient, Old and New: A Historical Perspective on Institutions and Uneven Development. In H. J. Chang (Ed.), *Institutional Change and Economic Development*. United Nations University Press.

Reinert, E. (2008). *How Rich Countries Got Rich and Why Poor Countries Stay Poor*. Constable & Robinson.

Richens, P. (2009). The Economic Legacies of the 'Thin White Line': Indirect Rule and the Comparative Development of Sub-Saharan Africa. *African Economic History, 37*, 33–102.

Robinson, C.J. (2000). *Black Marxism: The Making of the Black Radical Tradition*, University of California Press, Berkeley, California, USA.

Robinson, J. A. (2002). States and Power in Africa by Jeffrey I. Herbst: A Review Essay. *Journal of Economic Literature, 40*(2), 510–519.

Rodrik, D., Subramanian, A., & Trebbi, F. (2004). Institutions Rule: The Primacy of Institutions over Geography and Integration in Economic Development. *Journal of Economic Growth, 9*, 131–165.

Sachs, J. D. (2003). Institutions Don't Rule: Direct Effects of Geography on Per Capita Income. *NBER Working Paper No. 9490*. National Bureau of Economic Research.

Sachs, J. D. (2008). *Commonwealth: Economics for a Crowded Planet*. Penguin Books.

Sachs, J. D., & Malaney, P. (2002). The Economic and Social Burden of Malaria. *Nature, 415*, 680–685.

Salomon, R., & Wu, Z. (2012). Institutional Distance and Local Isomorphism Strategy. *Journal of International Business Studies, 43*(4), 343–367.

Slangen, A. H. L., & Beugelsdijk, S. (2010). The Impact of Institutional Hazards on Foreign Multinational Activity: A Contingency Perspective. *Journal of International Business Studies, 41*(6), 980–995.

Spolaore, E., & Wacziarg, R. (2013). How Deep are the Roots of Economic Development? *Journal of Economic Literature, 51*(2), 325–369.

Stilwell, S. (2014). *Slavery and Slaving in African History*. Cambridge University Press.

Tatah, M. (2017). *Africa in the Colonial Ages of Empire: Slavery, Capitalism, Racism, Colonialism, Decolonization, Independence as Recolonization*. Project Muse Langaa RPCIG.

Tedeschi, G. L. (2018). State History, Intergenerational Transmission and Institutional Trust in Africa. *CREDIT Research Paper No. 18/13*. Centre for Research in Economic Development and International Trade, University of Nottingham.

Tilley, H. (2011). *Africa as a Living Laboratory: Empire, Development, and the Problem of Scientific Knowledge, 1870–1950*. University of Chicago Press.

Tilley, H. (2016). Medicine, Empires, and Ethics in Colonial Africa. *AMA Journal of Ethics, 18*(7), 743–753.

Van Bavel, B. (2021). Market Dominance and Endogenous Decline: The Contribution of Historical Analysis. *Journal of Institutional Economics, 17*(1), 177–183.

Weingartner, K. (2020). 'The Fever': Questioning Malaria Management as a Colonial Legacy. *Development, 63*, 312–315.

Whatley, W. C. (2014). The Trans-Atlantic Slave Trade and the Origins of Political Authority in West Africa. In E. Akyeampong, R. H. Bates, N. Nunn, & J. A. Robinson (Eds.), *Africa's Development in Historical Perspective* (pp. 460–488). Cambridge University Press.

Whatley, W. C., & Gillezeau, R. (2011). The Impact of the Transatlantic Slave Trade on Ethnic Stratification in Africa. *American Economic Review: Papers and Proceedings, 101*, 571–576.

WHO. (2022). *Malaria Factsheet.* World Health Organization. Retrieved February, 2023, from https://www.who.int/news-room/fact-sheets/detail/malaria

World Bank. (2009). *World Development Report 2009: Reshaping Economic Geography*. World Bank.

Zaheer, S., & Mosakowski, E. (1997). The Dynamics of the Liability of Foreignness: A Global Study of Survival in Financial Services. *Strategic Management Journal, 18*(6), 439–463.

Zhang, Y., Xu, Z. P., & Kibriya, S. (2021). The Long-Term Effects of the Slave Trade on Political Violence in Sub-Saharan Africa. *Journal of Comparative Economics, 49*, 776–800.

Zhou, N., & Guillen, M. F. (2016). Categorizing the Liability of Foreignness: Ownership, Location, and Internalization Specific Dimensions. *Global Strategy Journal, 6*(4), 309–329.

Zouache, A. (2018). Institutions and the Colonisation of Africa: Some Lessons from French Colonial Economics. *Journal of Institutional Economics, 14*(2), 373–391.

CHAPTER 3

The Economic Policy Legacies Hampering FDI to Sub-Saharan Africa

Following the end of colonialism, post-independent[1] SSA countries have been shaped and hindered by colonial institutional and socio-economic legacies (Lyons & Jolley, 2018, p. 51). At its core, colonialism was devoted to the control and extraction of SSA's natural resource wealth. Hence, there was less attention paid to the socio-economic upliftment of the colonised peoples, nor the establishment of functional legitimate state administration, governance, and institutions (Tatah, 2017, pp. 145–146). Thus, new post-independent SSA states suffered from entrenched weak and fragile linkages between government institutions and society (Young, 1988), which in turn created a "deficit of legitimacy" (Thomson, 2000, p. 22), undermined social cohesion, and fostered civil conflict, coups, and wars (Lyons & Jolley, 2018, p. 58).

These institutional voids were also ossified by the liberation movements inherent nationalism, which, although necessary for the fight against colonialism, began to hinder post-independent economic policies. As Kalu (2016) explains, "the African nationalist movements focused exclusively on wresting political power from the European colonial masters without giving enough consideration to what to do with political independence.

[1] This chapter uses the term 'post-independent' rather than 'post-colonial' because independence only equates to post-colonialism once all vestiges and legacies of colonialism are eradicated (Ndlovu-Gatsheni & Mhlanga, 2013).

S. Gossel, *The Promise and Peril of FDI in Sub-Saharan Africa*, Palgrave Studies in African and Development Economics, https://doi.org/10.1007/978-3-032-01320-0_3

The early nationalist movements operated on the erroneous belief that Africa's problems would dissipate once the European colonial master handed over political power to Africans. There was little or no conscious effort to interrogate and dismantle the political arrangements and public service structures that fostered exploitation of the majority for the benefit of the colonial masters. The nationalist movements perhaps underestimated or incorrectly understood the impacts of institutions on social progress. The new African leaders simply stepped into power and inherited all the extractive structures set up by colonial Europe. In effect, what became of the independent African states was simply the replacement of white colonial masters with black rulers, or the replacement of European by African slave masters."

However, the view that post-independent African leaders merely continued along the tracks set by the colonial imperialists, and that SSA is a hopeless continent, doomed to live off debt and official development assistance (ODA) (The Economist, 2000), fails to take account of the international Cold War geopolitical dynamics and developmental distortions of the World Bank and IMF's neoliberal reform agendas. Over the decades, post-independent SSA has been shaken by the pressures and tensions between domestic policy ideology and international realpolitik.

Although SSA is increasingly taking its rightful place on the global stage, decades after most of SSA gained independence, the region unfortunately remains at the periphery of the global product space; and after half a century of post-independence, still has only made limited leeway in shifting from low-skilled resource extractive-based economies towards higher skills-based, technologically advanced beneficiation and manufacturing. Hence, SSA persistently ranks as the poorest region in the world, and FDI to SSA continues to lag FDI investment to other developing regions. In order to reach the Millennium Development Goals (UN, 2000), SSA requires an annual growth rate of 7%, which in turn requires an investment ratio of 25% of GDP (Loots & Kabundi, 2012). World Bank data however shows that over the period of 2010–2020, SSA's average economic growth rate, gross fixed capital formation as a percentage of GDP, and gross savings as a percentage of GDP only averaged 3.0%, 21.2%, and 20.2% respectively. Thus, the region continues to use foreign savings in the form of foreign debt, ODA, and FDI to fill the financing gap. Over the course of the last few decades, capital to SSA has swung in tandem with these economic policy waves with the period of African Socialism and then neoliberalism being primarily funded by ODA and debt whereas the post-millennium period has seen the rise of FDI. Hence, FDI to SSA is a relatively recent phenomenon.

While blame for SSA's persistent governance and economic strife has been laid at the feet of the African elites (Carmody, 2016, p. 4; van de Walle, 2002, 2003), the neo-colonial system (Bond, 2006), or the politicisation of aid (Moyo, 2009), in many circumstances these detrimental factors are the outcomes of conflicting economic ideologies that have plagued SSA over the post-independent period. This chapter therefore explores how post-independent economic policies and global geopolitics shaped SSA's FDI flows. The discussion commences with a review of the three post-independent political economic waves: First, African Socialism and the Cold War; second, Neoliberalism, the Washington Consensus, and Structural Adjustment Programs; and third, the AU, NEPAD, and globalisation. Thereafter, the chapter explores the effects and implications of these policy waves on SSA's FDI inflows.

3.1 The Rise and Fall of African Socialism

Upon achieving independence, SSA countries were in desperate need of socio-economic development, having gained control of states burdened with high levels of poverty and unemployment, low levels of education and skills, lacking physical infrastructure beyond that needed for natural resource extraction; and suffering from weak bureaucratic capacity, political fragmentation, and patrimonialism (Akyeampong, 2017; Sun, 2019). It was thus hoped that the natural resource endowments that had been the *raison d'être* for colonialism could provide a foundation for rapid economic growth and development (Collier & Gunning, 1999; Lundgren et al., 2013).

In order to break free from their colonial experiences of racism, inequality, economic subdevelopment, and stratified and divided societies, post-independent leaders advocated for development based on an ideology of *African Socialism*[2] (Christensen & Laitin, 2019, p. 244). Broadly, the guiding principles of African Socialism were political and economic autonomy, self-reliance, Africanisation of business, Pan-Africanism, and non-alignment (Akyeampong, 2017). It was thus envisaged that socio-economic development would be driven by a unique form of socialism that would

[2] A term first used in the Kenyan Ministry of Economic Planning and Development sessional paper number 10 in 1965.

embed a post-independent African identity while actively avoiding the formation of social class structures (Yacouba & Wologueme, 2018). Philosophically however, there were a range of African Socialisms (Sun, 2019), such as Julius Nyerere and Patrice Lumumba's 'Pan-Africanism,' Kwame Nkrumah's "Scientific Socialism," Kenneth Kaunda's humanism, and Leopold Senghor's "Neritude" (Otunnu, 2015).

Post-independence, SSA's leaders were however faced with a choice between capitalist and socialist ideologies. Although socialism was viewed as more relevant for agrarian-based development, there were fears that adopting socialism or communism would bind newly independent SSA countries to Russia or China and thus limit Western aid and assistance (Hunter, 2022, p. 468). Capitalism was however viewed with suspicion as it was feared that Western capital could diminish the accomplishment and intent of political independence, opening the door to neo-colonialism (Akyeampong, 2017), which Nkrumah (1966: x) described as "the worst form of imperialism. For those who practice it, it means power without responsibility and for those who suffer from it, it means exploitation without redress". African Socialism thus advocated for a mix between capitalist and socialist development by combining the capitalist economic principles with socialist prevention of class-conflicts. This would be achieved by 'Africanising' the socialist state, separating socialism from Marxist-Leninism (Sun, 2019), and integrating the "African personality" (Nkrumah, 1970). African socialism was thus conceived as a means to develop decolonised economies while fortifying "an attitude of mind" (Nyerere, 1967) that would 'decolonize the African psyche' (Biko, 2004; Fanon, 1967).

Practically, African Socialism adopted a range of developmental trajectories, evidenced by the revisionist and pragmatic socialists in Guinea, Ghana, Senegal, Mali, Tanzania, and Zambia; the military coup leaders in Benin, Burkina Faso, Congo, Madagascar, and Somalia; and socialist orientated liberation governments in Angola, Ethiopia, Mozambique, and Zimbabwe (Lösch, 1990). Crucial to most African Socialists however was the collectivism of agriculture, such as Nyerere's *ujamaa vijijini* (or 'familyhood' in Swahili) (Inukai, 1974). It was envisaged that 'villagisation' would overcome colonial marginalisation and ethnic fragmentation by restoring Africa's traditionally egalitarian values and culture (Otunnu, 2015) while the relocation of the rural populations would make it easier to deliver social and educational services (Shivji, 2010, pp. 120–133).

The implementation and outcomes of villagisation were however economically and socially harmful, mainly as a result of droughts and famines, mismanagement and uneconomic agricultural policies, and the global financial crises of the 1970s and 1980s (Otunnu, 2015). The forced relocation of the rural population however reinforced the class divide and entrenched rural underdevelopment (Sheridan, 2004)[3] while the taxation of agricultural production destroyed the ability of farmers to invest, expand, or produce more efficiently (Acharya, 1981). For example, in Tanzania, devastation of the agricultural sector due to price controls, taxation, expropriation, and government intervention led to agricultural output growth below population growth and the country thus slid from being a net food exporter in 1970 to having to import one million tons of grain to avert starvation in 1981 (Libby, 1987, p. 254 quoted in Ayittey, 2019). By 1984, tonnage of all export crops was 20% less than it had been in 1970, and basic food crops were 50% less (Zinsmeister, 1987, p. 33) while the effective expropriation rate for Ghanaian cocoa farmers was 90%, and Gambian peanut producers and Tanzanian maize farmers was 80%. Hence, instead of fostering egalitarian post-colonialism, villagisation led to "economic stagnation, political centralisation, and a clear-eyed cynicism" (Sheridan, 2004).

In addition to agriculture, state-centric economic policies included price controls, foreign exchange appreciation, monopolisation of international trade, regulation of the private sector, the establishment of state-owned enterprises, and import substitution industrialisation (ISI) (UN, 2008). However, allowing the foreign exchange rate to appreciate (to support urban consumption-fuelled import-led growth) eventually produced trade deficits, depleted foreign currency reserves, and encouraged high debt burdens (Christensen & Laitin, 2019, pp. 251–252). Price controls created artificial shortages and stimulated the formation of illicit markets, which in many cases were only unified after the exchange rate reforms in the mid-1980s (Agenor, 1992). Throughout the 1960s and 1970s there was a dramatic increase in the number and scope of state-owned enterprises (SOE). For example, the number of SOEs in Tanzania rose from 80 in 1967 to 400 in 1981; in Kenya, from 20 in 1963 to 60 in 1969; and in Ghana, from none in 1959 to nearly 400 in the early 1960s (D'almeida, 1986, p. 56). Yet, the performance of these SOEs suffered from

[3] In Tanzania for example, from 1973 to 1977, 11.1 million people were moved to 8000 *ujamaa* villages (Zinsmeister, 1987).

low-capacity utilisation and efficiency rates, clientelistic over-staffing, and perpetual unprofitability, which eventually proved so financially unsustainable that by the 1980s, many SSA countries required financial assistance from the IMF and World Bank[4] (World Bank, 2005).

The policy of import substitution entails the domestic trade and tariff protected production of goods that are typically sourced internationally. Diversification of the economy thus relies on increasing domestic production and technological capacity by shifting the economy away from agriculture to manufacturing (Bruton, 1998; Adewale, 2017). In theory, the resulting current account deficit should be corrected by international capital inflows, and over time, as the export structure migrates from primary to more sophisticated manufactured goods, the current account should then revert to equilibrium (Bruton, 1998). ISI had been widely adopted in many Latin American and South Asian countries throughout the 1950s and 1960s, and was adopted in SSA by Nigeria, Tanzania, and Zambia in the 1960s; Ghana and Madagascar in the early 1970s; and Burundi, Ethiopia, Senegal, and Sudan thereafter (Mendes et al., 2014).

Fuelled by petrodollars from the oil booms of the 1970s, ISI initially had a positive effect on SSA's economic growth and productivity (Archibong et al., 2021), but in time, as the capital dried up, two detrimental policy outcomes became apparent. First, policies enacted to isolate the nascent domestic producers from foreign competition and for exchange rate over-valuation led to inefficient and mispriced production that eroded the comparative advantage of natural resources and labour, thus rendering SSA even more reliant on natural resource extraction (Christensen & Laitin, 2019, p. 257). Second, foreign investment was prioritised over domestic investment via taxation exemptions, preferential credit access, low customs duty, duty-free imports, and favourable exchange rates (Stein, 1994). Consequently, domestic industrialisation and skills development stagnated while foreign investment was devoted to capital-intensive non-durable goods, which could not be easily exported because of small markets, large distances between markets, and poor infrastructure (Bruton, 1998). Thus, instead of balancing the current account, foreign capital was often repatriated, yielding persistent current account deficits and negative net capital accounts (Mendes et al., 2014).

[4]For example, when Nkrumah was overthrown in a coup in 1966, Ghana was effectively bankrupt (Aryeetey & Fosu, 2008, p. 297) and only 4 out of 64 state enterprises were able to breakeven (Garlick, 1971, p. 141 quoted in Ayittey, 2019).

Yacouba and Wologueme (2018) thus conclude that the failure of African Socialism can be ascribed to three ideological shortcomings. First, it was unable to overcome the colonial class divide between the privileged and disenfranchised. While it was believed that education would narrow the gap and foster indigenous pride, in reality, the economic side-effects of African Socialism deprived the education systems of necessary resources and thus although literacy rates improved, intellectual and academic outcomes were poor (Otunnu, 2015). In addition, many of the elite who studied abroad were seduced by neo-colonialism and became alienated from their cultural heritage, both of which undermined the ideological foundations of African Socialism. Second, it was not clear that the general populace understood or identified with socialism, which is one of the reasons so many of the African Socialist leaders, such as Nkrumah and Keita, were overthrown in military coups. Related to this, the third failing is that African Socialism did not adequately include a strategy for the use of military power for domestic protection and support of the socialist ideology. Consequently, the military became a repressive threat to the civilian population and to the political leadership (as evidenced by the 25 coup d'états that occurred between January 1963 to December 1969). Hence, African Socialism was unable to inculcate a uniquely African form of socialism nor to develop an economically sustainable alternative to capitalism.

In the 1970s and 1980s, the leaders of many liberation movements in SSA believed that the failures of African Socialism did not necessarily mean that state-led socialism was not applicable to SSA, but rather that Afro-Marxism was the higher path to the African socialist destination (Munslow, 1986, pp. 10–11). The non-aligned focus of African Socialism thus transitioned into a more overtly Communist aligned *Afrocommunism* or *Afro-Marxism* (Lösch, 1990). In time however, Cold War politics increasingly forced a narrowing of African foreign policy and developmental ideology into the binary choice between the West, particularly the United Kingdom (UK) and the United States of America (US), and the Union of the Soviet Socialist Republics (USSR) (Speich, 2019). SSA was thus obliged to adapt to a "form of global coloniality that dramatized the emergence of two competing imperialist empires, one claiming to be spreading international socialism and the other to be defending western capitalist-Christian civilization" (Ndlovu-Gatsheni, 2015, p. 32).

Throughout the 1970s and 1980s, Africa rapidly became a chessboard of brutal 'hot wars' in Angola, Mozambique, and South West Africa (present-day Namibia); proxy conflicts between the West and USSR underscored by the supply of weapons and advisors (Cooper, 2019, p. 239); or by the propping up of ideologically aligned dictators, such as the USSR support of Mengistu Haile Mariam of Ethiopia, who claimed to be a Marxist, and the USA support of Mobutu Sese Seko of Zaire (present-day Democratic Republic of the Congo) who claimed to be opposing communism (Schmidt, 2013). During the 1980s, the USSR was supportive of many socialist governments and liberation movements in SSA. Yet, when the USSR fell in 1989, Russia had little left to benefit SSA; ideologically and financially bereft, Russia's support for SSA dwindled, leaving SSA USD 17 billion indebted to Russia (Faleg & Secrieru, 2020).

In addition, the exploitation, expropriation, and misappropriation of state resources, associated with African Socialism and the fall of the USSR, coupled with the Cold War weapons readily available to warlords, criminals, proxy combatants, ruling elites, and insurgents, led to significant political and social crises in many SSA countries, including civil wars in Burundi, Cote D'Ivoire, Guinea-Bissau, Liberia, Nigeria, Rwanda, Sierra Leone, and Uganda (Kalu, 2016; Cooper, 2019, p. 239). Hence, instead of the economic development that African Socialism was supposed to generate, most SSA countries entered the post-Cold War world still suffering from the colonial legacies of extractive institutions and elitist predatory political systems.

3.2 The Rise and Fall of Neoliberalism

The origins of neoliberalism are contested, but the underlying principles are derived from the economic theories of Fredrich Hayek and Milton Friedman. Basically, neoliberalism rejects Keynesian economics and the welfare state, arguing that state economic intervention is "the road to serfdom" (Hayek, 1944), and instead, free markets can produce more efficient and beneficial outcomes (Connell & Dados, 2014). In developed countries, neoliberal policies were therefore regarded as a free market revolt against Keynesian state involvement in the economy, which it was claimed led to decreased corporate profitability and share prices, high inflation, and the creation of the welfare 'nanny state' (Dumenil & Levy, 2004). The ideology of neoliberalism spread via institutions such as the Mont Pelerin Society, the Chicago School of economics, and corporate foundations and think-tanks before being adopted as government policy by US President Ronald Reagan and UK Prime Minister Margaret

Thatcher in the 1980s—giving rise to "Reaganomics" and "Thatcherism" (Jackson, 2010).

By the early 1980s, many SSA countries were facing debt crises and thus turned to the Bretton Woods institutions for debt relief. By this stage, neoliberalism had become accepted dogma at the IMF and World Bank, leading to the promulgation of "Washington Consensus" accompanied by "Structural Adjustment Programs" (SAPs) (Connell & Dados, 2014). The term Washington Consensus was coined by the economist John Williamson in 1989 to refer to a set of Washington-based market-oriented policy reforms that were advocated as remedies for Latin America's economic malaise (Archibong et al., 2021). These policies coalesced into SAPs, which were prescribed for debt relief and financial assistance (Naiman & Watkins, 1999; Mkandiwire & Soludo, 1999). SAPs typically consist of a combination of stabilisation and structural adjustment policies. Stabilisation policies include IMF administered short-run prescriptions that focus on economic crisis mitigation whereas structural adjustment policies fall under the remit of the World Bank and focus on long-run macroeconomic restructuring (Hope & Kayira, 1997).

It was hoped that SAPs would remedy SSA's price distortions, overvalued exchange rates and wages, and facilitate the liberalisation of agricultural and commodity prices and subsidies (Due & Gladwin, 1991; Chari et al., 2020). Neoliberal austerity reforms advocated for the liberalisation of SSA's trade, investment, and labour markets; deregulation of domestic markets, privatisation of state-owned enterprises, devaluation of SSA's currencies, fiscal discipline, and the rationalisation of welfare spending, thus shifting the economic foundations of SSA's political economies from African Socialism to free-market capitalism (Gibbon et al., 1992; Mkandawire & Olukoshi, 1996; Heidhues et al., 2004). During the 1980s and early 1990s, 46 African countries sought assistance from the IMF, 84 structural adjustment loans were granted by the World Bank (IMF, 2012; van der Geest, 1994, p. 189), and over 200 SAPs were implemented (Harrison, 2019).

In the short run, many SSA countries benefited from the liberalisation of inefficient, over-regulated trade regimes, heightened competition, and the privatisation of over-indebted state-owned enterprises (Hope & Kayira, 1997; Williams, 2007). However, over the long run, the reforms failed to stimulate economic growth and development; GDP per capita growth was negative and volatile, inflation remained stubbornly high, agriculture and industrial output fell, while poverty and unemployment remained largely unaffected (Babatunde, 2012). In addition, the adoption of reforms without the ability to increase tax revenues meant that most SSA countries had no choice other than to cut expenditure on socially beneficial services such as infrastructure, education, and social services, which then worsened the urban-rural divide (Heidhues et al., 2004; Poku & Whitman, 2018, pp. 3–4).

Many of the detrimental effects were ascribed to the over-emphasis of export-orientated liberalisation, an insufficient understanding of SSA's social and political circumstances (Stein, 1994; Heidhues & Obare, 2011) and conflating structural adjustment with poverty alleviation programs (van de Walle, 1994). Proponents counter that the reasons for the failure of the reforms can be ascribed to incomplete and haphazard implementation (World Bank, 2001), inefficient or uncoordinated sequencing (Cornia & Helleiner, 1994; World Bank, 2000), the decline in demand for SSA's primary products during the 1980s and 1990s (Mkandiwire & Soludo, 1999), and the effects of high inflation on real incomes (Due & Gladwin, 1991; Ekpo, 1992). Nevertheless, the evidence shows that rather than reversing SSA's grim social and economic circumstances, the neoliberal reforms undermined SSA's long-run development instead (Owusu, 2003).

In addition to the Washington Consensus and SAP reforms, SSA countries also underwent significant restructuring of their public sectors, driven by the ideology of "New Public Management" (NPM). NPM arose from public choice theory, principal-agent theory, and transaction cost economics in the 1980s (Kaboolian, 1998). As a reaction against Weberian hierarchical bureaucratic structures, NPM assumes that private sector managerialism can improve the efficiency and effectiveness of the public sector by adopting results-oriented management, output-oriented budgeting, information management programmes, contracting in the state, costing and monetisation of state functions, capacity-building, and performance-based incentives for public servants (Stiglitz & Heertje, 1989; OECD, 1995; Therkildsen, 2001, p. 3). In common with free-market reforms, NPM included public sector programs of 'downsizing', 'agencification', 'contracting', 'outsourcing', and 'right-sizing' (Cheung, 1996; Wollmann, 2003; Harrison, 2005).

The first countries to undertake NPM decentralisation in SSA were Botswana, Côte d'Ivoire, Ghana, Kenya, Nigeria, Tanzania, and Uganda during the 1990s (Cabral, 2011). NPM, along with SAPs and Washington Consensus, was viewed as a necessary free market reform to undo the economic damage inflicted by African Socialism (Tshombe & Dassah, 2018,

p. 20), as well as to rectify the resultant underperformance, corruption, inefficiency, and over-staffed state bureaucracies (Hope, 1997, 2001; Hope & Chikulo, 1999). One of the principal commonalities between Washington Consensus, SAPs, and NPM is that they all require political commitment to democratic governance and public sector decentralisation (Kettl, 2000; Tshombe & Dassah, 2018, p. 22). Hence, the World Bank and IMF advocated for twice as many reforms in SSA than in other developing regions (Therkildsen, 2001, p. 3), mainly because governments in Africa were deemed to be "sick and in need of doctors, obtainable from the private sector" (Basheka & Tshombe, 2018, p. 2).

The adoption of NPM in SSA is ongoing, uneven, and incomplete (Conyers, 2007; Rubakula, 2014) but one success has been the adoption of Medium-Term Expenditure Frameworks (MTEF) in many SSA countries,[5] which has enhanced sustainable expenditure over the long-term by encouraging medium-term budgetary planning (Gollwitzer, 2010), the privatisation of state-owned enterprises (ADB, 1999), and decentralisation of the civil service (Hope, 2001). Significant challenges persist however, mainly arising from the region's weak capacity, lack of political will, and entrenched corruption and patrimonialism (Engida & Bardill, 2013). In addition, questions remain about the relevance and institutional efficacy of adopting NPM systems that are more appropriate for Western democratic capitalist economies than for SSA's developing political, fiscal, and administrative structures (Jütting et al., 2004; Doorgapersad, 2011).

Despite the devolution of Washington Consensus, SAPs, and NPM, the lingering effects of these policies continue to shape SSA's socio-economic and institutional landscape. By overriding the African Union's (AU) Pan-African agenda, the reforms led to deindustrialisation and over-dependence on ODA (Gottschalk & Eduzie, 2014, p. 197) while the cuts in public welfare expenditure necessitated a commensurate increase in private non-governmental organisations (NGO) donor funding to maintain the provision of health, education, and social support (Harrison, 2005). In addition, the restructuring of SOEs had technical and political ramifications (Pitcher, 2004). Technically, government involvement in the SOEs increased rather than decreased because the valuation, transaction, and sale of the SOEs to

[5] Between 1992 and 2001, 13 African countries adopted MTEFs (all of them under the World Bank except for Namibia) and by 2004 18 African countries had reached grant inclusive budget surpluses (Gollwitzer, 2010).

the private sector depended on government approval, participation, and facilitation. Politically, governments used the opportunity of SOE restructuring and rationalisation to exact rents, buy political support, increase public involvement in the private sector, maintain or expand elite power and control, and blame outsiders for government failures (Johnston & Kouzmin, 1998).

As the 1990s wore on, the efficacy of SAPs was increasingly challenged by ongoing low growth rates in the least developed countries, by the Mexican crisis of 1994–1995, and by the rapid development of the non-SAP "Asian Tigers" (Pender, 2001). Hence by 1999, as the socio-economic damage from Washington Consensus, SAPs, and NPM became abundantly evident, and as a result of criticisms from institutions such as the Organization of African Unity (OAU) and United Nations International Children's Emergency Fund (UNICEF), World Bank President James Wolfensohn announced the replacement of neoliberal SAPs with the "Comprehensive Development Framework" (CDF). The CDF posited "that there was a set of structural, social, and human aspects of how societies develop that should be measured using an analytical framework in much the same way as the traditional financial metrics of development like GDP, investment, trade, and financial flows" (Kharas, 2020). The CDF thus focussed on three principles: Societal development (encompassing economic, social, political, environmental, and cultural aspects), poverty reduction, and country ownership of developmental policy (World Bank, 1999). The CDF thus "signalled a shift away from the donor-led development assistance strategy of the past two decades to the development of a country strategy led by a country itself" (Owusu, 2003).

In time, the CDF has been shown to be less coercive or punitive than Washington Consensus, and SAPs, and are thus deemed to be more inclusive and adaptable to a country's lived experience (Rodrik, 2006; Owusu, 2006). The World Bank (2003) assessment of CDF in three SSA countries (Burkina Faso, Ghana, and Uganda) and three developing countries (Bolivia, Romania, Vietnam) concluded that the CDF is shaped by country-specific economic, political, and social factors, and these characteristics in turn affect institutional development. CDF strategies are therefore less likely to succeed in fractionalised societies with weak institutions but have been found to have beneficial developmental effects on economic growth, poverty reduction, human development, and aid effectiveness. Harper-Shipman's (2019) assessment of CDF in Kenya is however less complimentary, finding that in practise, CDF tends to be less flexible than envisaged as it is tied to neoliberal ideology and tends to overlook crucial country-specific developmental characteristics. Nevertheless, the CDF was integrated into the Millennium Development Goals of 2000, the Monterrey Consensus of 2002, and the Sustainability Development Goals of 2015 (World Bank, 2003: ix).

3.3 From OAU to AU Agenda 2063

The Organization of African Unity (OAU) was born on 25 May 1963, headquartered in Addis Ababa, Ethiopia, the OAU was envisaged to allow Africa to "henceforth speak with one voice and be in a position to resist imperial rule and neo-colonialism. This singular development was watershed in inter-African relations" (Edo & Olanrewaju, 2012). The OAU's five stated objectives were "(a) To promote the unity and solidarity of the African States; (b) To coordinate and intensify their cooperation and efforts to achieve a better life for the peoples of Africa; (c) To defend their sovereignty, their territorial integrity and independence; (d) To eradicate all forms of colonialism from Africa; and (e) To promote international cooperation, having due regard to the Charter of the United Nations and the Universal Declaration of Human Rights" (OAU, 1963, II(1)).

The OAU was initially able to overcome a range of ideological, ethnic, religious, and colonial divisions; most demonstrably its ability to channel diplomatic financial, military, and logistical assistance to the liberation movements in South Africa, Rhodesia (Zimbabwe), and Namibia (EI-Khawas, 1978). However, in subsequent decades, three significant shortcomings bedevilled the OAU. First, the OAU had no military organisation and thus was incapable of resolving the various border disputes, civil wars, and coups on African soil (Kufuor, 2005). Second, the OAU was unable to counter the rampant military dictatorships, single-party regimes, unaccountable governments, and flagrant human rights abuses, which eventually led the OAU to be derided as a 'club of dictators' (Kimenyi, 2015). Third, the OAU failed to evolve into an economic union, and instead encouraged economic integration based on colonial foundations, such as Francophone, Anglophone, and Portuguese Countries, Arab League countries, and Commonwealth countries; or on regional location, such as the West African States (ECOWAS), Southern African Development Coordinating Commission (SADCC), North Africa-Greater Area Free Trade Area, and Central Africa-Economic Community of the Great Lakes countries (ibid.).

By the turn of the millennium, African leaders were hoping to shift from the OAU's objectives of colonial liberation and post-independent integration, to instead focus on the interests of Africa's citizens in a rapidly globalising world (Ogo, 2018). The OAU Extraordinary Meeting of the Heads of State and Government at Sirte in September 1999 finally formalised the transformation of the OAU. The Sirte Declaration provided the basis for the replacement of the OAU with a new Pan-African institution that would be "endowed with supranational competencies to enact common policies and compliance mechanisms among African member states to achieve the continent's Pan-African goals" (Gottschalk & Edozie, 2014, p. 31). The African Union (AU) was established on 26th May 2001 in Addis Ababa, Ethiopia, and formally launched on 9 July 2002 in South Africa. The vision of the AU is for "an integrated, prosperous and peaceful Africa, driven by its own citizens and representing a dynamic force in global arena" (Adeniyi et al., 2016). It was thus envisaged that the AU would "function as a vehicle to achieve an integrated, interdependent Africa imbued with the ideals of justice and peace and underpinned by political, economic, social, and cultural integration that would enable the continent to make the best of its human and material resources. As a suprastate the AU ensures the progress and prosperity of its citizens by taking advantage of the opportunities offered by a globalized world" (Gottschalk & Edozie, 2014, p. 184).

Following its inception, the AU has had success in quelling conflicts and post-election violence in many African countries through the AU's African Peace and Security Architecture and Peace and Security Council and forced the return to civilian rule in SSA countries that experienced military coups (Elischer & Lawrance, 2022). While progress of the AU on stimulating inter-African trade has been slow, the AU has increasingly devoted attention to removing the myriads of tariffs hampering Africa's trade and development and to pay more attention to international cooperation and development opportunities between the AU and the international community (Adeniyi et al., 2016). Ongoing concerns and weaknesses however relate to the AU's limited ability to influence the governance of individual states, to pre-empt political instability, coups, or conflicts; and to alleviate the non-military hardships facing Africa's citizens, such as environmental degradation and disasters, corruption and organised crime, and famine and disease (Bakare, 2014).

These weaknesses arise in part from the AU's inability to be self-funded. Unlike members of other regional blocs, such as the European Union

(EU), Association of Southeast Asian Nations, Arab League, or the Organization of American States, most of the AU member states are too poor to pay their membership dues and thus the AU is reliant on external funding, half of which comes from the former colonial powers (Gottschalk & Edozie, 2014, p. 196). The AU's approved budget for 2022 was USD 650 million (compared to the EU's budget of 168 billion Euros), comprising USD 176 million for operations, USD 195 million for AU programs, and USD 279 million for peace and security. While AU member states fund 72% of the operations and program costs, the entire peace and security budget is donor funded (Nantulya, 2022).

Among the most important AU programs, envisaged to overcome SSA's significant developmental and governance deficits however is the "New Partnership for Africa's Development" (NEPAD),[6] which was promulgated on 23rd October 2001 by South African President Thabo Mbeki, Nigerian President Olusegun Obasanjo, and Senegalese President Abdoulaye Wade under the auspices of the AU. NEPAD was born in the historic intersection between "the growing Afro-pessimism in the West, especially in the donors and scholarly circles, the declining level of aid to Africa after the Cold War, and indeed, the emergence of a new crop of democratically elected leaders in Africa" (Agbu, 2003, p. 78). NEPAD seeks to minimise SSA's developmental reliance on ODA (NEPAD, 2001, p. 1), arguing that Africa has failed to gain from globalisation because of "structural impediments, resources outflows and unfavourable terms of trade" and thus argues that to reduce poverty and marginalisation, SSA will need to actively engage with globalisation to "produce the results of ethics, equity, inclusion, human security and sustainable development" (Mbeki, 1999, quoted in Owusu, 2003). This is to be achieved "by bridging existing gaps in priority sectors to enable the continent to catch up with developed parts of the world" (Raji, 2015, p. 15), particularly the G8 countries (UK, Canada, Japan, Germany, France, Italy, and Russia) (Bobo, 2014).

NEPAD is premised on five core principles: (i) good governance and the entrenchment of democracy, (ii) peace and security, (iii) sound economic policymaking and execution, (iv) productive partnerships, and (v) domestic ownership and leadership (Agbu, 2003). The stated goals of NEPAD were to achieve a sustained average GDP growth rate of above 7%

[6] NEPAD arose from the integration of the "Millennium African Renaissance Programme", "Compact for African Recovery," and the "Omega Plan" (Agbu, 2003).

annually over the period of 2000–2015, reducing the number of people living in extreme poverty by half, enrol all children of school age in primary schools, make progress eliminating gender disparities in the enrolment in primary and secondary education, reduce infant and child mortality ratios by two-thirds, reduce maternal mortality ratios by three-quarters, provide access for all who need reproductive health services, and implement strategies for sustainable development to reverse the loss of environmental resources (NEPAD, 2001, p. 15).

At the core of NEPAD is Mbeki's concept of the "African Renaissance", which argues that "economic development results from fostering the productive forces of capitalism, and that political stability and accountability draw authority and legitimacy from the will of the people. To Mbeki, African rebirth hinges on its greater integration into the global economic and political system" (Owusu, 2003). NEPAD places primary importance on good governance and socio-economic development and thus makes provision for an African Peer Review Mechanism (APRM), which assesses and monitors the quality of governance to ensure governments are compliant with AU's Declaration on good governance (Jiboku & Okeke-Uzodike, 2016).

Like many of the programs that preceded it, NEPAD is espoused to be "African-generated, African-owned, African-led, African-operated" (Ojieh, 2014, p. 87), but in reality, it suffers from a lack of transparency, policy coherence, coercion, and tends to be guided by the interests of government (Signe, 2018, pp. 97–98). In addition, NEPAD requires an annual inflow of USD 64 billion and is therefore significantly reliant on financial support from the G8 nations (Akinboade & Lalthapersad-Pillay, 2009). Hence, NEPAD has been criticised as being inherently elitist, neo-liberal, imperialist, and neo-colonial (Ogo, 2018; Omotola, 2010; Raji, 2015). Over the last two decades, evidence indicates that although NEPAD has contributed to better governance and administration, and entrenched SSA as a development partner in international resource mobilisation, the lived reality of SSA's populace is still far removed from the stated goals of NEPAD, and the envisaged economic reforms and progress continue to be hobbled by Africa's political leadership (Signe, 2018, pp. 119–120). In addition, the region is still heavily reliant on foreign aid and debt, and international economic relations are still skewed in favour of G8 donor countries while "the World Trade Organization's disposition towards Africa oscillates between exclusion and marginalisation" (Omotola, 2010).

In recent years, NEPAD has increasingly been absorbed into the AU's "Agenda 2063", which was ratified at the 50th Anniversary of the OAU in Addis Ababa on 26th May 2013. Agenda 2063 defines Africa's aspirations for inclusive economic growth and sustainable development for the next fifty years. The seven 'aspirations' are: "(1) A prosperous Africa based on inclusive growth and sustainable development, (2) An integrated continent, politically united and based on the ideals of Pan-Africanism and the vision of Africa's Renaissance; (3) An Africa of good governance, democracy, respect for human rights, justice and the rule of law; (4) A peaceful and secure Africa; (5) An Africa with a strong cultural identity, common heritage, shared values and ethics; (6) An Africa whose development is people-driven, relying on the potential of African people, especially its women and youth, and caring for children; and (7) Africa as a strong, united, resilient and influential global player and partner" (African Union Commission, 2015, p. 2).

Despite these ideals, Agenda 2063 is likely to suffer from the same limitations and shortcomings that have bedevilled the AU and NEPAD. First, Agenda 2063 is dependent on a competent, professional, efficient, and apolitical public administration across the political, legal, bureaucratic, and policy dimensions of state (Forje, 2019, pp. 181–182). Yet SSA's public administration suffers from endemic corruption, poor leadership, weak governance, factionalism, clientelism, and politicisation (Southall, 2003a, 2003b). Second, in most SSA countries, the social contract between the government and the citizenry is very weak, political promises remain unfulfilled, and legitimate demands are ignored with impunity (Nwebo, 2018). Third, there are concerns that Agenda 2063 does not take adequate account of a dynamic multipolar geopolitical world and thus underappreciates the historic impediments to Africa's economic development, the instability arising from the uneven globalisation of capital and trade, and the growing threats of the War on Terror and climate change (Kararach et al., 2022).

Hence, even before the compounding effects of the Covid pandemic, the aspirations of Agenda 2063 are unlikely to be achieved unless African states reform their public administrations to be apolitical and appropriately structured for a rapidly changing ICT integrated, high skills, globalised world (Forje, 2019); strengthen their parliamentary democracies and

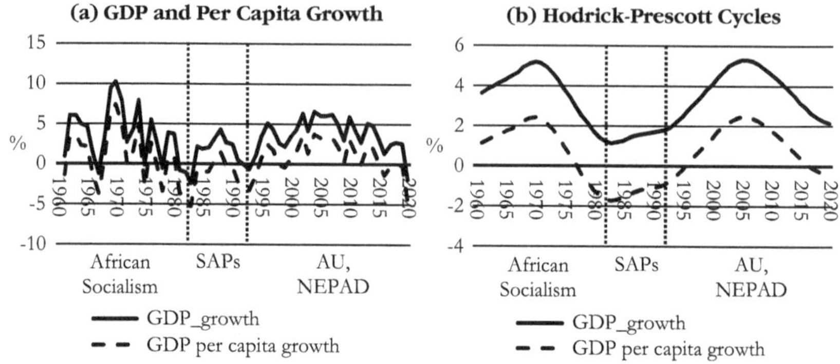

Fig. 3.1 GDP and per capita growth in SSA. (Data source: World Development Indicators)

enhance the legal impartiality, reach, and strength (Nwebo, 2018); and take advantage of financial globalisation to shift from ODA to long-term FDI, remittances, and trade (Kararach et al., 2022). The future success of Agenda 2063 and NEPAD thus hinges on the efficacy of the African Continental Free Trade Agreement (ACFTA) launched in July 2019, which aims to create a single African market, eliminating tariffs on 90% of goods, and unlocking a combined potential GDP of USD 3.4 trillion (El-Badawy et al., 2022).[7]

The effects of these policy waves can be seen from Fig. 3.1a and b, which shows the annual economic growth and per capita GDP growth rates, and Hodrick-Prescott filtered cyclicality over the period of 1960–2020. During the African Socialism and Cold War period, economic and per capita growth peaked in 1970 at 10.3% and 7.4% respectively but declined over the next decade, reaching a trough of −2.5% and −5.3% in 1983. Over the next decade of Washington Consensus SAP reforms, from 1984 to 1993, growth remained stagnant, averaging just 1.8% and −1.0% respectively. However, during the subsequent period of the AU, NEPAD, and heightened globalisation, growth recovered, rising from 1.1% and −1.5% in 1994, to a peak of 6.1% and 3.3% in 2007 before falling to African Socialism levels after the 2008 global financial crisis. Hence, over the decade from 1998 to 2007, average growth was 4.8% and 2.0% but averaged 3.1% and 0.4% thereafter.

[7] The ACFTA is discussed further in Chap. 6.

3.4 From ODA to FDI in SSA

SSA's experience with international capital has encompassed two significant overlapping waves. The first was USD 1 trillion in ODA over the 50-year period of 1960–2010 (Kabonga, 2016) while the second is the USD 640 billion in FDI from 1990 to current. Thus, for most of SSA's post-independent period, the region has relied on ODA rather than FDI. In theory, ODA should foster economic development by using foreign donor capital to overcome domestic capital constraints and thus filling the savings, foreign exchange, and fiscal gaps (Bacha, 1990). Yet, despite the promise of ODA, the economic outcomes have been disappointing, fuelling anger, recriminations, blame, and cynicism.

According to Neo-Colonial Dependency theory, which arose from Marxism in the 1950s, the goal of ODA was to make poor countries dependent on OECD countries, thus ensuring higher living standards for wealthy countries at the developmental expense of poor countries (Kabonga, 2016). False Paradigm theory, which originated in the 1960s, further argues that SSA's under-development can be attributed to the Global North's inappropriate policy prescriptions, which are based on a lack of understanding of Africa's characteristics, circumstances, and challenges (Momoh, 2016). Dambisa Moyo (2009) argues in her influential book that ODA has had three detrimental effects on SSA's development. First, ODA slows economic growth by eroding export competitiveness, increases inflation, and erodes the real value of savings. Second, ODA negatively affects African social and cultural well-being by patronisingly portraying Africans as eternally helpless, childishly dependent, and thus in need of rescue by wealthy Western countries (many of which are former colonisers). Third, ODA corrupts African governments, erodes democracy, and weakens accountability.

However, ODA dependency is also an outcome of the failures of African Socialism. Throughout the 1960s and 1970s, SSA's adherence to African Socialism had the economic effects of stifling economic growth, trade diversification, and capital flows (Saka & Momoh, 2015). International companies had little interest in domestic industrialisation in SSA and were more concerned with hampering nationalistic policies that would broaden domestic competition or interfere with their operations (Southall, 2016, p. 27). Consequently, SSA was unable to reap the benefits of international capital, and by the 1970s, SSA had become the most ODA dependent and over-indebted region in the world (Momoh, 2016). The advent of neoliberalism during the 1980s and 1990s, however, increasingly tied ODA provision to World Bank and IMF SAPs (Gulseven, 2020). SSA countries were therefore no longer granted ODA simply based on economic need, but rather, had to demonstrate their adherence to the IMF and World Bank's stipulated policy reforms.

As can be seen from Fig. 3.2a and b, throughout the 1970s and 1980s SSA's external public debt levels rose precipitously, from an average of 27.8% of gross national income (GNI) in the 1970s (averaging USD 36.1 billion annually) to 74.8% of GNI in the 1980s (averaging USD 213.9 billion annually). Over the same time, ODA increased from an average of 2.5% of GNI during the 1970s (averaging USD 3.1 billion annually) to an average of 3.7% of GNI during the 1980s (averaging USD 10.2 billion annually). Figure 3.2c further shows that during the decades of African

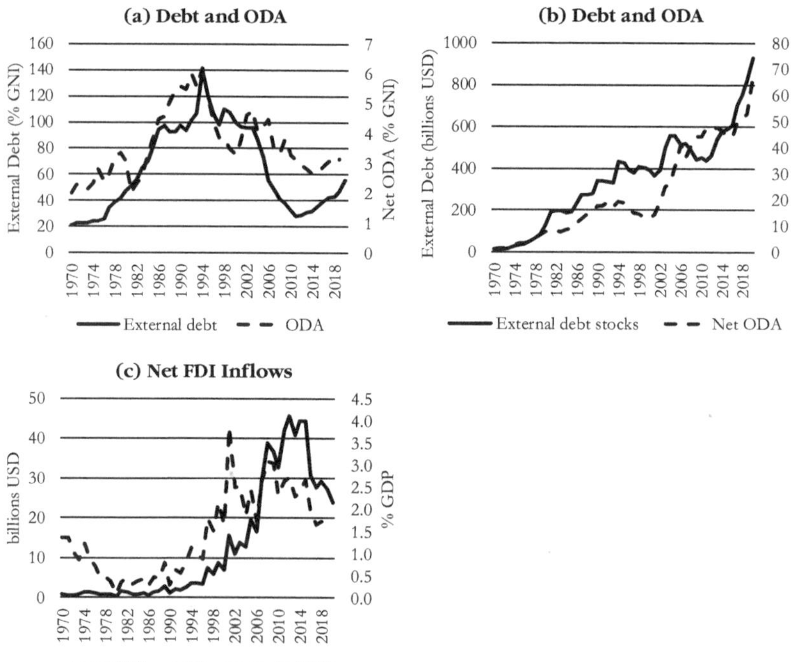

Fig. 3.2 ODA, foreign debt, and FDI to SSA. (Data source: World Development Indicators)

Socialism and SSA's debt crises in the 1970s and 1980s, FDI inflows to SSA averaged just 0.9% of GDP (an annual average of USD 931.7 million) and 0.4% of GDP (USD 1.2 billion annually) respectively, accounting for only 0.7% and 1% of the FDI inflows to emerging regions over these two decades.

This small share of global FDI can be attributed to a combination of both international and domestic factors. Internationally, the oil crises in 1973 and 1979 negatively impacted demand and prices for African commodity exports while the stagflation induced rising interest rates worsened SSA's debt costs (Owusu, 2003). This led to persistent budget deficits in the heavily indebted SSA countries, dampening growth, investment, and social upliftment (Onyeiwu & Shrestha, 2004); limiting macroeconomic reform choices, and damaging economic and financial institutions (Obadan, 2004, pp. 172–173). Domestically, the African Socialism inspired distrust of free markets (Okafor et al., 2015) along with the politically motivated expansion of the public service, excessive intervention in the economy, and state subsidisation for failing state-owned enterprises (Siebritz & Calitz, 2007) negated an investment environment conducive for FDI. Thus, throughout the 1970s and 1980s, domestic policy choices coupled with a fraught international political and financial economic environment deterred foreign capital, entrenching SSA as an investment destination with high political and economic risk exposure, low-quality labour, poor infrastructure, and highly inefficient and costly financial systems (Pigato, 2000; Ezeoha & Cattaneo, 2012).

From the mid-1990s however, the neoliberal reforms set in motion a strategic shift away from reliance on debt and ODA to include development finance and FDI as well. This change coincided with a migration of loanable funding from bilateral and multilateral lending institutions away from SSA to emerging countries in Eastern Europe (Arnold, 1991; Hutchful, 1991; Gabriele et al., 2000) coupled with heightened financial globalisation, and higher oil and commodity prices (Delechat et al., 2010). Hence, based on the experiences of the Asian Tigers, the IMF and World Bank increasingly touted FDI rather than ODA as a means to stimulate SSA's economic development, reduce poverty and unemployment, and stimulate domestic industries (Omeje, 2021, pp. 43–44).

Ideologically however, there was lingering distrust of foreign capital among SSA's political elite, who feared that foreign companies would act "as agents of imperialism and exploitation" (Glaister et al., 2020) and could use FDI to establish neo-colonial links and control (Moss et al.,

2004; Kemmanang & Zamke, 2021). Among the policies that have constrained FDI to SSA are the threat of expropriation and government intervention, the transfer of ownership of foreign firms to locals through violence (such as in Uganda and Zimbabwe) or through legally prescribed transfers (such as in Kenya, South Africa, and Zambia), restrictions on foreign ownership, "partial reform syndrome", and inefficient bureaucratic barriers (Moss et al., 2004).

The reformation of the OAU into the AU accompanied by the adoption of NEPAD subsequently improved the investment climate of SSA and FDI responded positively accordingly. As shown in Fig. 3.2c, FDI increased from an average of 1.1% of GDP during the 1990s (averaging USD 4.0 billion annually), rising to 2.5% of GDP in the early 2000s (averaging USD 20.0 billion annually), and then to 2.2% of GDP over the last decade (an annual average of USD 36.5 billion). In contrast, Fig. 3.2a and b shows that average external debt levels declined from 107.9% of GNI during the 1990s (averaging USD 379.4 billion), to 73.0% of GNI during the first decade of the millennium (averaging USD 474.0 billion), and then down to 36.1% in the last decade (an annual average of USD 593.4). Over the same period, average ODA moderated from 4.9% of GNI (averaging USD 16.9 billion annually), to 4.0% (averaging USD 29.2 billion annually), and 3.0% of GNI (averaging USD 47.5 billion annually) respectively.

Despite the rise in FDI since the 1990s, inflows are still below the volumes of other emerging regions. Table 3.1 shows that during the 1990s, early 2000s, and from 2010–2020, FDI to SSA totalled just 3.2%, 4.7%, and 3.9% respectively of the total flows.

Table 3.2 further shows that over the period of 1990–2020, FDI flowed to only a relatively small selection of SSA countries with only 12 out of 43 countries (27.9% of the sample) receiving above average inflows, accounting for 74.7% of total inflows to SSA (USD 494.8 billion). However, among these top 12 recipients, 41.4% of the FDI inflows were directed to the two countries of South Africa (USD 97.1 billion) and Nigeria (USD 95.4 billion), which cumulatively comprise 30.9% of total FDI to SSA. In addition, five of the top 12 recipients are natural resource export-dependent countries with a total of USD 115.8 billion of inflows, which comprises 24.9% of the total inflows among the top 12 recipients.

Table 3.1 Regional net FDI inflows

Region	*1970–1979*	*1980–1989*	*1990–1999*	*2000–2009*	*2010–2020*	*Total*
(a) Total net FDI inflows (billions USD):						
East Asia and Pacific	31.1	130.7	752.1	2289.1	6226.1	9429.1
Latin America and Caribbean	25.8	66.3	423.4	1167.2	2748.1	4430.8
Middle East and North Africa	3.7	35.8	57.0	592.6	633.8	1322.9
Sub-Saharan Africa	9.3	12.5	40.2	200.3	388.2	650.4
Total	69.9	245.3	1272.8	4249.2	9996.1	15833.3
(b) % total FDI inflows:						
East Asia & Pacific	44.5%	53.3%	59.1%	53.9%	62.3%	59.6%
Latin America & Caribbean	36.9%	27.0%	33.3%	27.5%	27.5%	28.0%
Middle East & North Africa	5.3%	14.6%	4.5%	13.9%	6.3%	8.4%
Sub-Saharan Africa	13.3%	5.1%	3.2%	4.7%	3.9%	4.1%

Data source: World Development Indicators

Table 3.2 Net FDI inflows to SSA

		Total net FDI inflows (billions USD)				*Net FDI inflows (% of GDP)*			
Rank	*Country*	*1990–1999*	*2000–2009*	*2010–2020*	*Total*	*1990–1999*	*2000–2009*	*2010–2020*	*Average*
1	South Africa	8.50	42.45	46.16	97.11	0.5	1.8	1.1	1.1
2	Nigeria	8.11	40.71	46.59	95.41	2.0	2.1	1.0	1.7
3	Mozambique*	0.92	3.92	38.62	43.45	2.2	4.6	23.9	10.2
4	Ghana	1.13	7.84	34.34	43.31	1.7	3.8	6.0	3.8
5	Congo*	0.24	7.11	26.96	34.30	0.1	3.4	5.0	2.8
6	Sudan	0.92	12.83	15.58	29.33	0.8	3.9	2.3	2.4
7	Ethiopia	0.68	3.11	23.49	27.27	0.8	2.8	3.0	2.2
8	Democratic Republic of Congo*	0.03	4.91	17.83	22.77	1.5	1.3	1.1	1.3
9	Tanzania	1.20	6.43	14.53	22.15	1.4	3.3	3.0	2.6
10	Zambia*	1.44	5.21	12.31	18.96	4.1	5.5	4.8	4.8
11	Uganda	0.91	4.38	10.17	15.46	1.6	4.1	3.0	2.9
12	Equatorial Guinea*	1.08	5.77	8.42	15.27	44.7	16.3	4.6	21.9
13	Gabon*	−0.44	3.17	11.16	13.89	−0.9	3.0	6.3	2.8
14	Kenya	0.53	1.28	11.19	13.00	0.6	0.5	1.3	0.8
15	Liberia	0.72	1.21	10.06	11.99	–	11.3	35.0	23.1
16	Cote d'Ivoire	2.32	3.18	5.86	11.36	0.7	8.3	10.7	6.5
17	Madagascar	0.19	3.85	6.26	10.30	0.5	4.4	4.8	3.2
18	Cameroon	0.27	2.32	7.63	10.21	0.3	1.3	2.0	1.2
19	Namibia	0.94	4.26	4.73	9.93	2.6	6.3	3.5	4.2
20	Senegal	0.59	2.03	6.47	9.09	0.9	1.7	2.9	1.9
21	Niger*	0.11	1.20	6.96	8.26	0.4	1.9	6.3	2.9
22	Chad	0.22	2.82	3.77	6.81	1.5	11.8	3.1	5.5

23	Mali*	0.26	1.84	4.46	6.57	1.0	2.7	3.0	2.2
24	Botswana	0.16	3.44	2.48	6.08	0.3	4.0	1.5	1.9
25	Guinea*	0.20	1.31	4.31	5.82	0.6	2.6	4.6	2.6
26	Zimbabwe	0.91	0.43	3.83	5.17	1.3	0.7	1.7	1.3
27	Sierra Leone	0.03	0.54	4.46	5.03	0.5	3.2	10.6	4.8
28	Somalia	0.01	0.45	3.16	3.62	0.6	–	6.2	3.4
29	Malawi	0.13	0.77	2.62	3.52	0.8	2.0	3.5	2.1
30	Rwanda*	0.04	0.38	2.59	3.01	0.2	0.9	2.9	1.3
31	Togo	0.02	0.66	2.32	3.00	0.1	3.1	3.6	2.3
32	Burkina Faso*	0.07	0.34	2.56	2.97	0.3	0.6	1.6	0.8
33	Benin*	−0.02	0.10	2.33	2.41	−0.1	0.1	1.7	0.6
34	Djibouti	0.02	0.71	1.64	2.37	0.5	8.2	6.7	5.1
35	Eswatini	0.64	0.51	0.57	1.72	4.6	2.2	1.2	2.6
36	Gambia	0.15	0.52	0.75	1.43	2.2	5.4	4.4	4.0
37	Lesotho	0.23	0.42	0.71	1.35	2.6	3.2	2.7	2.8
38	Eritrea	0.16	0.27	0.62	1.05	3.3	2.3	3.8	3.2
39	Central African Republic*	0.01	0.30	0.27	0.58	0.2	1.8	1.1	1.0
40	Guinea-Bissau	0.03	0.08	0.27	0.38	1.3	1.3	2.1	1.5
41	Burundi	0.00	0.02	0.26	0.28	0.0	0.2	0.9	0.4
42	South Sudan*	0.00	0.00	−0.56	−0.56	–	–	−0.7	−0.7
43	Angola*	5.74	12.19	−21.15	−3.22	8.9	7.5	−2.5	4.6
	Total	39.42	195.24	387.59	622.24	–	–	–	–
	Average	0.92	4.54	9.01	14.47	2.37	3.79	4.53	3.66

Sample period: 1990–2020. * indicates natural resource export dependent

Data source: World Development Indicators

References

Acharya, S. (1981). Perspectives and Problems of Development in Sub-Saharan Africa. *World Development, 9*, 109–147.

ADB. (1999). *African Development Report*. African Development Bank, Oxford University Press.

Adeniyi, O., Opara, N. M., Adeyemo, T., Ekeria, A. I., & Faith-Lois, B. (2016). African Union and the Challenges of Development. *Journal of African Union Studies, 5*(2–3), 67–89.

Adewale, A. R. (2017). Import Substitution Industrialisation and Economic Growth – Evidence from the Group of BRICS Countries. *Future Business Journal, 3*, 138–158.

African Union Commission. (2015). *Agenda 2063: The Africa We Want*. Retrieved March, 2023, from https://www.afdb.org/fileadmin/uploads/afdb/Documents/Policy-Documents/Agenda2063_Popular_Version_English.pdf

Agbu, O. (2003). Origin, Challenges and Prospects. *The Indian Journal of Political Science, 64*(1–2), 97–115.

Agenor, P. R. (1992). Parallel Currency Markets in Developing Countries: Theory, Evidence, and Policy Implications. *Essays in International Finance, 188*. International Finance Section. Princeton University.

Akinboade, O. A., & Lalthapersad-Pillay, P. (2009). The NEPAD Initiative and the Prospects of Business Opportunities in the Rest of Africa for South African Firms based in Gauteng. *Development Southern Africa, 26*(1), 131–155.

Akyeampong, E. (2017). African Socialism: Or the Search for an Indigenous Model of Economic Development. *African Economic History Working Paper Series No. 36/2017*. Harvard University.

Archibong, B., Coulibaly, B., & Okonjo-Iweala, N. (2021). Washington Consensus Reforms and Lessons for Economic Performance in Sub-Saharan Africa. *The Journal of Economic Perspectives, 35*(3), 133–156.

Arnold, M. W. (1991). Africa in the 1990s. *The Fletcher Forum of World Affairs, 15*(1), 9–22.

Aryeetey, E., & Fosu, A. K. (2008). Chapter 2: Economic Growth in Ghana, 1960–2000. In B. Ndulu, S. O'Connell, J. P. Azam, R. H. Bates, A. K. Fosu, J. W. Gunning, & D. Njinkeu (Eds.), *The Political Economy of Economic Growth in Africa 1960–2000* (pp. 289–324). Cambridge University Press.

Ayittey, G. B. N. (2019). How Socialism Destroyed Africa. *Presentation at the Heritage Foundation, Washington DC, USA*. Retrieved May, 2022, from https://www.africanliberty.org/2019/03/14/how-socialism-destroyed-africa/

Babatunde, M. A. (2012). Africa's Growth and Development Strategies: A Critical Review. *African Development, 37*(4), 141–178.

Bacha, E. L. (1990). A Three-gap Model of Foreign Transfers and the GDP Growth Rate in Developing Countries. *Journal of Development Economics, 32*(2), 279–296.

Bakare, A. R. (2014). African Union and the Developmental Transformation of Africa: Challenges, Achievement and Prospects. *European Journal of Sustainable Development, 3*(1), 67–86.

Basheka, B. C., & Tshombe, L. M. (2018). *New Public Management in Africa: Emerging Issues and Lessons.* Routledge.

Biko, S. (2004). *I Write What I Like: Selected Writings.* Picador Africa.

Bobo, B. F. (2014). Towards a Conceptual Framework for African Capacity Building: A Stand-Alone Perspective. *Journal of Third World Studies, 31*(1), 149–184.

Bond, P. (2006). *Looting Africa: The Economics of Exploitation.* Scottsville Books.

Bruton, H. J. (1998). A Reconsideration of Import Substitution. *Journal of Economic Literature, 36*(2), 903–936.

Cabral, L. (2011). Decentralization in Africa: Scope, Motivations and Impact on Service Delivery and Poverty. *Overseas Development Institute Working Paper No. 02.* Future Agriculture Consortium, University of Sussex.

Carmody, P. (2016). *The New Scramble for Africa* (2nd ed.). Polity Press.

Chari, A., Henry, P. B., & Reyes, H. (2020). The Baker Hypothesis. *NBER Working Paper No. 27708.* National Bureau of Economic Research.

Cheung, A. B. L. (1996). Public Sector Reform and the Re-legitimation of Public Bureaucratic Power, The Case of Hong Kong. *International Journal of Public Sector Management, 9*, 37–50.

Christensen, D., & Laitin, D. D. (2019). *African States since Independence: Order, Development, and Democracy.* Yale University Press.

Collier, P., & Gunning, J. W. (1999). Why Has Africa Grown Slowly? *Journal of Economic Perspectives, 13*(3), 3–22.

Connell, R., & Dados, N. (2014). Where in the World Does Neoliberalism Come From? The Market Agenda in Southern Perspective. *Theory and Society, 43*(2), 117–138.

Conyers, D. (2007). Decentralisation and Service Delivery: Lessons from Sub-Saharan Africa. *IDS Bulletin, 38*(1), 18–32.

Cooper, F. (2019). *Africa Since 1940: The Past of the Present.* Cambridge University Press.

Cornia, G. A., & Helleiner, G. K. (1994). *From Adjustment to Development in Africa: Conflict, Controversy, Convergence, Consensus?* Macmillan.

D'almeida, A. F. (1986). La Privatization des Enterprises Publiques en Afrique au Sud du Sahara. *Le Mois en Afrique*, 245–246.

Delechat, C., Ramirez, G., Wagh, S., & Wakeman-Linn, J. (2010). How Global Financial Markets Affect Sub-Saharan Africa. *IMF Staff Paper No. 57.* International Monetary Fund.

Doorgapersad, S. (2011). Paradigm Shift from New Public Administration to New Public Management: Theory and Practice in Africa. *Journal for Trans-Disciplinary Research in Southern Africa, 7*, 235–250.

Due, J. M., & Gladwin, C. H. (1991). Impacts of Structural Adjustment Programs on African Women Farmers and Female-Headed Households. *American Journal of Agricultural Economics, 73*(5), 1431–1439.

Dumenil, G., & Levy, D. (2004). *Capital Resurgent: Roots of the Neoliberal Revolution.* Harvard University Press.

Edo, V.O. & Olanrewaju, M.A. (2012). "An Assessment of the Transformation of the Organization of African Unity (O.A.U.) to the African Union (A.U.), 1963-2007," *Journal of the Historical Society of Nigeria*, 21, 41–69.

EI-Khawas, M. A. (1978). The Quiet Role of OAU In Africa's Liberation. *New Directions, 5*(2), 16–19.

Ekpo, A. H. (1992). Economic Development under Structural Adjustment: Evidence from Selected West African Countries. *Journal of Social Development in Africa, 7*(1), 25–43.

El-Badawy, E., Munasinghe, S., Bukarti, A. B., & Bianchi, B. (2022, March). Security, Soft Power and Regime Support: Spheres of Russian Influence in Africa. *Tony Blaire Institute for Global Change.* Retrieved March, 2023, from https://institute.global/policy/security-soft-powerand-regime-support-spheres-russian-influence-africa

Elischer, S., & Lawrance, B. (2022). Reassessing Africa's New Post-Coup Landscape. *African Studies Review, 65*(1), 1–7.

Engida, T. G., & Bardill, J. (2013). Reforms of the Public Sector in the Light of the New Public Management: A Case of Sub-Saharan Africa. *Journal of Public Administration and Policy Research, 5*, 1–7.

Ezeoha, A. E., & Cattaneo, N. (2012). FDI Flows to Sub-Saharan Africa: The Impact of Finance, Institutions, and Natural Resource Endowment. *Comparative Economic Studies, 54*, 597–632.

Faleg, G., & Secrieru, S. (2020). Russia's Forays into Sub-Saharan Africa: Do You Want to be My Friend, Again? *Brief No. 6.* European Union Institute for Security Studies (EUISS).

Fanon, F. (1967). *Black Skin, White Masks.* Grove Press.

Forje, W. (2019). *In the Heat of Africa's Underdevelopment: Africa at the Crossroads - Time to Deliver.* Langaa RPCIG.

Gabriele, A., Boratav, K., & Parikh, A. (2000). Instability and Volatility of Capital Flows to Developing Countries. *The World Economy, 23*, 1031–1056.

Garlick, P. (1971). *African Traders and Economic Development.* Clarendon Press.

Gibbon, P., Bangura, Y., & Ofstad, A. (1992). *Authoritarianism, Democracy and Adjustment: The Politics of Economic Reform in Africa.* The Scandinavian Institute of African Studies.

Glaister, K. W., Driffield, N., & Lin, Y. (2020). Foreign Direct Investment to Africa: Is There a Colonial Legacy? *Management International Review, 60*, 315–349.

Gollwitzer, S. (2010). Budget Institutions and Fiscal Performance in Africa. *CREDIT Research Paper No. 10/02.* Centre for Research in Economic Development and International Trade, University of Nottingham.

Gottschalk, K., & Edozie, R. K. (2014). *The African Union's Africa: New Pan-African Initiatives in Global Governance.* Michigan State University Press.

Gulseven, Y. (2020). Reconsidering Development Aid: A Systemic Analysis. *World Review of Political Economy, 11*(2), 232–255.

Harper-Shipman, T. D. (2019). How Comprehensive is Comprehensive? Using Wangari Maathai as a Critique of the World Bank's Contemporary Development Model. *Third World Quarterly, 40*(4), 633–650.

Harrison, G. (2005). Economic Faith, Social Project and a Misreading of African Society: The Travails of Neoliberalism in Africa. *Third World Quarterly, 26*(8), 1303–1320.

Harrison, G. (2019). Authoritarian Neoliberalism and Capitalist Transformation in Africa: All Pain, No Gain. *Globalizations, 16*(3), 274–288.

Hayek, F. A. (1944). *The Road to Serfdom.* University of Chicago Press.

Heidhues, F., Atsain, A., Nyangito, H., Padilla, M., Ghersi, G., & Le Vallée, J. C. (2004). Development Strategies and Food and Nutrition Security in Africa: An Assessment. *Discussion Paper No. 38.* IFPRI.

Heidhues, F., & Obare, G. (2011). Lessons from Structural Adjustment Programmes and their Effects in Africa. *Quarterly Journal of International Agriculture, 50*(1), 55–64.

Hope, K. R. (1997). *African Political Economy: Contemporary Issues in Development.* M.E. Sharpe.

Hope, K. R. (2001). The New Public Management: Context and Practice in Africa. *International Public Management Journal, 4*, 119–134.

Hope, K. R., & Chikulo, B. C. (1999). *Corruption and Development in Africa: Lessons from Country Case-Studies.* Macmillan.

Hope, K. R., & Kayira, G. (1997). Development Policies in Southern Africa: The Impact of Structural Adjustment Programmes. *South African Journal of Economics, 65*(2), 259–273.

Hunter, E. (2022). African Socialism. In M. Van der Linden (Ed.), *The Cambridge History of Socialism* (pp. 455–473). Cambridge University Press.

Hutchful, E. (1991). Eastern Europe: Consequences for Africa. *Review of African Political Economy, 50*, 51–59.

IMF. (2012). Looking to the Future: The IMF in Africa. In J. M. Boughton (Ed.), *Tearing Down the Walls: The International Monetary Fund 1990–1999.* International Monetary Fund.

Inukai, I. (1974). African Socialism and Agricultural Development Strategy: A Comparative Study of Kenya and Tanzania. *The Developing Economies, 12*(1), 3–22.

Jackson, B. (2010). At the Origins of Neo-Liberalism: The Free Economy and the Strong State, 1930–1947. *The Historical Journal, 53*(1), 129–151.

Jiboku, P. A., & Okeke-Uzodike, U. (2016). Regional Economic Integration and the Governance Challenge in Africa: Missing Links in the African Peer Review Mechanism. *African Development, 41*(2), 47–70.

Johnston, J., & Kouzmin, A. (1998). Who Are the Rent Seekers? From the Ideological Attack on Public Officials to the 'Pork Barrel' Par Excellence - Privatization and Out-Sourcing as Oligarchic Corruption. *Administrative Theory & Praxis, 20*(4), 491–507.

Jütting, J., Corsi, E., Kauffmann, C., McDonnell, I., Osterrieder, H., Pinaud, N., & Wegner, L. (2004). Decentralisation and Poverty in Developing Countries: Exploring the Impact. *Working Paper No. 236*. OECD Development Centre, Organization for Economic Cooperation and Development.

Kabonga, I. (2016). Dependency Theory and Donor Aid: A Critical Analysis. *Africanus: Journal of Development Studies, 46*(2), 29–39.

Kaboolian, L. (1998). The New Public Management: Challenging the Boundaries of the Management vs. Administration Debate. *Public Administration Review, 58*(3), 189–193.

Kalu, K. (2016). State–Society Relations, Institutional Transformation and Economic Development in Sub-Saharan Africa. *Development and Policy Review, 35*, O234–O245.

Kararach, G., Besada, H., & Shaw, T. (2022). African Development, Political Economy and the Road to Agenda 2063. In *Development in Africa*. Bristol University Press.

Kemmanang, L. F., & Zamke, J. J. D. (2021). Does the Quality of Institutions Matter for Foreign Investment Concentration in Africa? Understanding the Controversial Role of International Aid. *Review of Development Economics, 26*, 354–374.

Kettl, D. F. (2000). *The Global Public Management Revolution: A Report on the Transformation of Governance*. Brookings Institution.

Kharas, H. (2020). Jim Wolfensohn—A Man with Ideas Before His Time. *Brookings Future Development*. Retrieved May, 2022, from https://www.brookings.edu/blog/future-development/2020/12/02/jim-wolfensohn-a-man-with-ideas-before-his-time/

Kimenyi, M. S. (2015). *An African Union for an Emerging Continent: Reforms to Increase Effectiveness*. Brookings Institute Africa Growth Initiative. Retrieved May, 2022, from https://www.brookings.edu/wp-content/uploads/2016/07/african-union-kimenyi-2.pdf

Kufuor, K. O. (2005). The Collapse of the Organization of African Unity: Lessons from Economics and History. *The Journal of African Law, 49*(2), 132–144.

Libby, R. T. (1987). *The Politics of Economic Power in Southern Africa*. Princeton University Press.

Loots, E., & Kabundi, A. (2012). Foreign Direct Investment to Africa: Trends, Dynamics and Challenges. *South African Journal of Economic and Management Sciences, 15*(2), 128–141.

Lösch, D. (1990). Socialism in Africa. *Intereconomics, 25*(6), 300–306.

Lundgren, C. J., Thomas, A. H., & York, R. C. (2013). *Boom, Bust, or Prosperity? Managing Sub-Saharan Africa's Natural Resource Wealth.* International Monetary Fund.

Lyons, T., & Jolley, D. (2018). Chapter 5: Post-Independence Africa: Challenges and Opportunities. In T. Binns, K. Lynch, & E. Nel (Eds.), *The Routledge Handbook of African Development.* Routledge.

Mbeki, T. (1999). Statement at the 35th Ordinary Session of the OAU Assembly of Heads of State and Government, July 13, Algiers, Algeria.

Mendes, A. P. F., Bertell, M. A., & Teixeira, R. F. A. P. (2014). Industrialization in Sub-Saharan Africa and Import Substitution Policy. *Brazilian Journal of Political Economy, 34*(1), 120–138.

Mkandawire, T., & Olukoshi, A. (1996). *Between Liberalisation and Oppression: The Politics of Structural Adjustment in Africa.* CODESRIA Books.

Mkandiwire, T., & Soludo, C. C. (1999). *Our Continent, Our Future: African Perspectives on Structural Adjustment.* CODESRIA, Council for the Development of Social Science Research in Africa, World Press.

Momoh, Z. (2016). African Solutions to African Problems. *Journal of African Union Studies, 5*(1), 39–62.

Moss, T. J., Ramachandran, V., & Shah, M. K. (2004). Is Africa's Scepticism of Foreign Capital Justified? Evidence from East African Firm Survey Data. *Working Paper No. 41.* Center for Global Development, World Bank.

Moyo, D. (2009). *Dead Aid: Why Aid Is Not Working and How There Is Another Way for Africa.* Penguin Books.

Munslow, B. (1986). *Africa: Problems in the Transition to Socialism.* Zed Books.

Naiman, R., & Watkins, N. (1999). A Survey of the Impacts of IMF Structural Adjustment in Africa: Growth, Social Spending, and Debt Relief. *Center for Economic and Policy Research.* Retrieved March, 2023, from https://www.cepr.net/documents/publications/debt_1999_04.htm

Nantulya, P. (2022). The African Union at 20: Much Accomplished, More Challenges Ahead. *Africa Centre for Strategic Studies.* Retrieved March, 2023, from https://africacenter.org/spotlight/african-union-20-much-accomplished-more-challenges-ahead/

Ndlovu-Gatsheni, S. J. (2015). Genealogies of Coloniality and Implications for Africa's Development. *African Development, 40*(3), 13–40.

Ndlovu-Gatsheni, S. J., & Mhlanga, B. (2013). *Bondage of Boundaries and Identity Politics in Postcolonial Africa: The 'Northern Problem' and Ethno-Futures* (pp. 1–23). Africa Institute of South Africa.

NEPAD. (2001). *New Partnership for Africa's Development.* Department of International Relations and Cooperation, South African Government. Retrieved May, 2022, from http://www.dirco.gov.za/au.nepad/nepad.pdf

Nkrumah, K. (1966). *Neo-Colonialism: The Last Stage of Imperialism.* International Publishers.

Nkrumah, K. (1970). *Consciencism.* Modern Reader Paperbacks.

Nwebo, O. E. (2018). The African Union Agenda 2063 and the Imperative of Democratic Governance. *The Law and Development Review, 11*(2), 259–276.

Nyerere, J. (1967). Socialism: An Attitude of Mind. *East Africa Journal, 4*, 24–30.

OAU. (1963). *OAU Charter.* https://au.int/sites/default/files/treaties/7759-file-oau_charter_1963.pdf

Obadan, M. I. (2004). *Foreign Capital Flows and External Debt: Perspective on Nigeria and the LDCs Group.* Broadway Press Ltd.

OECD. (1995). *Governance in Transition: Public Management Reforms in OECD Countries.* Organization for Economic Cooperation and Development.

Ogo, N. C. (2018). African Union and the Challenge of Continuity in Programme Implementation. *Journal of African Union Studies, 7*(2), 7–23.

Ojieh, C. O. (2014). The 'Africanness' of the New Partnership for Africa's Development (NEPAD) and Goals' Attainment. *International Journal of African and Asian Studies, 3*, 86–93.

Okafor, G., Piesse, J., & Webster, A. (2015). The Motives for Inward FDI into Sub-Saharan African Countries. *Journal of Policy Modeling, 37*, 875–890.

Omeje, K. (2021). *The Failure and Feasibility of Capitalism in Africa.* Palgrave Macmillan.

Omotola, J. S. (2010). The Challenges of Development in Africa. *World Affairs: The Journal of International Issues, 14*(2), 22–46.

Onyeiwu, S., & Shrestha, H. (2004). Determinants of Foreign Direct Investment in Africa. *Journal of Developing Societies, 20*(1–2), 89–106.

Otunnu, O. (2015). Mwalimu Julius Kambarage Nyerere's Philosophy, Contribution, and Legacies. *African Identities, 13*(1), 18–33.

Owusu, F. (2003). Pragmatism and the Gradual Shift from Dependency to Neoliberalism: The World Bank, African Leaders and Development Policy in Africa. *World Development, 31*(10), 1655–1672.

Owusu, F. (2006). *Discourse on Development from Dependency to Neoliberalism: Beyond the African Tragedy. Discourses on Development and the Global Economy.*

Pender, J. (2001). From 'Structural Adjustment' to 'Comprehensive Development Framework': Conditionality Transformed? *Third World Quarterly, 22*(3), 397–411.

Pigato, M. (2000). *Foreign direct investment in Africa: Old Tales and New Evidence.* World Bank.

Pitcher, A. M. (2004). Conditions, Commitments, and the Politics of Restructuring in Africa. *Comparative Politics, 36*(4), 379–398.

Poku, N., & Whitman, J. (2018). *Africa Under Neoliberalism*. Routledge.

Raji, S. (2015). Africa and the Philosophy of the New Partnership for Africa's Development (NEPAD). *Journal of African Foreign Affairs, 2*(1–2), 27–48.

Rodrik, D. (2006). Goodbye Washington Consensus, Hello Washington Confusion? *Journal of Economic Literature, 44*(4), 973–987.

Rubakula, G. (2014). The New Public Management and its Challenges in Africa. *Public Policy and Administration Research, 4*(4), 85–96.

Saka, L., & Momoh, Z. (2015, March 12–13). New Partnership for Africa's Development and Africa's Development. *Presented at the International Multi-Disciplinary Academic Conference on African Transformation and Development*. Cambridge Publications and Research International, University of Ilorin.

Schmidt, E. (2013). *Foreign Intervention in Africa*. Cambridge University Press.

Sheridan, M. J. (2004). The Environmental Consequences of Independence and Socialism in North Pare, Tanzania, 1961–88. *The Journal of African History, 45*(1), 81–102.

Shivji, I. G. (2010). The Village in Mwalimu's Thought and Political Practice. In C. Chachage & A. Cassam (Eds.), *Africa's Liberation: The Legacy of Julius Nyerere*. Pambazuka.

Siebritz, F., & Calitz, E. (2007). The Legacy and Challenge of Fiscal Policy in Sub-Saharan Africa. *South African Journal of Economics, 75*(2), 221–235.

Signe, L. (2018). *African Development, African Transformation: How Institutions Shape Developmental Strategy*. Cambridge University Press.

Southall, R. (2003a). Democracy in Southern Africa: Moving Beyond a Difficult Legacy. *Review of African Political Economy, 96*, 255–272.

Southall, R. (2003b). Democracy in Africa: Fragile and Necessary. *Journal of Contemporary African Studies, 21*, 121–130.

Southall, R. (2016). *Liberation Movements in Power: Party & State in Southern Africa*. University of KwaZulu-Natal Press.

Speich, D. (2019). The Kenyan Style of 'African Socialism': Developmental Knowledge Claims and the Explanatory Limits of the Cold War. *Diplomatic History, 33*(3), 449–466.

Stein, H. (1994). Theories of Institutions and Economic Reform in Africa. *World Development, 22*(12), 1833–1849.

Stiglitz, J. E., & Heertje, A. (1989). *The Economic Role of the State*. Blackwell in Association with Bank Insinger de Beaufort NV.

Sun, J. Y. (2019). Historicizing African Socialisms: Kenyan African Socialism, Zambian Humanism, and Communist China's. *International Journal of African Historical Studies, 52*(3), 349–374.

Tatah, M. (2017). *Africa in the Old Empire of Territorial Colonization: Slavery, Capitalism, Racism, Colonialism, Decolonization, Independence as Recolonization*. Project Muse Langaa RPCIG.

The Economist. (2000). *The Hopeless Continent*. Retrieved April, 2024, from https://www.economist.com/weeklyedition/2000-05-13
Therkildsen, O. (2001). *Efficiency, Accountability and Implementation: Public Sector Reform in East and Southern Africa*. UNRISD.
Thomson, A. (2000). *An Introduction to African Politics*. Routledge.
Tshombe, L. M., & Dassah, M. O. (2018). New Public Management Reform in Africa: Theoretical Review. In B. C. Basheka & L. M. Tshombe (Eds.), *New Public Management in Africa: Emerging Issues and Lessons*. Routledge.
UN. (2000). *United Nations Millennium Declaration A/RES/55/2*. United Nations General Assembly.
UN. (2008). *Economic Development in Africa: Export Performance following Trade Liberalization, Some Patterns and Policy Perspectives*. United Nations.
van de Walle, N. (1994). Review Essay: Adjustment Alternatives and Alternatives to Adjustment. *African Studies Review, 37*(3), 103–117.
van de Walle, N. (2002). Elections without Democracy: Africa's Range of Regimes. *Journal of Democracy, 13*(2), 66–80.
van de Walle, N. (2003). Presidentialism and Clientelism: Africa's Emerging Party Systems. *The Journal of Modern African Studies, 41*(2), 297–321.
van der Geest, W. (1994). The Bargaining Process of Policy Based Lending. In W. van der Geest (Ed.), *Negotiating Structural Adjustment in Africa*. James Currey.
Williams, G. (2007). Why Structural Adjustment Is Necessary and Why It Doesn't Work. *Review of African Political Economy, 21*(60), 214–225.
Wollmann, H. (Ed.). (2003). *Evaluation in Public-Sector Reform: Concepts and Practice in International Perspective*. Edward Elgar.
World Bank. (1999). *Global Economic Prospects and the Developing Countries*. Oxford University Press.
World Bank. (2000). *Can Africa Claim the 21st Century?* Oxford University Press.
World Bank. (2001). *Aid and Growth in Africa*. Oxford University Press.
World Bank. (2003). *Toward Country-led Development: A Multi-Partner Evaluation of the Comprehensive Development Framework Synthesis Report*.
World Bank. (2005). The Evolution of Enterprise Reform in Africa: From State-Owned Enterprises to Private Participation in Infrastructure—And Back? *ESMap Technical Paper No. 083/05*.
Yacouba, C., & Wologueme, B. (2018). From the Failure of African Socialism, How to Set a New Trend for a New Generation? *Open Journal of Social Sciences, 6*, 27–36.
Young, C. (1988). The African Colonial State and its Political Legacy. In D. Rothchild & N. Chazan (Eds.), *The Precarious Balance: State and Society in Africa* (pp. 25–66). Westview Press.
Zinsmeister, K. (1987). East African Experiment: Kenyan Prosperity and Tanzanian Decline. *Journal of Economic Growth, 2*(2), 1–28.

CHAPTER 4

The Relationship Between Democracy and FDI in Sub-Saharan Africa

Africa has experienced three periods of democratisation (Guseh & Oritsejafor, 2005). The first was the long struggle for independence from colonial rule, lasting throughout the nineteenth and twentieth centuries. The second covered the short period of optimism following independence in the 1960s to despair by the end of the 1970s with the collapse of African Socialism accompanied by the client-patron neo-patrimonial rule of military and authoritarian 'Big Men' (Sigman & Lindberg, 2020; Dulani, 2020, p. 104).[1] By the mid-1980s, 42 out of 47 countries on the continent were led by military or single-party governments (Cheeseman, 2018, p. 214). The third started with the fall of the USSR in 1989 and the subsequent emergence of pro-democracy movements.[2] In common with many formally autocratic countries in Latin America and Asia, SSA underwent rapid democratisation in tandem with the globalisation of trade, capital, labour, and technology (Gossel, 2017). This was driven by domestic pressure for improved civil liberties and political rights from

[1] Exemplified by Teodoro Obiang Nguema Mbasogo, Mbasogo of Equatorial Guinea who is 82 and has been in power for 45 years, Denis Sassou Nguesso of the Congo who is 79 and been in power for 40 years, and Paul Biya of Cameroon who is 91 and been in power for 42 years (Loungou, 2024).

[2] Huntington (1991) refers to this period as the 'third wave' of democratisation. The 'first wave' occurred in 1828–1928, which was reversed in the wake of the Great Depression, and the 'second wave' in 1943–1962, which was separated by reversal waves in 1958–1975.

S. Gossel, *The Promise and Peril of FDI in Sub-Saharan Africa*, Palgrave Studies in African and Development Economics,
https://doi.org/10.1007/978-3-032-01320-0_4

students, activists, unionists, and burgeoning opposition parties coupled with a focus on democratisation and governance from international lenders and donors. Consequently, the elite faced unprecedented popular and economic pressure to liberalise their political systems (Bratton et al., 2004, p. 14), reform personalised and authoritarian leadership systems (Bratton & van der Walle, 1997; Cheeseman, 2010; Maltz, 2007; Posner & Young, 2007, 2018), adopt pluralistic governance with regular and competitive elections, and undertake constitutional reforms that would limit presidential powers (Bratton & van der Walle, 1997). From 1988 to 1994, the proportion of African countries that held elections increased from 25% to 84% (Van Ham & Lindberg, 2015).

The regional Polity V democracy data in Fig. 4.1a shows that before the early 1990s, Africa's democracy levels lagged the other regions in the world whereas after 1992, Africa underwent a rapid spate of democratisation while Asia remained largely undemocratic (South America had already undergone democratisation in the 1980s). Figure 4.1b however further shows that during the pre-1990s, the Polity V rankings of SSA's resource-dependent countries were more autocratic than among less resource-dependent SSA countries (averaging −6.7 and −4.7 respectively over the period of 1970–1989) and this pattern continued in the post-liberalisation years (averaging 0.3 and 1.2 respectively during 1990–2018).

Table 4.1 categorises 43 SSA countries according to their average Polity V scores over the period of 1990–2018. As can be seen, only six countries fall in the democratic range of 6–10 (Madagascar, Lesotho, Namibia, Benin, Botswana, and South Africa) while three countries fall in the

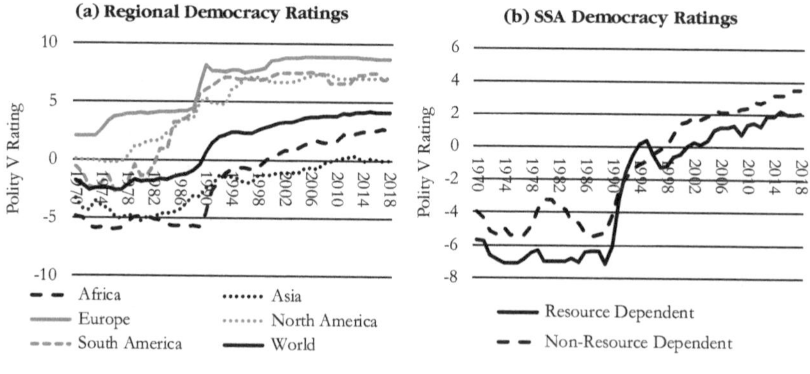

Fig. 4.1 Polity V democracy ratings. (Data source: ourworldindata.org, Polity V)

Table 4.1 SSA Polity V categories

Autocracies		*Anocracies*				*Democracies*	
Eswatini	−8.1	Sudan*	−5.4	South Sudan*	0.0	Madagascar	5.7
Eritrea	−6.7	Cameroon	−4.4	Somalia	1.0	Lesotho	5.9
Equatorial Guinea*	−6.0	Rwanda*	−4.4	Democratic Republic of Congo*	1.1	Namibia	6.0
		Angola*	−2.9	Burundi	1.3	Benin*	6.2
		Uganda	−2.9	Central African Republic*	1.3	Botswana	7.8
		Gambia	−2.8	Nigeria	1.5	South Africa	8.6
		Togo*	−2.7	Sierra Leone	2.6		
		Zimbabwe	−2.2	Guinea-Bissau	2.6		
		Chad*	−1.8	Liberia*	3.0		
		Congo-Brazzaville*	−1.7	Mozambique*	3.4		
		Gabon	−1.7	Niger*	3.7		
		Ethiopia	−1.2	Malawi	3.9		
		Tanzania	−1.2	Kenya	4.2		
		Burkina Faso*	−1.0	Senegal	4.5		
		Djibouti	−0.8	Mali*	4.5		
		Cote d'Ivoire	−0.6	Ghana	4.6		
		Guinea*	−0.5	Zambia*	4.7		

* indicates resource-dependent countries

autocratic range of −6 to −10 (Swaziland, Eritrea, and Equatorial Guinea). The majority of SSA countries thus fall in the 'grey zone' of −5 to 5 variously categorised as Anocratic (Marshall et al., 2014, p. 35), partially free (Freedom House, 2022), hybrid (Morlino, 2008), or pseudo-democratic (Diamond, 2002).

These regimes are characterised by populist politics, unaccountable leadership, impervious decision-making processes, and public institutions that are weak and lack credibility (Dumludag, 2009). State capacity is therefore poor while state decision-making structures are bloated with public sector participants. These features lead to a contradiction between formal institutions and informal practises whereby the formal institutions suffer from a trust deficit, while the informal practices (such as presidentialism, clientelism, and corruption) take precedence (Menocal et al., 2008). This in turn hampers democratisation because the state lacks the necessary institutional and administrative capacity necessary to respond to democratic pressures. Political change is thus typically driven by the political elite rather than by the electorate (ibid.) and consequently, anocratic regimes tend to solve political contestation and instability, with repression and conflict (Regan & Bell, 2010).

However, among the anocratic SSA countries, there is a wide variation in the 'strength of the state'[3] and thus Morlino (2008) argues that anocratic regimes, or 'regimes in transition,' can be further broken down into three categories based on the seven Freedom House indicators. The first are *democracies without law*, which are states that suffer from electoral illegality and the inadequate protection of civil rights as a result of dysfunctional or absent legal institutions. Democracies without law are thus characterised by poor rule of law (*RL*), weak electoral processes (*EP*), and low functioning government (*FG*). The second are *protected democracies*, which are states that place limits on the freedom to vote, overtly or covertly stifle dissent and opposition politics, and attempt to control the electoral process. Protected democracies are thus characterised by low political pluralism and participation (*PPP*). The third are *limited or illiberal democracies*, which are states that have democratic foundations and multi-party electoral procedures but suffer from conditional civil liberties, limited opposition party activities, and a monopoly on the media. These weakly democratic states are thus characterised by poor freedom of expression

[3]Where *state* refers to the monopoly of "legitimate use of force" (Linz & Stepan, 1996, p. 7), and the right "to command, regulate, and extract" (ibid., p. 16).

and beliefs (*FEB*), association and organisational rights (*AOR*), and personal autonomy and individual rights (*PAIR*).

Table 4.2 summarises the averages of the Freedom House data for 43 SSA countries over the period of 2006–2022 normalised to lie between 0 and 1. The results indicate that there are 30 SSA countries that can be considered as democracies without law, three protected democracies, and 12 limited democracies. Table 4.2 further indicates that among the democracies without law, the most common weaknesses are functional government (FG) (12 countries) and rule of law (RL) (12 countries) while protected democracies and limited democracies suffer from deficiencies in political pluralism and participation (PPP), and personal autonomy and individual rights (PAIR) respectively. Hence, Table 4.2 suggests that SSA suffers from pervasive weaknesses in democratic governance and individual rights.

These systemic deficiencies are an outcome of both post-colonial institutional voids and the effects of post-Washington Consensus 'partial reform syndrome', which combined to instigate the 'rentier state' (Mahdavy, 1970; Beblawi & Luciani, 1987), characterised by dependence on natural resource rent-seeking opportunities and neo-patrimonial clientelism (Pitcher, 2012, p. 8). Rentier states do not rely on taxation revenues (Luciani, 1997; Ndikumana & Abderrahim, 2010; McGuirk, 2013; Mlambo, 2022) and are thus unresponsive to the needs and demand of citizens (Desierto, 2018) and lack the impetus to develop sophisticated institutions (Mkandawire, 2001). In addition, most of SSA's political parties are relatively new and hence "suffer from a chronic lack of finances and lack internal democratic procedures. They are uncertain of their membership and weakened by factional in-fighting and ethno-regional cleavages. Many fail to campaign on substantive issues and serve as personalistic vehicles for Africa's Big Men" (Pitcher, 2012, p. 22).

These deficiencies in turn discourage manufacturing-based FDI in favour of resource extractive FDI, potentially locking resource-dependent SSA countries into an extractive cycle of patron-clientelism and democratic dysfunction. The remainder of this chapter thus initially explores the association between democracy and economic growth before considering the effects of the political resource curse and finally focusses more explicitly on the relationship between democratisation, elections, and FDI.

Table 4.2 SSA regimes

Democracies without law [30]			*Protected democracies [3]*			*Limited democracies [10]*		
Angola*	FG	0.10	Botswana	PPP	0.65	Benin*	PAIR	0.63
Burkina Faso*	FG	0.39	Chad*	PPP	0.07	Ethiopia	AOR	0.13
Burundi	FG	0.16	Rwanda*	PPP	0.14	Ghana	PAIR	0.64
Cameroon	RL	0.09				Lesotho	PAIR	0.56
Central African Republic*	RL	0.10				Malawi	PAIR	0.44
Congo*	EP	0.08				Mali*	PAIR	0.35
Cote d'Ivoire	FG	0.27				Namibia	PAIR	0.59
Democratic Republic of Congo*	RL	0.01				Niger*	PAIR	0.38
Djibouti	FG	0.19				Tanzania	FG, AOR, PAIR	0.51
Equatorial Guinea*	EP, FG, AOR	0.00				Zambia*	PAIR	0.48
Eritrea	EP, AOR	0.00						
Eswatini	EP	0.00						
Gabon	EP	0.12						
Gambia	FG	0.19						
Guinea*	FG	0.19						
Guinea-Bissau	FG	0.17						
Kenya	RL	0.38						
Liberia*	RL	0.42						
Madagascar	FG	0.38						
Mozambique*	RL	0.44						
Nigeria	RL	0.27						
Senegal	RL	0.60						
Sierra Leone	FG	0.52						
Somalia	EP	0.00						
South Africa	RL	0.63						
South Sudan*	RL	0.04						
Sudan*	RL	0.01						
Togo*	FG	0.34						
Uganda	EP	0.27						
Zimbabwe	RL	0.11						

Lowest Freedom House component and related score normalized between 0 and 1. *[#]* indicates the number of countries, * indicates resource-dependent countries. RL = Rule of Law, EP = Electoral Process, FG = Functioning of Government, PPP = Political Pluralism and Participation, FEB = Freedom of Expression and Belief, AOR = Associational and Organisational Rights, PAIR = Personal Autonomy and Individual Rights

4.1 Democracy and Capitalism

Since the end of the Cold War, it has been presumed that democracy and neoliberal capitalism naturally go together (Crouch, 2016). However, due to widening social and political inequality and the concentration of economic and political power, resources, and wealth arising from unfettered globalisation, this positive association has increasingly been called into question (Merkel, 2014). Neoliberal shareholder capitalism (Friedman, 1970) elevates shareholders' interests over social, environmental, and public interests, and has the effect of "framing all aspects of life in economic terms, undermining state administrative capacity and eroding state legitimacy" (Williams, 2021). This naturally erodes democracy as the financial interests of corporate power undermine and supplant the democratic legitimacy and sovereignty of the state (George, 2015, pp. 1, 12, 17). The rise of global multinationals has thus shown that instead of being equal partners, capitalism erodes democracy while dramatically expanding the power of corporations (Williams, 2021).

However, as a result of the 2008–2009 global financial crisis, ongoing climate emergency, and anti-globalisation trends, neoliberal capitalism may shift towards 'stakeholder capitalism' (Schwab, 2020), which "holds that corporations should support 'long-term' value creation rather than maximising shareholder value at the expense of key stakeholders such as customers, employees, suppliers and communities" (Bailey, 2020). The political effects of moving away from narrow neoliberal capitalism could be the re-emergence of the state and socialist left-leaning policies (Panitch & Gindin, 2012; Panitch et al., 2019) that put "people and planet before profit" (Bailey, 2020).

In SSA, these debates are nonetheless largely academic because the region's economic development is dependent on international capital markets, exposing SSA to the toxic brew of neo-colonial capitalism and weak democratic rights while international capitalism has enabled the ruling elites to limit democratisation by exploiting class divisions thereby cementing a "symbiotic relationship between these two forces, namely, the international monopolies and the new ruling elites" (Ndi, 2011). Governance in post-colonial SSA has therefore developed into competitive clientelism rather than electoral democracy (Joseph, 2014). According to Sayre Schatz (1984), SSA is beholden to "pirate capitalism," which is characterised by reliance on capitalistic production, business-friendly domestic policies to attract foreign investment, and nationalistic government policies of 'indigenisation' to nurture domestic entrepreneurship and ownership of the economy. These elements place government at the centre of the conflicts between designing policies to attract international capital while simultaneously introducing policies that favour domestic business.

Since the end of the Cold War, financial globalisation and liberalisation in SSA have worsened the detrimental mix between capitalism and weak governance, exaggerated by the "reliance on technocrats and big corporations, domestic and international, who are shielded from democratic constituents" (Edozie, 2008). Consequently, political reforms are less about expanding democratic rights and meeting the needs of the public, and more about enacting policies to benefit corporate interests and ensure unaccountability (Williams, 2021). Post-independent democracy in SSA therefore tends to be "ad hoc, dysfunctional, poorly funded, and sometimes ill-suited to local conditions" (Herbst, 2009).

According to Amartya Sen, democracy is "the process of expanding the real freedoms that people enjoy" (Sen, 1999, p. 4). These "real freedoms" include economic opportunity, political freedom, social freedom (the opportunity to have a healthy, educated, and fulfilled life), transparent legal and business environments, and security from crime and government aggression. Unfortunately, SSA has been unable to enjoy these real freedoms because many SSA countries are still controlled by single-party rule, political and class fragmentation, and remain dependent on neo-liberal and neo-colonial capitalism (Ndi, 2011). Consequently, SSA's development is based on cheap labour for resource extraction by supressing rather than encouraging democratic and economic rights, and thus if SSA is to enjoy the real freedom, there will need to be "the abandonment of patrimonial political and economic philosophies, the collapse of old social institutions, the disintegration of the moral bonds of tribal societies, creed, and race, and the inducement of rational, profit maximizing attitudes on the part of the masses" (ibid.).

4.2 Democracy and Economic Growth

Seymour Lipset's (1959, p. 80) Modernisation Theory was among the first to link democracy and economic development by positing that democratisation is driven by the modernisation of the state, particularly wealth accumulation, education, urbanisation, and industrialisation (Chisadza & Bittencourt, 2019). Modernisation theory thus argues that countries democratise when they become too complex to be controlled by an authoritarian regime (Barro, 1999). In contrast, the New Institutionalists (North & Thomas, 1973; North, 1990, 1991) hypothesise that institutional development rather than economic development drives democratisation, primarily because the system of democracy is reliant on functional public institutions that can limit elitist predation and enhance property rights protection. More recently however, studies have argued that both economic and institutional development are prerequisites for democratisation because political and economic development are interlinked (Acemoglu et al., 2008).

Critics further contend however that economic development is more important for the survival of democracy than for the process of democratisation (Przeworski, 1988; Przeworski & Limongi, 1997; Cheibub & Vreeland, 2011, p. 169). Hence, economic development can even lead to democratic collapse if the political institutions are too weak to control the instability associated with the process of democratisation (Moore, 1966; Huntington, 1968, 1991; Pereira et al., 1993). This contention is borne out by historical evidence. Over the period of 1960–2004, 35% of new democracies failed globally and 63% failed in SSA (Kapstein & Converse, 2008, p. 93). A reason for the high failure rate in SSA is because countries that suffer from low per capita income and high levels of inequality, poverty, and ethnic fragmentation are especially susceptible to democratic reversal (ibid., p. 48).

Empirical studies that examine the relationship between economic growth and democracy report mixed results. One strand of the literature finds that economic growth promotes democracy in accordance with Modernisation theory (Helliwell, 1994; Barro, 1996, 1999, 2015; Heo & Tan, 2001; Epstein et al., 2006), whereas a second strand reports that democracy promotes economic growth (North, 1990; Feng, 1997; Rodrik, 1998; Lake & Baum, 2001; Baum & Lake, 2003; Knutsen, 2012; Acemoglu et al., 2019), a third strand argues that democracy negatively affects economic growth (de Haan & Siermann, 1995a, 1995b; Krieckhaus, 2006; Burke & Leigh, 2010; Narayan et al., 2011; Fayad et al., 2011; Aisen & Veiga, 2013), and a fourth strand reports that democracy impacts economic growth indirectly (Alesina et al., 1996; Sturm & de Haan, 2001;

Tavares & Wacziarg, 2001; Kurzman et al., 2002; Doucouliagos & Ulubaşoğlu, 2008).[4]

In the case of SSA, while there is empirical evidence that democracy drives economic growth in accordance with the New Institutionalists (Bates et al., 2012; Fayissa & Nsiah, 2013; Masaki & van de Walle, 2014; Chisadza & Bittencourt, 2019), there is wide variation among SSA countries. For example, Narayan et al. (2011) find that Modernisation theory applies to Botswana, Chad, Cote d'Ivoire, Gabon, and Niger; New Institutionalism applies to Madagascar, Rwanda, South Africa, and Swaziland; and democracy negatively effects real income in Gabon and Sierra Leone. Despite this heterogeneity, studies of SSA find that the relationship is positive once SSA countries have undertaken an intermediate level of reforms (Fosu, 2008; Knutsen, 2012), reached a moderate level of income (Fayissa & Nsiah, 2013), or attained better levels of governance (Asongu et al., 2021).

In the early stages of democratisation however, corruption is used to overcome weak regulatory and institutional capacity which then tends to hamper democratisation in the later stages of development (Gossel, 2018). A possible reason for this relates to the accumulation of democratic capital, which Persson and Tabellini (2009) define as the time it takes "for citizens to learn to cherish and respect democracy as a valuable form of government." The more repeat elections, the greater the accumulation of democratic capital, the more likely democracy will survive; and the resultant certainty and stability therefore lower risk premia, attract capital inflows, and stimulate economic growth accordingly. Hence, it is possible that the weak association between democratisation and economic growth in SSA is because the region has not yet accumulated sufficient democratic capital.

One of the most significant channels through which democracy interacts with economic growth is exports. The strong rule of law and property rights protection in democratic regimes improves export competitiveness (Barro, 1996) and product sophistication (Yu, 2010), while the increased trade openness drives export diversification and internationalisation (Makhlouf et al., 2015). Studies show that democratic institutions reduce trade uncertainty and facilitate international transactions

[4] Acemoglu et al. (2019) posit that the two possible reasons for the variation in the literature are: first, because most studies only focus on GDP per capita; and second, they do not take adequate cognisance of the nonlinearity and heterogeneity of democratization.

(Martinez-Zarzoso & Marquez-Ramos, 2019), improve consumer rights, and legally enforce product-related regulations (Yu, 2010). In addition, more democratic countries with diversified exports tend to have better human rights because the populace and leaders enjoy the economic trade benefits, and the government has the taxation available to develop a sophisticated state (Peterson, 2017).

In contrast, more autocratic countries tend to be reliant on a narrow range of unsophisticated products while the higher political instability negatively affects exports as a result of factors that include production uncertainty, lower investment, higher risk premia, potential capital and labour disruptions (Gyimah-Brempong & Traynor, 1999; Fosu, 2003), price shocks, and taxation volatility (Peterson, 2017). Furthermore, autocratic states that are overly reliant on natural resource exports tend to be associated with greater levels of repression (Smith, 2008; Bueno de Mesquita & Smith, 2009; DeMeritt & Young, 2013; Conrad & DeMeritt, 2013) even though trade in resource-dependent autocratic states may benefit from the suppression of labour demands (Mitchell & McCormick, 1988; De Soysa & Vadlammanati, 2013). In addition, authoritarian regimes tend to undermine economic growth by threatening to renegotiate trade agreements (Handley & Limao, 2017); and establish a 'shadow state' that hinders trade by widening the ethical standards between importing and exporting countries, and the distortions associated with hidden taxes, corruption, and patronage (Anderson & Marcouiller, 2002; Dutt & Traca, 2010; Horsewood & Voicu, 2012).

Studies of SSA find empirical evidence that democratisation and trade are interlinked, reporting that although exports of goods and services are positively affected by democracy, deepening human rights and democratic institutions (Animashaun & Ubabukoh, 2021), primary commodity exports are only positively affected by voice and accountability (Bah et al., 2021) and the quality of political governance (Asongu et al., 2021). Hence, many SSA countries are prone to a vicious cycle whereby natural resource dependence entrenches neocolonial elitism and poor human rights while also eroding trade diversification.

4.3 'Political Resource Curse'

There are generally two negative effects of natural resource dependence on democratisation. First, the intermingling between international companies and resource-rich states to extract and apportion the rents ("reaping what one doesn't sow") sidelines the citizenry. Second, rentier states are less reliant on direct taxation, which negates accountability and transparency ("no taxation means no representation") (Mcferson, 2010, p. 344). Tom Burgis (2015, p. 73) calculates that in Africa, governments bring in USD 10 from resource extraction and export taxes compared to just USD 6 from income and company taxes. Consequently, many African states are highly reliant on resource taxes to fund government income, for example, in Mali 20% of government income is derived from resource taxes, rising to 50% in Chad, 70% in Nigeria, and 98% in South Sudan. More specifically, in 2011, the five largest multinational mining companies in Zambia (Vedanta, First Quantum, Glencore, African Barrick Gold, and CNMC Luanshya Copper Mines) derived a total product value of USD 6.3 billion but paid only USD 1.1 billion in CIT (17%). Of this amount however, USD 853 million was paid by First Quantum (80% of the CIT) whereas the remaining four companies only paid USD 217 million (an average CIT rate of 6.67%) (War on Want, 2015).

At its worst, this patron-client association between international mining companies and the political elite can negatively affect political economic development by financing conflicts and rebellions, by fostering political conflict between in-government or outside government actors seeking to gain control of the resource rents (Collier, 2010), and by perpetuating and supporting authoritarianism (Collier & Hoeffler, 2004; Jensen & Wantchekon, 2004; Ross, 2012). This has been dramatically demonstrated by the high number of coups that have occurred in western Africa over the last few years as weak democracy, corruption, economic hardship, and poverty and inequality sowed the conditions ripe for the return of military rulers in Mali, Guinea, and Burkina Faso (Laniran, 2022), and more recently in Gabon, Niger, Chad, and Sudan (Al Jazeera, 2023). Even excluding coups, the interaction between resource dependence and capitalism continues to hobble democratisation in SSA because "attempts to introduce genuine multi-party democracy are invariably scuttled by an incumbent hegemonic party that persistently manipulates the electoral process to remain in power, thereby leaving the state with a form of dysfunctional rentier democracy tempered with sporadic outbursts of violence from below and militarized repression from above" (Omeje, 2021, p. 88).

It has however been argued that the quality of institutions will determine whether natural resources are a blessing or a curse rather than the natural resources *per se* (Mehlum et al., 2006). The institutional view argues that natural resources hinder institutional development, delay democratisation, reduce the level of civil liberties, and weaken the rule of law (Leite & Weidmann, 1999; Isham et al., 2005; Sala-i-Martin & Subramanian, 2008; Zalle, 2019). Although the political resource curse can, in theory, be reversed by reforming institutions (Humphreys et al., 2007), this is typically difficult in reality because the quality of institutions prior to resource dependence is usually poor to start with and then gets eroded further. Consequently, resource-dependent countries lack the institutional capacity to constrain a ruler's policy discretion, and the resource revenues undermine the development of 'good' institutions and entrench 'bad' institutions, thus hindering democratisation and equitable wealth creation (Jensen & Wantchekon, 2004; Wiens, 2014).

In addition to institutional quality, natural resource dependence also affects a country's stock of human capital because dependence encourages human capital to shift from the industrial sector to the natural resources sector (Zalle, 2019). Although this reallocation can positively affect economic development if the country has well-developed human capital markets (Bravo-Ortega & de Gregorio, 2005), in countries with limited pools of human capital (such as in SSA), this reallocation can hamper diversification (Gylfason, 2001) and prolong the resource curse (Gylfason & Zoega, 2006). Natural resources may also affect the relationship between FDI and democracy because political repression is more likely to attract resource extractive FDI than diversified FDI (Adam & Filippaios, 2007). Hence, although the long-term nature of FDI should make it more receptive to deepening democracy, natural resources are usually tightly controlled by governments in the host country. Thus, extractive FDI must maintain close ties with governments in order to gain access to the natural resources, which is easier if the relationship is with autocratic regimes (Asiedu & Lien, 2011). It is therefore unsurprising that around 70% of the world's resource-rich states are rentier autocracies (Mailey, 2015) and that extractive FDI in SSA is impervious to institutional quality in resource-dependent states (especially oil-producing states) (Feulefack & Kamajou, 2015; Feulefack & Ngassam, 2020).

During colonialism, the natural resources of developing countries were used to benefit the socio-economic development and political control of the colonial powers and thus the rich nations grew richer while the wealth and resources of colonial and post-colonial states were drained away (Mlambo, 2022). Dependency Theory argues that the post-colonial capitalist global economy is still structured to ensure pre-eminence of the West at the core and dependence of emerging countries at the periphery (Emeh,

2013). Africa is exceptionally resource rich but is also disproportionately resource export dependent (Burgis, 2015, pp. 6–7). Thus, post-colonial reliance on natural resource extractive FDI has entrenched neo-colonial dependence and under-development in SSA (Omeje, 2021, pp. 89–90). This is because many SSA countries specialise in natural resource extraction while the developed world and emerging countries in Asia produce finished goods. Ownership of the means of production is therefore in the hands of foreign investors, and the profits from resource extraction are consequently repatriated to the home countries rather than growing and developing the economies of the host countries (Matunhu, 2011; Scott, 2012, p. 100). Hence, there is little evidence of a beneficial relationship between FDI, institutions, and economic growth in resource-dependent SSA countries (Asiedu & Lien, 2011; Agbloyor et al., 2016; Mlambo, 2022).

Furthermore, the disparate power dynamics between weak resource-dependent SSA states and powerful multinational resource companies has entrenched corruption and institutional dysfunction in many SSA countries. Foreign investors who are readily willing to conduct business that is illegal, immoral, or exploitative will have a comparative advantage over more ethical competitors (Mailey, 2015). Predatory companies can therefore exploit financially constrained, partially open, diplomatically isolated countries; or those that have weak institutions, rule of law, and civil rights. Hence, "these predatory corporations are not merely bystanders conducting business as usual in an unsavoury environment. They often proactively empower unaccountable leaders and frequently benefit directly from conflict and political crises" (ibid.).

An example is Sable Mining Africa Ltd.'s activities in Liberia. As detailed in the Global Witness report (2019), Sable Mining (initially named BioEnergy Africa) is a company listed on London's Alternative Investment Market and founded by controversial businessmen Philippe-Henri Edmonds (former English team spin bowler) and Andrew Groves.[5] Sable Mining arrived in Liberia in 2010 hoping to secure the mining rights to the last available iron ore concession in the Wologizi Mountain. Sable allegedly then hired Varney Sherman, a very well-connected lawyer (Sherman subsequently became the Chairman of President Ellen Johnson Sirleaf's Unity Party), who advised Sable that the Wologizi concession was ear-marked for public auction. The only way that the company could avoid

[5] Edmonds and Groves are alleged to have made millions from insider trading, stock market scams, bribery, hacking, shell companies, and overpricing assets (ibid.).

being outbid was to change the new Public Procurement and Concessions Act by bribing senior officials to allow the insertion of a loophole that would declare the area as non-bidding and thus allow Sable to win the contract without a tender. Over the next few months, Sable allegedly paid over USD 960,000 in bribes through Sherman's law firm (the transactions were recorded as "consulting fees") to among others, the Representative of Speaker of the House (Alex Tyler), the Chairman of National Investment Committee (Richard Tolbert), the Minister of State for Finance Economic and Legal Affairs (Morris Saytumah), the Chairman of Public Procurement and Concessions Commission (Willie Belleh), the Director of National Security Agency (Fombah Sirleaf), Senator Sumo Kupee, Speaker of the Senate (Cletus Wotorson), the Head of IE Sports Association (Richard Tolbert), and the Departmental Minister of Ministry of Lands, Mines and Energy (Ernest Jones).

Despite these activities, Sable was not awarded the concession because "certain people high up in Liberia had promised it to various parties from different countries and had not cross-checked" (ibid.). However, Groves then used the lessons learnt in Liberia to secure interests in the Nimba iron-ore project in Guinea, and the Lubu coal project in Zimbabwe (Mail & Guardian, 2018). In the meantime, Trace Compendium (2019) reports that on 12th May 2016, Liberian President Ellen Johnson Sirleaf with cooperation from the British authorities instituted an inquiry into Sable Mining's activities in Liberia, and on the 25th of May, the Liberian grand jury indicted Sable Mining on bribery charges. However, on the 13th of February 2018, all charges against Sable Mining and Andrew Groves were suddenly dropped by the Liberian courts, and on the 31st of July 2019, the charges against the senior officials charged with corruption were dropped "due to the prosecution being unable to prove [the charges] beyond all reasonable doubt."

4.4 Democratisation and FDI

In recent decades, theorists have posited that multinational companies will invest abroad for a variety of reasons, which include to take advantage of skills, technological, and cost of capital disparities (Lall, 1980; Hymer, 1976, pp. 34–38); to gain from ownership, location, or internalisation advantages (the eclectic paradigm of Dunning, 1981, 2001, 2008); to meet the needs of domestic markets (horizontal or market-seeking FDI); to export from locations that can offer abundant natural resources, raw materials, or low labour and production costs (vertical or efficiency seeking FDI) (Michalet, 1997, pp. 12–15); to enhance the capabilities of the company (strategic asset-seeking FDI) (Meyer, 2015); or to benefit from the availability of skilled labour, technological research institutes, innovative capacity, and technological adoption (Dumludag, 2009).

All these motives however suggest that FDI commonly entails significant capital investment and normally has long investment horizons (World Bank, 1999). It has therefore been argued that FDI should be attracted to more democratic countries because democratic institutions offer enhanced property rights protection, policy and regulatory stability, and lower corruption and expropriation risks (North & Weingast, 1989; Globerman & Shapiro, 2002, 2003; Harms & Ursprung, 2002; Jensen, 2003; Jakobson & de Soysa, 2006; Li, 2009). In addition, countries with well-developed political rights can withstand the instability of political change and ensure that political decisions do not negatively affect the investment environment (Bremmer, 2005).

Critics counter however that most emerging countries, including those in SSA, suffer from a range of impediments (such as low productivity levels, high inflation, underdeveloped infrastructure, narrow skills bases, limited market size, and low savings rates) and are therefore desperate to attract FDI (Mody & Murshid, 2005). Consequently, multinational investors can take advantage of this desperation by investing in less democratic countries that can limit the multinationals exposure to wage, labour, and tax demands, while gaining an opportunity to negotiate directly with the political elite (Resnick, 2001; Busse, 2004; Gehlbach & Keefer, 2011). Hence, liberalisation can hinder democratisation if the ensuing free market capitalism constrains governments, labour markets, and civil society (Adams et al., 1999; Mittelman, 2000).

Li and Resnick (2003) however argue that whether the relationship between democracy and FDI is positive or negative depends on the recipient's stage of institutional development because at the advent of democratisation the naturally unstable institutions will discourage FDI, but as democratic governance deepens, the accompanying property rights and the rule of law will then attract FDI. In addition, investing in countries with poor political rights could be expensive because weak political institutions are more likely to bend to the will of the political elite (Olson, 1993; Keefer, 2007) thus raising sovereign risk and endangering investment as a result of possible expropriation or unpredictable government intervention (Wei, 2000; Jensen, 2003, 2008; Li, 2009). Likewise, investment in countries with poor civil liberties will also be risky because of the weak legal systems that are malleable to government abuse, poor property rights protection, and weak enforcement of government commitments (North & Weingast, 1989; Merkel, 2004; Acemoglu, 2008). Hence, it is likely that FDI investors will either be attracted to the nefarious opportunities in countries with weak institutions and political elitism in the early stages of democratisation, or to the market opportunities and property rights protection in countries with maturing democratic institutions.

Consequently, there are three possible associations between financial globalisation and democratisation. First, free markets and democracy can mutually reinforce each other (Gill, 1997; Rodrik, 1997; Armijo, 1999) as liberalisation of economic markets stimulates democratisation and thus weakens the authority of the predatory elite (Acemoglu et al., 2005). Second, free markets and democracy can develop in tandem (Hayek, 1944; Fukuyama, 1991; Bhagwati, 1993; Friedman, 1999); and third, free markets can undermine democracy as discussed above (Rodrik, 2012). However, even in countries with maturing democratic institutions, it is possible that international investors can derail democratisation by capturing public policy for their own benefit, use the threat of disinvestment for coercion, or to fund civil and financial repression (Fayad et al., 2011).

Although there are relatively few studies that empirically explore the relationship between democracy and FDI in SSA, de Mauro (2013) and Akhtaruzzaman et al. (2018) find that FDI is attracted by democracy while Onyeiwu and Shrestha (2004) and Suliman and Mollick (2009) find that FDI is attracted by civil liberties to a greater extent than by political rights, and Gangi and Abdulrazak (2012) note that this applies particularly to voice and accountability, government effectiveness, and rule of law. Cleeve (2012) finds that FDI is attracted by deepening institutional quality to a greater extent than declining political risk while Gossel (2018) shows that FDI is more affected by the long-run accumulation of democratic capital than by contemporaneous democratisation. Dwumfour and Ntow-Gyamfi (2018) however find that the positive association is more applicable to high-income SSA countries whereas low- and middle-income SSA countries are more affected by the resource curse and Matima and Gossel (2023) further report that FDI in non-resource-dependent SSA countries is attracted by declining political risks and improved institutional quality whereas FDI to resource-dependent SSA countries is attracted by institutional investment protection. Ajide (2024) however shows that egalitarian and deliberative democracies significantly attract FDI followed by participative democracy whereas liberal democracy and electoral democracy are insignificant.

The relationship between net FDI inflows and the democracy indicators tabulated in Table 4.3 indicates that on average, resource-dependent SSA countries have Polity democracy ratings that are over two times less democratic than non-dependent SSA countries, and civil liberties and political rights that are 10% and 20% worse respectively. Economically, although resource-dependent SSA countries have marginally higher economic growth rates than non-dependent SSA countries, their GDP per capita and trade levels are 40% and 10% lower respectively. In addition, resource-dependent SSA countries have received 30% less FDI than non-dependent countries.

Figure 4.2 further shows that after political liberalisation in the early 1990s, there was a rapid improvement in the democracy metrics in SSA, and this liberalisation was accompanied by rising FDI inflows. From 1990–1999, resource-dependent countries received a total of USD 12.0 billion while non-dependent SSA countries received USD 27.4 billion. Thereafter, this gap widened still further, from 2000–2009, dependent SSA countries received USD 62.1 billion while non-dependent SSA countries received USD 132.4 billion; and from 2010–2020, dependent SSA countries received USD 137.6 billion while non-dependent SSA countries received USD 248.3 billion. Thus, over the last three decades, non-dependent countries have consistently received around twice as much FDI

Table 4.3 Natural resource-related democracy and economic performance

Average	*Measure*	*(a) Resource dependent [18]*	*(b) Non-dependent [24]*	*(a)/(b)*
Democracy	Polity2	−2.59	−1.19	2.2
Civil liberties	Freedom House	5.26	4.63	1.1
Political rights	Freedom House	5.62	4.82	1.2
GDP growth	Annual %	3.86	3.79	1.0
GDP per capita	Constant 2015 USD	1129.91	1766.35	0.6
Trade	% of GDP	58.26	64.40	0.9
Net FDI inflows	Millions USD	254.54	371.60	0.7

[#] indicates the number of SSA countries in the sample.

Data sources: World Development Indicators (1970–2020), Polity V (1970–2018), Freedom House (1972–2020)

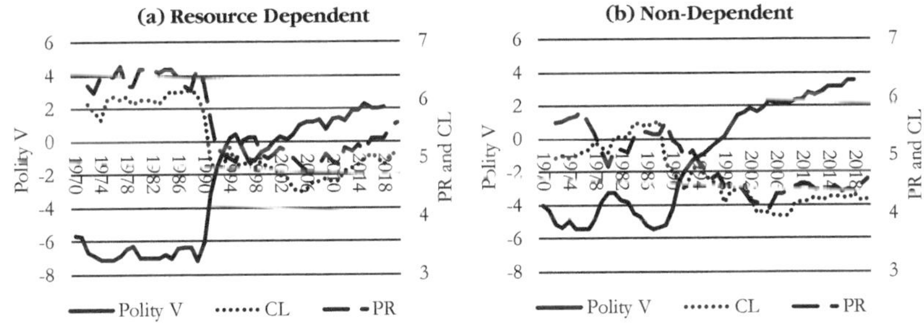

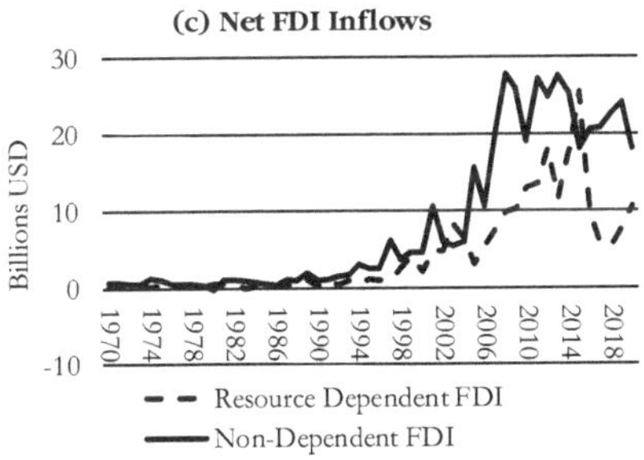

	ϱFDI	
Democracy	Resource Dependent	Non-Dependent
Polity 2	69.8%	82.6%
Civil liberties	-55.7%	-70.3%
Political rights	-56.1%	-68.2%

Fig. 4.2 FDI and democracy. (Data sources: Polity V, Freedom House, World Development Indicators)

inflows than natural resource-dependent SSA countries. Furthermore, considered in combination with the disparate democracy metrics, this also suggests that FDI is more attracted to democratic SSA countries and thus does not adhere to the autocracy-seeking FDI hypothesis of Resnick (2001).

This is borne out by Table 4.4, which segments the democracy and economic averages of 43 SSA countries over the post-liberalisation period of 1990–2020 based on the average Polity scores. As can be seen, SSA countries that have Polity scores above zero naturally have higher civil liberties and political rights than SSA countries with average Polity scores below zero (30% and 50% respectively). However, SSA countries with below-zero Polity averages have 30% higher economic growth, 40% higher GDP per capita, and 10% better trade levels than SSA countries with above-zero Polity averages. Despite these disparities, SSA countries with above-zero average Polity scores received twice as much FDI inflows than SSA countries with below-zero average Polity scores.

Table 4.4 Post-liberalisation democracy and economic performance

Average	*Measure*	*(a) Polity < 0 [21]*	*(b) Polity > 0 [22]*	*(a)/(b)*
Democracy	Polity2	−2.88	4.01	−0.7
Civil liberties	Freedom House	5.17	3.97	1.3
Political rights	Freedom House	5.86	3.85	1.5
GDP growth	Annual %	4.46	3.43	1.3
GDP per capita	Constant 2015 USD	1799.92	1299.82	1.4
Trade	% of GDP	66.67	60.91	1.1
Net FDI inflows	Millions USD	303.56	607.30	0.5

[#] indicates the number of SSA countries in the sample

Data sources: World Development Indicators (1990–2020), Polity V (1990–2018), Freedom House (1990–2020)

4.5 Elections and FDI

Over the course of the last half a century, most SSA countries have moved away from authoritarian liberation governments towards holding multi-party elections (Mills & Herbst, 2012, p. 6). After averaging just three executive and seven legislative, parliamentary, or constituent assembly elections per year from 1970 to 1990, the annual average increased to nine executive and ten legislative, parliamentary, or constituent assembly elections from 1990 to 2020. Despite the increased frequency of elections, democratic development in SSA remains uneven, and in common with other regions in the world, democratisation over the last decade has slowed as governments have increasingly used the 'menu of manipulation' (Schedler, 2002) or "strategic rigging" (Klaas, 2018, p. 238) to conduct irregular, manipulated, and fraudulent elections supported by patronage, clientelism, and neopatrimonialism (Basedau et al., 2007; Collier & Vicente, 2012; Ronceray & Byiers, 2019).

Hence, although elections have become more common in SSA since the end of the Cold War, there has also been a commensurate rise in the frequency of adverse election events. As can be seen from Table 4.5, the most common methods for manipulating elections have been the use of government harassment of the opposition (NELDA 15) and post-election violence (NELDA 29). Despite these events, there are significant numbers of elections where the incumbent's party lost the election (NELDA 24) but in nearly half of these occurrences, the incumbent then extended their time in office (NELDA 9). These figures also highlight the weaknesses of election monitoring, because despite the increase in these

Table 4.5 Adverse election events

	Executive elections						Legislative/parliamentary/constituent assembly elections					
	1970–1979	*1980–1989*	*1990–1999*	*2000–2009*	*2010–2020*	*Total*	*1970–1979*	*1980–1989*	*1990–1999*	*2000–2009*	*2010–2020*	*Total*
(a) Elections (#):	34	39	81	81	109	344	62	78	110	93	112	455
(b) Nelda code event:												
9 Had the incumbent extended his or her term in office or eligibility to run in elections at any point in the past?	2	9	6	13	17	47	0	0	1	0	2	3
15 Is there evidence that the government harassed the opposition?	3	7	22	18	47	97	12	15	30	20	49	126
24 Did the incumbent's party lose?	0	0	15	18	26	59	3	3	25	16	18	65
29 Were there riots and protests after the election?	3	8	16	19	45	91	5	15	22	17	36	95

(*continued*)

Table 4.5 (continued)

		Executive elections						*Legislative/parliamentary/constituent assembly elections*					
		1970–1979	*1980–1989*	*1990–1999*	*2000–2009*	*2010–2020*	*Total*	*1970–1979*	*1980–1989*	*1990–1999*	*2000–2009*	*2010–2020*	*Total*
39	Was the incumbent replaced?	3	3	29	24	34	93	0	6	5	6	6	23
47	Were there allegations by Western monitors of significant vote-fraud?	0	0	7	11	15	33	0	2	7	14	16	39
Total		11	27	95	103	184	420	20	41	90	73	127	351

adverse election events, the number of times that Western election monitors raised concerns about vote fraud (NELDA 47) is significantly below the number of adverse election events. It is possible however that this is because Western election monitors are hesitant to allege election fraud that may then lead to election violence or socio-political instability (Dodsworth, 2019). Consequently, elections in most African countries do not yet act as a conflict processing mechanism and thus African leaders "are more than twice as likely to be killed, exiled or jailed after leaving office than those in any other part of the world" (Cheeseman and Klaas, 2018, p. 19).

In common with other developing regions in the world, elections in SSA reflect the legacies of colonialism (Szeftel, 1999; Fukuyama, 2014) and post-colonial institutional voids (Bratton & van der Walle, 1997; Wig & Tollefsen, 2016). However, unlike Asia or Latin America, SSA suffers from lower GDP per capita incomes, education levels, and a smaller middle class. Consequently, "the top stratum of political leaders in Africa remains wedded to a political economy in which wealth and power derive from personal control of the resources of the state. As such, incumbent elites are predisposed to resist reforms to a system that has served them well in the past" (Bratton et al., 2004, p. 14). This top-heavy elitism manifests in elections that suffer from endemic incumbency (Ncube, 2012), militarism, patrimonialism, patronage, and clientelism (Berman, 1998; Southall, 2003a, 2003b; Wantchekon, 2003), and the use of violence and socio-cultural and ethnic divisions as political tools (Berman et al., 2005; Bhasin & Gandhi, 2013).[6] In addition, the disproportionate access to power, resources, and wealth among the political class means that opposition forces can be co-opted and minimised (Dahl, 1971; Southall, 2001; Mills & Herbst, 2012, p. 15). Consequently, elections are less about ideology or improving the lives of the populace and more about capturing and controlling the flow of rents for the disproportionate benefit of the political elite (Page, 2018), which Michela Wrong (2009) famously summed it up in the title of her book, *It's Our Turn to Eat*.

Even in countries that have opposition politics, this does not necessarily equate to greater political stability because incumbent politicians can take advantage of weak institutions and selective rule of law and can use the resource rents to unfairly buy political support. Consequently, opposition

[6] According to Staffan Lindberg (2004, p. 61), roughly 80% of African elections witnessed some kind of electoral violence, even among elections that were deemed to be fair and free.

parties are commonly forced to use riots to counter the political power of incumbency, but this then creates a vicious cycle because incumbent politicians then use the actual or perceived threat of political instability to clamp down on or co-opt opposition parties, thus entrenching authoritarianism (Jensen & Wantchekon, 2004). Hence, at the level of the electorate there is only limited political recourse (Lewis-Beck & Stegmaier, 2000) and over time, this lack of democratic deepening then drives disillusionment of elections and democracy as a means to reduce poverty and underdevelopment (Lemon, 2007).

With regards to FDI, it is to be expected that international investors will be deterred by elections that are associated with heightened political instability and risk (Chen et al., 2019). However, FDI is a capital-intensive long-run investment and thus investors may be more focussed on policy risks and the process of democratisation rather than short-run election events or legislative changes (Persson & Tabellini, 2003; Gossel, 2018). Hence, in a democratically unstable environment, international investors may use elections to monitor political unrest, policy instability, and respect for the law. Non-violent free and fair elections should therefore positively affect FDI (Touchton, 2015) but it is also possible that unfair elections could attract FDI if investors can secure their investment directly with the political elite (Huntington & Dominguez, 1975; O'Donnell, 1978, 1988; Haggard, 1990; Resnick, 2001; Jensen, 2008). Consequently, international companies can use their investment as a proxy vote during election periods, by promising to increase or threatening to decrease (or delay) their investment if the election outcome is believed to be beneficial or detrimental to their post-election investment (Vaaler, 2008).

In the case of SSA, Gossel (2020) finds that although FDI is attracted by democracy, it is deterred by elections (especially liberation elections), and that FDI investors are more concerned with overt election manipulation than whether the election is deemed to be free and fair. Related to this, Youssouf et al. (2022) further find that FDI is deterred by frequent constitutional changes, as these tend to be associated with socioeconomic and political instability rather than reforms while Palmtag et al. (2025) report that FDI decreases pre-election violence in politically competitive regions but has no significant effect in regions where the incumbent or opposition parties predominate.

Figure 4.3 shows that, as mentioned previously, there has been a steady increase over time in elections and adverse election events. However, FDI inflows have not followed a similar pattern, rising dramatically after the

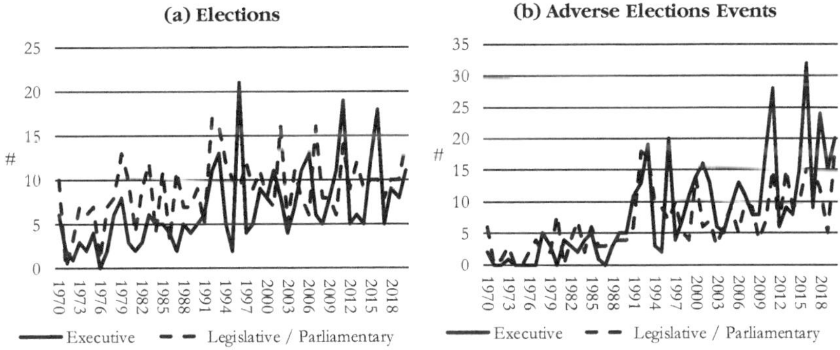

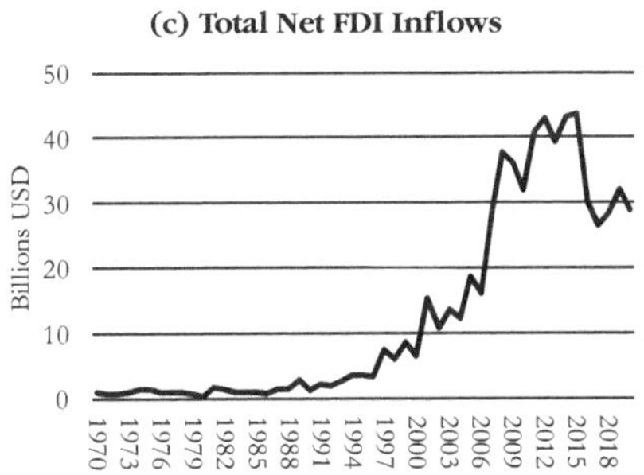

Election	ϱFDI
Executive	40.4%
Adverse executive events	56.9%
Legislative / parliamentary	22.7%
Legislative / parliamentary adverse events	46.9%

Fig. 4.3 Elections and FDI in SSA. (Data sources: NELDA, World Development Indicators)

early 2000s. The correlation coefficients between the election events and FDI also suggest that FDI is more sensitive to executive elections than to legislative/parliamentary elections. The correlation between FDI and executive elections and adverse election events are 40.4% and 56.9% respectively compared to the correlations between FDI and legislative/parliamentary elections and adverse election events of 22.7% and 46.9% respectively. A possible reason for this disparity is because FDI investors are more sensitive to the potential policy changes, risks, and instability associated with executive elections or because FDI investors do not have confidence that legislators and parliamentarians can restrain excessive presidentialism (Gossel, 2018).

References

Acemoglu, D. (2008). Oligarchic Versus Democratic Societies. *Journal of the European Economic Association, 6*, 1–44.

Acemoglu, D., Johnson, S., & Robinson, J. (2005). The Rise of Europe: Atlantic Trade, Institutional Change, and Economic Growth. *American Economic Review, 95*(3), 546–579.

Acemoglu, D., Johnson, S., Robinson, J., & Yared, P. (2008). Income and Democracy. *American Economic Review, 98*, 808–842.

Acemoglu, D., Naidu, S., Restrepo, P., & Robinson, J. A. (2019). Democracy Does Cause Growth. *Journal of Political Economy, 127*(1), 47–100.

Adam, A., & Filippaios, F. (2007). Foreign Direct Investment and Civil Liberties: A New Perspective. *European Journal of Political Economy, 23*(4), 1038–1052.

Adams, F., Gupta, S. D., & Mengisteab, K. (1999). Globalization and the Dilemmas of the State. In *Globalization and the Developing World: An Introduction*. Macmillan.

Agbloyor, E. K., Gyeke-Dako, A., Kuipo, R., & Abor, J. Y. (2016). Foreign Direct Investment and Economic Growth in SSA: The Role of Institutions. *Thunderbird International Review, 58*(5), 479–497.

Aisen, A., & Veiga, F. J. (2013). How Does Political Instability Affect Economic Growth? *European Journal of Political Economy, 29*, 151–167.

Ajide, K. B. (2024). Does the Presence of Democratic Traits Enhance Africa's Appeal for Foreign Direct Investment? *Economic Change and Restructuring, 57*, 239.

Akhtaruzzaman, M., Yang, S., & Omar, A. (2018). Are Resource Rich Countries More Attractive than Countries with Good Institutions to Foreign Direct Investors in Sub Saharan Africa? *International Journal of Economics and Finance, 10*(6), 65–74.

Al Jazeera. (2023, August 30). *Mapping Africa's Coups D'etat Across the Years*. Retrieved March, 2024, from https://www.aljazeera.com/news/2023/8/30/mapping-africas-coups-detat-across-the-years

Alesina, A., Ozler, S., Roubini, N., & Swagel, P. (1996). Political Instability and Economic Growth. *Journal of Economic Growth, 1*(2), 189–211.

Anderson, J. E., & Marcouiller, D. (2002). Insecurity and the Pattern of Trade: An Empirical Investigation. *Review of Economics and Statistics, 84*(2), 342–352.

Animashaun, J. & Ubabukoh, C. L. (2021). Is Human Rights Protection Good for Trade in Africa: Evidence from Proximity to Democratically 'Good' and 'Bad' Neighboring Countries. *Managing Global Transition, 19*(4), 285–305.

Armijo, L. E. (1999). Mixed Blessings: Expectations About Capital Flows and Democracy. In *Financial Globalization and Democracy in Emerging Markets*. Palgrave.

Asiedu, E., & Lien, D. (2011). Democracy, Foreign Direct Investment and Natural Resources. *Journal of International Economics, 84*(1), 99–111.

Asongu, S. A., Kossele, T. P. Y., & Nnanna, J. (2021). Not All that Glitters is Gold: Political Stability and Trade in Sub-Saharan Africa. *Crime, Law and Social Change, 75*, 469–485.

Bah, M., Ondoa, H. A., & Kpognon, K. D. (2021). Effects of Governance Quality on Exports in Sub-Saharan Africa. *International Economics, 167*, 1–14.

Bailey, K. (2020). Stakeholder Capitalism Against Democracy: Relegitimising Global Neoliberalism. *Journal of Australian Political Economy, 86*, 85–121.

Barro, R. J. (1996). Democracy and Growth. *Journal of Economic Growth, 1*(1), 1–27.

Barro, R. J. (1999). Determinants of Democracy. *Journal of Political Economy, 107*(S6), 158–183.

Barro, R. J. (2015). Convergence and Modernization. *The Economic Journal, 125*(585), 911–942.

Basedau, M., Erdmann, G., & Mehler, A. (2007). *Votes, Money and Violence: Political Parties and Elections in Sub-Saharan Africa*. Nordiska Afrikainstitutet/ University of KwaZulu-Natal Press.

Bates, R. H., Fayad, G., & Hoeffler, A. (2012). The State of Democracy in Sub-Saharan Africa. *International Area Studies Review, 15*(4), 323–338.

Baum, M. A., & Lake, D. A. (2003). The Political Economy of Growth: Democracy and Human Capital. *American Journal of Political Science, 47*(2), 333–347.

Beblawi, H., & Luciani, G. (1987). *The Rentier State*. Croom Helm.

Berman, B., Eyoh, D., & Kymlicka, W. (Eds.). (2005). *Ethnicity and Democracy in Africa*. James Curry.

Berman, B. J. (1998). Ethnicity, Patronage and the African State: The Politics of Uncivil Nationalism. *African Affairs, 97*, 305–341.

Bhagwati, J. (1993). Democracy and Development. In L. Diamond & M. F. Plattner (Eds.), *Capitalism, Socialism, and Democracy Revisited*. Johns Hopkins University Press.

Bhasin, T., & Gandhi, J. (2013). Timing and Targeting of State Repression in Authoritarian Elections. *Electoral Studies, 32*, 620–631.

Bratton, M., Mattes, R., & Gyimah-Boadi, E. (2004). *Public Opinion, Democracy, and Market Reform in Africa, Cambridge Studies in Comparative Politics*. Cambridge University Press.

Bratton, M., & van der Walle, N. (1997). *Democratic Experiments in Africa: Regime Transitions in Comparative Perspective*. Cambridge University Press.

Bravo-Ortega, C., & de Gregorio, J. (2005). The Relative Richness of the Poor? Natural Resources, Human Capital and Economic Growth. *Policy Research Working Paper No. 3484*. World Bank.

Bremmer, I. (2005). Managing Risk in an Unstable World. *Harvard Business Review, 83*, 51–60.

Bueno de Mesquita, B., & Smith, A. (2009). Political Survival and Endogenous Institutional Change. *Comparative Political Studies, 42*(2), 168–197.
Burgis, T. (2015). *The Looting Machine*. William Collins.
Burke, P. J., & Leigh, A. (2010). Do Output Contractions Trigger Democratic Change? *American Economic Journal: Macroeconomics, 2*(4), 124–157.
Busse, M. (2004). Transnational Corporations and Repression of Political Rights and Civil Liberties: An Empirical Analysis. *Kyklos, 57*(1), 45–66.
Cheeseman, N. (2010). African Elections and Vehicles for Change. *Journal of Democracy, 21*(4), 139–153.
Cheeseman, N. (2018). *Institutions and Democracy in Africa: How the Rules of the Game Shape Political Developments*. Cambridge University Press.
Cheibub, J. A., & Vreeland, J. R. (2011). Economic Development and Democratization. In N. J. Brown (Ed.), *The Dynamics of Democratization, Dictatorship, Development, and Diffusion*. Johns Hopkins University Press.
Chen, K., Nie, H., & Ge, Z. (2019). Policy Uncertainty and FDI: Evidence from National Elections. *The Journal of International Trade & Economic Development, 28*(4), 419–428.
Chisadza, C., & Bittencourt, M. (2019). Economic Development and Democracy: The Modernization Hypothesis in Sub-Saharan Africa. *The Social Science Journal, 56*, 243–254.
Cleeve, E. (2012). Impediments to Foreign Direct Investment Inflows to Sub-Saharan Africa. *Thunderbird International Business Review, 54*(4), 469–477.
Collier, P. (2010). The Political Economy of Natural Resources. *Social Research, 77*(4), 1105–1132.
Collier, P., & Hoeffler, A. (2004). Greed and Grievance in Civil War. *Oxford Economic Papers, 56*(4), 563–595.
Collier, P., & Vicente, P. C. (2012). Violence, Bribery, and Fraud: The Political Economy of Elections in Sub-Saharan Africa. *Public Choice, 153*(1–2), 117–147.
Conrad, C. R., & DeMeritt, J. H. (2013). Constrained by the Bank and the Ballot: Unearned Revenue, Democracy, and State Incentives to Repress. *Journal of Peace Research, 50*(1), 105–119.
Crouch, C. (2016). Capitalism, Inequality and Democracy. *Stato e mercato, Agosto, 107*(2), 159–182.
Dahl, R. (1971). *Polyarchy*. Yale University Press.
de Haan, J., & Siermann, C. L. J. (1995a). A Sensitivity Analysis of the Impact of Democracy on Economic Growth. *Empirical Economics, 20*(2), 197–215.
de Haan, J., & Siermann, C. L. J. (1995b). New Evidence on the Relationship between Democracy and Economic Growth. *Public Choice, 86*(1–2), 175–198.
de Mauro, A. (2013). Africa's Burden: Labour Markets, Natural Resources and the FDI 'Reliance-Rejection' Paradox. *MPRA Paper No. 50019*. Munich Personal RePEc Archive.

De Soysa, I., & Vadlammanati, K. C. (2013). Do Pro-Market Economic Reforms Drive Human Rights Violations? An Empirical Assessment, 1981–2006. *Public Choice, 155*(1–2), 163–187.
DeMeritt, J. H., & Young, J. K. (2013). A Political Economy of Human Rights: Oil, Natural Gas, and State Incentives to Repress. *Conflict Management and Peace Science, 30*(2), 99–120.
Desierto, D. A. (2018). Formal Models of the Political Resource Curse. *Economics of Governance, 19*, 225–259.
Diamond, L. J. (2002). Thinking About Hybrid Regimes. *Journal of Democracy, 13*(2), 21–35.
Dodsworth, S. (2019). Double Standards: The Verdicts of Western Election Observers in Sub-Saharan Africa. *Democratization, 26*(3), 382–400.
Doucouliagos, H., & Ulubaşoğlu, M. A. (2008). Democracy and Economic Growth: A Meta-Analysis. *American Journal of Political Science, 52*(1), 61–83.
Dulani, B. (2020). The Struggle for Presidential Term Limits. In G. Lynch & P. Von Doepp (Eds.), *Routledge Handbook of Democratization in Africa* (pp. 104–116). Routledge.
Dumludag, D. (2009). *Political Institutions and Foreign Direct Investment Flows into Developing Countries.* MPRA Paper No. 27327. Munich Personal RePEc Archive, University Library of Munich.
Dunning, J. H. (1981). *International Production and the Multinational Enterprise.* Allen and Unwin.
Dunning, J. H. (2001). The Eclectic (OLI) Paradigm of International Production: Past, Present and Future. *International Journal of the Economics of Business, 8*, 173–190.
Dunning, J. H. (2008). Space, Location and Distance in IB Activities: A Changing Scenario. In J. H. Dunning & P. Gugler (Eds.), *Foreign Direct Investment, Location and Competitiveness.* JAI Press.
Dutt, P., & Traca, D. (2010). Corruption and Bilateral Trade Flows: Extortion or Evasion? *The Review of Economics and Statistics, 92*(4), 843–860.
Dwumfour, R. A., & Ntow-Gyamfi, M. (2018). Natural Resources, Financial Development and Institutional Quality in Africa: Is There a Resource Curse? *Resources Policy, 59*, 411–426.
Edozie, R. K. (2008). New Trends in Democracy and Development: Democratic Capitalism in South Africa, Nigeria and Kenya. *Politikon, 35*(1), 43–67.
Emeh, I. E. J. (2013). Dependency Theory and Africa's Underdevelopment: A Paradigm Shift from Pseudo-Intellectualism: The Nigerian Perspective. *International Journal of African and Asian Studies, 1*, 116–128.
Epstein, D. L., Bates, R., Goldstone, J., Kristensen, I., & O'Halloran, S. (2006). Democratic Transitions. *American Journal of Political Science, 50*, 551–569.

Fayad, G., Bates, R. H., & Hoeffler, A. (2011). Income and Democracy: Lipset's Law Inverted. *OxCarre Research Paper No. 61*. Oxford Centre for the Analysis of Resource Rich Economies.

Fayissa, B., & Nsiah, C. (2013). The Impact of Governance on Economic Growth in Africa. *The Journal of Developing Areas, 47*(1), 91–108.

Feng, Y. (1997). Democracy, Political Stability and Economic Growth. *British Journal of Political Science, 27*, 391–418.

Feulefack, K. L., & Kamajou, F. (2015). Quality of Institutions and Foreign Direct Investment: The Case of Sub-Saharan Africa. *Applied Sciences Reports, 9*(2), 70–79.

Feulefack, K. L., & Ngassam, B. S. (2020). Natural Resources, Quality of Institutions and Foreign Direct Investment in Africa. *Economics Bulletin, 40*(1), 1–16.

Fosu, A. K. (2003). Political Instability and Export Performance in Sub-Saharan Africa. *Journal of Development Studies, 39*, 68–83.

Fosu, A. K. (2008). Democracy and Growth in Africa: Implications of Increasing Electoral Competitiveness. *Economics Letters, 100*, 442–444.

Freedom House (2022). *Freedom in the World*. https://freedomhouse.org/report/freedom-world

Friedman, M. (1970, September 13). The Social Responsibility of Business is to Increase its Profits. *The New York Times Magazine*. Retrieved March, 2023, from https://link.springer.com/chapter/10.1007/978-3-540-70818-6_14

Friedman, T. L. (1999). *The Lexus and the Olive Tree: Understanding Globalization*. Anchor Books.

Fukuyama, F. (1991). *The End of History and the Last Man*. Oxford University Press.

Fukuyama, F. (2014). *Political Order and Political Decay*. Profile Books.

Gangi, Y. A., & Abdulrazak, R. S. (2012). The Impact of Governance on FDI Flows to African Countries. *World Journal of Entrepreneurship, Management and Sustainable Development, 8*(2–3), 162–169.

Gehlbach, S., & Keefer, P. (2011). Investment Without Democracy: Ruling-Party Institutionalization and Credible Commitment in Autocracies. *Journal of Comparative Economics, 39*(2), 123–139.

George, S. (2015). *Shadow Sovereigns: How Global Corporations Are Seizing Power*. Polity Press.

Gill, S. (1997). Globalization, Democratization, and the Politics of Indifference. In J. H. Mittelmann (Ed.), *Globalization: Critical Reflections*. Lynne Rienner Publishers.

Global Witness. (2019). *The Deceivers*. Retrieved January, 2024, from https://www.globalwitness.org/thedeceivers/

Globerman, S., & Shapiro, D. (2002). Global Foreign Direct Investment Flows: The Role of Governance Infrastructure. *World Development, 30*(11), 1898–1919.

Globerman, S., & Shapiro, D. (2003). Governance Infrastructure and US Foreign Direct Investment. *Journal of International Business Studies, 34*(1), 19–39.
Gossel, S. J. (2017). Democratic Capital, Democratic Rights and FDI in Sub-Saharan Africa. *Journal of International Development, 29*(8), 1033–1061.
Gossel, S. J. (2018). Corruption, Democracy, and FDI in Sub-Saharan Africa. *Journal of Policy Modeling, 40*, 647–662.
Gossel, S. J. (2020). FDI and Elections in Sub-Saharan Africa. *The European Journal of Development Research, 32*(4), 1151–1172.
Guseh, J. S., & Oritsejafor, E. (2005). Democracy and Economic Growth in Africa: The Cases of Ghana and South Africa. *Journal of Third World Studies, XXII*(2), 121–137.
Gyimah-Brempong, K., & Traynor, T. L. (1999). Political Instability, Investment and Economic Growth in Sub-Saharan Africa. *Journal of African Economies, 8*, 52–86.
Gylfason, T. (2001). Natural Resources, Education, and Economic Development. *European Economic Review, 45*(4–6), 847–859.
Gylfason, T., & Zoega, G. (2006). Natural Resources and Economic Growth: The Role of Investment. *The World Economy, 29*, 1091–1115.
Haggard, S. (1990). *Pathways from the Periphery: The Politics of Growth in the Newly Industrializing Countries.* Cornell University Press.
Handley, K., & Limao, N. (2017). Policy Uncertainty, Trade and Welfare: Theory and Evidence for China and the US. *American Economic Review, 107*(9), 2731–2783.
Harms, P., & Ursprung, H. W. (2002). Do Civil and Political Repression Really Boost Foreign Direct Investments? *Economic Enquiry, 40*(4), 651–663.
Hayek, F. A. (1944). *The Road to Serfdom.* Chicago University Press.
Helliwell, J. F. (1994). Empirical Linkages between Democracy and Economic Growth. *British Journal of Political Science, 24*(2), 225–248.
Heo, U., & Tan, A. C. (2001). Democracy and Economic Growth: A Causal Analysis. *Comparative Politics, 33*(4), 463–473.
Herbst, J. (2009). Africans Like Markets: Why Don't They Favour Capitalism? *Critical Review, 21*(4), 415–422.
Horsewood, N., & Voicu, A. M. (2012). Does Corruption Hinder Trade for the New EU Members. *Economics: The Open-Access, Open-Assessment E-Journal, 6*, 1–28.
Humphreys, M., Sachs, J. D., & Stiglitz, J. E. (Eds.). (2007). *Escaping the Resource Curse.* Columbia University Press.
Huntington, S. P. (1968). *Political Order in Changing Societies.* Yale University Press.
Huntington, S. P. (1991). *The Third Wave: Democratization in the Late Twentieth Century.* University of Oklahoma Press.

Huntington, S. P., & Dominguez, J. I. (1975). Political Development. In F. I. Greenstein & N. W. Poldby (Eds.), *Handbook of Political Science* (Vol. 3, pp. 1–114). Addison-Wesley.

Hymer, S. H. (1976). *The International Operations of National Firms: A Study of Direct Foreign Investment*. The MIT Press.

Isham, J., Woolcock, M., Pritchett, L., & Busby, G. (2005). The Varieties of Resource Experience: Natural Resource Export Structures and the Political Economy of Economic Growth. *World Bank Economic Review, 19*(2), 141–174.

Jakobson, J., & de Soysa, I. (2006). Do Foreign Investors Punish Democracy? Theory and Empirics, 1984–2001. *Kyklos, 59*(3), 383–410.

Jensen, N., & Wantchekon, L. (2004). Resource Wealth and Political Regimes in Africa. *Comparative Political Studies, 37*(7), 816–841.

Jensen, N. M. (2003). Democratic Governance and Multinational Corporations: Political Regimes and Inflows of Foreign Direct Investment. *International Organization, 57*(3), 587–616.

Jensen, N. M. (2008). Political Risk, Democratic Institutions, and Foreign Direct Investment. *Journal of Politics, 70*(4), 1040–1052.

Joseph, R. (2014). Growth, Security, and Democracy in Africa. *Journal of Democracy, 25*(4), 61–75.

Kapstein, E. B., & Converse, N. (2008). *The Fate of Young Democracies*. Cambridge University Press.

Keefer, P. (2007). The Political Economy of Development. In C. Boix & S. C. Stokes (Eds.), *The Oxford Handbook of Comparative Politics*. Oxford University Press.

Klaas, B. (2018). Electoral Rules: The Relationship between Political Exclusion and Conflict. In N. Cheeseman (Ed.), *Institutions and Democracy in Africa*. Cambridge University Press.

Knutsen, C. H. (2012). Democracy, State Capacity, and Economic Growth. *World Development, 43*, 1–18.

Krieckhaus, J. (2006). Democracy and Economic Growth: How Regional Context Influences Regime Effects. *British Journal of Political Science, 36*(2), 317–340.

Kurzman, C., Werum, R., & Burkhart, R. E. (2002). Democracy's Effect on Economic Growth: A Pooled Time Series Analysis, 1951-80. *Studies in Comparative International Development, 37*(1), 3–33.

Lake, D. A., & Baum, M. A. (2001). The Invisible Hand of Democracy: Political Control and the Provision of Public Services. *Comparative Political Studies, 34*(6), 587 621.

Lall, S. (1980). Monopolistic Advantages and Foreign Involvement by U.S. Manufacturing Industry. *Oxford Economic Papers, 32*, 102–122.

Laniran, T. J. (2022, December 22). West Africa has Experienced a Wave of Coups – Superficial Democracy is to Blame. *The Conversation*. Retrieved January, 2024, from https://theconversation.com/west-africa-has-experienced-a-wave-of-coups-superficial-democracy-is-to-blame-195664

Leite, C. A., & Weidmann, J. (1999). Does Mother Nature Corrupt? Natural Resources, Corruption, and Economic Growth. *IMF Working Papers 1999/085*. International Monetary Fund.

Lemon, A. (2007). Perspectives on Democratic Consolidation in Southern Africa: The Five General Elections of 2004. *Political Geography, 26*, 824–850.

Lewis-Beck, M. S., & Stegmaier, M. (2000). Economic Determinants of Electoral Outcomes. *Annual Review of Political Science, 3*, 183–219.

Li, Q. (2009). Democracy, Autocracy, and Foreign Expropriation of Foreign Direct Investment. *Comparative Political Studies, 42*(8), 1098–1127.

Li, Q., & Resnick, A. (2003). Reversal of Fortunes: Democratic Institutions and Foreign Direct Investment Inflows to Developing Countries. *International Organization, 57*(1), 175–211.

Lindberg, S. I. (2004). The Democratic Quality of Multiparty Elections: Participation, Competition and Legitimacy in Africa. *Journal of Commonwealth and Comparative Studies, 42*(1), 61–104.

Linz, J., & Stepan, A. (1996). *Problems of Democratic Transition and Consolidation: Southern Europe, South America, and Post-Communist Europe*. Johns Hopkins University Press.

Lipset, M. (1959). Some Social Requisites of Democracy: Economic Development and Political Legitimacy. *American Political Science Association, 53*(1), 69–105.

Loungou, S. (2024, August 22). Africa's Ageing Leaders: Succession Race in Cameroon, Congo, and Equatorial Guinea Could Destabilise the Region. *The Conversation*. Retrieved March, 2025, from https://theconversation.com/africas-ageing-leaders-succession-race-in-cameroon-congo-and-equatorial-guinea-could-destabilise-the-region-235713

Luciani, G. (1997). Allocation Versus Production States: A Theoretical Framework. In H. Beblawi & G. Luciani (Eds.), *The Rentier State*. Croom Helm Publishing.

Mahdavy, H. (1970). The Patterns and Problems of Economic Development in a Rentier Stare: The Case of Iran. In M. A. Cook (Ed.), *Studies in Economic History of the Middle East*. Oxford University Press.

Mail & Guardian. (2018, May 25). Dodgy Mine Mogul's New Zim Play. Retrieved March, 2023, from https://mg.co.za/article/2018-05-25-00 dodgy-mine-moguls-new-zim-play/

Mailey, J. R. (2015). The Anatomy of the Resource Curse: Predatory Investment in Africa's Extractive Industries. *ACSS Special Report No. 3*. Africa Center for Strategic Studies.

Makhlouf, Y., Kellard, N. M., & Vinogradov, D. (2015). Trade Openness, Export Diversification, and Political Regimes. *Economic Letters, 136*, 25–27.

Maltz, G. (2007). The Case for Presidential Term Limits. *Journal of Democracy, 18*(1), 128–142.

Marshall, M. G., Gurr, T. R., & Jaggers, K. (2014). Political Regime Characteristics and Transitions, 1800–2013. *Polity IV Data User's Manual*. Center for Systemic Peace. Retrieved March, 2023, from www.systemicpeace.org

Martinez-Zarzoso, I., & Marquez-Ramos, L. (2019). Exports and Governance. Is Middle East and North Africa Different? *World Economics, 42*(1), 143–174.

Masaki, T., & van de Walle, N. (2014). The Impact of Democracy on Economic Growth in Sub-Saharan Africa, 1982–2012. *WIDER Working Paper 2014/057*. World Institute for Development Economics Research, United Nations University.

Matima, Z., & Gossel, S. J. (2023). The Relationship between FDI, Political Risk and Institutional Quality in Sub-Saharan Africa. *The Journal of International Trade & Economic Development, 32*(3), 461–474.

Matunhu, J. (2011). A Critique of Modernization and Dependency Theories in Africa: Critical Assessment. *African Journal of History and Culture, 3*(5), 65–72.

McFerson, H. M. (2010). Extractive Industries and African Democracy: Can the 'Resource Curse' be Exorcised? *International Studies Perspectives, 11*, 335–353.

McGuirk, E. F. (2013). The Illusory Leader: Natural Resources, Taxation and Accountability. *Public Choice, 154*(3–4), 285–313.

Mehlum, H., Moene, K., & Torvik, R. (2006). Institutions and the Resource Curse. *The Economic Journal, 116*, 1–20.

Menocal, A. R., Fritz, V., & Rakner, L. (2008). Hybrid Regimes and the Challenges of Deepening and Sustaining Democracy in Developing Countries. *South African Journal of International Affairs, 15*(1), 29–40.

Merkel, W. (2004). Embedded and Defective Democracies. *Social Science Research, 11*, 33–58.

Merkel, W. (2014). Is Capitalism Compatible with Democracy. *Zeitschrift Fur Vergleichende Politikwissenschaft, 8*(2), 109–128.

Meyer, K. (2015). What is Strategic Asset Seeking FDI? *The Multinational Business Review, 23*(1), 57–66.

Michalet, C. A. (1997). *Strategies of Multinationals and Competition for Foreign Direct Investment: The Opening of Central and Eastern Europe*. World Bank Publications.

Mills, G., & Herbst, J. (2012). *Africa's Third Liberation*. Penguin Books.

Mitchell, N. J., & McCormick, J. M. (1988). Economic and Political Explanations of Human Rights Violations. *World Politics, 40*(4), 476–498.

Mittelman, J. H. (2000). *The Globalization Syndrome*. Princeton University Press.

Mkandawire, T. (2001). Thinking about Developmental States in Africa. *Cambridge Journal of Economics, 25*(3), 289–313.

Mlambo, C. (2022). Politics and the Natural Resource Curse: Evidence from Selected African States. *Cogent Social Science, 8*, 1–17.

Mody, A., & Murshid, A. P. (2005). Growing Up with Capital Flows. *Journal of International Economics, 65*(1), 249–266.

Moore, B. (1966). *Social Origins of Dictatorship and Democracy: Lord and Peasant in the Making of the Modern World*. Beacon Press.

Morlino, L. (2008). Hybrid Regimes or Regimes in Transition? *FRIDE Working Paper No. 70* (pp. 1–16).

Narayan, P. K., Narayan, S., & Smyth, R. (2011). Does Democracy Facilitate Economic Growth or Does Economic Growth Facilitate. *Economic Modelling, 28*, 900–910.

Ncube, M. (2012). *Elections and Political Fragility in Africa*. African Development Bank.

Ndi, A. (2011). Why Liberal Capitalism Has Failed to Stimulate a Democratic Culture in Africa: Rethinking Amartya Sen's Theory about Development as Freedom. *Journal of Developing Societies, 27*(2), 177–200.

Ndikumana, L., & Abderrahim, K. (2010). Revenue Mobilization in African Countries: Does Natural Resource Endowment Matter? *African Development Review, 22*(3), 351–365.

North, D. C. (1990). *Institutions, Institutional Change, and Economic Performance*. Cambridge University Press.

North, D. C. (1991). Institutions. *Journal of Economic Perspectives, 5*(1), 97–112.

North, D. C., & Thomas, R. (1973). *The Rise of the Western World*. Cambridge University Press.

North, D. C., & Weingast, B. R. (1989). Constitutions and Commitment: The Evolution of Institutions Governing Public Choice in Seventeenth-Century England. *Journal of Economic History, 49*(4), 803–832.

O'Donnell, G. A. (1978). Reflections on the Patterns of Change in the Bureaucratic Authoritarian State. *Latin American Research Review, 13*(1), 3–38.

O'Donnell, G. A. (1988). Bureaucratic Authoritarianism. Argentina, 1966–73. In *Comparative Perspective*. University of California Press.

Olson, M. (1993). Dictatorship, Democracy and Development. *American Political Science Review, 87*(3), 567–576.

Omeje, K. (2021). *The Failure and Feasibility of Capitalism in Africa*. Palgrave Macmillan.

Onyeiwu, S., & Shrestha, H. (2004). Determinants of Foreign Direct Investment in Africa. *Journal of Developing Societies, 20*(1–2), 89–106.

Page, T. M. (2018). *A New Taxonomy for Corruption in Nigeria*, Carnegie Endowment for International Peace. Retrieved March, 2023, from https://carnegieendowment.org/files/CP_338_Page_Nigeria_FINAL.pdf

Palmtag, T., Paula, K., & Rommel, T. (2025). Beyond Economic Development? Foreign Direct Investment and Pre-Election Violence. *Journal of Peace Research, 62*(2), 246–261.

Panitch, L., & Gindin, S. (2012). *The Making of Global Capitalism: The Political Economy of American Empire*. Verso.

Panitch, L., Gindin, S., & Maher, S. (2019). *The Socialist Challenge Today: Syriza, Corbyn, Sanders*. Merlin Press.

Pereira, B., Carlos, L., Maravall, J. M., & Przeworski, A. (1993). *Economic Reforms in New Democracies: A Social Democratic Approach*. Cambridge University Press.

Persson, T., & Tabellini, G. (2003). *The Economic Effects of Constitutions*. MIT Press.

Persson, T., & Tabellini, G. (2009). The Nexus of Political and Economic Change. *American Economic Journal: Macroeconomics, 1*(2), 88–126.

Peterson, T. M. (2017). Export Diversity and Human Rights. *Journal of Conflict Resolution, 61*(8), 1740–1767.

Pitcher, A. (2012). *Party Politics and Economic Reform in Africa's Democracies*. Cambridge University Press.

Posner, D. N., & Young, D. J. (2007). The Institutionalization of Political Power in Africa. *Journal of Democracy, 18*(3), 126–140.

Posner, D. N., & Young, D. J. (2018). Term Limits: Leadership, Political Competition and the Transfer of Power. In N. Cheeseman (Ed.), *Institutions and Democracy in Africa: How the Rules of the Game Shape Political Developments: 260–278*. Cambridge University Press.

Przeworski, A. (1988). Democracy as a Contingent Outcome of Conflicts. In I. Elster & R. Slagstad (Eds.), *Constitutionalism and Democracy*. Cambridge University Press.

Przeworski, A., & Limongi, F. (1997). Modernization: Theories and Facts. *World Politics, 49*(2), 155–183.

Regan, P. M., & Bell, S. R. (2010). Changing Lanes or Stuck in the Middle: Why Are Anocracies More Prone to Civil Wars? *Political Research Quarterly, 63*(4), 747–759.

Resnick, A. L. (2001). Investors, Turbulence, and Transition: Democratic Transition and Foreign Direct Investment in Nineteen Developing Countries. *International Interactions, 27*, 381–398.

Rodrik, D. (1997). *Has Globalization Gone Too Far?* Institute for International Economics.

Rodrik, D. (1998). Why Do More Open Economics Have Bigger Governments? *Journal of Political Economy, 106*(5), 997–1032.

Rodrik, D. (2012). *The Globalization Paradox: Why Global Markets, States, and Democracy Can't Coexist*. Oxford University Press.

Ronceray, M., & Byiers, B. (2019). Elections in Africa – Playing the Game or Bending the Rules? *Discussion Paper No. 261*. European Centre for Development Policy Management (ECDPM).

Ross, L. M. (2012). *The Oil Curse: How Petroleum Wealth Shapes the Development of Nations*. Princeton University Press.

Sala-i-Martin, X., & Subramanian, A. (2008). Addressing the Natural Resource Curse: An Illustration from Nigeria. In D. P. Collier, C. C. Soludo, & C. Pattillo

(Eds.), *Economic Policy Options for a Prosperous Nigeria* (pp. 61–92). Palgrave Macmillan.

Schatz, S. P. (1984). Pirate Capitalism and the Inert Economy of Nigeria. *The Journal of Modern African Studies, 22*(1), 45–57.

Schedler, A. (2002). Elections Without Democracy: The Menu of Manipulation. *Journal of Democracy, 13*(2), 36–50.

Schwab, K. (2020, October 12). We must move on from Neoliberalism in the post-COVID era. *World Economic Forum web blog post.* Retrieved April, 2023, from https://www.weforum.org/agenda/2020/10/coronavirus-covid19-recovery-capitalismenvironment-economics-equality

Scott, T. S. (2012). *Globalization and the Cultures of Business in Africa.* Indiana University Press.

Sen, A. (1999). *Development as Freedom.* Oxford University Press.

Sigman, R., & Lindberg, S. I. (2020). Neopatrimonialism and Democracy. In G. Lynch & P. Von Doepp (Eds.), *Routledge Handbook of Democratization in Africa* (pp. 17–37). Routledge.

Smith, A. (2008). The Perils of Unearned Income. *Journal of Politics, 70*(3), 780–793.

Southall, R. (2001). Conclusion: Emergent Perspectives on Opposition in South Africa. *Democratization, 8*, 275–284.

Southall, R. (2003a). Democracy in Southern Africa: Moving Beyond a Difficult Legacy. *Review of African Political Economy, 96*, 255–272.

Southall, R. (2003b). Democracy in Africa: Fragile and Necessary. *Journal of Contemporary African Studies, 21*, 121–130.

Sturm, J.-E., & de Haan, J. (2001). How Robust Is the Relationship between Economic Freedom and Economic Growth? *Applied Economics, 33*(7), 839–844.

Suliman, A. H., & Mollick, A. V. (2009). Human Capital Development, War and Foreign Direct Investment in Sub-Saharan Africa. *Oxford Development Studies, 37*(1), 47–61.

Szeftel, M. (1999). Political Crisis and Democratic Renewal in Africa. In J. Daniel, R. Southall, & M. Szeftel (Eds.), *Voting for Democracy: Watershed Elections in Contemporary Anglophone Africa* (pp. 1–18). Aldershot.

Tavares, J., & Wacziarg, R. (2001). How Democracy Affects Growth. *European Economic Review, 45*(8), 1341–1378.

Touchton, M. (2015). Campaigning for Capital: Fair Elections and Foreign Investment in Comparative Perspective. *International Interactions, 42*(2), 271–294.

Trace Compendium. (2019). Sable Mining Africa Limited. *Trace International.* Retrieved March, 2023, from https://www.traceinternational.org/TraceCompendium/Detail/739?class=casename_searchresult&type=1

Vaaler, P. M. (2008). How Do MNCs Vote in Developing Country Elections? *The Academy of Management Journal, 51*(1), 21–43.

Van Ham, C., & Lindberg, S. I. (2015). From Sticks to Carrots: Electoral Manipulation in Africa, 1986–2012. *Government and Opposition, 50*(3), 521–548.

Wantchekon, L. (2003). Clientelism and Voting Behaviour: Evidence from a Field Experiment in Benin. *World Politics, 55*(3), 399–422.

War on Want. (2015). Extracting Minerals, Extracting Wealth: How Zambia is Losing $3 Billion a Year from Corporate Tax Dodging. Retrieved May, 2023, from https://waronwant.org/resources/extracting-minerals-extracting-wealth-how-zambia-losing-3-billion-year-corporate-tax

Wei, S. J. (2000). How Taxing is Corruption on International Investors? *Review of Economics and Statistics, 82*(1), 1–11.

Wiens, D. (2014). Natural Resources and Institutional Development. *Journal of Theoretical Politics, 26*(2), 197–221.

Wig, T., & Tollefsen, A. F. (2016). Local Institutional Quality and Conflict Violence in Africa. *Political Geography, 53*, 30–42.

Williams, M. (2021). The Crisis of Democracy: Neoliberal Capitalism, Authoritarianism and Reclaiming Democracy. In M. Williams & V. Satgar (Eds.), *Destroying Democracy: Neoliberal Capitalism and the Rise of Authoritarian Politics.* Wits University Press.

World Bank. (1999). *Global Economic Prospects and the Developing Countries.* Oxford University Press.

Wrong, M. (2009). *It's Our Turn to Eat: The Story of a Kenyan Whistle-Blower.* Harper Perennial Publishers.

Youssouf, N.-N., Joseph, K. M., & Thierry, Y. U. (2022). Constitutional Instability and Foreign Direct Investment in Africa. *Economics of Transition and Institutional Change, 32*, 3–23.

Yu, M. (2010). Trade, Democracy, and the Gravity Equation. *Journal of Development Economics, 91*, 289–300.

Zalle, O. (2019). Natural Resources and Economic Growth in Africa: The Role of Institutional Quality and Human Capital. *Resources Policy, 62*, 616–624.

CHAPTER 5

The Relationship Between Corruption and FDI in Sub-Saharan Africa

Corruption typically involves the illegal transfer of assets from public to private ownership, ranging from simple administrative bribery to complex kleptocratic capture of the state (Warf, 2016, 2017). The global cost of corruption is more than USD 3.6 trillion per year (equivalent to 5% of global GDP) (World Economic Forum, 2018), including USD 1 trillion in bribes paid by businesses and individuals (World Bank, 2018; Schlenther, 2016). In the case of SSA, the United Nations (2011) states that "Corruption is undoubtedly the most pressing governance and development challenge that Africa is confronted with today. Corruption has debilitating and corrosive effects on progress, stability, and development of the continent. It impedes economic growth by discouraging foreign investments, creates distortion in resource allocation and competitive markets, increases the cost of doing business, and reduces the net-value of public spending. It also reduces the quality of services and public infrastructure and the volume of tax revenues and encourages the misappropriation and misallocation of scarce resources. In the political realm, it undermines the rule of law, respect for human rights, accountability and transparency and weakens government institutions. This in turn erodes public legitimacy in government and compromises good governance. The social costs of corruption are also deleterious as it deepens income inequality, poverty and adversely affects good moral values in the society. In general, corruption is

S. Gossel, *The Promise and Peril of FDI in Sub-Saharan Africa*, Palgrave Studies in African and Development Economics, https://doi.org/10.1007/978-3-032-01320-0_5

a challenge to sustainable economic development, peace, and good governance."

In post-independent SSA, corruption has also hampered government's ability to reverse the region's significant poverty levels and instead has widened inequality and social instability as political leaders, public officials, and private sector companies and individuals have encouraged programs for illegal self-enrichment (Mbaku, 2010, p. 3). The effects of corruption in SSA have thus "exacerbated the conflict between economically dominant or rich groups (primarily the ethno-regional groups that captured the apparatus of government at independence) and the historically impoverished and marginalised communities" (ibid.). Corruption in SSA however has its roots in the legacies of colonialism. By its nature, colonialism imposed domestically unaccountable administration that protected the interests of foreign powers while institutionalising corruption, entrenching 'might is right', and fragmenting ethnic identities and societies (Zalanga, 2018).

Countries with high levels of ethnic fractionalisation tend to suffer from high levels of corruption because the political elite and public service often direct benefits to the members of their ethnic group while wilfully depriving public goods to the other members of society (Mauro, 1995; Hwang et al., 2011). In addition, colonialism and corruption have developmental legacies because colonial structures and conditions continue to shape post-independent SSA (Tatah, 2017, p. 186). This legacy however varies between SSA countries that were not colonised by Britain and those that were because countries that fell under British colonial rule tend to have better governance and control of corruption, and more efficient bureaucracies (La Porta et al., 1999; Treisman, 2000). In addition, colonies that had higher European settlement have higher levels of corruption, mainly as a result of the associated elitism (Angeles & Neanidis, 2015).

Corruption did not diminish after colonialism because political opposition was too oppressed, suppressed, or co-opted to threaten the ruling elite, while politicisation of the state bureaucracy entrenched clientelism. In addition, state power, resources, and opportunity were centralised under political leaders and 'Big Men', producing ineffective and weak legal and bureaucratic systems and inefficient allocation of resources that benefited the ruling elite rather than the public (Omeje, 2021, p. 37). Consequently, the 1960s were characterised by the replacement of the colonial elite with a post-independence elite who similarly could use wealth and power for their financial benefit, to entrench their hold on power, and ensure that the poor remained dependent (Zalanga, 2018).

In the 1970s and 1980s however, as many SSA countries fell into economic crises, the 'Washington Consensus' structural adjustment programs (SAPs) induced reforms and 'downsizing' curtailed the patronage available to the ruling elites and thus centralised corruption devolved into decentralised bribery even as citizens received less public goods and service as a result of the SAP-mandated public expenditure cuts (Shah, 2006). The neoliberal requirement that SSA countries privatise many public services and assets under the ideology of New Public Management (NPM) led to the rapid liberalisation of SSA's economies, "setting the stage for a new scramble for Africa" (Carmody, 2016, p. 21). This liberalisation then birthed a new round of patron-client corruption because international companies were readily willing to pay bribes and engage in illegal activities to secure lucrative government contracts (Jeffries, 1993).

In 2004, the African Union estimated that corruption during the 1990s cost SSA over USD 148 billion per year, equivalent to 50% of SSA's tax revenue, 25% of the region's GDP, or three times the amount of foreign aid received (GPAD, 2011). Despite the increased focus on "good governance" in the years after the SAPs (Mbaku, 2010, p. 32), corruption remains a significant developmental hindrance in SSA and has been identified as among the primary reasons why the region is unlikely to meet the Millennium Development Goals (UN-MDG, 2013; Economic Commission for Africa, 2009). Empirical studies have found that corruption in SSA hinders socio-economic development and good governance (Asongu, 2013; Bamidele, 2013; Omoteso & Mobolaji, 2013; Forson et al., 2017), worsens poverty (Justesen & Bjornskov, 2014), aggravates political instability (Farzanegan & Witthuhn, 2017), worsens ethnic violence (Bezemer & Jong-A-Pin, 2013), and disincentivises business and investment (Efobi, 2015).

As can be seen from Fig. 5.1, the Corruption Perception Index (CPI), averaged over the period of 2012–2020, shows that SSA remains the most corrupt region in the world. Hence, approximately 1.2 billion people living in SSA are denied their rightful access to social development benefits such as education, healthcare, and fixed investment because the capital is instead diverted for personal use by corrupt governments (Warf, 2017).

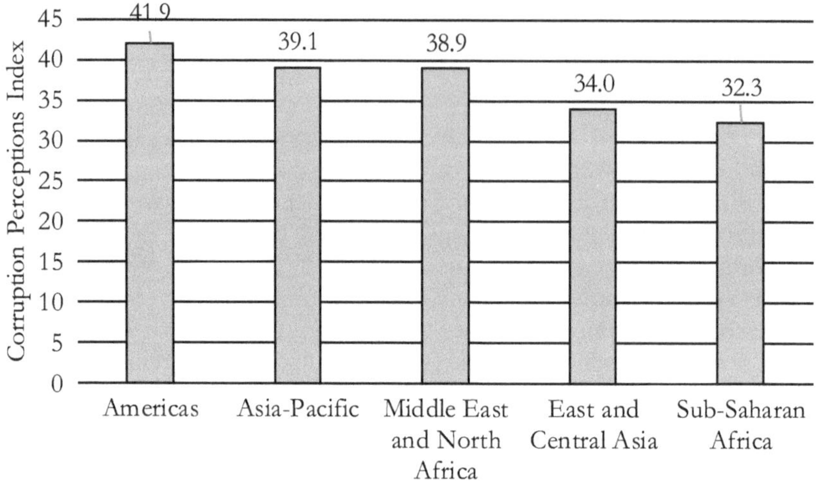

Fig. 5.1 Emerging country corruption perceptions indices. (Data source: Transparency International)

More specifically, the average CPI presented in Map 5.1 shows that all the SSA countries fall below the mid-point of 50 (except for Botswana)[1] and no country in SSA falls in the *Least Corrupt* category (CPI score of above 80). Only Botswana with an average CPI score of 62 falls in the *Slightly Corrupt* category whereas six countries (14% of SSA) (Ghana, Lesotho, Namibia, Rwanda, Senegal, and South Africa) fall in the *Moderately Corrupt* category; 30 countries (70% of SSA) are classified as *Very Corrupt*; and six countries (14% of SSA) (Equatorial Guinea, Guinea-Bissau, Sudan, Somalia, South Sudan, and Burundi) are deemed to be *Extremely Corrupt*.

Although the effects of corruption are often more readily apparent than the causes of corruption, Jain (2001) notes that corruption requires three preconditions: bureaucratic discretionary power, the ability to extract economic rents as a result of holding bureaucratic power,[2] and a low probability of being caught and penalised. It has however been argued that geography and cultural practises also shape the prevalence of corruption.

[1] The categories in Map 5.1 are derived from Warf (2017).

[2] The World Bank defines a resource rent as the difference between the production cost and sale price of a commodity.

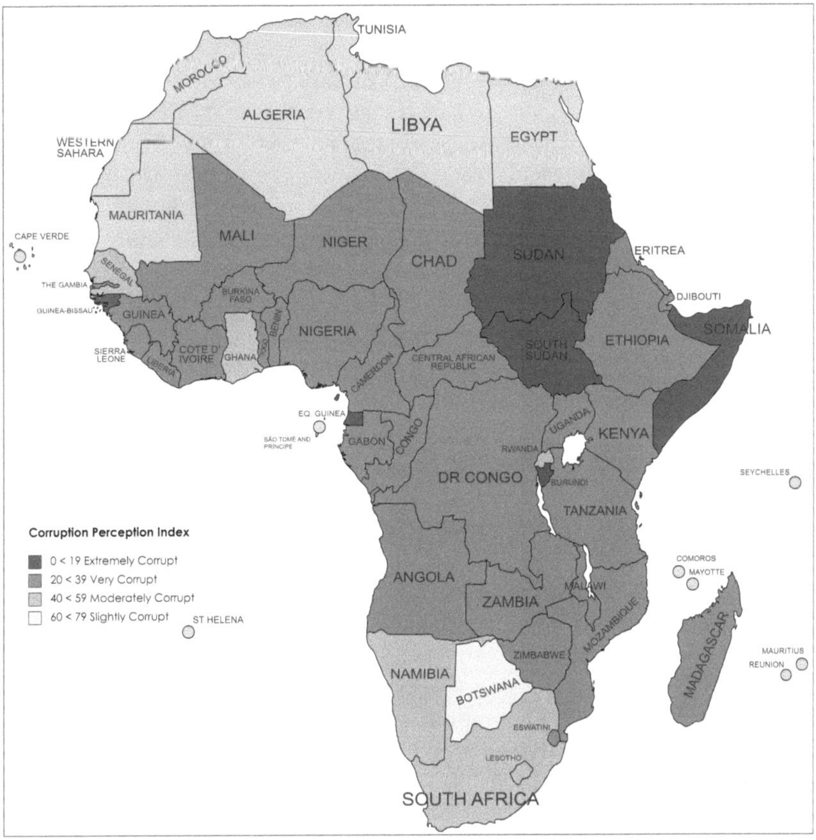

Map 5.1 Average corruption perceptions index (2012–2020). (Source: Author's compilation from Transparency International data, categorised from Warf (2017))

In the case of geography, corruption is commonly more prevalent in dispersed locations because the enforcement of the rule of law and the monitoring of bureaucratic activities is difficult (Goel & Nelson, 2010). Beyond physical geography, corruption is also shaped by geographic proximity whereby countries learn how to be corrupt from their close neighbours, suffer from negative spill-over effects arising from their neighbour's corrupt activities, or alternatively, differentiate themselves from their corrupt neighbours by focussing on controlling corruption (Goel & Nelson, 2007; Becker et al., 2009; Márquez et al., 2011; Sui et al., 2018; Borsky &

Kalkschmied, 2019; Khodapanah et al., 2020; Goel & Saunoris, 2014, 2022).

In addition to geography, culture embodies historical influences and thus "shapes the cultural norms that dictate corrupt acts" (Goel & Nelson, 2010). These cultural practises, behaviours, and values however make defining corruption difficult because a transaction deemed to be corrupt in one culture may be considered a normal part of doing business in another (Bardhan, 1997, p. 1330). For example, the culturally accepted practise of giving gifts (monetary or otherwise) as part of interpersonal exchanges is an accepted custom in many Asian, African, and Middle East countries, but is deemed to be bribery and corruption outside of those cultures (Warf, 2016). In addition, it has been noted that cultures that are more masculine tend to have higher corruption levels than societies where women hold a large proportion of leadership positions (Goetz, 2000; Swamy et al., 2001; Guvenli & Sanyal, 2012; Tuliao & Chen, 2017). Among the reasons cited are because women "may have higher standards of ethical behaviour and be more concerned with the common good" (Dollar et al., 2001, p. 427). Over time this masculinity factor becomes less significant as countries democratise, because democratic institutions foster equity and stimulate social, economic, and political leadership opportunities for women while also entrenching the rule of law (Sung, 2003).

Despite the colonial, geographic, and cultural complexities, corruption is nevertheless a sign of dysfunction in the management of the state (Rose-Ackerman & Palifka, 2016, p. 51). The remainder of this chapter therefore commences with a discussion on how SSA's post-colonial political economic development entrenched corruption before considering the relationship between democracy and corruption, and then democracy and political corruption. Thereafter, the chapter turns to the effects of capital flows, first by discussing illicit financial flows (IFFs), and finally the relationship between corruption and FDI.

5.1 Gatekeeper States and Dysfunctional Capitalism

The concept of a "Gatekeeper State" was first conceived by Fred Cooper (2018) who argued that most post-independent African countries were not in a position institutionally, fiscally, or economically to form functional states after independence. Consequently, the only developmental opportunity available was "to sit astride the interface between a territory and the rest of the world, collecting and distributing resources that derived from that point itself: customs revenue and foreign aid; permits to do business in the territory; entry and exit visas; and permission to move currency in and out" (ibid., p. 235). The economic repercussions however were unaccountable centralised government, policy contestation among the elite over access to the 'gate', and the corruption and crony capitalism associated with the rentier state (Auty, 2001; Gillies, 2020). Hence, Cooper argues that contention over the 'gate' is one of the key sources of socio-political and economic instability in SSA.[3]

According to Hillbom's (2012) examination of Botswana, there are six traits that characterise a gatekeeper state. First, the institutional structure derived from colonialism bequeathed insufficient financial resources, and thus the state must rely on natural resource for comparative advantage. Second, this reliance renders the state overly dependent on a small range of exploitable resources. Third, as a result, the state is unable to diversify the economy or enact a comprehensive development strategy. Fourth, there is the emergence of a dual society where the formal economy comprises resource exports and urban centres, but the rest of society is stuck in the informal economy, excluded from the state. Fifth, the state lacks the financial and political means for social and economic development and transformation. Finally, the dominance of the state in the economy fosters elite capture of the state. Hence, in a gatekeeper state, corruption is a symptom of greater systemic problems (Beresford, 2015).

The ability of a state to become a gatekeeper however depends on whether the natural resource endowment is easily lootable (for example oil, copper deposits, and diamonds). Such resources can easily be subject to predation as they are geographically widely dispersed and have low barriers to entry whereas non-lootable resources tend to be geographically concentrated, have high barriers to entry, and are characterised by high capital intensity (Dunning, 2008, p. 41). Resource rents accrue from natural resource returns in excess of labour, transport, and financial market

[3] Critics contend however that the concept of the Gatekeeper State is by its nature overly simplistic and does not adequately consider Gatekeeper politics, such as in South Africa under former President Zuma (Beresford, 2015) or in Zimbabwe under former President Mugabe (Gallagher, 2018). Andreasson (2018) notes that Gatekeeping is prevalent in many parts of the world, not just in Africa, and Brown (2018) argues that Gatekeeping is just one side-effect of financial globalisation.

returns on capital, and are thus state-owned windfalls (Sachs, 2007). Hence, lootable resources provide the fiscal foundation of a gatekeeper state without the complexity of direct taxation. Heightened private sector development however does not necessarily denote a decrease in natural resource rents because a formalised natural resource sector is easily taxable and relatively inelastic due to the significant sunk costs and immovable capital investment (Dunning, 2008, p. 40). Lootable resources therefore benefit the state directly whereas resource access granted to the private sector benefits the state indirectly.

SSA's gatekeeper states existed mainly from the 1940s to the mid-1970s, funded by international demand for natural resources but characterised by colonial bureaucratic structures and administrations (Hillbom, 2012). However, the decline in commodity demand in the late 1970s and 1980s in combination with SSA's debt crises eroded the architecture of the gatekeeper states. From the 1980s, with the advent of neoliberal reforms, the gatekeeper structure began to collapse as SAP reforms demanded liberalisation and privatisation, and economic stagnation starved the ruling elites of their ability to maintain their patronage networks (Cooper, 2002). The power to control the 'gate' further declined after the new millennium as a result of the reform of the OAU into the AU and the advent of NEPAD and other liberalisation policies, which have facilitated taxation and government expenditure reforms to improve transparency, efficiency, and service delivery (Dorman, 2018). These reforms have been coupled with improved democratisation and the rise of a technologically proficient emerging middle class, which has eroded centralised political structures and fostered greater formalised political opposition and accountability. In addition, the rising wealth of SSA and access to new credit facilities in emerging countries, such as China, have driven significant infrastructure development in the region, and the associated privatisation and technological advancements have removed the control of the gate (Hönke, 2018) while financial globalisation and financial sector development have shifted financial control of SSA's assets away from the international financial centres to the domestic banking system (Cobbett, 2018).

Despite the weakening of gatekeeping however, two forms of dysfunctional capitalism are still prevalent in many SSA countries: crony capitalism (or spoils consumption) and predatory capitalism (Beresford, 2015). Crony capitalism occurs when individuals and companies (multinational and domestic) have corrupt relationships with government officials and politicians to secure jobs, contracts, or unfair advantages over competitors

(Omeje, 2021, p. 128). Examples include the millions of USD paid to Nigerian officials in the 1990s by companies such as Shell Oil, Willbros, Kellogg Brown & Root (a subsidiary of Halliburton), and Eni for preferential oil and gas exploration, extraction, and build contracts in the lucrative Niger Delta; and to shield the companies from prosecution for environmental degradation and human rights abuses (Burgis, 2016, pp. 190–191). The financial and political backing from these companies also facilitated support for government military oppression, show trials, incarceration, and murder of opponents of the resource extraction (Amnesty International, 2017).

Predatory capitalism however can be defined as “a post-Darwinian trajectory of patron-clientelism and economic plunder characterised by extreme personalization of the state and looting of its resources by the governing oligarchy, with the result that there is a loss of any sense of public space or public policy” (Omeje, 2021, p. 141). Predatory capitalism can be state led, such as during the Presidencies of Jose Eduardo dos Santos in Angola and Teodoro Obiang Nguema Mbasogo in Equatorial Guinea, or private agent led, such as the activities of Dan Gertler in the Democratic Republic of Congo (DRC).

Jose dos Santos was president of Angola for over three decades from 1979 to 2017. During this time, his administration was characterised by endemic corruption, nepotism, and kleptocracy fuelled by the country’s natural resource wealth. After 2002, dos Santos used the state oil company (Sonangol) and its complex web of subsidiaries as the conduit to channel USD 24 billion of Angola’s wealth, funnelled through 400 banks and companies in 41 countries and tax havens (Freedberg et al., 2020; Drogin, 2022) to his family, dynastic crony capitalists, the political elite; and to buy support for the MPLA (Almeida, 2020; Harvey, 2022). After the oil price crashed in 2014, the oil rents dried up. With political rivals sensing weakness, dos Santos began putting in place contingency measures to protect his ill-gotten gains for when he was no longer in power. These included positioning his son (Jose Filomeno) as head of Angola’s USD 5 billion sovereign wealth fund, replacing the board of Sonangol with his daughter (Issabel) as CEO, and attempting to ensure that they received immunity from future presidential interference (Harvey, 2022). dos Santos stepped down in 2017 and despite these measures, Isabel’s Angolan assets were frozen, and she was fired from Sonangol on charges of USD 1 billion in corruption in 2019 (Omeje, 2021, p. 131). In 2020, Portugal ordered that all her bank accounts be frozen subject to a criminal investigation, and Jose was charged, convicted, and jailed for five years for illegally transferring USD 500 million from Angola's sovereign wealth fund into a Swiss bank account (ibid.). Unfortunately, the misappropriation of Angola's wealth has weakened the country's ability to overcome endemic poverty, inequality, and weak democratic and institutional quality, locking the country into a path of resource-dependent under-development (Bye et al., 2021).

A second example of state-led predatory capitalism is the Presidency of Teodoro Obiang Nguema Mbasogo in Equatorial Guinea. Over his long oligarchic reign commencing in 1979, President Nguema has used the country's oil and timber wealth "to establish companies or serve on the boards of multinationals that extract oil, market timber, or build major infrastructure projects" (ISS Africa, 2017) to benefit his family (his son Teodoro, nicknamed Teodorin, is the Vice President), ethnic inner circle, and foreign intermediaries. Despite becoming SSA's third largest oil producer and potentially among the wealthiest countries in the world on a per capita GDP basis, Equatorial Guinea suffers from among the world's worst levels of corruption, repression, poverty, and inequality (ibid.). In 2006, Forbes magazine estimated that the president and his associates had deposited USD 700 million in the US Riggs Bank (Riggs paid a USD 16 million fine in 2015) with the president, his son, and his nephew as the signatories for the accounts (Omeje, 2021, p. 135). Since 2007, Western authorities have been clamping down on the stolen wealth. In 2011, French authorities confiscated Teodorin's EUR 107 million mansion in Paris along with luxury cars, furniture, jewellery, art works, and collectables; in 2014, the US Department of Justice (DoJ) confiscated 28 sports cars, a Gulfstream jet, and a USD 30 million property in Malibu; in 2017, France seized EUR 100 million and Teodorin was convicted in abstention for embezzlement, handed a three-year suspended jail sentence, and fined EUR 30 million; in 2019, Swiss authorities seized and auctioned 25 luxury cars (ibid.); and in 2020, French authorities confiscated his EUR 107 million 101-room Parisian mansion and a 76 meter luxury yacht (Transparency International France, 2021).

Predatory capitalism however is not only limited to political leaders but can also include private actors. An example is Dan Gertler's activities in the DRC (and subsequently, Zimbabwe). Gertler comes from an esteemed family of Israeli diamond cutters and traders, but he used his long-running relationship with President Joseph Kabila to gain preferential export rights for the DRCs diamonds and minerals. Shortly, after starting his company, Dan Gertler International (DGI) in 1996, Gertler was offered the monopoly to mine all the diamonds in the DRC in exchange for facilitating a USD 20 million loan to assist then-President Laurent Kabila to fund the conflict against Rwandan and Ugandan invaders (Burgis, 2016, p. 48). After Laurent was assassinated in 2001, Gertler's relationship with Joseph paid off when his new company Emaxon Finance International (a subsidiary of DGI) was granted the four-year right to export 88% of the DRC's rough diamonds and a 5% discount on the purchase of diamonds in exchange for a USD 15 million loan for the DRC to modernise its mining equipment (Newsweek, 2003). The US Treasury claims that the sale of under-priced mining assets to Gertler-linked offshore companies costs the DRC USD 1.4 billion from 2010–2012 (Fabricius, 2022).

Over the next decade, Gertler amassed over USD 1 billion from mining interests in the DRC and Zimbabwe through a complex web of secret agreements and interlinked transactions conducted through tax havens (Burgis, 2016, p. 50) and with the financial backing of Glencore, the scandal-ridden Swiss mining multinational (Doherty & Pegg, 2017).[4] However, Gertler's dealings then began to garner attention from international authorities. In 2012, the IMF stopped a three-year USD 500 million loan to the DRC on suspicions that the companies involved in the transaction were under-pricing the underlying mining assets (Reuters, 2012). Fearing repercussions, in February 2013, Glencore bought out Gertler's shares in their shared assets in the DRC for USD 534 million (Doherty & Pegg, 2017). In 2016, the US DoJ alleged that Gertler was the "DRC partner" who had paid USD 100 million in bribes on behalf of the New York hedge fund Och-Ziff for preferential mining opportunities and prices (ibid.). In July 2017, Canadian authorities cancelled Emaxon's company registration; and in December 2017 and June 2018, the US Treasury sanctioned Gertler and blocked all his US assets on charges of corruption and human rights abuses under the Magnitsky Act (Fabricius, 2022).

President Kabila stepped down in December 2018 and Félix Antoine Tshisekedi Tshilombo succeeded him as president. In 2023, President Tshisekedi and Gertler negotiated a secret agreement to return Gertler's USD 2 billion in mining rights back to the DRC in exchange for the president lobbying the US government to drop the sanctions against Gertler (President Trump eased the sanctions during his last week in office but President Biden subsequently reinstated them) (Lipton, 2021). In December 2022, Glencore was ordered to pay USD 180 million to the

[4] See Anderson (2023) for a discussion of Glencore's activities in the DRC.

DRC for corruption during the period of 2007 to 2018 (Hodge, 2022) and in March 2023, the company was ordered to pay USD 700 million in fines (of which USD 125 million was ear-marked for the DRC) by a US Judge for violating the Foreign Corrupt Practices Act in seven countries (van Niekerk, 2023). It has however been claimed that Gertler still receives USD 200,000 per day in royalties from copper-cobalt interests in the DRC (Fabricius, 2022).

Taken to the extreme, predatory capitalism can morph into state capture, which is "a brand of oligarchy in which powerful families, dynasties and businesses collude with top state officials to hijack the policy machinery of the state to advance mutual interests" (Omeje, 2021, p. 133). South Africa's experience of state capture centres around the corrupt relationship between President Jacob Zuma and the wealthy Indian Gupta family during the years from 2009 to 2018 (Madonsela, 2019). As detailed in the six-volume Zondo Commission Report,[5] the Gupta family used their close financial relationship with President Zuma to secure preferential government contracts and access to the R500 billion annual procurement budget of the state-owned enterprises (SOEs); particularly, Eskom (power generation and transmission), Transnet (freight and logistics), Prasa (railways), Denel (defence), South African Airways (airline), and the South African Broadcasting Company (media) (Arum, 2019).

The *modus operandi* of state capture in South Africa entailed entrenching a Gupta-Zuma 'shadow state' in three ways (Alence & Pitcher, 2019; Momoniat, 2023). First, by appointing pliant ministers who would then oversee the replacement of competent board members in the SOEs and officials in financial oversight, procurement, and tenders with Gupta-Zuma associates (euphemistically known as 'cadre deployment') under the guise of socio-economic transformation. Second, by weakening the law enforcement and oversight institutions, such as the National Prosecuting Authority (NPA) and South African Revenue Services (SARS). Third, using Gupta controlled media and an international PR company (Bell Pottinger)[6] to try sway public opinion, divert attention, or create alternative narratives to the reports of state capture from established media houses.

A crucial feature of state capture is that these ministers, officials, and associates could then reap the benefits of their positions while also

[5] Available at https://www.statecapture.org.za/site/information/reports [accessed May 2024]

[6] Bell Pottinger was forced to close in September 2016 when the extent of its race baiting and media manipulation in South Africa were exposed (Segal, 2018).

facilitating corrupt transactions between the SOEs and colluding private sector multinationals in a range of sectors, including banks (Standard Bank, First National Bank, Standard Chartered, Bank of Baroda), consultancies (McKinsey, Bain & Company), accounting and advisory (KPMG, PwC), and IT services (SAP) along with a range of local private sector enablers (Open Secrets, 2022). State capture during the Zuma years significantly eroded the country's economic performance with economic growth trending to zero, drastically rising debt, and failure of the country's SOEs (Alence & Pitcher, 2019). As the scale of the graft was exposed by the Public Protector's reports, and the release of gigabytes of documents and emails from the Gupta server by two anonymous whistleblowers, Zuma came under increasing pressure to resign by the public, judiciary, media, and politicians including from some in the ruling African National Congress (ANC). Zuma was finally forced to resign after he lost the ANC's elective conference to Cyril Ramaphosa in December 2017 and the Gupta family fled to the United Arab Emirates (UAE) in 2018. Although President Ramaphosa labelled Zuma's Presidency "nine wasted years", South Africa's economy has not recovered and despite Ramaphosa's promises, no state capturers have been convicted of their crimes (Grootes, 2023).

These examples show that in weak states, dysfunctional capitalism is an outcome of dysfunctional governance, but the resultant negative feedback loops affect all facets of society. At the level of governance, dysfunctional capitalism undermines policy formulation, implementation, and resource allocation while at a political level, development and performance of public institutions are negated. This culture of "eating" and "squanderation" then filters down, consuming the organisations of service delivery, and undermining human and capital resources (Omeje, 2021, p. 145). Eventually the effects of dysfunctional capitalism spiral until they threaten the "institutionality and formal sovereignty of the state, further corroding the capacity of the state to effectively re-engineer capitalism and regulate the economy for the good of all" (ibid., p. 126). Hence, by its nature a neopatrimonial state is the architype of an anti-developmental state (Sandbrook, 2000, p. 97).

5.2 Corruption and Democratisation

It has been widely argued that democratic countries should experience lower levels of corruption than authoritarian countries because democratic societies have institutions to enforce accountability and the rule of law

(Moreno, 2002), independent media that make it more difficult to hide malfeasance (Brunetti & Weder, 2003; Chowdhury, 2004), competitive political systems that can 'punish' the incumbent government for corruption (Kolstad & Wiig, 2016), and competitive economic and financial markets (Bliss & Di Tella, 1997; Ades & Di Tella, 1999) that lessen the prospect of corrupt patron-client relationships (Emerson, 2006). In contrast more authoritarian regimes tend to divert the capital available for the populace for education, healthcare, and infrastructure to instead benefit the political and military elite, related companies and associates, and to extend their time in power (Besley & Persson, 2009; Acemoglu et al., 2010; Efobi, 2015; Dizaji et al., 2016).

The empirical evidence however is inconclusive, with some studies finding no significant association between democracy and corruption (Fisman & Gatti, 2002, pp. 336–338; Ades & Di Tella, 1999; Paldam, 2002; Gillanders, 2016) while others report that as hypothesised, corruption declines as democracy increases (Treisman, 2000; Chowdhury, 2004; Goel & Nelson, 2005; Serra, 2006; Billger & Goel, 2009). A possible reason for this disparity is because the relationship between corruption and democracy may be an inverted U-shape rather than linear whereby corruption rises initially as a country democratises, and then falls around a decade later (Rock, 2009) once democracy has consolidated (Mohtadi & Roe, 2003; Schneider & Schmitter, 2004, p. 84; Jetter et al., 2015).

It has additionally been argued that democratisation may heighten rather than lower the levels of corruption for three reasons. First, election campaigns require significant funding, and thus investors may only be willing to provide necessary capital in exchange for legislative or policy changes that favour their interests rather than the interests of the populace (Rose-Ackerman & Palifka, 2016, p. 351). Second, corruption could be used to buy votes or ensure party loyalty by offering a range of selective benefits such as "tax exemptions and subsidies, low-interest loans to selective layers of society, access to highly subsidized foreign currency for connected firms and individuals, public employment, land allocations, lucrative licenses for imports and exports, and discriminatory enforcements of the law" (Farzanegan & Witthuhn, 2017). Finally, the distribution of rents could be used to secure political power, security, and stability regardless of democratic developments (Acemoglu et al., 2004; Alesina et al., 2000; Robinson et al., 2006; Farzanegan & Witthuhn, 2017). Hence, it is possible that "the introduction of democracy has served to reinforce existing patron–client relationships, leading to the democratization of corruption rather than its reduction" (Kolstad & Wiig, 2016).

In addition to the opportunistic motives of the political elite, there may be rational reasons for voters to elect corrupt politicians. This may be because voters are not aware of the candidate's corrupt activities and preferences, or because voters may choose a candidate whom they know are corrupt but who have policy preferences closest to their own (Pani, 2011; Winters & Weitz-Shapiro, 2013). Over time however, as more corrupt leaders are elected, a corrupt parliament may prove even more ruinous than an autocratic regime (Ehrlich & Lui, 1999; Corchon, 2008). An example is Jacob Zuma, elected president of South Africa even though he was facing 783 charges of fraud and corruption, but he was deemed to be more consultative, inclusive, populist, and patrimonial compared to his predecessor, President Mbeki, who was alleged to be too neoliberal, autocratic, aloof, intellectual, and enriching only a narrow political elite (Giollabhuí, 2017). During the state capture years of Zuma's presidency, the ruling ANC protected him against six motions of no confidence and a motion to declare him unfit to hold office (PMG, 2017). Parliamentary protection was also commonly used as a demonstration of party loyalty, political allegiance, and a reaction against "counter-revolutionaries" (Herman, 2017). In addition, ANC MPs used their majority to obstruct official investigations, dismiss charges of corrupt activities and relationships, and shield themselves from oversight and accountability, even as the scale and costs of state capture became known (Doyle et al., 2022).

The claim that the democratic characteristics of transparency and accountability will lower the levels of corruption may also under-estimate the ease with which corrupt regimes can repurpose or weaken democratic institutions (Bac, 2001; Kolstad & Wiig, 2016) or even if there is transparency, when there is a high number of corrupt public officials, accountability may be unenforceable (Andvig & Moene, 1990; Rose-Ackerman & Palifka, 2016, p. 290). In addition, in many African states, the police are too ill-equipped and poorly trained, and lack the political support to tackle corruption and enforce the rule of law and instead, often suffer from their own pervasive corruption and politicisation (Medie, 2018, p. 140).

The negative relationship between governance and corruption is further compounded by the extent of natural resource endowment—"the paradox of plenty" (Karl, 1997, p. xv). As mentioned previously, in most resource export-dependent countries, resource rents supplant taxation revenues and are used to fund repression and ensure political control,

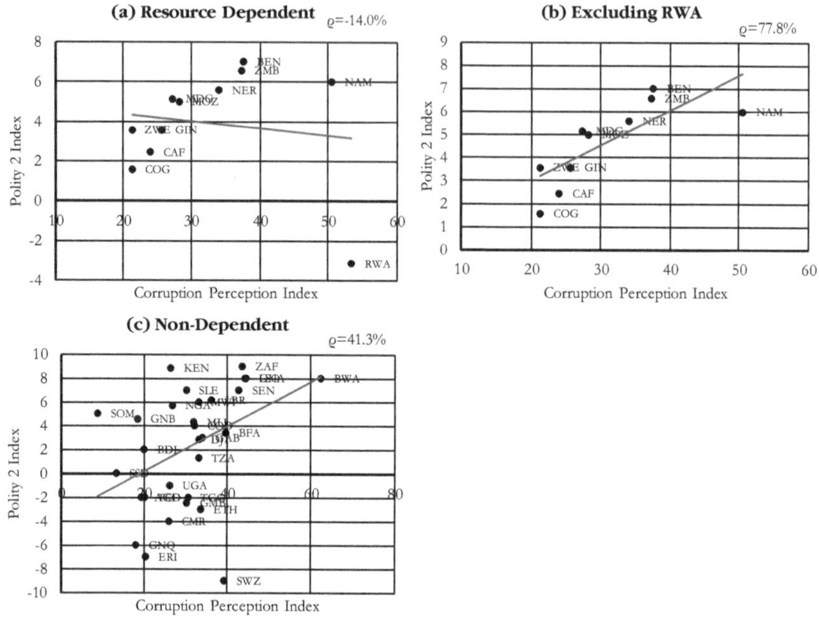

Fig. 5.2 Scatterplot of corruption and democracy in SSA. (Sources: Transparency International, Polity V)

power, and loyalty. Consequently, resource-dependent states suffer from high levels of political instability, civil conflict, and authoritarianism (Lindberg & Meerow, 2011, p. 186) because politics is dominated by struggles over access, control, and allocation of rents rather than to provide public goods and services (Auty, 2004; Ross, 1999; Gillies, 2020).

With regards to SSA, the scatterplots of democracy (Polity 2) and the Corruption Perceptions Index (CPI) in resource-dependent and non-dependent SSA countries (averaged over the period of 2012–2018)[7] presented in Fig. 5.2 show that once the outlier of Rwanda (RWA) is excluded, there is an inverse relationship between democracy and CPI in both sub-samples, suggesting that rising democracy is associated with falling corruption levels. However, it should be borne in mind that it is not possible

[7]The start date has been limited by the availability of CPI data and then end date by the availability of Polity V data.

to determine from these graphs whether many SSA states suffer from high levels of corruption because they have weak democratic institutions, or whether the democratic institutions are weakened by pervasive corruption. Nevertheless, studies report that countries in the early stages of democratisation usually do experience rising levels of corruption, mainly due to low GDP per capita, which makes the misuse of public funds by the new public officials an attractive option (Jetter et al., 2015).[8] Furthermore, assessments of the causal relationship between democracy and corruption suggest that the control of corruption leads to improved democracy rather than the reverse (Sekkat et al., 2024) while variations in the components of democracy may affect the type rather than the level of corruption (Stephenson, 2015). Hence, these studies suggest that SSA has high levels of corruption because the regions democracies are still nascent and thus the region's institutions are not deep enough to combat corruption, which in turn hinders democratisation.

5.3 Political Corruption

Inge Amundsen (2019, p. 181) defines political corruption as corruption that occurs at the highest levels of the political system and thus involves politicians, ministers, senior civil servants, and public officials whereas bureaucratic corruption occurs at the delivery level of the state. Political corruption thus "serves a function beyond greed and personal enrichment – it may keep the regime together and afloat. Political corruption not only gives the incentives for controlling the state, it is a means to maintain control of the state. The rulers will have no political will to eradicate political corruption as it gives them wealth and power, whereas bureaucratic corruption can be eradicated if the rulers so desire" (ibid., p. 1).

In the case of SSA, investors are first exposed to political corruption followed by bureaucratic corruption. However, companies may not only be subjected to corruption but can also be willing participants if a multinational firm and a host-country government official co-conspire in dishonest deals (Krifa-Schneider et al., 2022). Beyond political corruption, investors can also be exposed to bureaucratic corruption from lower-level government officials when the investment is operationalised (Straub, 2008, p. 247). Political and bureaucratic corruption thus turn public

[8] Jetter et al. report that this threshold is USD 2000.

wealth into a pyramid scheme with the rich and powerful at the top, who amass the greatest benefit for themselves; and the remainder then passing down to the lower levels, where corrupt officials sequentially take their share, until eventually, the scant remains reach the poor at the bottom (Cheeseman, 2015, p. 60).

An example of political corruption is the "tuna loans" scandal in Mozambique. In 2013 and 2014, three Mozambiquan public companies signed agreements with Credit Suisse and Privinvest (an Emirati Lebanese shipbuilding company) for USD 2 billion in loans for the establishment of state tuna fisheries (England, 2016). These "tuna bonds" were secured by secret government guarantees after Privinvest paid USD 136 million in bribes to Mozambiquan and Credit Suisse officials, and these bribes and the subsequent looting of the loaned funds were then purposefully concealed (Cotterill & Walker, 2023). In 2016, the secret agreements were exposed, and the IMF and other foreign donors halted financial support, which led to default of the loans and a set of international criminal investigations (Mucari et al., 2023). In 2021, Credit Suisse agreed to pay a fine of USD 475 million and wrote off USD 200 million of Mozambique's debts (ibid.). In December 2022, eleven Mozambiquan senior officials were found guilty of embezzlement and money laundering and were sentenced to 11 to 12 years of imprisonment (Frey, 2023). They include ex-President Guebuza's oldest son (Ndambi), the former head of the State Security Service (SISE) (Gregorio Leao), the former director of SISE Economic Intelligence (Antonio Carlos do Rosario), Guebuza's former political advisor (Renamo Matusse), and the former president's personal secretary (Ines Moiane) (Frey, 2023). In July 2023, the Mozambiquan ex-finance minister Manuel Chang (who signed the secret state guarantees) was extradited from South Africa to the US to stand trial on charges of corruption and money laundering (Mucari et al., 2023) while Mozambique's USD 3 billion case against Privinvest is still ongoing in the UK courts (Tobin, 2023).

One of the reasons that the political and private sector elites can readily engage in political corruption in SSA is because political parties, especially opposition parties, are commonly characterised by weak bureaucratic, organisational, and democratic structures. In contrast, incumbent governments have authoritarian legacies favouring personality-driven 'strong men', hegemonic leadership, and older men in top government structures ('old guard'), typically demanding loyalty to the party rather than to the electorate and distrust opposition or criticism (Gyimah-Boadi, 2007, pp. 25–26). In addition, as discussed in Chap. 4, SSA's political parties do not have ready sources of capital, mainly because membership contributions are not well organised, and are therefore dependent on external funding that can ensure political survival by buying popular support between elections, supporting strategic social groups, buying off political rivals and opposition, funding friendly civil society organisations and the media coverage, and the purchase of government institutions of oversight and control. Hence, "where state financing is provided, it tends to over-advantage ruling parties; where there are no state funding arrangements, campaign resources are secured on a freewheeling and self-help basis, with the incumbent siphoning off state resources and extorting from private business, while opposition parties forage" (Amundsen, 2019, p. 1).

Inge Amundsen (2019, p. 4) makes a distinction between "extractive political corruption" and "power-preserving political corruption" where the former focusses on the enriching of political office-bearers, their families, and political allies from activities such as public procurement bribery and corruption, embezzlement, economic crimes, and crony capitalism. *Extractive political corruption* however is associated with the use of corrupt practises to maintain, entrench, or perpetuate political power, and often makes use of "violence, intimidation, threats and manipulation of elections," as well as "buying friends (favouritism, co-optations, clientelism and nepotism), buying support from businesses (by favouring the businesses of political supporters), buying institutions of oversight and control (through appointments and inducements), the use of state resources to win elections, and buying judicial impunity".

As a result of SSA's dire need for external capital, corrupt multinationals can significantly harm development by compromising the public services and distorting public policy, causing environmental degradation by passing negative externalities on to society; and undermining human capital by engaging in discrimination, abuse, or exploitation (Mbaku, 2010, pp. 281–282). These companies become "so politically powerful in relation to the state that they are no longer a typical tenant of the state but a de facto co-landlord with the state" (Carmody, 2016, p. 99). Hence, Kenneth Omeje (2021, pp. 90–91) argues that SSA suffers from a pernicious form of rentier capitalism where unaccountable and compromised public leaders and functionaries are enmeshed with corporations, especially multinational mining companies. This creates financial economic structures where political office is personalised, elitist, and predatory while multinationals can maintain the powers and privileges entrenched during the colonial age. Corruption in most resource-dependent states is thus not an aberration or side-effect of ineffective governance, but rather, is a pernicious "mode of governance based on a transactional contract of extraction, or outward orientation, between domestically based elites and transnational companies, and the global powers in whose territories many of them are headquartered" (Carmody, 2016, p. 32).

It has however been argued that political corruption should be reduced by political decentralisation for two reasons. First, because corrupt bureaucrats can be easily replaced, and will therefore not want to draw attention to their corrupt activities by demanding large amounts; and second, because corporations will seek to pay the lowest bribe to the cheapest public official (Rose-Ackerman & Palifka, 2016, p. 344). The counter argument however is that if corruption entails a potentially career-ending risk, then a corrupt official may demand a sizeable bribe as compensation (ibid.). In addition, many poorly trained and incompetent public officials owe their positions to the incumbent leadership rather than to the public and thus may act with impunity so long as they have political support (Mbaku, 2010, p. 67). While it has been hypothesised that parliamentary systems should be less corrupt than presidential systems when the president is from one party while the legislative majority is from another (Persson et al., 2000, 2009), in SSA this is seldom the case because neopatrimonialism and patronage remain entrenched in both systems (Gyimah-Boadi, 2004, p. 22). Thus, a presidential system can be more corrupt than a parliamentary system if a corrupt president organises the state to extract rents while using state resources and institutions to shield himself/herself from parliamentary oversight or if parliament is as compromised as the corrupt leader (Kunicová & Rose-Ackerman, 2005; Kunicová, 2006).

5.4 Illicit Financial Flows and Capital Flight

Illicit financial flows (*IFF*) are defined as "money that is illegally earned, transferred, or utilised" (Kar & Cartwright-Smith, 2007, p. iv) and thus typically arise from corruption, illegal exploitation, and tax evasion (Le Billon, 2011). Related to, and overlapping with IFFs, is capital flight, which has been defined as unrecorded capital flows (Asongu & Odhiambo, 2019) or "a large-scale outflow of financial assets and capital from a nation due to events such as political or economic instability, currency devaluation or the imposition of capital controls" (Osei-Assibey et al., 2018). IFFs and capital flight are both a global and domestic governance problem arising from weak legal and political institutions, and inadequate regulatory and financial infrastructure (HLP, 2007, p. 51; Ndikumana & Boyce, 2022, pp. 3–4). It has been found that corporate activities comprise between 60% to 80% of IFFs while around 35% arises from criminal activities (Baker, 2005).

Over the last 50 years, African countries have lost between USD 1 trillion (Palan et al., 2010, p. 174; Kar & Cartwright-Smith, 2010; Kar & Leblanc, 2013) to USD 2 trillion (Ndikumana & Boyce, 2022, p. 1) in IFFs, equivalent to USD 88 billion per year (UNCTAD, 2020). This is more than all the ODA assistance received by Africa over the half century (HLP, 2007, p. 13) and is enough to wipe out the region's total external debt of around USD 250 billion while still leaving USD 600 billion over for poverty alleviation and economic growth (OECD, 2012). Hence, Ndikumana and Boyce (2011) state that SSA "is a net creditor to the rest of the world, in that the subcontinent's private external assets exceed its public external liabilities."

However, excluding the illegality of IFFs, capital flight can be a rational investor reaction to an adverse or deteriorating environment. As noted by Asongu and Odhiambo (2019), there are three reasons why investors may choose to disinvest. First, if political governance declines, political instability and violence will increase, institutional quality will decrease, and political risk will rise accordingly. Investors will thus fear that their capital and investment returns will be at risk and may therefore move the investment to a safer location abroad. Second, weak governance could lead to the formulation of policies that discourage foreign investment, leading to poor macroeconomic performance, deindustrialisation, and heightened disinvestment. Third, deteriorating or weak rule of law and control of corruption will likely lead to declining property rights and rising expropriation risks, thus undermining investor confidence and stimulating disinvestment accordingly. Once entrenched, these sentiments are very difficult to negate, which may be the reason for the persistence of capital flight once it begins (Ndikumana & Boyce, 2011).

Empirically, it has been found that that IFFs and capital flight hinder economic growth (Anetor, 2019; Antwi et al., 2024; Akinlo, 2024), and undermine industrialisation (Asongu & Odhiambo, 2019) and economic development (Boyce & Ndikumana, 2001). The most significant drivers of capital flight are found to be weak control of corruption (Osei-Assibey et al., 2018) and natural resource dependence (Kossele & Mbai-Akem, 2020). However, studies further report that capital flight arising from macroeconomic uncertainty is particularly harmful to the long-run economic growth potential of oil-exporting SSA countries (Salisu & Isah, 2021), and that political governance and institutional quality do not moderate the negative economic growth effects of capital flight (Asongu & Nwachukwu, 2017; Akinlo, 2024).

Map 5.2 shows that, averaged over the period of 2009–2018, the majority of SSA countries experienced IFFs in excess of 20% of total trade,

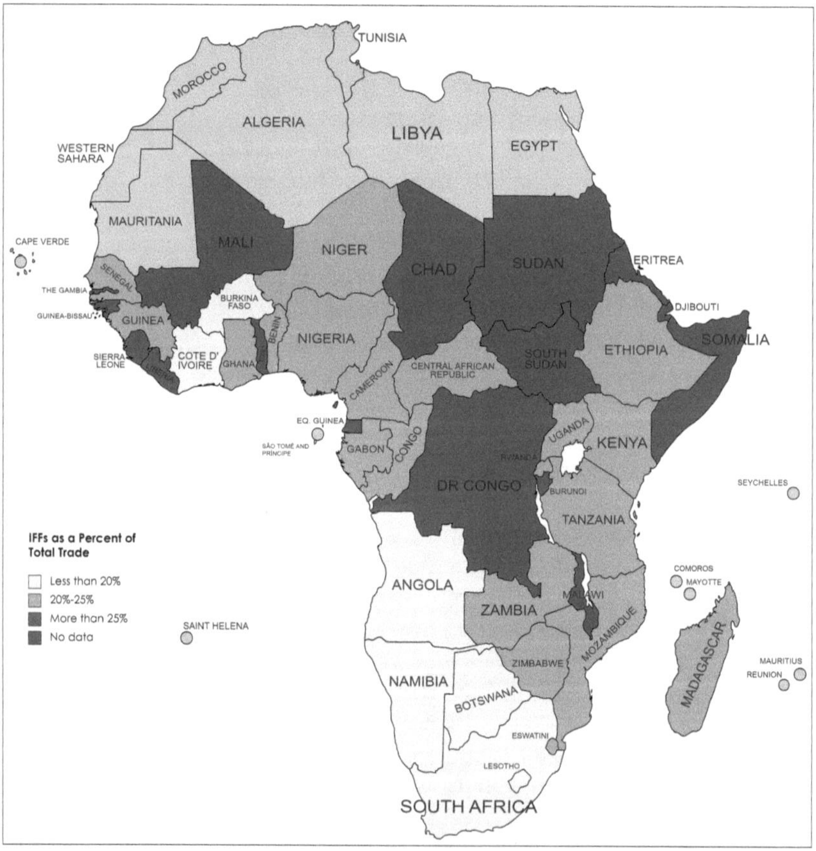

Map 5.2 Illicit financial flows as a percentage of total trade. (Source: Author's compilation from Global Financial Integrity data)

with the most afflicted countries being Burundi (25%), Mali (26%), Togo (27%), Malawi (29%), Sierra Leone (38%), and Gambia (42%).

Beyond the extraction of capital, IFFs remove taxation revenues, elevate economic and gender inequality, erode social bonds, reduce domestic resource mobilisation, lower sustainable economic growth, worsen poverty, weaken institutional quality, and lower public socio-economic expenditure (Aziani, 2018, p. vii; Nkurunziza, 2015; UNCTAD, 2020, p. 138; Ndikumana & Boyce, 2022, p. 241). Similarly, capital flight deprives SSA countries of the capital for economic growth and development (Akinlo, 2024) by negating tax revenues and driving debt dependence, leading to revenue and foreign exchange shortages, which disproportionately affect the poorer sectors of society; thus, widening wealth and income inequality (Ndikumana & Boyce, 2011) and the domestic savings and investment gap (Osei-Assibey et al., 2018).

However, IFFs are interwoven into SSA's developmental fabric. Colonial structural legacies coupled with post-colonial resource dependence have cemented external private and domestic state actors in SSA's domestic and regional affairs. As a result, the state does not have an accountable association with tax-paying citizens and does not have a fiscal responsibility to provide public goods and services (Ndikumana & Boyce, 2022, p. 236). The combination of weak state and external dependence means that these external actors wield disproportionate political power, which they use to protect their interests from outside scrutiny and beyond the rule of law while extracting resources and capital (Herbst, 2014, p. 134). Unsurprisingly, a central characteristic of IFFs is tax avoidance and evasion, especially by mining multinationals (IMF, 2021) and associated wealthy individuals, as well as public officials who channel bribes or fiscal resources through offshore subsidiaries and bank accounts into tax havens using loopholes in domestic and international tax regulations (Omeje, 2021, p. 99).

However, in addition to trade-related capital flight, there is also a significant relationship between external debt and capital flight. This phenomenon is commonly referred to as 'the revolving-door hypothesis' (Beja, 2006; Ndikumana & Boyce, 2011; Agyeman et al., 2022) and takes two forms—debt-fuelled or debt-driven capital flight (Beja, 2006). Debt-fuelled capital flight occurs when the debt-funded capital is channelled out of the country instead of being used for the intended investment purposes whereas debt-driven capital flight occurs when excessive borrowing undermines macroeconomic stability and development, which in turn stimulates disinvestment and capital flight. Over the course of the last fifty years, as SSA has shifted from donor reliance to increasingly diversified trade-led economic growth, the nature of Africa's IFFs has evolved accordingly. In the few decades after independence, a large portion of IFFs comprised ODA funds siphoned off into foreign bank accounts by public officials (Anderson et al., 2020). However, as ODA declined, and trade and FDI increased, IFFs from SSA became more complex as centralised public sector corruption transformed into decentralised private sector corruption, facilitated and directed through a web of international tax havens.

This system of financial impropriety is built into the global economy and is assumed to be a normal means of doing business. Wealthy companies and individuals actively seek ways to reduce or avoid their tax liabilities by employing a range of well-paid international intermediaries that artificially lower tax liabilities using complex corporate structures (such as subsidiaries and subordinates), financial arrangements (such as networks of 'shell companies' or asset revaluations), opaque corporate domicile, and tax loopholes (Otusanya et al., 2022). Consequently, the line between ethical and unethical financial transactions is typically blurred and there are numerous examples where financial institutions, particularly banks, are party to criminal activities.

It is estimated that there are between 50 to 60 tax havens in the world, acting as domicile for more than 2 million 'letterbox' companies, thousands of banks, equity and hedge funds, and insurance companies (The Economist, 2013). Tax havens are a significant component of the global financial infrastructure with half of all international bank lending and global trading activities, and between 30% to 50% of all FDI channelled via tax havens by banks, legal and accounting firms, and financial intermediaries (Christensen, 2011; Haberly & Wójcik, 2015; Bolwijn et al., 2018). It has been estimated that tax havens hold between USD 21 trillion to USD 32 trillion (Henry, 2012), which is around 8% of the world's household financial wealth and equivalent to 10% of world GDP (Zucman, 2014). Of this amount, the top 0.1% wealthiest households own about 80% and the top 0.01% own around 50% (Alstadsæter et al., 2018). Over and above this amount, USD 500 billion is added annually in tax evasion by high-net-worth individuals (Murphy, 2012; Shaxson, 2019).

Among the three most common methods that corporations use to funnel IFFs out of SSA are transfer mispricing, which entails using shell companies to move profits or assets to low-tax or no-tax jurisdictions without leaving a paper trail; trade mis-invoicing, where the price, quality, or quantity of traded goods and services between two parties is purposefully under- or over-stated; and thin capitalisation, where corporations shift capital or profits among group companies under the guise of inter-group loans (Moore et al., 2018, pp. 61–63). It has been estimated that SSA loses between USD 18 billion to USD 36 billion annually to this impropriety, equating to 6% to 13% of SSA's total government tax revenue, and 33% to 67% of total development assistance from OECD countries (ibid., pp. 64–65). Over the 10 years from 2002–2011, SSA lost between USD 242 billion to USD 407 billion from trade mis-invoicing alone (Kar & Leblanc, 2013), including imputed interest this rises to USD 607 billion (ACEP, 2015).

5.5 Corruption and FDI

There are two theories that describe the relationship between FDI and domestic corruption. The first posits that corruption acts as a "grabbing hand" (or "sand in the wheels") because paying bribes acts as an indirect tax (Wei, 2000; Habib & Zurawicki, 2002) and creates a range of financial distortions that include reduced profitability (Wei, 1997; Glass & Wu, 2002; Uhlenbruck et al., 2006; Demirbag et al., 2007), a waste of resources (Applebaum & Katz, 1987; Murphy et al., 1991; Shleifer & Vishny, 1993), higher contract-related risks (Boycko et al., 1995; Saha & Thampy, 2006), and lower the incentives to invest (Mauro, 1995; Ehrlich & Lui, 1999; Wei, 2000; Voyer & Beamish, 2004).

The second theory argues that if the costs of corruption are less than the financial benefits, then corruption may act as "helping hand" (or "greasing the wheels") because corruption may be necessary to speed up or circumvent bureaucratic processes, reduce fees, costs, and taxes; ensure an unfair competitive advantage, establish a preferential economic advantage (Lui, 1985; Wheeler & Mody, 1992; Bardhan, 1997; Egger & Winner, 2005; Woo, 2010, p. 72), or facilitate access to existing or new public investment opportunities (Carmichael, 1995; Tanzi & Davoodi, 2000; Cheung et al., 2012; Akcigit et al., 2018; Bandhari, 2021; Canen & Wantchekon, 2022). In many regions of the world (such as Asia, Eastern Europe, and SSA) that have weak institutions, over-regulation, or a culture of 'gifting', bribery is not just "a cost of doing business", it is a prerequisite for market entry, to gain market share, or to compete with corrupt competitors (Krifa-Schneider et al., 2022). Paying bribes however may still not provide certainty because any agreement between foreign investors and corrupt officials naturally has no legal status and thus there is little recourse if the contract or agreement is not honoured (Wei, 1997).

Regardless of whether corruption acts as a grabbing hand or a helping hand, it typically arises in socio-economic environments beset with structural limitations such as weak governance, patron-client relationships, patrimonial and clientelist networks, limited state constraints, and institutional voids (Meagher & Thomas, 2004; Luiz & Stewart, 2014; Gossel, 2018) coupled with individualistic motives arising from the limited remuneration, agency, and discretion of bureaucrats (Gossel, 2020). SSA in particular is a challenging environment because of the "weak institutional frameworks including poor regulatory systems, flawed judiciaries and political systems still in the process of consolidation. These institutional conditions, where the rules of the game are still fluid, are thought to provide settings ripe for corrupt behaviour as companies either opportunistically try to exploit these weaknesses, or out of frustration, succumb to pressure to 'get things done'" (Luiz & Stewart, 2014).

Although the company gains from market expansion or penetration, and higher revenues and profits, the country suffers from lower productivity and innovation (Fisman, 2001); and distorted, mispriced, and unequal infrastructure development and public service provision (Burgess et al., 2015; Rose-Ackerman & Palifka, 2016, p. 93). Alternatively, investors could attempt to limit their exposure to corruption by changing how they invest (Krifa-Schneider et al., 2022), such as by favouring joint ventures with local partners instead of establishing wholly owned entities (Smarzynska & Wei, 2000; Estrin & Prevezer, 2010; Demirbag et al., 2010).

With regards to SSA, studies find that FDI uses corruption to overcome SSA's weak regulatory environment and thus the helping hand (or grease the wheels) hypothesis holds initially. However, over time, as institutions develop and democracy deepens, the helping hand turns into the grabbing hand (or sand in the wheels) (Quazi et al., 2014; Ibrahim et al., 2015; Gossel, 2018), which accords with studies that find that the effect of corruption is related to a country's stage of development (Krifa-Schneider et al., 2022). The tolerable level of corruption where this transition occurs has been found to be around the mid-point on the World Banks' control of corruption index (Abotsi & Iyavarakul, 2015), but when averaged over the period of 2012–2020, only four SSA countries have scores above this threshold: Botswana (0.8), Lesotho (0.0), Namibia (0.3), and Rwanda (0.6).

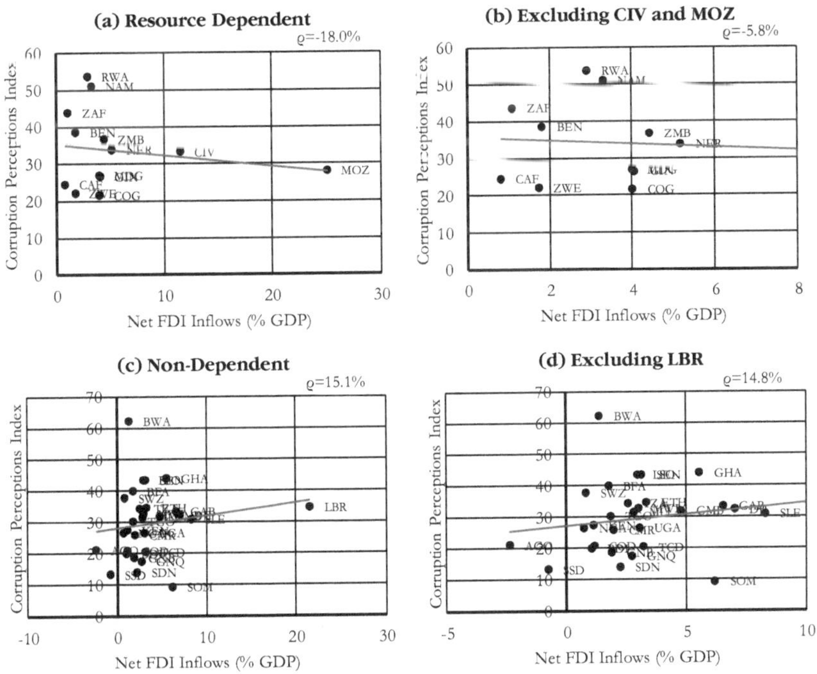

Fig. 5.3 Scatterplots of net FDI inflows and corruption perceptions index. (Data sources: World Bank, Transparency International)

The scatterplots of net FDI inflows and outflows against the corruption perceptions index (CPI) (averaged over 2012–2020) presented in Figs. 5.3 and 5.4 respectively indicate that there is a weak negative relationship between FDI and corruption in resource-dependent SSA countries but there is a stronger positive association in non-resource countries.

However, the Granger causality tests[9] between FDI and the CPI summarised in Table 5.1 suggest that there are no significant causal relationships between the FDI and the CPI in resource-dependent SSA countries whereas there is evidence of significant unidirectional causality running from net FDI inflows to the CPI in the full sample and the non-resource-dependent sub-sample. Hence, the correlations in Figs. 5.3a and 5.4a between FDI and the CPI in resource-dependent SSA states are likely

[9] The I(0) panel unit root test results are summarised in Appendix 1.

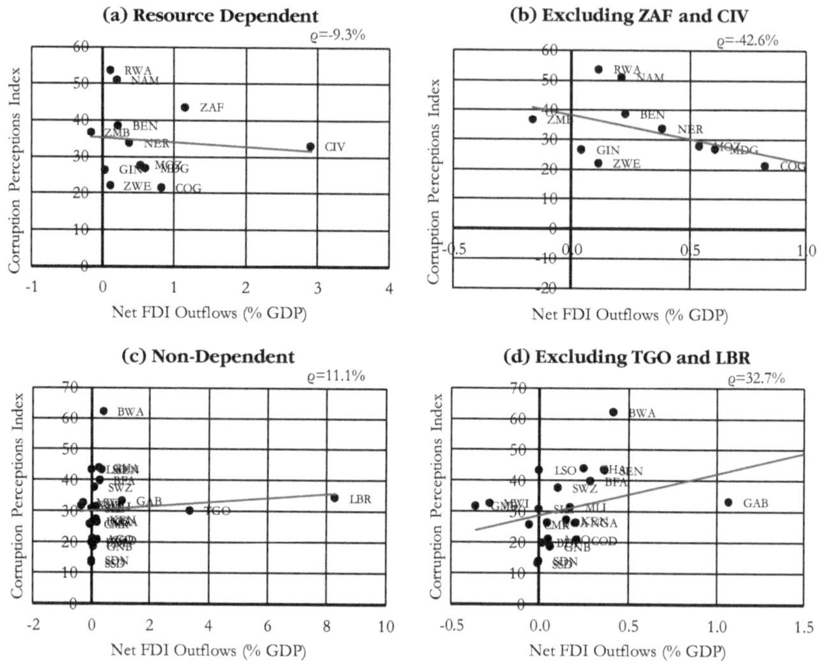

Fig. 5.4 Scatterplots of net FDI outflows and corruption perceptions index. (Data sources: World Bank, Transparency International)

Table 5.1 Granger causality results of net FDI and the corruption perceptions index

Null hypothesis	*Net FDI inflows*		*Net FDI outflows*	
	Obs	*F-statistic*	*Obs*	*F-statistic*
Full sample:				
CPI does not Granger cause net FDI	271	0.223	206	0.007
Net FDI does not Granger cause CPI		5.390***		0.906
Resource-dependent sub-sample:				
CPI does not Granger cause net FDI	91	0.236	84	0.484
Net FDI does not Granger cause CPI		2.206		1.123
Non-resource-dependent sub-sample:				
CPI does not Granger cause net FDI	180	0.809	122	0.135
Net FDI does not Granger cause CPI		3.868**		0.937

Pairwise Granger causality tests, sample period: 2012–2020, no. of lags = 2. ** and *** represent significance at the 5% and 1% level respectively affected by other exogenous factors whereas in non-resource SSA states, FDI leads to lower corruption.

As mentioned previously, a significant portion of SSA's natural resources is exploited by international companies (UNCTAD, 2007), and thus natural resource endowment remains a significant attractor of FDI (Asiedu 2006, 2013; Ezeoha & Cattaneo, 2012; Acheampong & Osei, 2014). However, resource-dependent countries are characterised by weak states and unaccountable governments, and it is therefore possible that in addition to the economic benefits associated with resource extraction, FDI may also be attracted by the ease with which capital can be repatriated. Hence, FDI may drive IFFs by extracting capital outside of official channels and will therefore be unrecorded in the host country's balance of payments (Ndikumana & Sarr, 2019). Consequently, FDI, corruption, and IFFs tend to be intertwined in resource-dependent states (Perez et al., 2012; Aleksynska & Havrylchyk, 2013).

There are three ways in which FDI can enable IFFs (Perez et al., 2012). First, the establishment of an overseas company or subsidiary could enable the company in the home country to transfer IFFs using transfer mispricing, trade mis-invoicing, or thin capitalisation. Second, investors can use IFFs to establish legitimate operations or businesses in the home country. Third, by using the host country as a mere transit point to shield the financial gains from taxation, expropriation, or accountability.[10] Empirically, Perez et al. find that about 29% of total FDI is channelled to countries that are known money laundering centres, and of this amount, around 20% is to launder IFFs.

The scatterplots of net FDI flows against IFFs (averaged over 2009–2018) in Figs. 5.5 and 5.6 show that there is a positive linear correlation between FDI inflows and IFFs but a negative correlation between FDI outflows and IFFs.

The Granger causality tests summarised in Table 5.2[11] however indicate that although there is weak unidirectional causality running from FDI inflows to IFFs in non-resource-dependent SSA countries, there is significant unidirectional causality from FDI outflows to IFFs. In contrast, there are no causal associations between FDI and IFFs in

[10] An example is the 'round tripping' of FDI from India via Mauritius (discussed further in Chap. 6).

[11] The I(0) panel unit root test results are summarised in Appendix 2.

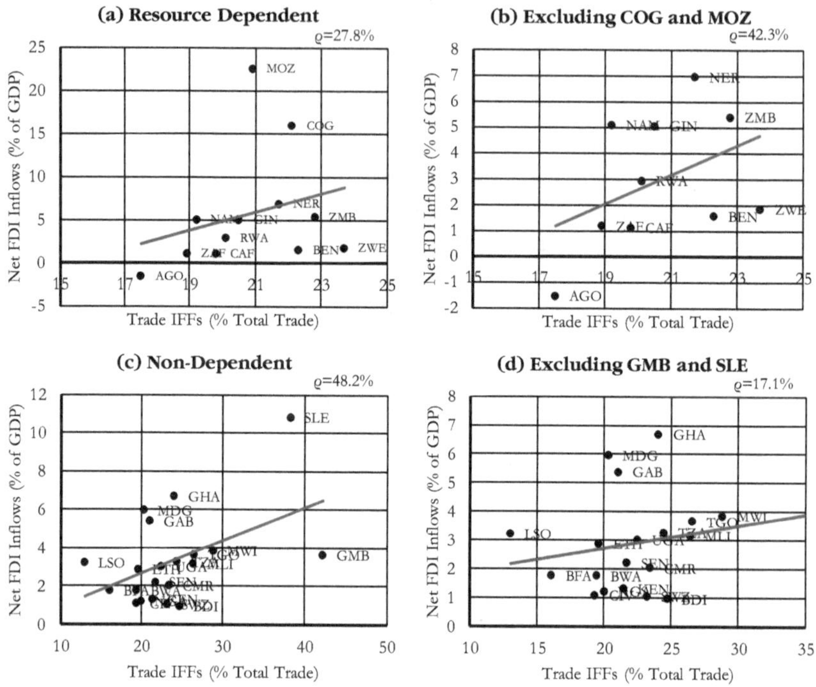

Fig. 5.5 Net FDI inflows and illicit financial flows. (Source: World Development Indicators, Global Financial Integrity)

resource-dependent countries. Hence, although the scatterplots show that FDI inflows have a positive association with IFFs, and FDI outflows have a negative association; the Granger test results suggest that FDI outflows causally drive IFFs in non-resource-dependent SSA countries whereas the association in resource-dependent SSA countries is shaped by other exogenous factors.

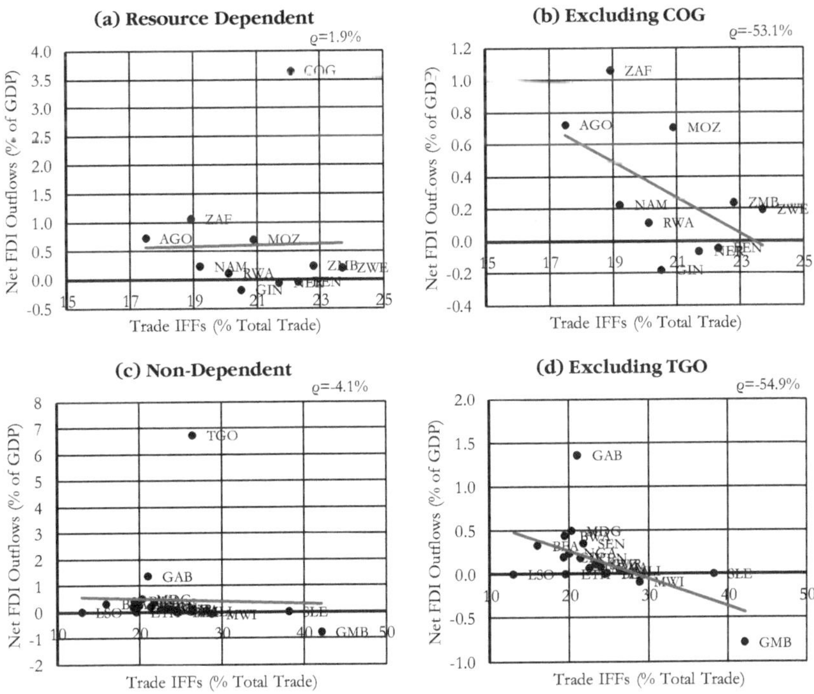

Fig. 5.6 Net FDI outflows and illicit financial flows. (Source: World Development Indicators, Global Financial Integrity)

Table 5.2 Granger causality results between net FDI and illicit financial flows

Null hypothesis	*Net FDI inflows*		*Net FDI outflows*	
	Obs	*F-statistic*	*Obs*	*F-statistic*
Full sample:				
IFF does not Granger cause net FDI	218	0.144	181	1.079
Net FDI does not Granger cause IFF		1.415		7.358***
Resource-dependent sub-sample:				
IFF does not Granger cause net FDI	87	0.070	77	0.169
Net FDI does not Granger cause IFF		0.725		0.096
Non-resource-dependent dub-sample:				
IFF does not Granger cause net FDI	131	2.697*	104	1.069
Net FDI does not Granger cause IFF		5.526***		10.409***

Pairwise Granger causality tests, sample period: 2009–2018, no. of lags = 2. *** and * represent significance at the 1% and 10% level respectively

Appendices

Appendix 1: Unit Root Test Results of Net FDI and the Corruption Perceptions Index

	Full sample	*Resource-dependent*	*Non-dependent*
Corruption Perception Index (2012–2020) [1]:			
Levin, Lin & Chu t-stat	−23.463***	−2.042**	−23.725***
Im, Pesaran and Shin W-stat	−1.960**	0.922	−2.922***
ADF - Fisher Chi-square	106.347*	19.716	86.631***
PP - Fisher Chi-square	101.518	28.333	73.185
Net FDI inflows (2012–2020) [1]:			
Levin, Lin & Chu t-stat	−7.483***	−4.008***	−6.304***
Im, Pesaran and Shin W-stat	−2.660***	−1.259*	−2.359***
ADF - Fisher Chi-square	138.643***	40.053**	98.590***
PP - Fisher Chi-square	177.905***	55.291***	122.614***
Net FDI outflows (2012–2020) [1]:			
Levin, Lin & Chu t-stat	−7.184***	−5.361***	−5.200***
Im, Pesaran and Shin W-stat	−2.524***	−1.270*	−2.207***
ADF - Fisher Chi-square	114.119***	37.389**	76.730***
PP - Fisher Chi-square	135.197***	40.395**	94.802***

***, **, * represent significance at the 1%, 5%, 10% level respectively. *[#]* indicates the automatic lag selected by the SIC. Probabilities for Fisher tests are computed using an asymptotic Chi-square distribution. All other tests assume asymptotic normality

Appendix 2: Unit Root Test Results of Net FDI and Illicit Financial Flows

	Full sample	*Resource-dependent*	*Non-dependent*
Illicit financial flows (2009–2018) [0]:			
Levin, Lin & Chu t-stat	−13.482***	−11.860***	−5.908***
Im, Pesaran and Shin W-stat	−5.371***	−5.192***	−2.833***
ADF - Fisher Chi-square	126.181***	60.641***	65.540***
PP - Fisher Chi-square	154.108***	78.467***	75.641***
Net FDI inflows (2009–2018) [0]:			
Levin, Lin & Chu t-stat	−9.619***	−5.859***	−7.690***
Im, Pesaran and Shin W-stat	−4.169***	−3.427***	−2.681***
ADF - Fisher Chi-square	147.770***	57.001***	90.769***
PP - Fisher Chi-square	179.560***	69.068***	110.493***
Net FDI outflows (2009–2018) [0]:			
Levin, Lin & Chu t-stat	−10.419***	−5.441***	−8.999***
Im, Pesaran and Shin W-stat	−4.529***	−2.247***	−3.998***
ADF - Fisher Chi-square	121.794***	40.880**	80.914***
PP - Fisher Chi-square	136.681***	49.196***	87.484***

***, **, * represent significance at the 1%, 5%, 10% level respectively. *[#]* indicates the automatic lag selected by the SIC. Probabilities for Fisher tests are computed using an asymptotic Chi-square distribution. All other tests assume asymptotic normality

References

Abotsi, A. K., & Iyavarakul, T. (2015). Tolerable Level of Corruption for Foreign Direct Investment in Africa. *Contemporary Economics, 9*(3), 249–270.

Acemoglu, D., Ticchi, D., & Vindigni, A. (2010). A Theory of Military Dictatorships. *American Economic Journal: Macroeconomics, 2*(1), 1–42.

Acemoglu, D., Verdier, T., & Robinson, J. A. (2004). Kleptocracy and Divide-and-Rule: A Model of Personal Rule. *Journal of the European Economic Association, 2*(2–3), 162–192.

ACEP. (2015). Illicit Financial Flows and the Extractive Industry in Ghana. *Africa Centre for Energy Policy*. Retrieved January, 2024, from http://acep.africa/wp-content/uploads/2019/11/Illicit-Financial-Flow-in-Ghanas-extractives.pdf

Acheampong, P., & Osei, V. (2014). Foreign Direct Investment (FDI) Inflows into Ghana: Should the Focus Be on Infrastructure or Natural Resources? Short-Run and Long-Run Analyses. *International Journal of Financial Research, 5*(1), 42–51.

Ades, A., & Di Tella, R. (1999). Rents, Competition, and Corruption. *American Economic Review, 89*, 982–993.

Agyeman, G., Sakyi, D., & Oteng-Abayie, E. F. (2022). External Debt and Economic Growth in Selected Sub-Saharan African Countries: The Role of Capital Flight. *Research in Globalization, 5*, 100091.

Akcigit, U., Baslandze, S., & Lotti, F. (2018). Connecting to Power: Political Connections, Innovation, and Firm Dynamics. *NBER Working Paper 25136*. National Bureau of Economic Research.

Akinlo, T. (2024). Does Institutional Quality Modulate the Effect of Capital Flight on Economic Growth in Sub-Saharan Africa? *Journal of Money Laundering Control, 27*(1), 60–75.

Aleksynska, M., & Havrylchyk, O. (2013). FDI from the South: The Role of Institutional Distance and Natural Resources. *European Journal of Political Economy, 29*, 38–53.

Alence, R., & Pitcher, A. (2019). Resisting State Capture in South Africa. *Journal of Democracy, 30*(4), 5–19.

Alesina, A., Baqir, R., & Easterly, W. (2000). Redistributive Public Employment. *Journal of Urban Economics, 48*(2), 219–241.

Almeida, H. (2020, October 15). Angola Says Stolen Assets Worth More Than $24 Billion Estimate. *Bloomberg*. Retrieved January, 2024, from https://www.bloomberg.com/news/articles/2020-10-15/angola-says-stolen-assets-worth-more-than-24-billion-estimate

Alstadsæter, A., Johannesen, N., & Zucman, G. (2018). Who Owns the Wealth in Tax Havens? Macro Evidence and Implications for Global Inequality. *Journal of Public Economics, 162*, 89–100.

Amnesty International. (2017). *A Criminal Enterprise? Shell's Involvement in Human Rights Violations in Nigeria in the 1990s*. Amnesty International.

Amundsen, I. (2019). *Political Corruption in Africa; Extraction and Power Preservation*. Edward Elgar.

Anderson, J.J., Johannsen, N., & Rijkers, B. (2020). "Elite Capture of Foreign Aid: Evidence from Offshore Bank Accounts," *Policy Research Working Paper No. 9150*, World Bank, New York, USA.

Anderson, P. (2023). Cobalt and Corruption: The Influence of Multinational Firms and Foreign States on the Democratic Republic of the Congo. *Journal for Global Business and Community, 14*(1). Retrieved January, 2024, from https://doi.org/10.56020/001c.72664

Andreasson, S. (2018). Energy Producers in Sub-Saharan Africa: Beyond the Gatekeeper State? *Third World Thematics, 3*(3), 381–397.

Andvig, J. C., & Moene, K. O. (1990). How Corruption May Corrupt. *Journal of Economic Behaviour and Organization, 13*(1), 63–76.

Anetor, F. O. (2019). Macroeconomic Determinants of Capital Flight: Evidence from the Sub-Saharan African Countries. *International Journal of Management, Economics and Social Sciences, 8*(1), 40–57.

Angeles, L., & Neanidis, K. C. (2015). The Persistent Effect of Colonialism on Corruption. *Economica, 82*(326), 319–349.

Antwi, S., Tetteh, A. B., Armah, P., Mukhtar, A.-M., & Duedu, L. A. (2024). An Empirical Investigation of Capital Flight and Economic Growth Nexus in Africa. *The Journal of International Trade & Economic Development*. https://doi.org/10.1080/09638199.2024.2389865

Applebaum, E., & Katz, E. (1987). Seeking Rents by Setting Rents: The Political Economy of Rent Seeking. *Economic Journal, 97*, 685–699.

Arum, N. (2019, July 15). State Capture: Zuma, the Guptas, and the Sale of South Africa. *BBC*. Retrieved March, 2024, from https://www.bbc.com/news/world-africa-48980964

Asiedu, E. (2006). Foreign Direct Investment in Africa: The Role of Natural Resources, Market Size, Government Policy, Institutions and Political Instability. *The World Economy, 29*(1), 63–77.

Asiedu, E. (2013). Foreign Direct Investment, Natural Resources and Institutions. *Working Paper* (3, pp. 1–38). International Growth Center.

Asongu, S. A. (2013). Fighting Corruption in Africa: Do Existing Corruption-Control Levels Matter? *International Journal of Development Issues, 12*(1), 36–52.

Asongu, S. A., & Nwachukwu, J. C. (2017). Fighting Capital Flight in Africa: Evidence from Bundling and Unbundling Governance. *Journal of Industry, Competition and Trade, 17*, 305–323.

Asongu, S. A., & Odhiambo, N. M. (2019). Governance, Capital Flight and Industrialisation in Africa. *Economic Structures, 8*(36), 1–22.

Auty, R. M. (Ed.). (2004). *Resource Abundance and Economic Development*. Oxford University Press.

Auty, R.M. (2001). *Resource Abundance and Economic Development*, Oxford University Press, Oxford, UK.

Aziani, A. (2018). *Illicit Financial Flows: An Innovative Approach to Estimation*. Springer.

Bac, M. (2001). Corruption, Connections and Transparency: Does a Better Screen Imply a Better Scene? *Public Choice, 107*, 87–96.

Baker, R. W. (2005). *Capitalism's Achilles Heel: Dirty Money and How to Renew the Free-Market System*. John Wiley and Sons.

Bamidele, O. (2013). Corruption, Conflict and Sustainable Development in African States. *The African Symposium, 13*(1), 42–54.

Bandhari, A. (2021). Political Determinants of Economic Exchange: Evidence from a Business Experiment in Senegal. *American Journal of Political Science, 66*(4), 835–852.

Bardhan, P. (1997). Corruption and Development: A Review of Issues. *Journal of Economic Literature, 35*(3), 1320–1346.

Becker, S. O., Egger, P. H., & Seidel, T. (2009). Common Political Culture: Evidence on Regional Corruption Contagion. *European Journal of Political Economy, 25*(3), 300–310.

Beja, E. L. (2006). Revisiting the Revolving Door: Capital Flight from Southeast Asia. *DESA Working Paper No. 16, ST/ESA/2006/DWP/16*. United Nations.

Beresford, A. (2015). Power, Patronage, and Gatekeeper Politics in South Africa. *African Affairs, 114*(455), 226–248.

Besley, T., & Persson, T. (2009). Repression or Civil War? *American Economic Review, 99*(2), 292–297.

Bezemer, D., & Jong-A-Pin, R. (2013). Democracy, Globalization and Ethnic Violence. *Journal of Comparative Economics, 41*, 108–125.

Billger, S. M., & Goel, R. K. (2009). Do Existing Corruption Levels Matter in Controlling Corruption?: Cross-Country Quantile Regression Estimates. *Journal of Development Economics, 90*(2), 299–305.

Bliss, C., & Di Tella, R. (1997). Does Competition Kill Corruption? *Journal of Political Economy, 105*, 1001–1023.

Bolwijn, R., Casella, B., & Rigo, D. (2018). An FDI-Driven Approach to Measuring the Scale and Economic Impact of BEPS. *Transnational Corporations, 25*(2), 107–144.

Borsky, S., & Kalkschmied, K. (2019). Corruption in Space: A Closer Look at the World's Subnations. *European Journal of Political Economy, 59*, 400–422.

Boycko, M., Shleifer, A., & Vishny, R. W. (1995). *Privatizing Russia*. MIT Press.

Boyce, J.K. & Ndikumana, L. (2001). "Is Africa a Net Creditor? New Estimates of Capital Flight from Severely Indebted Sub-Saharan African Countries, 1970-1996," *The Journal of Development Studies*, 38(2), 27–56.

Brown, W. (2018). Still One Size Fits All? Uneven and Combined Development and African Gatekeeper States. *Third World Thematics: A TWQ Journal, 3*(3), 1–22.

Brunetti, A., & Weder, B. (2003). A Free Press is Bad News for Corruption. *Journal of Public Economics, 87*(7–8), 1801–1824.

Burgess, R., Jedwab, R., Miguel, E., Morjaria, A., & Padró i Miquel, G. (2015). The Value of Democracy: Evidence from Road Building in Kenya. *American Economic Review, 105*(6), 1817–1851.

Burgis, T. (2016). *The Looting Machine: Warlords, Tycoons, Smugglers and the Systematic Theft of Africa's Wealth*. William Collins.

Bye, V., Inglês, P., & Orre, A. (2021). Angola After dos Santos: Change and Continuity. *Working Paper No. WP 2021:8*. Chr. Michelsen Institute.

Canen, N., & Wantchekon, L. (2022). Political Distortions, State Capture, and Economic Development in Africa. *Journal of Economic Perspectives, 36*(1), 101–124.

Carmichael, S. (1995). *Business Ethics: The New Bottom Line*. Demos.

Carmody, P. (2016). *The New Scramble for Africa*. Polity Press.

Cheeseman, N. (2015). *Democracy in Africa*. Cambridge University Press.

Cheung, Y. L., Rau, P. R., & Stouraitis, A. (2012). How Much Do Firms Pay as Bribes and What Benefits Do They Get? Evidence from Corruption Cases Worldwide. *NBER Working Paper 17981*. National Bureau of Economic Research.

Chowdhury, S. K. (2004). The Effect of Democracy and Press Freedom on Corruption: An Empirical Test. *Economics Letters, 85*(1), 93–101.

Christensen, J. (2011). The Looting Continues: Tax Havens and Corruption. *Critical Perspectives on International Business, 7*(2), 177–196.

Cobbett, E. (2018). Gatekeepers of Financial Power: From London to Lagos. *Third World Thematics: A TWQ Journal, 3*(3), 364–380.

Cooper, F. (2002). *Africa Since 1940: The Past of the Present*. Cambridge University Press.

Cooper, F. (2018). Gatekeeping Practices, Gatekeeper States and Beyond. *Third World Thematics: A TWQ Journal, 3*(3), 455–468.

Corchon, L. C. (2008). Forms of Governance and the Size of Rent-Seeking. *Social Choice and Welfare, 30*, 197–210.

Cotterill, J., & Walker, O. (2023, October 1). UBS Settles with Mozambique in Credit Suisse 'Tuna Bond' Case. *Financial Times*. Retrieved January, 2024, from https://www.ft.com/content/69290c72-08bf-43e8-be44-e14041acb603

Demirbag, M., Glaister, K. W., & Tatoglu, E. (2007). Institutional and Transaction Cost Influences on MNEs Ownership Strategies of their Affiliates: Evidence from an Emerging Market. *Journal of World Business, 42*, 418–434.

Demirbag, M., McGuinness, M., & Altay, H. (2010). Perceptions of Institutional Environment and Entry Mode. *Management International Review, 50*, 207–240.

Dizaji, S. F., Farzanegan, M. R., & Naghavi, A. (2016). Political Institutions and Government Spending Behaviour: Theory and Evidence from Iran. *International Tax and Public Finance, 23*, 522–549.

Doherty, B., & Pegg, D. (2017, December 22). Paradise Papers: US Puts Sanctions on Billionaire Over Dealings in DRC. *The Guardian*. Retrieved January, 2024, from https://www.theguardian.com/news/2017/dec/22/paradise-papers-us-sanctions-billionaire-dealings-drc

Dollar, D., Fisman, S., & Gatti, R. (2001). Are Women Really the 'Fairer' Sex? Corruption and Women in Government. *Journal of Economic Behaviour & Organization, 46*, 423–429.

Dorman, S. R. (2018). Beyond the Gatekeeper State? Studying Africa's States and State Systems in the Twenty-First Century. *Third World Thematics: A TWQ Journal, 3*(3), 311–324.

Doyle, M., Rault-Smith, J., & Alli, R. (2022). *A PMG Review of Parliamentary Oversight in Light of State Capture and the Zondo Report*. Parliamentary Monitoring Group.

Drogin, B. (2022, July 8). José Eduardo dos Santos, Who Plundered Angola, Dies at 79. *The Washington Post*. Retrieved January, 2024, from https://www.washingtonpost.com/obituaries/2022/07/08/jose-eduardo-dos-santos-angola-dictator-dead/

Dunning, T. (2008). Chapter 2: The Foundations of Rentier States Crude Democracy. In *Natural Resource Wealth and Political Regimes*. Cambridge University Press.

Economic Commission for Africa. (2009). *African Governance Report II*. Oxford University Press.

Efobi, U. (2015). Politicians' Attributes and Institutional Quality in Africa: A Focus on Corruption. *Journal of Economic Issues, 49*(3), 787–813.

Egger, P., & Winner, H. (2005). Evidence on Corruption as an Incentive for Foreign Direct Investment. *European Journal of Political Economy, 21*, 932–952.

Ehrlich, I., & Lui, F. T. (1999). Bureaucratic Corruption and Endogenous Growth. *Journal of Political Economy, 107*, S270–S293.

Emerson, P. M. (2006). Corruption, Competition and Democracy. *Journal of Development Economics, 81*, 193–212.

England, A. (2016, April 18). IMF Halts Mozambique Aid After Finding Undisclosed Debts of $1bn. *Financial Times*. Retrieved January, 2024, from https://www.ft.com/content/6c755214-057f-11e6-9b51-0fb5e65703ce

Estrin, S., & Prevezer, M. (2010). A Survey on Institutions and New Firm Entry: How and Why Do Entry Rates Differ in Emerging Markets? *Economic Systems, 34*(3), 289–308.

Ezeoha, A., & Cattaneo, N. (2012). FDI Flows to Sub-Saharan Africa: The Impact of Finance, Institutions, and Natural Resource Endowment. *Comparative Economic Studies, 54*, 597–632.

Fabricius, P. (2022, April 22). Why is the DRC President Withholding Details of the Deal to Recover Assets from the Controversial Mining Magnate? *Institute for Security Studies Africa*. Retrieved March, 2024, from https://issafrica.org/iss-today/tshisekedi-does-a-dodgy-deal-with-gertler

Farzanegan, M. R., & Witthuhn, S. (2017). Corruption and Political Stability: Does the Youth Bulge Matter? *European Journal of Political Economy, 49*, 47–70.

Fisman, R. (2001). Estimating the Value of Political Connections. *American Economic Review, 91*(4), 1095–1102.

Fisman, R., & Gatti, R. (2002). Decentralization and Corruption: Evidence Across Countries. *Journal of Public Economics, 83*, 325–345.

Forson, J. A., Buracom, P., Chen, G., & Baah-Ennumh, T. Y. (2017). Genuine Wealth Per Capita as a Measure of Sustainability and the Negative Impact of

Corruption on Sustainable Growth in Sub-Saharan Africa. *South African Journal of Economics, 85*(2), 178–195.

Freedberg, S. P., Alecci, S., Fitzgibbon, W., Dalby, D., & Reuter, D. (2020, January 19). How Africa's Richest Woman Exploited Family Ties, Shell Companies, and Inside Deals to Build an Empire. *ICIJ*. Retrieved January, 2024, from https://www.icij.org/investigations/luanda-leaks/how-africas-richest-woman-exploited-family-ties-shell-companies-and-inside-deals-to-build-an-empire/

Frey, A. (2023, April 4). Hidden Debts: Second Trial Under Preparation. *Club of Mozambique*. Retrieved February, 2024, from https://clubofmozambique.com/news/hidden-debts-second-trial-under-preparation-235479/

Gallagher, J. (2018). Zimbabwe's Consolidation as a Gatekeeper State. *Third World Thematics: A TWQ Journal, 3*(3), 1–16.

Gillanders, R. (2016). Corruption and Anxiety in Sub-Saharan Africa. *Economics of Governance, 17*, 47–69.

Gillies, A. (2020). Corruption Trends During Africa's Oil Boom, 2005 to 2014. *The Extractive Industries and Society, 7*, 1171–1181.

Giollabhuí, S. M. (2017). The Fall of an African President: How and Why did the ANC Unseat Thabo Mbeki? *African Affairs, 116*(464), 391–413.

Glass, A. J., & Wu, X. (2002). *Does Corruption Discourage Foreign Direct Investment and Innovation?* Unpublished working paper. Texas A&M University.

Goel, R. K., & Nelson, M. A. (2005). Economic Freedom versus Political Freedom: Cross-Country Influences on Corruption. *Australian Economic Papers, June*, 121–133.

Goel, R. K., & Nelson, M. A. (2007). Are Corrupt Acts Contagious? Evidence from the United States. *Journal of Policy Modeling, 29*(6), 839–850.

Goel, R. K., & Nelson, M. A. (2010). Causes of Corruption: History, Geography and Government. *Journal of Policy Modeling, 32*, 433–447.

Goel, R. K., & Saunoris, J. W. (2014). Global Corruption and the Shadow Economy: Spatial Aspects. *Public Choice, 161*, 119–139.

Goel, R. K., & Saunoris, J. W. (2022). Corrupt Thy Neighbour? New Evidence of Corruption Contagion from Bordering Nations. *Journal of Policy Modeling, 44*, 635–652.

Goetz, A. (2000). Political Cleaners: Women as the New Anti-Corruption Force? *Development and Change, 38*(1), 87–105.

Gossel, S. J. (2018). Corruption, Democracy, and FDI in Sub-Saharan Africa. *Journal of Policy Modeling, 40*, 647–662.

Gossel, S. J. (2020). FDI and Elections in Sub-Saharan Africa. *The European Journal of Development Research, 32*(4), 1151–1172.

GPAD. (2011). *Governance and Public Administration Division Combating Corruption, Improving Governance in Africa: regional Anti-Corruption*

Programme for Africa (2011–2016). United Nations, Economic Commission for Africa.

Grootes, S. (2023, October 30). MIA—President Ramaphosa and His Promise to Decisively Act Against the ANC and State Corruption. *Daily Maverick*. Retrieved January, 2024, from https://www.dailymaverick.co.za/article/2023-10-30-mia-president-ramaphosa-and-his-promise-to-decisively-act-against-the-anc-and-state-corruption/

Guvenli, T., & Sanyal, R. (2012). Perception and Understanding of Bribery in International Business. *Ethics & Behaviour, 22*(5), 333–348.

Gyimah-Boadi, E. (2004). Africa: The Quality of Political Reform. In E. Gyimah-Boadi (Ed.), *Democratic Reform in Africa: The Quality of Progress* (pp. 5–27). Lynne Rienner Publishers.

Gyimah-Boadi, E. (2007). Political Parties, Elections and Patronage: Random Thought on Neo-Patrimonialism and African Democratization. In M. Basedau, G. Erdmann, & A. Mehler (Eds.), *Votes, Money and Violence: Political Parties and Elections in Sub-Saharan Africa*. University of KwaZulu-Natal Press.

Haberly, D., & Wójcik, D. (2015). Regional Blocks and Imperial Legacies: Mapping the Global Offshore FDI Networks. *Economic Geography, 91*(3), 251–280.

Habib, M., & Zurawicki, L. (2002). Corruption and Foreign Direct Investment. *Journal of International Business Studies, 33*(2), 291–307.

Harvey, R. (2022, July 18). José Eduardo dos Santos – A Legacy of Kleptocracy. *Good Governance Africa*. https://gga.org/jose-eduardo-eduardo-dos-santos-a-legacy-of-kleptocracy/

Henry, J. S. (2012). The Price of Offshore Revisited: New Estimates for Missing Global Private Wealth, Income, Inequality and Lost Taxes. *Tax Justice Network*. Retrieved January, 2024, from http://taxjustice.nonprofitsoapbox.com/storage/documents/The_Price_of_Offshore_Revisited_-_22-07-2012.pdf

Herbst, J. (2014). *States and Power in Africa: Comparative Lessons in Authority and Control*. Princeton University Press.

Herman, P. (2017, May 29). ANC MPs Must Vote In Line with Caucus – NEC. *News24*. Retrieved February, 2024, from https://www.news24.com/news24/anc-mps-must-vote-in-line-with-caucus-nec-20170529

Hillbom, E. (2012). Botswana: A Development-Oriented Gate-Keeping State. *African Affairs, 111*(442), 67–89.

HLP. (2007). *Illicit Financial Flows*. Report of the High-Level Panel on Illicit Financial Flows from Africa, Commissioned by the AU/ECA Conference of Ministers of Finance, Planning and Economic Development.

Hodge, N. (2022, December 6). Glencore to Pay $180M in DRC Corruption Case. *Compliance Week*. Retrieved March, 2024, from https://www.complianceweek.com/regulatory-enforcement/glencore-to-pay-180m-in-drc-corruption-case/32420.article

Hönke, J. (2018). Beyond the Gatekeeper State: African Infrastructure Hubs as Sites of Experimentation. *Third World Thematics: A TWQ Journal, 13*(3), 347–363.

Hwang, J., Jung, K.-O., & Lim, E.-S. (2011). Corruption and Growth in an Ethnically Fragmented World. *The Journal of Developing Areas, 44*(2), 265–277.

Ibrahim, M., Kumi, E., & Yeboah, T. (2015). Greasing or Sanding the Wheels? Effect of Corruption on Economic Growth in Sub Saharan Africa. *African Journal of Economic and Sustainable Development, 4*(2), 157–173.

IMF. (2021). Tax Avoidance in Sub-Saharan Africa's Mining Sector. *Working Paper No. DP/2021/022*. International Monetary Fund.

ISS Africa. (2017). Equatorial Guinea's Web of Wealth and Repression. *Institute of Security Studies Africa*. Retrieved March, 2024, from https://issafrica.org/about-us/press-releases/equatorial-guineas-web-of-wealth-and-repression

Jain, A. (2001). Corruption: A Review. *Journal of Economic Surveys, 75*(1), 71–121.

Jeffries, R. (1993). The State, Structural Adjustment and Good Government in Africa. *The Journal of Commonwealth & Comparative Politics, 31*(1), 20–35.

Jetter, M., Agudelo, A. M., & Hassan, A. R. (2015). The Effect of Democracy on Corruption: Income is Key. *World Development, 74*, 286–304.

Justesen, M. K., & Bjornskov, C. (2014). Exploiting the Poor: Bureaucratic Corruption and Poverty in Africa. *World Development, 58*, 106–115.

Kar, D., & Cartwright-Smith, D. (2007). *Illicit Financial Flows from Developing Countries, 2002–2006*. Global Financial Integrity, Center for International Policy.

Kar, D., & Cartwright-Smith, D. (2010). *Illicit Financial Flows from Africa: Hidden Resource for Development*. Global Financial Integrity.

Kar, D., & Leblanc, B. (2013). *Illicit Financial Flows from Developing Countries: 2002–2011*. Global Financial Integrity.

Karl, T. L. (1997). *The Paradox of Plenty: Oil Booms and Petro-States*. University of California Press.

Khodapanah, M., Shabani, Z. D., Akbarzadeh, M. H., & Shojaeian, M. (2020). Spatial Spillover Effects of Corruption in Asian Countries: Spatial Econometric Approach. *Regional Science Policy & Practice, 14*(4), 699–717.

Kolstad, I., & Wiig, A. (2016). Does Democracy Reduce Corruption? *Democratization, 23*(7), 1198–1215.

Kossele, T. P. Y., & Mbai-Akem, M. G. N. (2020). Capital Flight and Extent of Corruption Control in the Least Corrupt African Countries: An Empirical Assessment. *Indian Growth and Development Review, 13*(3), 469–483.

Krifa-Schneider, H., Matei, I., & Sattar, A. (2022). FDI, Corruption and Financial Development Around the World: A Panel Non-Linear Approach. *Economic Modelling, 110*, 105809.

Kunicová, J. (2006). Democratic Institutions and Corruption. In S. Rose-Ackerman (Ed.), *International Handbook on the Economics of Corruption* (pp. 140–160). Edward Elgar.

Kunicová, J., & Rose-Ackerman, S. (2005). Electoral Rules and Constitutional Structures as Constraints on Corruption. *British Journal of Political Science, 35*(4), 573–606.

La Porta, R., Lopez-De-Silanes, F., Shleifer, A., & Vishny, R. (1999). The Quality of Government. *Journal of Law, Economics & Organisation, 15*(1), 222–279.

Le Billon, P. (2011). Extractive Sectors and Illicit Financial Flows. *U4 Issue 13.* CMI Anti-Corruption Resource Centre.

Lindberg, S. I., & Meerow, S. (2011). Persistent Authoritarianism and the Future of Democracy in Africa. In N. Brown (Ed.), *The Dynamics of Democratization: Dictatorship, Development, and Diffusion.* The John Hopkins University Press.

Lipton, E. (2021, March 8). Sanctions Are Reimposed on Israeli Billionaire Granted Relief Under Trump. *The New York Times.* Retrieved March, 2024, from https://www.nytimes.com/2021/03/08/us/politics/dan-gertler-sanctions.html

Lui, F. T. (1985). An Equilibrium Queuing Model of Bribery. *Journal of Political Economy, 93*, 760–781.

Luiz, J. M., & Stewart, C. (2014). Corruption, South African Multinational Enterprises and Institutions in Africa. *Journal of Business Ethics, 124*(3), 383–398.

Madonsela, S. (2019). Critical Reflections on State Capture in South Africa. *Insight on Africa, 11*(1), 113–130.

Márquez, M. A., Salinas-Jiménez, J., & del Mar Salinas-Jiménez, M. (2011). Exploring Differences in Corruption: The Role of Neighbouring Countries. *Journal of Economic Policy Reform, 14*(1), 11–19.

Mauro, P. (1995). Corruption and Growth. *Quarterly Journal of Economics, 110*(3), 681–712.

Mauro, P. (1998). Corruption and the Composition of Government Expenditure. *Journal of Public Economics, 69*, 263–279.

Mbaku, J. M. (2010). *Corruption in Africa: Causes Consequences, and Cleanups.* Lexington Books.

Meagher, P., & Thomas, M. (2004). A Corruption Primer: An Overview of Concepts in the Corruption Literature. *Discussion Papers on Institutions and Development No. 04/03.* Centre for Institutional Reform, and the Informal Sector (IRIS), University of Maryland.

Medie, P. A. (2018). The Police: Laws, Prosecutions and Women's Rights in Liberia. In N. Cheeseman (Ed.), *Institutions and Democracy in Africa.* Cambridge University Press.

Mohtadi, H., & Roe, T. L. (2003). Democracy, Rent Seeking, Public Spending and Growth. *Journal of Public Economics, 87*(3–4), 445–466.

Momoniat, I. (2023, April 10). How and Why Did State Capture and Massive Corruption Occur in South Africa? *IMF Public Financial Management Blog.* Retrieved January, 2024, from https://blog-pfm.imf.org/en/pfm-blog/2023/04/how-and-why-did-state-capture-and-massive-corruption-occur-in-south-africa

Moore, M., Prichard, W., & Fjeldstad, O. (2018). *Taxing Africa: Coercion, Reform and Development.* Zed Books.

Moreno, A. (2002). Corruption and Democracy: A Cultural Assessment. *Comparative Sociology, 1*(3–4), 495–507.

Mucari, M., Ridley, K., & Tobin, S. (2023, September 29). Explainer: Why Has Mozambique Sued Credit Suisse Over the 'Tuna Bonds'? *Reuters.* Retrieved January, 2024, from https://www.reuters.com/business/finance/why-has-mozambique-sued-credit-suisse-over-tuna-bonds-2023-09-29/

Murphy, K. M., Shleifer, A., & Vishny, R. W. (1991). The Allocation of Talent: Implications for Growth. *Quarterly Journal of Economics, 106*, 503–530.

Murphy, R. (2012). *Closing the European Tax Gap: A Report for Group of the Progressive Alliance of Socialists and Democrats in the European Parliament.* Tax Research LLP.

Ndikumana, L., & Boyce, J. K. (2011). Capital Flight from Sub-Saharan Africa: Linkages with External Borrowing and Policy Options. *International Review of Applied Economics, 25*(2), 149–170.

Ndikumana, L., & Boyce, J. K. (2022). Why Care About Capital Flight? In L. Ndikumana & J. K. Boyce (Eds.), *On the Trail of Capital Flight from Africa: The Takers and the Enablers.* Oxford University Press.

Ndikumana, L., & Sarr, M. (2019). Capital Flight, Foreign Direct Investment and Natural Resources in Africa. *Resources Policy, 63*, 101427.

Newsweek. (2003, December 7). Sifting Through A Dark Business. Retrieved January, 2024, from https://www.newsweek.com/sifting-through-dark-business-131907

Nkurunziza, J. D. (2015). Capital Flight and Poverty Reduction in Africa. In I. Ajayi & L. Ndikumana (Eds.), *Capital Flight from Africa: Causes, Effects and Policy Issues* (pp. 81–110). Oxford University Press.

OECD. (2012). *Development Aid at a Glance.* Organisation for Economic Co-operation and Development Table 2.2.9.

Omeje, K. (2021). *The Failure and Feasibility of Capitalism in Africa.* Palgrave Macmillan.

Omoteso, K., & Mobolaji, H. I. (2013). Corruption, Governance and Economic Growth in Sub-Saharan Africa: A Need for the Prioritisation of Reform Policies. *Social Responsibility Journal, 10*(2), 316–330.

Open Secrets. (2022). *Wanted: The State Capture Conspirators.* Open Secrets.

Osei-Assibey, E., Domfeh, K. O., & Danquah, M. (2018). Corruption, Institutions and Capital Flight: Evidence from Sub-Saharan Africa. *Journal of Economic Studies, 45*(1), 59–76.

Otusanya, O. J., Liu, J., & Lauwo, S. G. (2022). Influence of Tax Dodging on Tax Justice in Developing Countries: Some Theory and Evidence from Sub-Saharan Africa. *Journal of Financial Crime, 30*(2), 332–360.

Palan, R., Murphy, R., & Chavagneux, C. (2010). *Tax Havens: How Globalization Really Works.* Cornell University Press.

Paldam, M. (2002). The Cross-Country Pattern of Corruption: Economics, Culture and the Seesaw Dynamics. *European Journal of Political Economy, 18*(2), 215–240.

Pani, M. (2011). Hold Your Nose and Vote: Corruption and Public Decisions in a Representative Democracy. *Public Choice, 148*(1–2), 163–196.

Perez, M. F., Brada, J. C., & Drabek, Z. (2012). Illicit Money Flows as Motives for FDI. *Journal of Comparative Economics, 40*, 108–126.

Persson, T., & Tabellini, G. (2009). The Nexus of Political and Economic Change. *American Economic Journal: Macroeconomics, 1*(2), 88–126.

Persson, T., Roland, G., & Tabellini, G. (2000). "Comparative Politics and Public Finance," *Journal of Political Economy*, 108(6), 1121–1161.

PMG. (2017, August 7). Infographic: Motions of No Confidence – The Zuma Years. *Parliamentary Monitoring Group*. Retrieved March, 2024, from https://pmg.org.za/blog/infographic-motions-no-confidence-zuma-years

Quazi, R., Vemuri, V., & Soliman, M. (2014). Impact of Corruption on Foreign Direct Investment in Africa. *International Business Research, 7*(4), 1–10.

Reuters. (2012, December 3). IMF Halts Congo Loan over Mining Contract Concerns. Retrieved January, 2024, from https://www.reuters.com/article/idUSL5E8N3F6G/

Robinson, J. A., Torvik, R., & Verdier, T. (2006). Political Foundations of the Resource Curse. *Journal of Development Economics, 79*(2), 447–468.

Rock, M. T. (2009). Corruption and Democracy. *Journal of Development Studies, 45*(1), 55–75.

Rose-Ackerman, S., & Palifka, B. J. (2016). *Corruption and Government: Causes, Consequences, and Reform.* Cambridge University Press.

Ross, M. (1999). The Political Economy of the Resource Curse. *World Politics, 51*(2), 297–322.

Sachs, J. D. (2007). How to Handle the Macroeconomics of Oil Wealth. In M. Humphreys, J. D. Sachs, & J. E. Stiglitz (Eds.), *Escaping the Resource Curse.* Columbia University Press.

Saha, B., & Thampy, T. (2006). Extractive Bribe and Default in Subsidized Credit Programs. *Journal of Economic Behavior and Organization, 60*, 182–204.

Salisu, A. A., & Isah, K. O. (2021). Capital Flight-Growth Nexus in Sub-Saharan Africa: The Role of Macroeconomic Uncertainty. *The Journal of Developing Areas, 55*(1), 167–184.

Sandbrook, R. (2000). *Closing the Circle: Democratization and Development in Africa.* Zed Books.

Schlenther, B. O. (2016). Addressing Illicit Financial Flows in Africa How Broad is the Whole of Government Approach Supposed to be? *Journal of Financial Crime, 23*(4), 1074–1091.

Schneider, C. Q., & Schmitter, P. C. (2004). Liberalization, Transition and Consolidation: Measuring the Components of Democratization. *Democratization, 11*(5), 59–90.

Segal, D. (2018, February 4). How Bell Pottinger, P.R. Firm for Despots and Rogues, Met Its End in South Africa. *The New York Times*. Retrieved March, 2024, from https://www.nytimes.com/2018/02/04/business/bell-pottinger-guptas-zuma-south-africa.html

Sekkat, K., Fhima, F., & Nouira, R. (2024). Does the Control of Corruption Cause Progress in Democracy and if so, Through which Channels? A Threshold Non-Linear Analysis. *Democratization*. Retrieved August, 2024, from https://doi.org/10.1080/13510347.2024.2326842

Serra, D. (2006). Empirical Determinants of Corruption: A Sensitivity Analysis. *Public Choice, 126*, 225–256.

Shah, A. S. (2006). Corruption and Decentralized Public Governance. *Policy Research Working Paper No. 3824*. World Bank.

Shaxson, N. (2019). Tackling Tax Havens. *International Monetary Fund*. Retrieved May, 2023, from https://www.imf.org/en/Publications/fandd/issues/2019/09/tackling-global-tax-havens-shaxon

Shleifer, A., & Vishny, R. (1993). Corruption. *Quarterly Journal of Economics, 108*(3), 599–617.

Smarzynska, B. K., & Wei, S.-J. (2000). Corruption and the Composition of Foreign Direct Investment – Firm-Level Evidence. *Policy Research Working Paper Series 2360*. The World Bank.

Stephenson, M. C. (2015). Chapter 4: Corruption and Democratic Institutions: A Review and Synthesis. In S. Rose-Ackerman & P. Lagunes (Eds.), *Greed, Corruption, and the Modern State*. Edward Elgar Publishing.

Straub, S. (2008). Opportunism, Corruption and the Multinational Firm's Mode of Entry. *Journal of International Economics, 74*, 245–263.

Sui, B., Feng, G. F., & Chang, C. P. (2018). The Pioneer Evidence of Contagious Corruption. *Quality & Quantity, 52*, 945–968.

Sung, H.-E. (2003). Fairer Sex or Fairer System? Gender and Corruption Revisited. *Social Forces, 82*(2), 703–723.

Swamy, R., Knack, S., & Azfar, O. (2001). Gender and Corruption. *Journal of Development Economics, 64*(1), 25–55.

Tanzi, V., & Davoodi, H. (2000). Corruption, Growth, and Public Finances. *Working Paper No. 00/182*. International Monetary Fund.

Tatah, M. (2017). *Africa in the Colonial Ages of Empire: Slavery, Capitalism, Racism, Colonialism, Decolonization, Independence as Recolonization*. Langaa RPCIG.

The Economist. (2013, February 16). Storm Survivors: Special Report: Offshore Finance. Retrieved January, 2024, from https://www.economist.com/sites/default/files/20130216_offshore_finance.pdf

Tobin, S. (2023, October 19). Mozambique's $3.1 bln Lawsuit Against Shipbuilder Politically Motivated, UK Court Told. *Reuters*. Retrieved January, 2024, from https://www.reuters.com/business/mozambiques-31-bln-lawsuit-against-shipbuilder-politically-motivated-uk-court-2023-10-19/

Transparency International France. (2021, July 30). Definitive Conviction of Teodorin Obiang in France Sends Strong Message, Allows Asset Restitution to Equatorial Guinea. Retrieved January, 2024, from https://www.transparency.org/en/press/teodorin-obiang-conviction-asset-recovery-equatorial-guinea-france

Treisman, D. (2000). The Causes of Corruption: A Cross-National Study. *Journal of Public Economics, 76*(3), 399–457.

Tuliao, K. V., & Chen, C. W. (2017). CEO Duality and Bribery: The Roles of Gender and National Culture. *Management Decision, 55*(1), 218–231.

Uhlenbruck, K., Rodriguez, P., Doh, J., & Eden, L. (2006). The Impact of Corruption on Entry Strategy: Evidence from Telecommunications Projects in Emerging Economies. *Organization Science, 17*, 402–414.

UNCTAD. (2007). *World Investment Report: Transnational Corporations, Extractive Industries and Development*. United Nations Conference on Trade and Development.

UNCTAD. (2020). *Economic Development in Africa Report 2020: Tackling Illicit Financial Flows for Sustainable Development in Africa*. United Nations Conference on Trade and Development.

United Nations. (2011). *Combating Corruption, Improving Governance in Africa: Regional Anti-Corruption Programme for Africa (2011–2016)*. Economic Commission for Africa, Governance and Public Administration Division (GPAD) Programme Document. Retrieved January, 2024, from https://repository.uneca.org/handle/10855/23273

UN-MDG. (2013). *The Millennium Development Goals Report*. Retrieved January, 2024, from http://www.un.org/millenniumgoals/pdf/report-2013/mdg-report-2013-english.pdf

Van Niekerk, P. (2023, March). After Impoverishing Millions Around the World for Decades, Glencore Finally Gets Slapped by US Courts. *Daily Maverick*. Retrieved January, 2024, from https://www.dailymaverick.co.za/article/2023-03-09-after-impoverishing-millions-around-the-world-for-decades-glencore-finally-gets-slapped-by-u%E2%80%A6

Voyer, P. A., & Beamish, P. W. (2004). The Effect of Corruption on Japanese Foreign Direct Investment. *Journal of Business Ethics, 50*, 211–224.

Warf, B. (2016). Global Geographies of Corruption. *GeoJournal, 81*(5), 657–669.

Warf, B. (2017). Geographies of African Corruption. *PSU Research Review, 1*(1), 20–38.

Wei, S. J. (1997). Why is Corruption So Much More Taxing than Tax? Arbitrariness Kills. *NBER Paper No. w6255*. National Bureau of Economic Research.

Wei, S. J. (2000). How Taxing is Corruption on International Investors? *Review of Economics and Statistics, 82*, 1–11.

Wheeler, D., & Mody, A. (1992). International Investment Location Decisions: The Case of U.S. Firms. *Journal of International Economics, 33*, 57–76.

Winters, M. S., & Weitz-Shapiro, R. (2013). Lacking Information or Condoning Corruption: When Do Voters Support Corrupt Politicians? *Comparative Politics, 45*(4), 418–436.

Woo, J. Y. (2010). The Impact of Corruption on a Country's FDI Attractiveness: A Panel Data Analysis, 1984–2004. *Journal of International and Area Studies, 17*(2), 71–91.

World Bank. (2018, September). Global Cost of Corruption at Least 5 Per Cent of World Gross Domestic Product, Secretary-General Tells Security Council, Citing World Economic Forum Data. Retrieved January, 2024, from https://press.un.org/en/2018/sc13493.doc.htm

World Economic Forum. (2018, December). Corruption Is Costing the Global Economy USD 3.6 Trillion Dollars Every Year. Retrieved January, 2024, from https://www.weforum.org/agenda/2018/12/the-global-economy-loses-3-6-trillion-to-corruption-each-year-says-u-n

Zalanga, S. (2018). The Political Economy of Corruption. In S. O. Oloruntoba & T. Falola (Eds.), *The Palgrave Handbook of African Politics, Governance and Development* (pp. 869–882). Palgrave Macmillan.

Zucman, G. (2014). Taxing Across Borders: Tracking Personal Wealth and Corporate Profits. *Journal of Economic Perspectives, 28*(4), 121–148.

CHAPTER 6

The Effects of China, India, and Russia's Competing Strategies on FDI to Sub-Saharan Africa

In Africa, trade volumes, wealth accumulation, capital inflows, and international integration still trail behind the rest of the world. While the continent comprises 17% of the globe population, Africa only comprises 3% of the global economy (Cilliers, 2023) despite having the most youthful and fastest growing population in the world (Hastings, 2022). It has been estimated that Africa's population will reach 1.7 billion people by 2030, of which around 50% will live in the seven countries of Democratic Republic of Congo (DRC), Egypt, Ethiopia, Kenya, Nigeria, Tanzania, and South Africa. In addition, the middle and upper classes are expected to increase from 35% to 43% of the population, having a shared consumer and business expenditure of USD 6.7 trillion and household consumption of USD 2.5 trillion, of which nearly half will be spent in the three countries of Nigeria (20%), Egypt (17%), and South Africa (11%) (Signe, 2018).

A crucial factor in SSA's development will be the African Continental Free Trade Agreement (ACFTA). According to UNCTAD (2021), the ACFTA will be "a game changer for development ambitions in Africa" as it will encourage inclusive growth and further the AU's aims of the 2030 Agenda for Sustainable Development and Agenda 2063 by establishing the largest free trade area since the inception of the World Trade Organisation (WTO) (Tralac, 2019). Progress towards economic integration in Africa began during the 1970s with the formation of the eight African Regional Economic Communities (RECs), but it was only after

S. Gossel, *The Promise and Peril of FDI in Sub-Saharan Africa*, Palgrave Studies in African and Development Economics, https://doi.org/10.1007/978-3-032-01320-0_6

the adoption of the Abuja Treaty in 1991 that the RECs focussed on becoming integrated free trade blocs (Woolfrey et al., 2019). However, progress of the RECs towards African integration has been mixed. As can be seen from Table 6.1, some countries are not well integrated, many RECs are dominated by the most powerful economies in their respective RECs, and many countries fall in overlapping RECs (UNCTAD, 2021).

Table 6.2(a) further shows that the Community of Sahel-Saharan States (CEN-SAD) has the highest levels of GDP, trade, and FDI, which is unsurprising since it has the highest number of member states (25). In contrast, the East African Community (EAC) has the lowest economic indicators even though the Arab Maghreb Union (AMU) has less member states (8 versus 5 respectively), possibly reflecting the fragile conflict-ridden economies of South Sudan, Burundi, and the DRC. Table 6.2(b) shows that the South African Development Community (SADC) has the lowest tariff rates whereas the Economic Community of Central African States (ECCAS) has the highest. Between these two poles, the remaining RECs have tariffs that average around 10.6%. With regards to commodity dependence in Table 6.2(c), the Economic Community of West African States (ECOWAS) has the highest exports of agricultural products (12.14% of merchandise exports), the Economic Community of Central African States (ECCAS) and the Arab Maghreb Union (AMU) have the highest oil rents (13.26% and 13.05% of GDP respectively), and the South African Development Community (SADC) have the highest ores and metals exports (17.02% of merchandise exports). Consequently, inter-African trade has been hampered by low levels of complementarity and diversification, weak productive capacities, high tariff and non-tariff trade regimes (UNCTAD, 2021).

It is envisaged that over the next decade, the ACFTA will dismantle 97% of tariffs, boosting inter-African trade by 52% to USD 450 billion by 2035 (Mold, 2022). Despite this immense potential however, Mude (2020) points out that there are five complexities that the ACFTA will have to overcome. First, African states have historically been hesitant to yield their economic and regulatory sovereignty. Second, it is unclear how it will be possible to protect existing RECs from ACFTA-related intra-REC competition. Third, the ACFTA envisages the establishment of a dispute settlement mechanism to reduce or mitigate inter-state disputes, but this mechanism is likely to suffer from similar institutional weaknesses that bedevil SSA's other conflict resolution systems, such as the AU's Peace and Security Council. Fourth, many of the RECs are dominated by

Table 6.1 Regional Economic Communities

Country	*AMU*	*CEN-SAD*	*COMESA*	*EAC*	*ECCAS*	*ECOWAS*	*IGAD*	*SADC*
Algeria	x							
Angola					x			x
Benin		x				x		
Botswana								x
Burkina Faso		x				x		
Burundi			x	x	x			
Cabo Verde						x		
Cameroon					x			
Central African Republic		x			x			
Chad		x			x			
Comoros		x	x					x
Congo					x			
Cote d'Ivoire		x				x		
Democratic Republic of Congo			x	x	x			x
Djibouti		x	x				x	
Egypt		x	x					
Equatorial Guinea					x			
Eritrea		x	x				x	
Eswatini			x					x
Ethiopia			x				x	
Gabon					x			
Gambia		x				x		
Ghana		x				x		
Guinea		x				x		
Guinea-Bissau		x				x		
Kenya			x	x			x	
Lesotho								x
Liberia						x		
Libya	x	x	x					
Madagascar			x					x
Malawi			x					x
Mali		x				x		
Mauritania	x	x						
Mauritius			x					x

(*continued*)

Table 6.1 (continued)

Country	*AMU*	*CEN-SAD*	*COMESA*	*EAC*	*ECCAS*	*ECOWAS*	*IGAD*	*SADC*
Morocco	x	x						
Mozambique								x
Namibia								x
Niger		x				x		
Nigeria		x				x		
Rwanda			x	x	x			
Sao Tome and Principe					x			
Senegal		x				x		
Seychelles			x					x
Sierra Leone		x				x		
Somalia		x		x			x	
South Africa								x
South Sudan				x			x	
Sudan		x	x				x	
Tanzania				x				x
Togo		x						
Tunisia	x	x						
Uganda			x	x			x	
Zambia			x					x
Zimbabwe			x					x
Total	5	25	19	8	11	14	8	16

AMU = Arab Maghreb Union; CEN-SAD = Community of Sahel-Saharan States; COMESA = Common Market for Eastern and Southern Africa; EAC = East African Community; ECCAS = Economic Community of Central African States; ECOWAS = Economic Community of West African States; IGAD = Intergovernmental Authority on Development; SADC = Southern African Development Community

a few economies (such as Nigeria in CEN-SAD and ECOWAS, and South Africa in SADC) and it is unclear how the ACFTA will lessen these economic rivalries while also fostering development of the region's weaker states. Finally, there is the risk that the adoption of the ACFTA common tariffs will be undercut by the overlapping tariff structures of the RECs.

Despite Africa being "the last frontier market" (Signe, 2018), over the last two decades, Western countries have failed to secure their trade and investment in the region and only returned their gaze to the continent after China, India, and Russia's economic and political activities threatened to usurp Western interests. Since the global financial crisis, US trade

Table 6.2 Economic performance of the Regional Economic and Monetary Communities

Metric	*Measure*	*AMU [5]*	*CEN-SAD [25]*	*COMESA [19]*	*EAC [8]*	*ECCAS [11]*	*ECOWAS [14]*	*IGAD [8]*	*SADC [15]*
(a) Economic performance:									
Total GDP	Constant 2015 billions USD	7558.60	23734.08	14189.38	2846.44	3649.66	10977.19	4065.88	10942.13
Total exports of goods and services	Constant 2015 billions USD	2112.74	4323.92	3456.71	579.30	1187.68	822.51	1595.08	3062.49
Total imports of goods and services	Constant 2015 billions USD	2315.96	4864.08	3873.88	656.96	1270.54	993.15	1387.87	3259.40
Total net FDI inflows	Billions USD	125.37	454.57	309.84	49.18	86.39	195.91	86.36	225.77
(b) Tariffs:									
Average all products tariff rate	Applied weighted mean as %	11.49	11.23	9.27	9.25	12.74	10.53	10.34	6.37
Average manufactured products tariff rate	Applied weighted mean as %	11.48	11.21	9.13	8.20	12.05	10.38	10.89	6.21
Average primary products tariff rate	Applied weighted mean as %	11.28	11.66	9.80	12.28	15.42	10.99	11.10	6.51

(*continued*)

Table 6.2 (continued)

Metric	*Measure*	*AMU [5]*	*CEN-SAD [25]*	*COMESA [19]*	*EAC [8]*	*ECCAS [11]*	*ECOWAS [14]*	*IGAD [8]*	*SADC [16]*
(c) Commodities:									
Average agricultural raw materials exports	% of merchandise exports	0.45	9.49	4.21	6.07	8.84	12.14	8.39	2.97
Average oil rents	% of GDP	13.05	3.27	3.00	2.14	13.26	1.01	2.99	2.23
Average ores and metals exports	% of merchandise exports	13.20	9.58	11.15	10.28	12.04	9.26	1.72	17.02

[#] indicates the number of SSA countries in the sample. AMU = Arab Maghreb Union; CEN-SAD = Community of Sahel-Saharan States; COMESA = Common Market for Eastern and Southern Africa; EAC = East African Community; ECCAS = Economic Community of Central African States; ECOWAS = Economic Community of West African States; IGAD = Intergovernmental Authority on Development; SADC = Southern African Development Community

Data source: World Development Indicators (2000–2020)

with Africa fell from USD 142 billion in 2008 to USD 64 billion in 2021, accounting for around 1% of the USA's international commerce (Hastings, 2022). Countries such as China, India, and Russia have taken note and are actively seeking to entrench themselves as SSA's development partners and future beneficiaries of the region's potential and opportunities.

In the case of China and India, this attention generally coincides with their own economic liberalisation and renewed globalisation strategies. China's economic transformation is unprecedented in economic history, in the three decades after Deng Xiaoping's economic liberalisation, beginning in the 1970s, annual economic growth averaged 10% and trade volumes increased 70 times (Carmody, 2016, p. 72). Over the last two decades, China's GDP increased eight times, rapidly rising from being sixth to the second largest economy in the world, the largest trading economy in the world, the second largest source of FDI outflows, and the world's largest recipient of FDI inflows (Abegunrin & Manyeruke, 2020, p. 31). This rapid growth and development necessitated significant imports of raw materials, including a third of the world's steel production, 40% of the world's cement, 26% of the world's copper, and 40% of the world's oil output (Carmody, 2016, p. 72).

For Africa, China's emergence offers a means to cement a mutually beneficial economic and political alliance (Abegunrin & Manyeruke, 2020). China is Africa's largest trading partner, infrastructure financier, and the fastest growing source of FDI (Sun et al., 2017). China is also becoming a significant technological partner for Africa and "Chinese companies have become market leaders in African digital infrastructure, mostly because their Western competitors decided early in this century, badly mistakenly, that the local people were too poor to afford cellphones" (Hastings, 2022). By 2030, China is expected to cut between 85 and 100 million low-cost labour-intensive manufacturing jobs as the country moves away from low-skilled manufacturing while Africa will add 11 million new entrants into the labour market each year (ibid.). Africa will thus soon have the largest pool of available labour in the world, creating the opportunity for the continent to become the next manufacturing and supply centre (Sun, 2017).

Following India's economic liberalisation in the 1990s, the country has been an active investor in SSA, particularly in the manufacturing sectors of textiles, pharmaceuticals, automobiles, and machinery (Gopaldas, 2022) along with financial services and ICT (Khan & Arora, 2017). India has thus quickly risen to become Africa's third largest trading partner behind

China and the USA. In 2022, India's total trade with Africa was around USD 89 billion, which was about one third of China's trade with Africa (IISD, 2022). While it is not possible for India to compete with China on an investment or trade volume basis, it has been successful in establishing itself as a significant developmental partner alongside China by combining the "corporate sector, cultural and political linkages, an active diaspora, and the experience of Indian businesses in navigating complex and diverse landscapes" (Gopaldas, 2022).

Russia in contrast may not have as large an economic footprint in SSA as China and India, but it does have significant soft power from the USSR's support of many of SSA's liberation movements and socialist governments during the Cold War. However, during 2016–2020, Russia accounted for only 2% of Africa's total trade, and in 2020, before the Russian invasion of Ukraine, exports from Africa to Russia were just USD 1.4 billion (0.4% of Africa's total exports) while imports from Russia were USD 8.5 billion (1.7% of Africa's total imports) (EIU, 2022). While both China and India have promoted themselves as more impartial developmental partners than Western countries, claiming to offer trade, investment, credit, and technical and human resources without the common Western conditions of "governance, fairness and sustainability" (Chakrabarti & Ghosh, 2014), Russia's modern interaction with the continent is as much political as economic.

In the years after the fall of the Berlin Wall, Russia gradually re-established economic interests in SSA's natural resource extraction, food supply, weaponry, and energy provision (Lopes, 2022). Hence, as China and India cemented their power and dominance in SSA, Russia turned to military supply and services to tie African countries to its political and diplomatic vision. Even before the Russian invasion of Ukraine, this strategy was deemed to be vitally important both for the supply of strategic natural resources (such as uranium, manganese, bauxite, and chromium) and to project Russia's political power on the world stage (El-Badawy et al., 2022).

Nevertheless, while Russia seeks to position itself alongside other powerful nations, this is undercut by its relatively small economy, which is the 11th largest economy in the world (Lopes, 2022). In addition, Russia has gained a reputation for fomenting instability in SSA through its use of mercenaries, especially the infamous Wagner Group (Hastings, 2022). It could however be argued that African leaders are aware that Russia is trying to 'punch above its weight' and therefore "play the game because they benefit from rivalries between Russia and the West and the constant questioning of the latter's hegemony" (Lopes, 2022). Russia does not pressure African leaders to accept its transactional bilateral engagements and, rather than complex negotiations, prefers to enter agreements through closed-door political connections, thus ensuring that the resultant rents underpinning the transactions are kept secret (ibid.).

The complex interactions between China, India, and Russia in SSA have been further compounded by the war in Ukraine. SSA has been a region of contestation between the world powers for the last half-century (Giles, 2013), and this has only increased in the wake of the Russian invasion. Russia's economy is overly dependent on natural resources and is suffering from the side-effects of an aging population (in common with many other nations in Europe and Asia) (Lukyanets et al., 2021). Consequently, Russia has sought to use the power of its allies, especially China, to project its own resilience. Hence, "the war in Ukraine serves as a proxy for the confrontation between Russia and the West, and it allows Russia to check the solidity of its alliance with China. At the same time, Russia serves as a proxy between the West and China regarding shaping future global governance" (Lopes, 2022).

Even before the war in Ukraine, SSA was suffering from the socio-economic hardships arising from the Covid pandemic, the subsequent stimulus policies in developed countries, and the global supply chain disruptions, plunging eight SSA countries into debt distress and a further 13 at risk of debt distress (Chingono, 2024). Coupled with the geopolitical instability in the wake of the Russian invasion, SSA has experienced significantly negative food insecurity. In 2020, African countries imported USD 4 billion of wheat, maize, barley, rye, and vegetable or seed oils from Russia (EIU, 2022). Wheat imports alone made up about 90% of Africa's USD 4 billion trade with Russia and around half of Africa's USD 1.5 billion trade with Ukraine (McBain, 2022).[1] Following the invasion however, oil, food, and fertiliser prices increased by 40%, 10%, and 55% respectively (ODI, 2024). Hence, it has been estimated that extreme poverty in SSA will increase by 18 million Africans in 2022 and a further 21 million in 2023 (Lopes, 2022).

[1] The SSA countries that are most reliant on wheat imports are the Democratic Republic of Congo, Sierra Leone, Zambia, Ethiopia, Malawi, Sudan, Mozambique, and Burundi (EIU, 2022).

In addition to affecting food supply and prices, the war in Ukraine is also reshaping global geopolitics. Although Russia's influence in Africa predates the Ukraine war, the extent to which Russia can continue to militarily and politically support weak and unstable SSA governments will depend on the losses it suffers in Ukraine. Having already lost a conservative estimate of 50,000 soldiers (Kinetz, 2023), and 21,000 Wagner Group mercenaries (Knight et al., 2023), it is unclear whether Russia will have the resources to continue its operations in Africa. In addition, the international sanctions imposed on Russia by Western nations will complicate Russia's trade and investment in SSA, making the pre-invasion strategy of military support in exchange for natural resources more difficult (EIU, 2022). Before the war, Russia signed deals with several African countries to supply nuclear energy. However, the cost of the war for Russia and high debt levels in Africa could mean that the capital to finance the agreements may be unavailable (Lopes, 2022).

The war in Ukraine is also affecting China's Belt and Road Initiative (BRI), which is at the core of China's developmental strategy. The BRI encompasses six corridors: the New Eurasian Land Bridge (NELB); China-Mongolia-Russia Corridor; China-Central Asia-West-Asia Economic Corridor; China-Indochina Peninsula Economic Corridor; China-Pakistan Economic Corridor; and the Bangladesh-China-India-Myanmar Economic Corridor (Mendez et al., 2022). It is envisaged that the BRI will facilitate greater policy coordination among countries along the BRI corridors, heighten and develop infrastructure connectivity, stimulate and support trade, deepen financial integration, promote development of a unified financial system, promote cultural and academic interactions, and promote travel and tourism (ibid.).

Although Russia's invasion will affect all six BRI corridors, it is likely to affect the NELB the worst because of this corridor's sizeable geographic span, running 10,900 km from China's east coast through Kazakhstan, Moldova, Russia, Belarus, Poland, and Germany (Wilson, 2022). Besides being the most expensive of the BRI corridors, and thus the most difficult to finance, the NELB also encompasses the increasingly sceptical EU member states of Poland and Germany, as well as the perceived Russia-friendly countries of Kazakhstan, Moldova, Belarus (Mendez et al., 2022). In addition, the underlying ideology of the BRI is that all member countries will endeavour to become more open by removing trade and investment barriers, but in the wake of the Russian invasion, countries in Europe are increasingly seeking to shore up EU security and reduce dependence on China, often at the risk of inter-regional co-operation (Brinza et al., 2024).

With rising East-West tensions, China is having to balance competing demands and priorities. On the one hand, Russia is China's second-largest provider of oil and third largest provider of natural gas; but on the other hand, close ties to Russia complicate the development of the NELB, which is reliant on EU support (Mendez et al., 2022). Perhaps sensing an opportunity to take advantage of a slower BRI, the US launched the USD 600 billion Partnership for Global Infrastructure Investment at the 2022 G-7 Summit,[2] which aims "to mobilize hundreds of billions of dollars in infrastructure financing – delivering energy, physical, digital, health, and climate-resilient infrastructure."[3] However, despite being conceived as a direct challenge to China's BRI, this initiative suffers from a lack of funding and has been received with cynicism by many African leaders (Hastings, 2022).

The Russia-Ukraine conflict has however been beneficial for India's international position. Perhaps as a result of being unencumbered by ambitious global and regional developmental plans, India has been able to successfully manage its international relationships better than China. By positioning itself as a counterbalance to China, India has been able to fill the gulf between the West and East by continuing to buy weapons and oil from Russia, while also calling for greater representation of developing countries in multinational organisations such as the United Nations Security Council (Gopaldas, 2022). This chapter further explores how China, India, and Russia have each adopted different strategies to engage with SSA politically and economically, while also exploring the implications for SSA's FDI in the ongoing contestation between the West and East.

[2] https://www.state.gov/bureaus-offices/secretary-of-state/office-of-the-u-s-special-coordinator-for-the-partnership-for-global-infrastructure-and-investment/ [accessed May 2024]

[3] https://www.whitehouse.gov/briefing-room/statements-releases/2023/05/20/fact-sheet-partnership-for-global-infrastructure-and-investment-at-the-g7-summit/ [accessed May 2024]

6.1 China

China has a long history of economic and political engagement with Africa, but modern China-Africa relations can generally be divided into three phases (Adisu et al., 2010). The first, from around 1850 to the 1950s, was mainly associated with the colonial labour needed in the agriculture, mining, and railway sectors along with the small-scale entrepreneurship that supplied the needs of the Chinese labourers. The second, from 1960 to the 1980s, coincided with the rise of African Socialism and the establishment of the People's Republic of China. During this time, China-Africa relations were largely political as China sought to challenge the economic and political hegemony of the West. After Deng Xiaoping's economic and political reforms, commencing in 1976, China moved away from isolationism while seeking to attract foreign investment and expand the domestic workforce. Gradually, China focussed its attention on the African continent as a ready source of much-needed natural resources and as a potential market for low-cost consumer goods (Abegunrin & Manyeruke, 2020, p. 29). The third period, from the 1990s to today, has been characterised by the globalisation strategy of 'Going Out' (*zou chu qu*) (Biggeri & Sanfilippo, 2009), which focusses on natural resource extraction and the internationalisation of Chinese companies coupled with the use of international diplomacy as a means to garner support for China's policies (Pannell, 2008).

At the dawn of the millennium, China formalised its interaction with SSA with the launch of the Forum on China-Africa Cooperation (FOCAC). Held every three years, FOCAC provides institutional support for bilateral and multilateral cooperation, built on "solidarity and cooperation based on equality, consultation, consensus, friendship, partnership, and mutual benefit" (Kinyondo, 2019). In tandem with China's evolving relationship with Africa, these benefits have evolved over time (Yu, 2022a, 2022b). In the initial phase, from 2000 to 2006, the focus of FOCAC was on broadening tariff-free imports from China, but from 2006 to the launch of the BRI, the focus expanded to include FDI, ODA (in the form of preferential loans and credit), and development finance.

In 2013, China launched the six trillion dollar "One Belt One Road Initiative" (BRI) (often referred to the Chinese Marshal Plan), which actively sought to "improve infrastructure, trade, financial integration, and people-to-people bonds across more than 70 countries (accounting for half of the world's population) in Asia, Africa, and Europe" using overland corridors ('belts') and maritime shipping lanes ('roads') (Abegunrin & Manyeruke, 2020, p. 31). As part of BRI, China has established ten centres to promote and facilitate Chinese investment and trade in SSA (Fijałkowski, 2011). Consequently, since 2015, FOCAC has shifted attention from trade and financial linkages to more explicit political cooperation under the philosophy of 'development for peace', in contrast to the Wests ideology of 'democracy for development' (Pádraig, 2016, pp. 183–193). Yet, in the wake of the Covid pandemic, FOCAC has not been as high level as in prior years. Economic slowdowns and the effects of the Russian invasion have also shifted the focus of FOCAC away from state-led development to private company supported development (Chen et al., 2024).

China's involvement in Africa has however been challenged by the West, which argues that the BRI and FOCAC are merely "neo-colonialism or a giant debt trap" (Abegunrin & Manyeruke, 2020, p. 47). The conflicting views of China's involvement in Africa have been characterised as the difference between the West's liberal "Washington Consensus," with its focus on good governance and conditionality (Williamson, 2012; Gokcekus & Suzuki, 2016) versus China's "Beijing Consensus" (Ramo, 2004), which does not consider governance or conditionality and thus "unlike many Western investors, corruption, crime and bureaucracy did not seem to disturb Chinese investors particularly" (Gu, 2009).

Critics have further argued that the increased presence of China in Africa has offset the reform pressure on African countries to improve human rights, strengthen institutions, and deepen governance (Halper, 2012, p. 76), and has therefore extended the durability of undemocratic and corrupt regimes (Gokcekus & Suzuki, 2016; Taylor, 2016, p. 86). Although there is evidence that SSA countries such as Egypt, Ethiopia, Mali, and Tanzania have benefited economically and politically from China's involvement (Berthelemy, 2011), at the same time China has been accused of eroding democratic governance, stability, and peace in SSA, particularly in Liberia, Sudan, and Zimbabwe (Mlambo et al., 2016). In addition, China's willingness to tolerate corruption and undermine environmental protection, human rights, and fair labour laws (Taylor, 2012, p. 111) in countries such as Algeria, Angola, Equatorial Guinea, Nigeria, Congo Republic, Sudan, and Zambia suggests that China's focus is on establishing extractive relationships to gain access to the primary commodities needed for its ongoing domestic industrialisation rather than for mutually beneficial development (Sutherland et al., 2020).

However, China's tolerance of corruption in investment destinations may simply be because Chinese state and private investors are used to dealing with high levels of corruption back in China and are more willing to invest in riskier destination because of Chinese government support (Lu et al., 2014; Quer et al., 2018). Furthermore, the necessity of gaining access to vital natural resources for development and growth in China my over-ride concerns about investing in corrupt SSA countries because the investments form part of larger political ambitions (Munjal et al., 2022). The polarity of West versus East may also be simplistic because it is typically framed within the ideological standards of the West. Consequently, the expected conduct of private companies when undertaking international business implicitly assumes conformity to the Western ideals of democratic free market governance and reforms (Ado & Su, 2016).

Despite the ideological differences, the evidence indicates that Chinese investment in SSA has benefited the region by raising the export prices of commodities, expanding the capacity of SSA countries to extract resources, and significantly improving infrastructure and manufacturing, which in turn have heightened employment, broadened market access, and lowered the prices of manufactured goods (Klaver & Trebilcock, 2011; Calabrese & Tang, 2022). In addition, Chinese firms employ 89% local labour, 64% of Chinese firms provide skills training to their employees, and 44% of firms employ local managers (Sun et al., 2017). Despite these benefits, the long-run gains are however debatable for three reasons. First, it is unclear whether the benefits from China's infrastructure investment in SSA outweigh the side-effects of cheap sub-standard labour, which in turn hinders domestic companies and employment (Ndhlovu, 2014). Second, the insular practises of Chinese firms raise doubts about the potential technological, human capital, and employment spillover effects (Liu, 2014). Third, it is possible that the ability of Chinese firms to out-compete SSA firms have deindustrialising and destabilising socio-economic effects on SSA's already weak manufacturing sectors (Giovannetti & Sanfilippo, 2009; Kaplinsky, 2008; Kaplinsky & Morris, 2008, 2009; He, 2020).

These complexities become more readily apparent in the context of SSA's human rights record. Unlike the West, which strongly considers human rights, democratic governance, and control of corruption when allocating aid and trade, China's policy of non-interference coupled with its poor record of domestic human rights adherence means that China channels investment to SSA countries regardless of SSA's poor human rights record (Doriye, 2010; De Grauwe et al., 2012). Critics argue however that historically, Western nations used free market capitalism to gain entry into resource-rich countries to similarly exploit natural resources while promoting liberal democracy as a means to curtail excessive government intervention in the economy (Taylor, 2016, p. 84).

The duality of "Washington Consensus" versus "Beijing Consensus" may thus be simplistic and could more meaningfully be viewed through the lens of Joseph Nye's "hard power" versus "soft power" (Nye, 2004). According to Nye, hard power is where a country uses economic inducement and military threats to get its way (Nye, 1990, p. 166) whereas soft power (Nye, 2009, p. 160) is the nurturing of allure to a country's "culture, political ideals and values, and foreign policy" (Repnikova, 2022, p. 2). Soft power is therefore "based on the assumption that an ability to attract others can change their preferences in a way that they act in the interests of the country projecting attractiveness" (Fijałkowski, 2011). Hard power thus tends to be overt while soft power is covert. In reality however, most countries (including China) tend to use a mix of hard and soft power, which Nye refers to as "smart power" (Nye, 2009).

China's foreign policy and economic involvement in SSA are not purely cultural or ideological (Power & Mohan, 2010), but instead focus on "international institution building, agenda setting, mobilization of coalitions, and ability to fulfil commitments" (Li, 2009, p. 26). China has been particularly successful in promoting the claim that it engages with foreign countries without political conditions, unlike the West, and that its interactions with SSA are underpinned by a 'brotherly partnership' that seeks to counter neo-colonialism and ensure a 'win-win' for the developing world built around South-South Cooperation (Bodomo, 2017, p. 36). In reality, these claims are incomplete because China does impose conditions, such as the non-recognition of Taiwan under the One-China policy (ibid., p. 36), and rather than being 'brotherly partnerships', China's labour relations and practises have often simply exported the exploitation common in Chinese companies to Chinese-owned and controlled companies in SSA (Carmody, 2016, p. 76), leading to the destruction of local industries, environmental degradation, and the flouting of labour standards (Koumou & Manyi, 2016).

A core feature of China's development model focusses on "economic development, flexibility and experimentation, strong leadership of the state in guiding and correcting the reform process, and the combination of active participation in globalization and autonomy" (Repnikova, 2022, p. 6). The 'soft power' goal of this strategy is to displace the democratic neo-liberal free market capitalism of the Washington Consensus and Bretton Woods institutions with authoritarian capitalism (Hou, 2014). Critics argue that China's model of state-led development offers limited alternatives to the West because, in common with neo-liberalism, China's model is also founded "on the exploitation of its vast pool of cheap labour, attracting foreign investment, and an increasingly liberalised economy" (ibid.). In addition, many developing countries were following developmental paths of industrialisation, and infrastructure and manufacturing development independently, and thus the 'China model' may exaggerate China's developmental influence rather than provide a replicable developmental path (Repnikova, 2022, p. 6). Furthermore, there are claims that China's use of soft power is merely to "cajole client states into accepting Chinese contracts" (Power & Mohan, 2010) while China's rapacious demand for natural resources has driven up commodity prices, cemented a neo-colonial relationship with African states, and entrenched an unequal trade relationship where SSA exports raw materials and imports the finished and cheap manufactured goods (Biggeri & Sanfilippo, 2009; Schiere, 2010).

In tandem with China's heightened economic activity in SSA, there has also been a significant rise in Chinese FDI. As can be seen from Fig. 6.1a, FDI stocks from China to Africa increased from just USD 491.2 million in 2003 to USD 43.4 billion in 2020 while FDI stocks from the USA increased from USD 19.8 billion in 2003, peaked at USD 69.0 billion in 2014, and then declined to USD 47.5 billion by 2020. Figure 6.1b further shows that while FDI flows from the USA peaked at USD 10.4

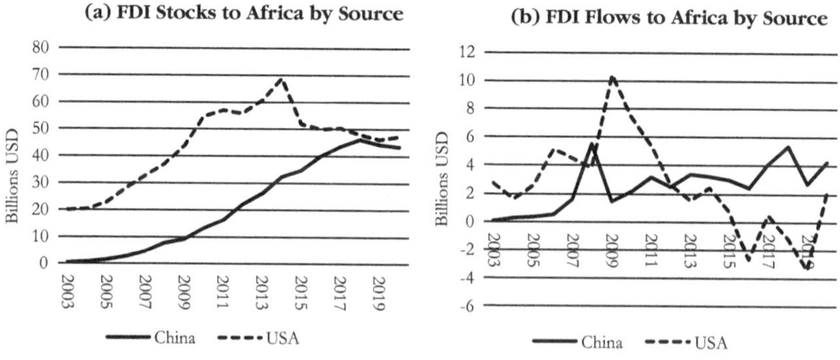

Fig. 6.1 China's FDI to SSA. (Data source: SAIS-CARI)

billion in 2009 and then declined thereafter, reaching USD 2.1 billion in 2020, FDI flows from China steadily increase from just USD 74.8 million in 2003 to USD 4.2 billion in 2020. Hence, FDI stocks from China to SSA are now nearly equal to those from the USA while FDI flows are double.

The accelerating influence of China in SSA has already challenged the economic and political footprint of the West (Ado & Su, 2016), crowding out FDI from the USA (Donou-Adonsou & Lim, 2018), and challenging the pre-eminence of FDI from the OECD (Yao & Wang, 2014). Empirically, it has also been found that Chinese FDI to SSA has significantly boosted economic growth (Whalley & Weisbrod, 2012; Doku et al., 2017), domestic per capita incomes (Donou-Adonsou & Lim, 2018; Zhang, 2021), employment (Khodeir, 2016), and industrialisation (Darko & Xu, 2022).

Figure 6.2 however shows that over the period of 2003–2020, most Chinese FDI was directed to SSA countries with significant natural resources[4] and growing markets for Chinese consumer goods. Excluding South Africa, which is both natural resource dependent and a significant consumer market, a total of USD 16.1 billion (49.8%) of Chinese FDI

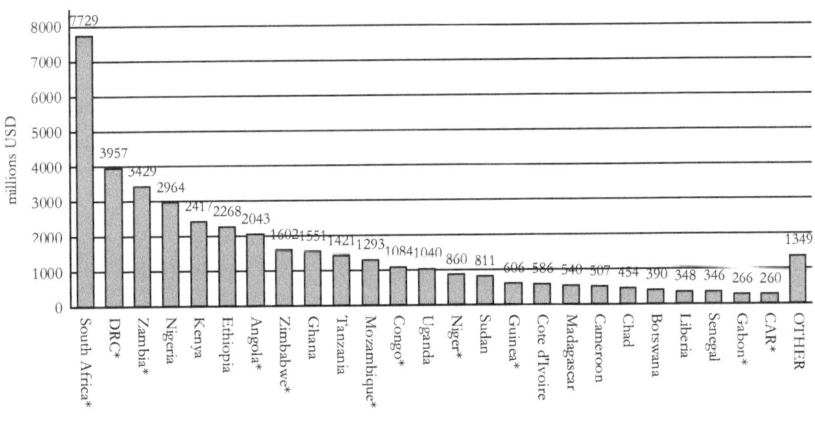

Fig. 6.2 Total Chinese FDI to SSA. (Data source: SAIS-CARI, 2003–2020, * indicates natural resource dependent)

[4] A country is deemed to be natural resource dependent if the average oil rents or ore and metal exports exceed 25% of GDP or merchandise exports respectively (IMF, 2012).

flowed to 17 natural resource SSA countries while USD 16.3 billion (50.2%) flowed to non-dependent countries.[5] This relatively even split between resource-dependent and non-dependent SSA countries supports studies such as Benfratello et al. (2023) who find that Chinese FDI is now as much market-seeking as resource-seeking.

However, a crucial difference between the West's interaction with SSA and China is that the West separated FDI, aid, and trade decades ago (Kaplinsky & Morris, 2009) whereas China views these three investment channels as an integrated portfolio. Consequently, Chinese infrastructure investment in host countries tends to attract Chinese FDI to that country, and Chinese FDI in turn stimulates trade (and vice versa) (Busse et al., 2016). Historically, Western FDI facilitated the exports of goods into international markets whereas Chinese FDI facilitated the exports of natural resources to China (ibid.). Hence, the West's FDI to SSA tended to be market-seeking whereas China's FDI tended to be resource-seeking (Ross, 2015). However, after the global financial crisis in 2008, there is evidence that China's FDI shifted to being equally market-seeking (Shan et al., 2018; Darko & Xu, 2022). In addition, Western FDI commonly entered investment destinations via stock markets and was thus beholden to risk appetite whereas China's FDI was channelled via its state-owned enterprises and thus reflected political rather than purely profit motives (Globerman & Shapiro, 2009; Morck et al., 2008; Kolstad & Wiig, 2012; Li, Van Assche, Fu, et al., 2022; Li, Van Assche, Li, & Qian, 2022). This strategy bolstered the competitiveness of Chinese firms with government support (Luo et al., 2010), which increased the willingness of China's FDI to invest in natural resource countries that had high political risk and weak institutions (Kang, 2018).

More recently however, Chinese FDI has moved away from being primarily state led and the number of private Chinese enterprises engaged in FDI investment in SSA is estimated to number over 10,000 of which a third are in manufacturing (Sun et al., 2017). Although, critics counter that in common with state-led FDI investors, these private investors are more focussed on establishing long-run relationships with SSA governments than primarily or exclusively on commercial success (Hong & Sun, 2006; Asongu & Aminkeng, 2013). However, this may be a necessity because as shown in Fig. 6.3, most of the Chinese FDI was directed to the

[5] Excludes the SSA countries of Benin, Burkina Faso, Equatorial Guinea, Eritrea, Namibia, Rwanda, and South Sudan, which are grouped under the Other category in Fig. 6.3.

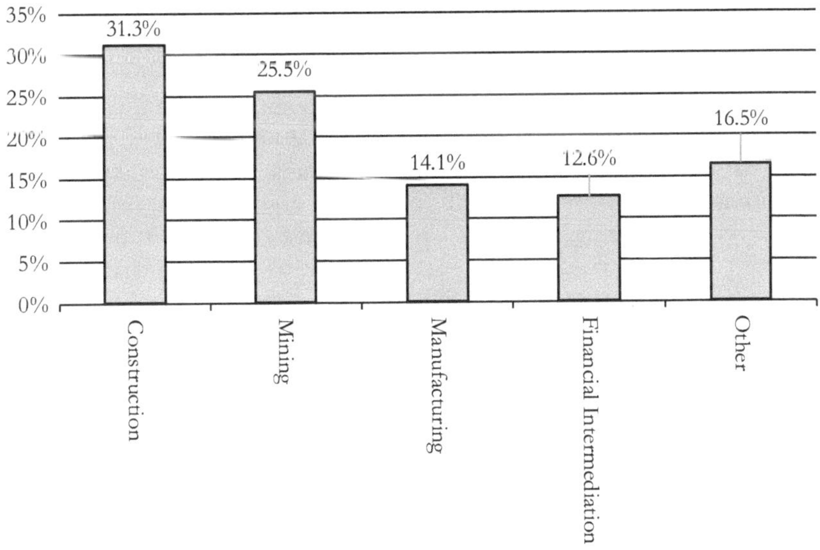

Fig. 6.3 Chinese FDI composition to SSA (Figure 6.3 excludes the two sectors of leasing and commercial services, and scientific research and technological services due to paucity of the data.). (Data source: SAIS-CARI, 2013–2020)

construction (USD 92.2 billion) and mining (USD 75.0 billion) sectors, which typically requires government approvals and involvement.

In addition, among the studies that find that Chinese FDI is attracted by natural resources (Asiedu, 2006; Buckley et al., 2007; Sanfilippo, 2010; Ramasamy et al., 2012), it is unclear whether the motive is primarily resource endowment (Shan et al., 2018) or the attractiveness of weak institutions in resource-dependent countries (Kolstad & Wiig, 2012). Hence, Chinese FDI may be tolerant of weak institutions rather than being attracted by weak institutions for three reasons. First, the domestic institutional environment in China has higher corruption levels and weaker stock market regulations compared to the West, which means that the potential risks and costs of regulatory laxity and corruption are not as great for Chinese investors as they would be for Western investors (Kolstad & Wiig, 2012). Second, Chinese investors have more experience dealing with corruption domestically and are therefore less hesitant and better equipped to enter other corrupt countries (Buckley et al., 2007). Third, the risks of dealing with corrupt governments could be mitigated by

Chinese political support (Qian & Baek, 2011) and Chinese investors can use their personal networks to substitute for weak institutions in destination countries (Shafer et al., 2007).

The scatterplots of Chinese FDI and SSA's institutional quality index (IQI)[6] (averaged over the period of 2003–2020) in Fig. 6.4 suggest that, with the exception of South Africa (ZAF), China invests primarily in SSA countries with weak institutional quality and high resource dependence. However, considering that SSA is characterised by poor institutional quality with an average −0.75, it is not possible to conclude that most of China's FDI is purposefully directed to SSA countries that have below-average institutional quality.

The Granger causality results in Table 6.3 further show that there is no significant associations between FDI and IQI.[7] Hence, the claim that Chinese FDI is attracted to SSA by weak institutions may be simplistic, mainly because political considerations (Kolstad & Wiig, 2012; Ramasamy et al., 2012) and access to natural resources take precedence (Munjal et al., 2022).

6.2 India

Evidence of India's interaction with SSA can be traced back thousands of years, long predating China's involvement on the continent (Bhattacharya, 2010, p. 63). During colonial times, Great Britain sent thousands of Indians to work on plantations as indentured labour, 'free' traders, and as part of the colonial military establishment (Paul, 2014). Indians in Africa therefore served as "an ethnicized intermediate class, with Europeans controlling the 'commanding heights' of large-scale commercial agriculture, banking, manufacturing and mining, and indigenous Africans supplying manual labour" (Pádraig, 2016, p. 111). More recently, India and Africa both shared a struggle against colonialism, and after independence, both adopted a geopolitical stance of non-alignment while facing similar socio-economic and demographic challenges (Gopaldas, 2022). Today there are

[6] The institutional quality index (IQI) is measured as the average of the World Bank's six World Governance Indicators (Control of Corruption, Rule of Law, Government Effectiveness, Regulatory Quality, Political Stability and Absence of Violence/Terrorism, and Voice and Accountability).

[7] The I(0) panel data unit root test results are summarised in Appendix.

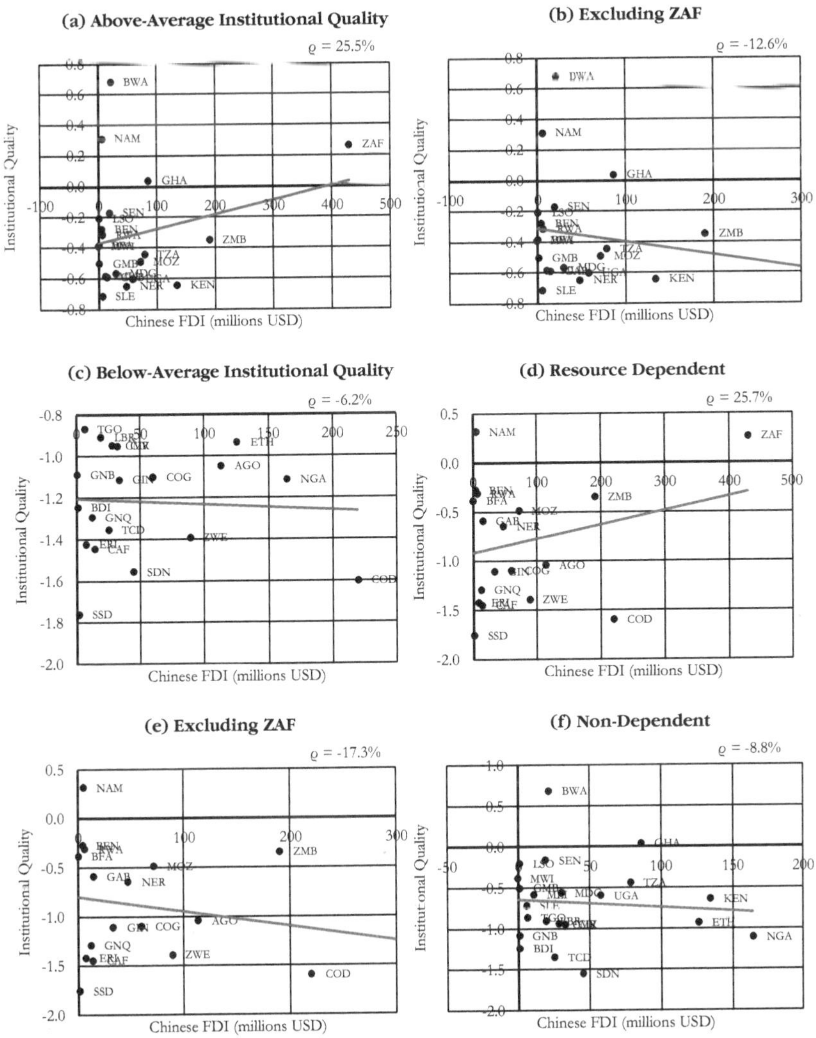

Fig. 6.4 Scatterplot of Chinese FDI flows and SSA's institutional quality. (Data sources: SAIS-CARI, World Bank)

Table 6.3 Granger causality results between Chinese FDI flows and SSA's IQI

	IQI does not Granger cause FDI		*FDI does not Granger cause IQI*	
	F-statistic	*Prob.*	*F-statistic*	*Prob.*
All *[40]*	0.934	0.334	0.000	0.993
Above average IQI *[21]*	2.233	0.136	0.391	0.532
Below average IQI *[19]*	0.100	0.752	1.386	0.240
Resource dependent *[18]*	1.539	0.216	0.049	0.825
Non-dependent *[22]*	0.100	0.752	0.326	0.568

Pairwise Granger Causality Tests. Sample: 2003–2020. Lags = 1. [#] indicates the number of countries

around two million people of Indian descent in Africa (Bhattacharya, 2010, p. 63).

India commenced a process of economic liberalisation in the early 1990s while shifting its foreign policy orientation towards the West, Middle East, and Southeast Asia (Carmody, 2016, p. 104). However, the need for natural resources to power its fast-growing economy sparked India's reengage with SSA (Alam & Gupta, 2014) while India's expertise in diverse sectors such as heavy industry, mining, infrastructure, ICTS, and pharmaceuticals attracted the interest of SSA (Bhattacharya, 2010, p. 69). India's foreign policy thus shifted from Gandhian idealism and Nehruvian non-alignment to pragmatic economic growth and development orientated policies (ibid., p. 67).

Although Indian investments in SSA increased significantly after the 1990s, China was more successful in establishing its economic and political footprints on the continent, and by the turn of the millennium, India had become increasingly concerned that it was losing opportunities in Africa to China. In 2002, India then commenced with a trade and investment program entitled "Focus Africa", which has since established trade relations with 24 African countries (Alam & Gupta, 2014). Simultaneously, India removed its foreign exchange restrictions, making it easier for Indian companies to invest overseas (Chakrabarty, 2017). In 2008, the "Africa-India Forum" was enacted, which holds triannual meetings, alternating between New Delhi and African capitals that focus on trade and investment; and socio-economic, institutional, and technological development (Bodomo, 2017, p. 60). In the last decade, Indian companies have thus used managerial proficiency and low-cost production methods to enter resource-rich countries in SSA, particularly those that are English speaking (Paul, 2014) to establish themselves as crucial development partners (Chakrabarti & Ghosh, 2014).

Simplistically, it has been claimed that China is a manufacturing hub while India is a services hub, but in the case of Africa, both countries are courting the same governments for access to the same natural resources and offering similar trade and developmental benefits (Pádraig, 2016, pp. 104–105). The main difference, however, is that India's developmental cooperation comprises non-governmental organisations, state-owned companies, and private enterprises whereas China's engagement is founded primarily on state capitalism (Chakrabarti & Ghosh, 2014). India's approach therefore tends to be more focussed on local production, transparency, and skills development (Gopaldas, 2022). Consequently, the investment and interactions of Indian companies in Africa give the impression of being more uncoordinated and 'messier' than China's state-backed activities (Pádraig, 2016, p. 104).

The evolution of Indian FDI to SSA has mirrored India's changing foreign policy priorities. In the pre-globalisation period, Indian companies focussed on expanding the supply of intermediate products via greenfield investment in low-income Asian and African countries (Paul, 2014). With the advent of globalisation however, the FDI motives of Indian companies have expanded from purely market-seeking to market- and resource-seeking, while establishing forward and backward linkages to expand and diversify their business activities and markets (ibid.).

Although India and China have adopted similar developmental cooperation strategies, to entrench their economic and political power in the global economy, they both actively compete in SSA to a greater extent than they partner (Chakrabarti & Ghosh, 2014). As an alternative to China's BRI, India established 18 diplomatic missions in Africa and promulgated the India-Japan-Africa Growth Corridor in 2018, which makes use of the existing maritime corridors with India and the financial support of Japan (Kurzydlowski, 2020). In addition, India has attempted to establish a military presence in SSA by contributing troops to the UN peacekeeping missions, a commitment that China has been reluctant to undertake (Gopaldas, 2022). Both India and China believe that their international investment and trade in SSA will translate into greater soft power; for China, the objectives are to reinforce adherence to the One China policy and China's political agenda at multilateral organisations, while India seeks to garner support for its stance on climate change and agricultural trade, and for a permanent seat at the UN Security Council (Chakrabarti & Ghosh, 2014).

Figure 6.5 summarises India's changing geographic FDI strategy over time (Chaudhry et al., 2018). During India's first stage of internationalisation, from 1975 to 1990, most FDI outflows were in greenfield investments in manufacturing, services, and extractive industries, primarily in East Asia and Pacific (31.0%) and Europe and Central Asia (24.1%). During India's second stage of internationalisation, from 1991 to 2001 however, most FDI switched to brownfield investments in the developed countries, primarily North America (29.2%), Europe and Central Asia (26.9%), followed by East Asia and Pacific (17.7%). Over the period of 2012–2020, a sizeable portion of India's FDI that formally flowed to North America has since been reallocated to investments in Europe and Central Asia (32.6% or USD 71.5 billion), East Asia and Pacific (22.6% or USD 49.7 billion), and SSA (17% or USD 37.8 billion).

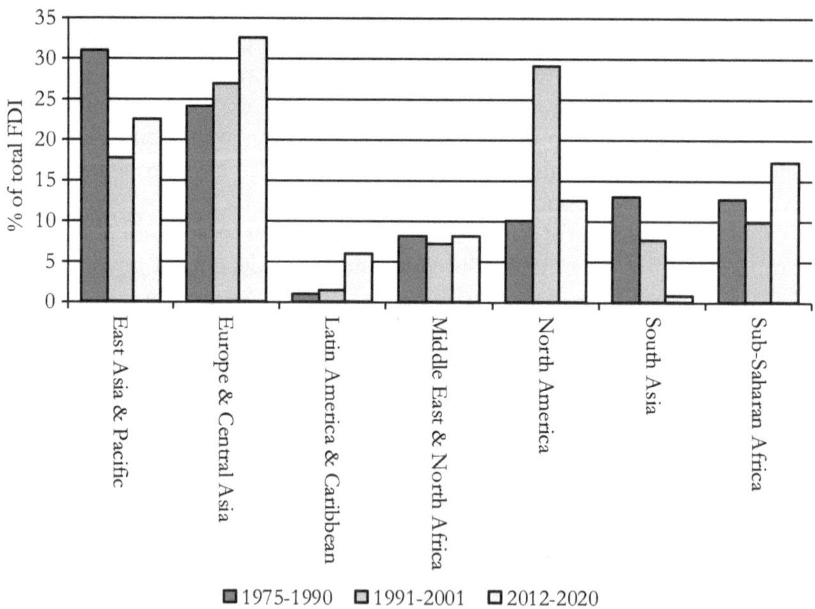

Fig. 6.5 India's regional FDI strategies. (Source: Author's compilation based on Chaudhry et al. (2018) and Reserve Bank of India data)

With regards to FDI to SSA, Fig. 6.6 shows that over the period of 2012 2020, Indian FDI totalled USD 37.8 billion (comprising 17.2% of Indian FDI outflows) but peaked at USD 8.3 billion in 2014, mainly due to the investment by the Oil and Natural Gas Corporation Videsh Ltd. (OVL) in Mozambique's oil and gas industry (Chakrabarty, 2017). Since then, however, India's FDI to SSA has steadily declined, reaching USD 1.8 billion in 2019 before rising to USD 3.6 billion in 2020.

While China's FDI has primarily focussed on the construction and mining sectors, Fig. 6.7 indicates that 31.3% of India's FDI to SSA is concentrated in manufacturing (USD 11.8 billion) and 24.0% in financial services (USD 9.1 billion). However, of the 597 Indian companies that invested in Africa during 2008–2016, just 11 companies comprise 80% of India's FDI to the region (Chakrabarty, 2017). Thus, Indian FDI to SSA is much more geographically concentrated than FDI from China and tends to focus on the sectors that China is less invested in, possibly because India does not have the necessary resources or political will to explicitly compete with China in SSA.

It has been claimed that unlike FDI from China, FDI from India is less tolerant of corruption, mainly because domestic political and bureaucratic pressure to control corruption is greater in India than it is in China (Munjal et al., 2022). In theory, this means that Indian FDI is

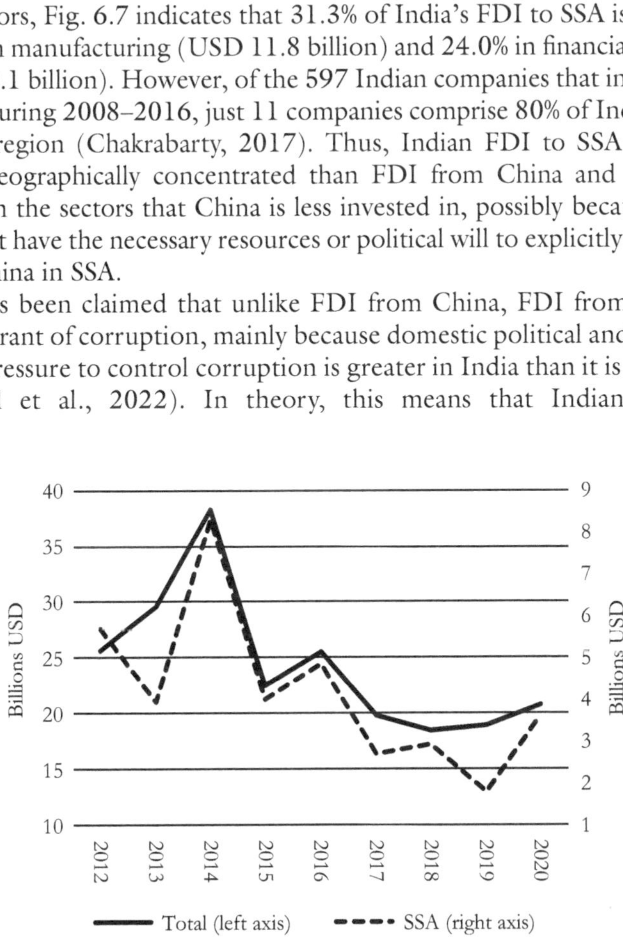

Fig. 6.6 Indian FDI outflows. (Data source: Reserve Bank of India)

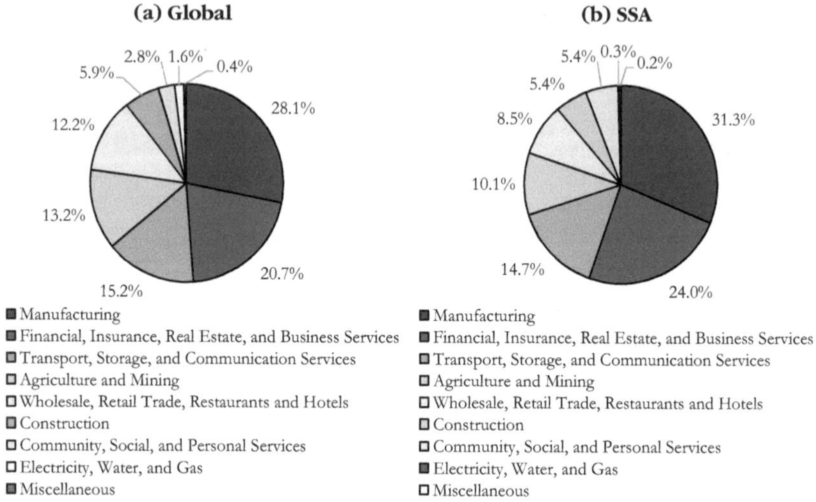

Fig. 6.7 Indian Sectoral FDI. (Data source: Reserve Bank of India)

channelled to countries that have better institutional quality, and consequently, Indian investors spend less time and money dealing with 'greasing the wheels' of corrupt bureaucracy (ibid.). Yet, over the period of 2012–2020, 88.4% (USD 33.4 billion) of FDI from India to SSA was channelled through Mauritius, which until recently had the status of a tax haven and double-taxation legislation. Thus, a large share of Indian FDI to SSA was actually just 'round-tripped' via Mauritius back to India for the purposes of tax evasion (Chaudhry et al., 2018).[8] With regards to the remaining 11.6% (USD 4.4 billion) of Indian FDI, Fig. 6.8 shows that the bulk flowed to Mozambique, mainly into the agriculture and mining sector (USD 3.1 billion), followed by South Africa, predominately into financial services (USD 243.7 million) and manufacturing (USD 128.1 million).

[8] To avoid tax-revenue losses arising from this 'round tripping', the government of India renegotiated the Double Taxation Avoidance Agreement in May 2016, which then came into effect in 2019 (Chaudhry et al., 2018).

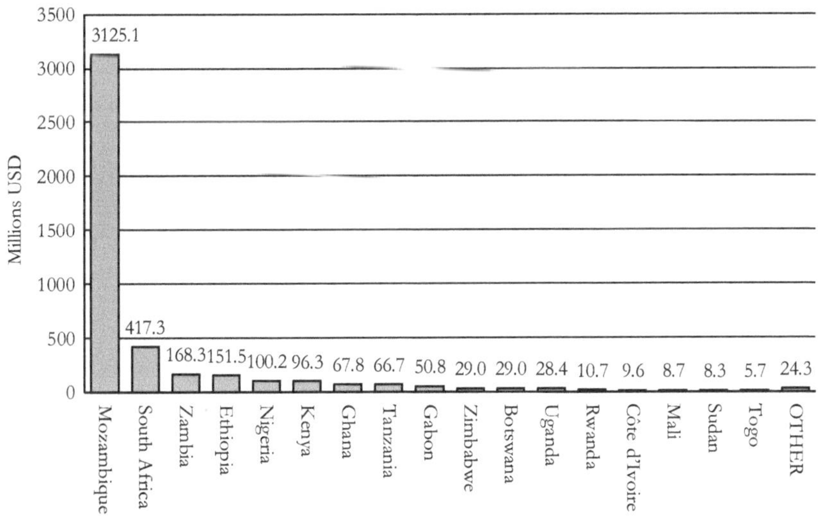

Fig. 6.8 Indian FDI to SSA (excluding Mauritius). (Data source: Reserve Bank of India)

6.3 Russia

Compared to China and India, Russia has been slower to turn its attention to the opportunities in SSA, but like China and India, Russia also has a long political relationship with many SSA countries. During the years of African Socialism, the Soviet leader Nikita Khrushchev sought to hasten SSA's shift to socialism by circumventing capitalism and thus entrenching the USSR as a developmental partner (Giles, 2013). As the 1960s progressed, and African Socialism fell into socio-economic instability, the USSR was forced to re-evaluate its position in SSA and to focus on commercial rather than political relations (Faleg & Secrieru, 2020). Subsequently, Cold War conflicts in many SSA countries provided an opportunity for the USSR to provide covert and overt military support, which included troops, military equipment, and KGB advisors; and the opportunity for SSA's leaders (past and future) to gain Soviet education, entrenching distrust of the West and solidifying Russia's position as an anti-colonial partner (Giles, 2013).

With the fall of the USSR in 1991, Russia's involvement in SSA was significantly curtailed as Russian leaders focussed their attention on domestic socio-economic stability and recovery. After the dawn of the new millennium, Russia's re-engagement with SSA focussed on 'soft' involvement in "conflict resolution, humanitarian assistance, and debt relief," as well as on establishing cultural centres (Russian Schools Abroad) in Mali, Algeria, Kenya, Guinea, and Sudan (ibid.). Over time, Russia has also sought to increase diplomatic relationships while publicising its historic anti-colonial role in SSA. Similar to China's engagement with SSA, Russia has also promoted itself as ideologically agnostic as a means of countering the West's conditionality. In contrast however, rather than focussing on soft power, Russia has increasingly offered SSA leaders the tools of hard power.

Since 2010, the Russian leader, Vladimir Putin, has aggressively sought to reverse the lost power and prestige of the USSR that followed the Perestroika and Glasnost introduced by Mikhail Gorbachev (which Putin termed "the greatest geopolitical catastrophe of the century") (Amusan, 2018). This included military involvement in the war in Syria, commencing in September 2015, expansionist wars in eastern Ukraine after the annexation of Crimea in February 2014, as well as alliances with the anti-Western states of Iran, North Korea, and China (Chomsky, 2012; Unnikrishnan & Purushothaman, 2017). Consequently, over the last two decades, Russia has increasingly viewed SSA as yet "another battleground where established and rising powers clash for resources, market shares and political influence" (Faleg & Secrieru, 2020).

Although Russia is one of SSA's fastest growing trade partners, it still lags far behind the EU and China. In 2020, Russian trade to SSA was only USD 14 billion, which was just 4.7% of SSA's trade with the EU (USD 295 billion) and 5.5% of SSA's trade with China (USD 254 billion) (Fabricus, 2023a). In common with other countries in the world, Russia hopes to gain access to SSA's rich natural resources while securing new export markets for its domestic products and skills. Russian companies are producing aluminium in Nigeria and uranium in Niger (Neethling, 2019); mining for diamonds and gold in Angola, Central African Republic, the Democratic Republic of Congo, Sudan, and Zimbabwe; and expanding gas and oil extraction in Guinea, Mozambique, Nigeria, and South Sudan (El-Badawy et al., 2022).

What Russia loses out on merchandise trade it seeks to make up for in military trade. Although the USA is the world's largest weapons exporter, with an annual value of USD 175.1 billion in 2020 (US Department of State, 2021), Russia was second with annual sales amounting to USD 15 billion (Green, 2022). Before the invasion of Ukraine, Russia accounted for 35% of weapon exports to Africa, compared to China at 17%, USA at 9.6%, and France at 6.9%; and Africa remains the second largest importer of Russian weapons globally (especially Algeria, Angola, Burkina Faso, Egypt, Ethiopia, Morocco and Uganda) (Khanyile, 2022). In 2019, at the Russia-Africa Summit, Russia signed 50 contracts and Memoranda of Understanding with more than 30 African countries to provide USD 12.2 billion worth of economic, military, environmental goods and services, and 16 contracts for nuclear cooperation (Rampe, 2023). It is however unclear how the war in Ukraine will affect Russia's ability to honour these agreements.

Despite claims that Russia's involvement in SSA is for anti-jihadist activities, there is significant evidence that Russia uses military engagement as a means to "to establish and deepen security ties with African armies and secure access to infrastructure to ensure the resupply and maintenance of its navy" (Faleg & Secrieru, 2020). In addition, Russia has widely engaged in covert interventions using state-backed militias and destabilising technologies. Despite the African Convention for the Elimination of Mercenaryism, ratified in Libreville in 1977 and coming into effect in 1985, Russia has fomented or supported political and civil instability in SSA via state-backed militias, especially the Wagner Group.[9]

Founded by Russian oligarch, Yevgeny Prigozhin, the Wagner Group first gained notoriety after its fighters were involved in Russia's annexation of Crimea and supported pro-Russian separatists in Ukraine (Al Jazeera, 2022). Wagner is estimated to have around 5000 members in Africa consisting of former Russian soldiers, convicts, and foreign nationals (Rampe, 2023) and is organised as a fusion between the Executive Outcomes mercenary business model with Russia's low-cost, low-risk strategy to challenge Western interests in Africa (van Niekerk, 2022). After 2017, Wagner Group mercenaries are known to have been active in the conflicts in Central African Republic, Libya, Mozambique, Mali, and Sudan frequently accompanied by reports of human rights abuses against civilians (Fabricius, 2022). One of the main reasons for Wagner's success in Africa is Russia's ready supply of weaponry, provided with little political conditions and no need for transparency (El-Badawy et al., 2022).

[9] In 2024, the Russian Ministry of Defence rebranded Wagner's African activities as "the Africa Corps" (Arduino, 2024).

This template of providing military security in exchange for lucrative natural resources is exemplified by its activities in the Central African Republic (CAR). In 2018, between 400 and 1000 Wagner mercenaries assisted the government of President Faustin-Archange Touadéra to repel rebel attacks on Bangui, the capital of CAR. In exchange for military support, Wagner was granted control of the Ndassima gold mine and unrestricted logging rights (Rampe, 2023). Thereafter, Touadéra appointed a Russian as his National Security Advisor, Wagner troops as his presidential guard, and swiftly replaced any CAR politicians critical of Russian influence. In 2020, when Touadéra was seeking re-election, Russia deployed its 'tools of manipulation' to ensure a favourable outcome for Touadéra. Today there are around 2300 Wagner mercenaries in CAR, many of whom have been accused of engaging in extrajudicial killings, rapes, torture, and arbitrary detentions (Siegle, 2021a).

In addition to military supply and assistance, Russia has also simultaneously weaponised and monetised information technologies and strategic communications ("StratCom") to generate Russia-friendly publicity and media channels and have been offered to SSA leaders as "a package of services for regime survival" (Faleg & Secrieru, 2020). In recent years, Russia's StratCom has interfered in SSA's democratisation by spreading fake news using trolls and bots; and menacing opposition parties and leaders using cybersurveillance, social media manipulation, and the surreptitious support of preferred candidates (ibid.; Mills & Hartley, 2023). In addition, StratCom has assisted autocratic leaders to resist domestic and international democratic pressure; hide election manipulation, fraud and repression; disseminate manipulated polling figures, and promulgate election pronouncements from fake election organisations (ibid.). After the Russia-Africa Summit in 2019, Facebook announced that Russian StratCom disinformation campaigns and electoral manipulation had been deployed in Cameroon, Central African Republic, Democratic Republic of Congo, Madagascar, Libya, and Sudan (El-Badawy et al., 2022).

However, Russia's tools of manipulation are not employed randomly (Siegle, 2021b). Among Africa's most fragile states, Russia has offered political and military support to incumbent leaders in exchange for natural resources (in the Central African Republic, Republic of Congo, Gabon, Guinea, Madagascar, Mozambique, South Sudan, and Zimbabwe) whereas in weak democratic countries (such as Madagascar, Mozambique, and Zimbabwe), Russia has used various tools of manipulation to support Russia-friendly political leaders (Gossel, 2023). In more mature democracies, "Russia has sought to undermine faith in the democratic process itself by raising questions about the effectiveness of democracy, exaggerating electoral weaknesses, overstating the ineffectiveness of the electoral process, and portraying the relationship between democracy and security as a zero-sum game" (ibid.). As can be seen from Map 6.1 overleaf, Russia has supplied military weapons to 11 African countries, military training to eight countries, StratCom "counter-terrorism" services to seven countries, and intelligence and surveillance to two countries.

Map 6.1 Russia's military involvement in Africa. (Source: Author's compilation from Scorpio (2019))

Despite the frequency of elections in Africa, 25% of the region's leaders have been in power for longer than 20 years while less than ten out of Africa's 54 countries impartially protect civil and political rights and allow fair political competition and popular participation (Siegle, 2021b). While not being the sole cause, Russia's activities in SSA have significantly contributed to the worst bout of civil instability since independence with six military coups after 2021 (El-Badawy et al., 2022). The socio-economic disruptions of the Covid pandemic and the war in Ukraine, and particularly the resultant heightened food insecurity, have weakened many already unstable governments in SSA (Kammer et al., 2022). Russia claims that it can 'repair' this dysfunction but in reality, stokes or worsens the instability, or facilitates 'constitutional coups' for its own gain (El-Badawy et al., 2022). Following the aborted Wagner mutiny in Russia in June 2023, and the death of Prigozhin in a plane crash in August 2023, it is unclear what the future of Wagner in Africa will entail (Siegle, 2023). While there were claims that Wagner's fighters would be absorbed into the Russian army or stationed in Belarus, before his death, Prigozhin claimed that Wagner would refocus its lucrative activities in Africa (Reuters, 2023). With the death of Wagner's leadership, there is the risk that Wagner could shatter into rival fractions, all fighting each other (and possibly Putin) for a share of Africa's spoils, further destabilising the region (Davis, 2023).

In addition to the physical benefits associated with military and StratCom assistance, Russia has sought to gain diplomatically by swaying countries to vote in its interests at the United Nations (Faleg & Secrieru, 2020). In this regard, Africa is of particular importance as nearly a quarter of the UN is composed of African states. This creates the contradictory position whereby it is in Russia's interests to promote regional peace and security in SSA countries that are therefore more likely to vote in Russia's political positions at the UN, while at the same time, Russia's sales of weaponry and use of anti-democratic cyber-technologies ferment instability on the continent (Giles, 2013).

Given Russia's destabilising activities, it is unsurprising that Russia is not a significant FDI contributor to SSA. Globally, Russian FDI rose significantly from an average of just USD 10 billion before 1999 to USD 363.5 billion in 2007, and then levelled off at an average of USD 378.6 from 2017 to 2020 (Kuznetsov, 2021). Yet Russia accounts for less than 1% of FDI to SSA (Irwin-Hunt, 2020; Thomas, 2022) and indications are that similar to Indian FDI to Mauritius, around 75% of Russian FDI is 'round-tripped' via offshore entities and tax havens, stimulated by Russia's weak stock market, undeveloped banking system, inefficient regulation, and high transaction costs (Bulatov, 2017). The bulk of the remaining Russian FDI is invested by state-owned or oligarchical companies in natural resources (particularly in the oil and gas and metals sectors) where Russian companies have a competitive advantage, have amassed significant export revenues before expansion, and further Russian interests abroad (Kalotay & Sulstarova, 2010). Examples include investments in oil and gas in Cameroon, Congo, Ghana, Mozambique, and Nigeria; and mining of diamonds in Angola, aluminium and Bauxite in Guinea, aluminium in Nigeria, gold in Sudan, and platinum in Zimbabwe (EIU, 2022).

Whether Russia's diplomatically orientated expansion has been a success is doubtful, as evidenced by SSA member's vote at the UN in March 2022 on a resolution calling on Russia to halt its invasion and withdraw its forces from Ukraine. Of all member states, 28% of all the votes were cast by African countries. The majority of SSA members (28 SSA countries) that voted in favour of the resolution are mostly western-aligned democracies (including Botswana, Cabo Verde, Ghana, Malawi, Mauritius, Niger, Nigeria, Kenya, Seychelles, Sierra Leone, and Zambia) compared to the one SSA country (Eritrea) that voted against the resolution, while the 17 SSA countries that abstained are reliant on Russia for military and political support (such as CAR, Sudan, and Mali), have patronage relationships with Russia and make use of Russian soft power (such as Algeria, Angola, Burundi, Guinea, Equatorial Guinea, Madagascar, Mozambique, South Sudan, Uganda, and Zimbabwe), or are attempting to appear non-aligned (such as Morocco, Namibia, Senegal, and South Africa) (Siegle, 2022; Tawat, 2022). In addition, unlike the Russia-Africa Summit in 2019, which was attended by 43 African heads of state or senior government officials, the 2023 Summit was only attended by 16 leaders. Furthermore, although the African leaders adopted the explicitly pro-Kremlin declaration, they expressed unhappiness with Russia's unilateral ending of the Black Sea Grain Initiative, called for Russia to respect the UN principle of sovereignty and territorial integrity, and for a negotiated end to the Ukraine war (Fabricus, 2023b, 2023c).

After the Russian invasion of Ukraine, Russia's economy is increasingly disconnected from the international financial system as a result of international sanctions, and thus, Russia's ability to continue to finance FDI in SSA is debatable. In addition, mercenary activities typified by the Wagner Group and other military operatives in Africa (13 countries have foreign military operations on the continent) could pose a risk to future FDI flows

(Atta-Asamoah, 2019). Of the top ten FDI investors in Africa, half are from the West (as are four out of the top five) (EY, 2023), and thus African leaders that sign up to "Russia's lawless international order" potentially jeopardise their inflows from the West (Siegle, 2022). In addition, the ability to entrench a pro-Kremlin bias on the continent has been hampered by Russia's low levels of trade and investment, outdated understanding of SSA's socio-political landscape, and the limited success of its disinformation and political manipulation (Faleg & Secrieru, 2020). The evidence therefore suggests that over the last two decades, Russia's involvement in SSA has been more opportunistic and detrimental compared to China and India's engagement with the continent.

Appendix

Unit Root Test Results of Chinese FDI and Institutional Quality

Sample	*All*	*IQI sub-sample*		*Resources sub-sample*	
		Above ave.	*Below ave.*	*Dependent*	*Non-dependent*
FDI:					
Levin, Lin & Chu t*	−4.987***	−4.262***	−2.855***	−9.005***	0.043
Im, Pesaran and Shin W-stat	−7.600***	−5.861***	−4.867***	−7.633***	−3.413***
ADF - Fisher Chi-square	237.802***	126.067***	111.736***	132.906***	104.896***
PP - Fisher Chi-square	270.680***	147.753***	122.927***	136.551***	134.129***
IQI:					
Levin, Lin & Chu t*	−3.338***	−2.183***	−2.833***	−3.349***	−1.237
Im, Pesaran and Shin W-stat	−1.531*	−0.318	−1.850**	−1.509*	−0.698
ADF - Fisher Chi-square	104.104**	42.501	61.603***	50.973**	53.132
PP - Fisher Chi-square	174.528***	48.163	126.365***	75.015***	99.513***

***, **, * represent significance at the 1%, 5%, 10% level respectively. Sample: 2003–2020. Automatic selection of maximum lags. Automatic lag length selection based on SIC: 0 to 3. Newey-West automatic bandwidth selection and Bartlett kernel

References

Abegunrin, O., & Manyeruke, C. (2020). *China's Power in Africa: A New Global Order*. Springer International Publishing AG.

Adisu, K., Sharkey, T., & Okoroafo, S. C. (2010). The Impact of Chinese Investment in Africa. *International Journal of Business and Management, 5*(9), 3–9.

Ado, A., & Su, Z. (2016). China in Africa: A Critical Literature Review. *Critical Perspectives on International Business, 12*(1), 40–60.

Al Jazeera. (2022). Russia's Yevgeny Prigozhin Admits Owning Wagner Mercenary Force. Retrieved August, 2023, from https://www.aljazeera.com/news/2022/9/26/russias-prigozhin

Alam, M. B., & Gupta, A. K. (2014). India's Policy Towards Africa. *World Affairs: The Journal of International Issues, 18*(2), 88–99.

Amusan, L. (2018). Seeking Relevance in the Age of Globalisation. *Journal of African Union Studies, 7*(1), 151–172.

Arduino, A. (2024, February 14). Wagner Group is Now Africa Corps. What this Means for Russia's Operations on the Continent. *The Conversation*. Retrieved May, 2024, from https://theconversation.com/wagner-group-is-now-africa-corps-what-this-means-for-russias-operations-on-the-continent-223253

Asiedu, E. (2006). Foreign Direct Investment in Africa: The Role of Natural Resources, Market Size, Government Policy, Institutions and Political Instability. *The World Economy, 29*(1), 63–77.

Asongu, S. A., & Aminkeng, G. A. (2013). The Economic Consequences of China–Africa Relations: Debunking Myths in the Debate. *Journal of Chinese Economics and Business Studies, 11*(4), 261–277.

Atta-Asamoah, A. (2019). Proceed with Caution: Africa's Growing Foreign Military Presence. *Institute for Security Studies*. Retrieved May, 2024, from https://issafrica.org/iss-today/proceed-with-caution-africas-growing-foreign-military-presence

Benfratello, L., D'Ambrosio, A., & Sangrigoli, A. (2023). Foreign Direct Investments in Africa: Are Chinese Investors Different? *Journal of Business Research, 155*, 113383.

Berthelemy, J. C. (2011). China's Engagement and Aid Effectiveness in Africa. *Working Paper No. 129*. African Development Bank.

Bhattacharya, S. B. (2010). Chapter 5: Engaging Africa: India's Interests in the African Continent, Past and Present. In F. Cheru & C. Obi (Eds.), *The Rise of China and India in Africa: Challenges, Opportunities and Critical Interventions*. Bloomsbury Academic & Professional.

Biggeri, M., & Sanfilippo, M. (2009). Understanding China's Move into Africa: An Empirical Analysis. *Journal of Chinese Economics and Business Studies, 7*(1), 31–54.

Bodomo, A. (2017). *The Globalization of Foreign Investment in Africa*. Emerald Publishing.
Brinza, A., Bērziņa-Čerenkova, U. A., Le Corre, P., Seaman, J., Turcsányi, R., & Vladisavljev, S. (2024). De-Risking or De-Coupling – The Future of the EU Strategy Towards China. *European Parliament Report EP/EXPO/AFET/FWC/2019–01/LOT4/R/07*. European Union.
Buckley, P. J., Clegg, L. J., Cross, A. R., Liu, X., Voss, H., & Zheng, P. (2007). The Determinants of Chinese Outward Foreign Direct Investment. *Journal of International Business Studies, 38*(4), 499–518.
Bulatov, A. (2017). Offshore Orientation of Russian Federation FDI. *Transnational Corporations, 24*(2), 71–89.
Busse, M., Erdogan, C., & Mühlen, H. (2016). China's Impact on Africa – The Role of Trade, FDI and Aid. *Kyklos, 69*(2), 228–262.
Calabrese, L., & Tang, X. (2022). Economic Transformation in Africa: What is the Role of Chinese Firms? *Journal of International Development, 35*, 43–64.
Carmody, P. (2016). *The New Scramble for Africa*. Polity Press.
Chakrabarti, S., & Ghosh, I. (2014). FDI in Africa: A Comparison of the Indian and Chinese Experience. *Procedia - Social and Behavioral Sciences, 157*, 340–352.
Chakrabarty, M. (2017). Indian Investments in Africa: Scale, Trends, and Policy Recommendations. *ORF Occasional Paper No. 142*. Observer Research Foundation.
Chaudhry, D., Tomar, P., & Joshi, P. (2018). Deconstructing Indian Overseas Foreign Direct Investments: Historical & Contemporary Trends. *Oxfam Discussion Papers*. Retrieved June, 2023, from https://www.oxfamindia.org/sites/default/files/2018-10/FINAL%20DP_OFDI_1.4.pdf
Chen, W., Fornino, M., & Rawlings, H. (2024). Navigating the Evolving Landscape between China and Africa's Economic Engagements. *IMF Working Paper No. 037*. International Monetary Fund.
Chingono, N. (2024, February 28). Africa's Debt to Stay Above Pre-Pandemic Levels Through 2025, UN Official Says. *Reuters*. Retrieved May, 2024, from https://www.reuters.com/world/africa/africas-debt-stay-above-pre-pandemic-levels-through-2025-un-official-says-2024-02-28/#:~:text=Africa
Chomsky, N. (2012). *Making the Future: The Unipolar Imperial Moment*. Hamish Hamilton.
Cilliers, J. (2023, April 18). How the Ukraine War Ends, and Implications for Africa. *Institute for Security Studies*. Retrieved May, 2024, from https://issafrica.org/iss-today/how-the-ukraine-war-ends-and-implications-for-africa
Darko, E. M., & Xu, K. (2022). The Effect of Chinese Foreign Direct Investment on Africa's Industrialization Process. *International Journal of Emerging Markets, 19*(10), 3139–3159.

Davis, J. M. (2023, July 18). Opinion: With Their Leader Still Missing, Who Will Control Wagner Forces in Africa? *CNN Opinion*. Retrieved June, 2024, from https://edition.cnn.com/2023/07/18/opinions/wagner-group-africa-mali-putin-prigozhin-davis/index.html

De Grauwe, P., Houssa, R., & Picillo, G. (2012). African Trade Dynamics: Is China a Different Trading Partner? *Journal of Chinese Economics and Business Studies, 10*(1), 15–45.

Doku, I., Akuma, J., & Owusu-Afriyie, J. (2017). Effect of Chinese Foreign Direct Investment on Economic Growth in Africa. *Journal of Chinese Economic and Foreign Trade Studies, 10*(2), 162–171.

Donou-Adonsou, F., & Lim, S. (2018). On the Importance of Chinese Investment in Africa. *Review of Development Finance, 8*, 63–73.

Doriye, E. (2010). The Next Stage of Sovereign Wealth Investment: China Buys Africa. *Journal of Financial Regulation and Compliance, 18*(1), 23–31.

EIU. (2022, March 16). Russia-Ukraine War Complicates Russian Operations in Africa. *The Economist Intelligence Unit*. Retrieved May, 2024, from https://country.eiu.com/article.aspx?articleid=1561950939&Country=Egypt&topic=Economy&subtopic=Ope_2

El-Badawy, E., Munasinghe, S., Bukarti, A. B., & Bianchi, B. (2022, March). Security, Soft Power and Regime Support: Spheres of Russian Influence in Africa. *Tony Blaire Institute for Global Change*. Retrieved May, 2024, from https://institute.global/insights/geopolitics-and-security/security-soft-power-and-regime-support-spheres-russian-influence-africa

EY. (2023). A Pivot to Growth. Ernst & Young Global Ltd., *Africa Attractiveness 2023*. Retrieved May, 2024, from https://www.ey.com/en_za/attractiveness/21/africa-attractiveness-report-

Fabricius, P. (2022). Wagner is Being Used in Africa as a Proxy to Target Civilians. *Institute for Security Studies*. Retrieved May, 2024, from https://issafrica.org/iss-today/wagner-is-being-used-in-africa-as-a-proxy-to-target-civilians

Fabricus, P. (2023a, August 4). Lacklustre Russia-Africa Summit a Vanity Boost for Putin but a Damp Squib for the Continent. *Daily Maverick*. Retrieved August, 2023, from https://www.dailymaverick.co.za/article/2023-08-04-lacklustre-russia-africa-summit-a-vanity-boost-for-putin-but-a-damp-squib-for-the-continent/

Fabricus, P. (2023b, July 30). Putin Rejects Ramaphosa's Appeal to Reinstate Black Sea Grain Initiative. *Daily Maverick*. Retrieved August, 2023, from https://www.dailymaverick.co.za/article/2023-07-30-putin-rejects-ramaphosas-appeal-to-reinstate-black-sea-grain-initiative/

Fabricus, P. (2023c, July 31). Russia-Africa Summit Declaration is Tantamount to an Implicit African Endorsement of Putin's War. *Daily Maverick*. Retrieved May, 2024, from https://www.dailymaverick.co.za/article/2023-07-31-russia-africa-summit-declaration-is-tantamount-to-an-implicit-african-endorsement-of-putins-%E2%80%A61/10

Faleg, G., & Secrieru, S. (2020). Russia's Forays into Sub-Saharan Africa: Do You Want to be My Friend, Again? *Brief No. 6*. European Union Institute for Security Studies (EUISS).

Fijałkowski, L. (2011). China's 'Soft Power' in Africa? *Journal of Contemporary African Studies, 29*(2), 223–232.

Giles, K. (2013). *Russian Interests in Sub-Saharan Africa*. Strategic Studies Institute, US Army War College.

Giovannetti, G., & Sanfilippo, M. (2009). Do Chinese Exports Crowd-Out African Goods? An Econometric Analysis by Country and Sector. *The European Journal of Development Research, 21*(4), 506–530.

Globerman, S., & Shapiro, D. (2009). Economic and Strategic Considerations Surrounding Chinese FDI in the United States. *Asia Pacific Journal of Management, 26*(1), 163–183.

Gokcekus, O., & Suzuki, Y. (2016). Mixing Washington Consensus with Beijing Consensus and Corruption in Africa. *The Singapore Economic Review, 61*(2), 1–14.

Gopaldas, R. (2022, October 24). With India on the Rise Globally, Africa Could Benefit from a More Engaged and Ambitious New Delhi. *Institute for Security Studies*. Retrieved February, 2024, from https://issafrica.org/iss-today/a-new-chapter-in-india-africa-relations

Gossel, S. J. (2023, February 2). Trying to Make Sense of the Senseless—South Africa's Bizarre Fealty to Russia. *Daily Maverick*. Retrieved May, 2024, from https://www.dailymaverick.co.za/article/2023-02-02-trying-to-make-sense-of-the-senseless-south-africas-bizarre-fealty-to-russia/

Green, A. M. A. (2022). Russian Weapon Exports. *Wilson Centre*, Retrieved May, 2024, from https://www.wilsoncenter.org/blog-post/russian-weapon-exports

Gu, J. (2009). China's Private Enterprises in Africa and the Implications for African Development. *European Journal of Development Research, 21*, 570–587.

Halper, S. (2012). *The Beijing Consensus: Legitimizing Authoritarianism in Our Time*. Basic Books.

Hastings, M. (2022, October 2). The West Is Ceding Africa's Promise to China's Exploitation. *Bloomberg*. Retrieved July, 2023, from https://www.bloomberg.com/opinion/articles/2022-10-02/max-hastings-us-and-the-west-are-losing-africa-to-china-s-exploitation

He, Y. (2020). The Impact of Imports from China on African Textile Exports. *Journal of African Trade, 7*(1–2), 60–68.

Hong, E., & Sun, L. (2006). Dynamics of Internationalization and Outward Investment: Chinese Corporations' Strategies. *The China Quarterly, 187*, 610–634.

Hou, X. (2014). Dissecting China's Rise: Controversies over the China Model. *China Perspectives, 2*(98), 61–67.

IISD. (2022, September 25). India Seeks to Strengthen its Longstanding Ties with Africa. *International Institute for Sustainable Development.* Retrieved June, 2023, from https://www.iisd.org/articles/news/india-strengthen-ties-africa#:~:text=India%20is%20trying%20to%20strengthen,an%20increase%20in%20Chinese%20exports

IMF. (2012). *Regional Economic Outlook: Sub-Saharan Africa.* International Monetary Fund.

Irwin-Hunt, A. (2020, September 15). Russia's Ongoing Charm Offensive in Africa. *FDI Intelligence.* Retrieved July, 2023, from https://www.fdiintelligence.com/content/feature/russias-ongoingcharm-offensive-in-africa-7834

Kalotay, K., & Sulstarova, A. (2010). Modelling Russian Outward FDI. *Journal of International Management, 16*, 131–142.

Kammer, A., Azour, J., Selassie, A. A., Goldfajn, I., & Rhee, C. Y. (2022, March 15). How War in Ukraine Is Reverberating Across World's Regions. *IMF Blog.* Retrieved July, 2023, from https://www.imf.org/en/Blogs/Articles/2022/03/15/blog-how-war-in-ukraine-is-reverberating-across-worlds-regions-031522

Kang, Y. (2018). Regulatory Institutions, Natural Resource Endowment and Location Choice of Emerging-Market FDI: A Dynamic Panel Data Analysis. *Journal of Multinational Financial Management, 45*, 1–14.

Kaplinsky, R. (2008). What Does the Rise of China Do for Industrialisation in Sub-Saharan Africa? *Review of African Political Economy, 35*(115), 7–22.

Kaplinsky, R., & Morris, M. (2008). Do the Asian Drivers Undermine Export-Oriented Industrialisation in SSA? *World Development, 36*(2), 254–273.

Kaplinsky, R., & Morris, M. (2009). Chinese FDI in Sub-Saharan Africa: Engaging with Large Dragons. *European Journal of Development Research, 21*, 551–569.

Khan, S. M., & Arora, K. (2017). Scope of India's and China's Investment in African Continent. *Procedia Computer Science, 122*, 691–697.

Khanyile, M. B. (2022, March 27). Sanctions Against Russia Will Affect Arms Sales to Africa: The Risks and Opportunities. *The Conversation.* Retrieved August, 2023, from https://theconversation.com/sanctions-against-russia-will-affect-arms-sales-to-africa-the-risks-and-opportunities-180038

Khodeir, N. A. (2016). The Impact of Chinese Direct Investments on Employment in Africa. *Journal of Chinese Economic and Foreign Trade Studies, 9*(2), 86–101.

Kinetz, E. (2023, July 10). How Many Russians Have Died in Ukraine? Data Shows What Moscow Hides. *Associated Press.* Retrieved August, 2023, from

https://apnews.com/article/russia-ukraine-war-military-deaths-facd75c2311ed7be660342698cf6a409
Kinyondo, A. (2019). Is China Recolonizing Africa? *World Affairs, 182*(2), 128–164.
Klaver, M., & Trebilcock, M. (2011). Chinese Investment in Africa. *The Law and Development Review, 4*(1), 168–217.
Knight, M., Kostenko, M., & Chen, H. (2023, July 1). 21,000 Wagner Mercenaries Killed in Ukraine and 'World Wants to Kill' Putin, Zelensky Says. *CNN*. Retrieved January, 2024, from https://edition.cnn.com/2023/07/01/world/wagner-losses-ukraine-zelensky-prigozhin-intl-hnk/index.html#:~:text=At%20least%2021%2C000%20Wagner%20mercenaries,most%20powerful%20group%E2%80%9D%20was%20fighting
Kolstad, I., & Wiig, A. (2012). What Determines Chinese Outward FDI? *Journal of World Business, 47*, 26–34.
Koumou, R. F. M., & Manyi, W. (2016). Effects of Chinese Foreign Direct Investment in Africa. *Journal of Finance and Accounting, 4*(3), 131–139.
Kurzydlowski, C. (2020, June 27). What Can India Offer Africa? *The Diplomate*. Retrieved May, 2023, from https://thediplomat.com/2020/06/what-can-india-offer-africa/
Kuznetsov, A. V. (2021). Direct Investment from Russia Abroad: Changes Since 2018. *Herald of the Russian Academy of Sciences, 91*(6), 700–707.
Li, J., Van Assche, A., Fu, X., Li, L., & Qian, G. (2022). The Belt and Road Initiative and International Business Policy: A Kaleidoscopic Perspective. *Journal of International Business Policy, 5*(2), 135–151.
Li, J., Van Assche, A., Li, L., & Qian, G. (2022). Foreign Direct Investment Along the Belt and Road: A Political Economy Perspective. *Journal of International Business Studies, 53*(5), 902–919.
Li, M. (2009). *Soft Power: China's Emerging Strategy in International Politics*. Lexington Books.
Liu, Z. (2014). Human Capital Externalities in Cities. *Journal of Economic Geography, 14*(3), 621–649.
Lopes, C. (2022). The Untamed Impact of a Faraway Shock: Africa and the War in Ukraine. *Strategic Review for Southern Africa, 44*(1), 9–24.
Lu, J., Liu, X., Wright, M., & Filatotchev, I. (2014). International Experience and FDI Location Choices of Chinese Firms: The Moderating Effects of Home Country Government Support and Host Country Institutions. *Journal of International Business Studies, 45*, 428–449.
Lukyanets, A., Okhrimenko, I., & Egorova, M. (2021). Population Aging and Its Impact on the Country's Economy. *Social Science Quarterly, 102*(2), 722–736.
Luo, Y., Xue, Q., & Han, B. (2010). How Emerging Market Governments Promote Outward FDI: Experience from China. *Journal of World Business, 45*, 78–79.

McBain, W. (2022, April). Africa Braces for Food Price Inflation as Russia-Ukraine War Continues. *African Business* (pp. 22–24).

Mendez, A., Forcadell, F. J., & Horiachko, K. (2022). Russia–Ukraine Crisis: China's Belt Road Initiative at the Crossroads. *Asian Business & Management, 21*, 488–496.

Mills, G., & Hartley, R. (2023, January 26). Friendship or Fiendship? South Africa's Weird Love for Russia Poses Serious Questions. *Daily Maverick*. Retrieved July, 2023, from https://www.dailymaverick.co.za/article/2023-01-26-friendship-or-fiendship-south-africas-weird-love-for-russia-poses-serious-questions/

Mlambo, C., Kushamba, A., & Simawu, M. B. (2016). China-Africa Relations: What Lies Beneath? *The Chinese Economy, 49*, 257–276.

Mold, A. (2022). The Economic Significance of Intra-African Trade: Getting the Narrative Right. *Brookings Global Working Paper No. 44*. United Nations Economic Commission for Africa in Kigali.

Morck, R., Yeung, B., & Zhao, M. (2008). Perspectives on China's Outward Foreign Direct Investment. *Journal of International Business Studies, 39*(3), 337–350.

Mude, T. (2020). The African Continental Free Trade Agreement and Intra-African Trade Transformative Integration or Neo-liberal Organised Hypocrisy? *Africa Insight, 50*(1), 41–53.

Munjal, S., Varma, S., & Bhatnagar, A. (2022). A Comparative Analysis of Indian and Chinese FDI into Africa: The Role of Governance and Alliances. *Journal of Business Research, 149*, 1018–1033.

Ndhlovu, T. (2014, September 18). China's African Ambitions Stumble in Botswana. *Al-Jazeera*. Retrieved July, 2023, from https://www.aljazeera.com/news/africa/2014/08/chinas-african-ambitions-stumble-botswana-201482312611222505.html

Neethling, T. (2019). Russia Steps Up Efforts to Fill Gaps Left by America's Waning Interest in Africa. *The Conversation*. Retrieved March, 2023, from https://theconversation.com/russia-steps-up-efforts-to-fill-gaps-left-by-americas-waning-interest-in-africa-125945/

Nye, J. S. (1990). Soft Power. *Foreign Policy, 80*, 153–171.

Nye, J. S. (2004). *Soft Power: The Means to Success in World Politics*. Public Affairs.

Nye, J. S. (2009). Get Smart: Combining Hard and Soft Power. *Foreign Affairs, 88*(4), 160–163.

ODI. (2024, January 31). Impact of the Russia–Ukraine War on Africa: Policy Implications for Navigating Shocks and Building Resilience. Retrieved August, 2024, from https://odi.org/en/publications/impact-of-the-russia-ukraine-war-on-africa-policy-implications-for-navigating-shocks-and-building-resilience/

Pádraig, C. (2016). Other New Economic Power Interests and Relations with Africa. In *The New Scramble for Africa*. Polity Press.
Pannell, C. W. (2008). China's Economic and Political Penetration in Africa. *Eurasian Geography and Economics, 49*(6), 706–730.
Paul, A. (2014). Indian Foreign Direct Investment: A Way to Africa. *Procedia – Social and Behavioral Sciences, 157*, 183–195.
Power, M., & Mohan, G. (2010). Towards a Critical Geopolitics of China's Engagement with African Development. *Geopolitics, 15*(3), 462–495.
Qian, X., & Baek, K. (2011). An Analysis on Political Risks and the Flow of Foreign Direct Investment in Developing and Industrialized Economies. *Economics, Management, and Financial Markets, 4*, 60–91.
Quer, D., Claver, E., & Rienda, L. (2018). The Influence of Political Risk, Inertia and Imitative Behavior on the Location Choice of Chinese Multinational Enterprises: Does State Ownership Matter? *International Journal of Emerging Markets, 13*(3), 518–535.
Ramasamy, B., Yeung, M., & Laforet, S. (2012). China's Outward Foreign Direct Investment: Location Choice and Firm Ownership. *Journal of World Business, 47*(1), 17–25.
Ramo, J. C. (2004). *The Beijing Consensus*. The Foreign Policy Centre.
Rampe, W. (2023, May 23). What Is Russia's Wagner Group Doing in Africa? *Council on Foreign Relations*. Retrieved July, 2023, from https://www.cfr.org/in-brief/what-russias-wagner-group-doing-africa
Repnikova, M. (2022). *Chinese Soft Power*. Cambridge University Press.
Reuters. (2023, July 29). Wagner Ready to Increase Africa Presence, Prigozhin Tells Local Media. Retrieved May, 2024, from https://www.reuters.com/world/africa/wagner-ready-increase-africa-presence-prigozhin-tells-local-media-2023-07-28/
Ross, A. G. (2015). An Empirical Analysis of Chinese Outward Foreign Direct Investment in Africa. *Journal of Chinese Economic and Foreign Trade Studies, 8*(1), 4–19.
Sanfilippo, M. (2010). Chinese FDI to Africa: What Is the Nexus with Foreign Economic Cooperation? *African Development Review, 22*, 599–614.
Schiere, R. (2010). *China's Development Challenges, Economic Vulnerability and Public Sector Reforms*. Routledge.
Scorpio. (2019). Exclusive: Advance into Africa—An Audit of Russia's Growing Economic and Military Footprint on the Continent. *Daily Maverick*. Retrieved May, 2023, from https://www.dailymaverick.co.za/article/2019-11-15-exclusive-advance-into-africa-an-audit-of-russias-growing-economic-and-military-footprint-on-the-continent/
Shafer, W. E., Fukukawa, K., & Lee, G. M. (2007). Values and the Perceived Importance of Ethics and Social Responsibility: The US versus China. *Journal of Business Ethics, 70*(3), 265–284.

Shan, S., Lin, Z., Li, Y., & Zeng, Y. (2018). Attracting Chinese FDI in Africa: The Role of Natural Resources, Market Size and Institutional Quality. *Critical Perspectives on International Business, 14*(2/3), 139–153.

Siegle, J. (2021a, 17 September). Russia's Asymmetric Strategy for Expanding Influence in Africa. *LSE Blogs*. Retrieved June, 2023, from https://blogs.lse.ac.uk/africaatlse/2021/09/17/russia-asymmetric-strategy-expanding-influence-in-africa-security-moscow/

Siegle, J. (2021b, September 24). Russia in Africa: Undermining Democracy Through Elite Capture. *Africa Centre for Strategic Studies*. Retrieved July, 2023, from https://www.printfriendly.com/p/g/fvhnVH

Siegle, J. (2022, March 9). Why Russia is on a Charm Offensive in Africa. The Reasons Aren't Pretty. *The Conversation*. Retrieved July, 2023, from https://theconversation.com/why-russia-is-on-a-charm-offensive-in-africa-the-reasons-arent-pretty-187711

Siegle, J. (2023, September 4). Russia in Africa: Prigozhin's Death Exposes Putin's Real Motives on the Continent. *The Conversation*. Retrieved May, 2024, from https://theconversation.com/russia-in-africa-prigozhins-death-exposes-putins-real-motives-on-the-continent-212707

Signe, L. (2018, March 14). Capturing Africa's High Returns. *Brookings*. Retrieved May, 2023, from https://www.brookings.edu/opinions/capturing-africas-high-returns/

Sun, I. Y. (2017, May–June). The World's Next Great Manufacturing Center. *Harvard Business Review*. Retrieved November, 2022, from https://hbr.org/2017/05/the-worlds-next-great-manufacturing-center

Sun, I. Y., Jayaram, K., & Kassiri, O. (2017). *Dance of the Lions and Dragons: How Are Africa and China Engaging, and How Will the Partnership Evolve?* McKinsey Global Institute.

Sutherland, D., Anderson, J., Bailey, N., & Alon, I. (2020). Policy, Institutional Fragility, and Chinese Outward Foreign Direct Investment: An Empirical Examination of the Belt and Road Initiative. *Journal of International Business Policy, 3*, 249–272.

Tawat, M. (2022). Russia-Ukraine War: Decoding How African Countries Voted at the UN. *The Conversation*. Retrieved August, 2023, from https://theconversation.com/russia-ukraine-war-decoding-how-african-countries-voted-at-the-un-178663

Taylor, I. (2016). Chapter 3: Chinese Interests and Strategies in Africa. In C. Pádraig (Ed.), *The New Scramble for Africa*. Polity Press.

Taylor, S. D. (2012). Chapter 4: Foreign Investment Beyond Compradorism and Primary Commodities. In *Globalization and the Cultures of Business in Africa: From Patrimonialism to Profit*. Indiana University Press.

Thomas, D. (2022). Vladimir Putin's Russia Has Little to Offer Africa. *African Business*. Retrieved January, 2023, from https://african.business/2022/03/trade-investment/vladimir-putins-russia-has-little-strong-to-offer-africa/

Tralac. (2019). African Continental Free Trade Area Legal Texts and Documents. Retrieved July, 2024, from http://www.tralac.org/resources/ourresources/6730-continental-free-trade-area-cfta.html

UNCTAD. (2021). *Economic Development in Africa Report 2021: Reaping the Potential Benefits of the African Continental Free Trade Area for Inclusive Growth*. United Nations Conference on Trade and Development.

Unnikrishnan, N., & Purushothaman, U. (2017). Russia in Middle-East: Playing the Long Game? *India Quarterly, 73*(2), 251–258.

US Department of State. (2021, January 20). U.S. Arms Transfers Increased by 2.8 Percent in FY 2020 to $175.08 Billion. Retrieved July, 2024, from https://www.state.gov/u-s-arms-transfers-increased-by-2-8-percent-in-fy-2020-to-175-08-billion/

Van Niekerk, N. (2022). Wagner Group: Putin's Grim Reapers Giving Mercenaries a Bad Name, Now Embedded in Africa. *Daily Maverick*. Retrieved June, 2023, from https://www.dailymaverick.co.za/article/2022-08-25-wagner-group-putins-grim-reapers-giving-mercenaries-a-bad-name-now-embedded-in-africa/

Whalley, J., & Weisbrod, A. (2012). The Contribution of Chinese FDI to Africa's Pre Crisis Growth Surge. *Global Economy Journal, 12*(4), 1850271.

Williamson, J. (2012). Is the 'Beijing Consensus' Now Dominant? *Asia Policy, 13*, 1–16.

Wilson, E. (2022, March 3). War in Ukraine Threatens BRI, Disrupts China-Europe Rail Freight. *EuroMoney*. Retrieved May, 2024, from https://www.euromoney.com/article/29sc7mbhcs98zytzn14hs/opinion/war-in-ukraine-threatens-bri-disrupts-china-europe-rail-freight

Woolfrey, S., Apiko, P., & Pharatlhatlhe, K. (2019). Nigeria and South Africa: Shaping Prospects for the African Continental Free Trade Area. *ECDPM Discussion Paper No. 242*. Retrieved August, 2023, from https://ecdpm.org/work/nigeria-and-south-africa-shaping-prospects-for-the-african-continental-free-trade-area

Yao, S., & Wang, P. (2014). Has China Displaced the Outward Investments of OECD Countries? *China Economic Review, 28*, 55–71.

Yu, S. Z. (2022a, February 3). What is FOCAC? Three Historic Stages in the China-Africa Relationship. *London School of Economics Blog*. Retrieved July, 2023, from https://blogs.lse.ac.uk/africaatlse/2022/02/03/what-is-focac-three-stages-the-new-china-africa-relationship-trade-economics/

Yu, S. Z. (2022b, February 4). FOCAC and the Future of China-Africa Relations. *London School of Economics Blog*. Retrieved July, 2023, from https://blogs.lse.ac.uk/africaatlse/2022/02/01/focac-the-future-of-china-africa-relations-trade-forum-cooperation/

Zhang, K. H. (2021). How Does South-South FDI Affect Host Economies? Evidence from China-Africa in 2003–2018. *International Review of Economics and Finance*, *75*, 690–703.

CHAPTER 7

The Relationship Between Financial Sector Development and FDI in Sub-Saharan Africa

Many SSA countries liberalised their financial systems and markets in the 1980s and 1990s in accordance with the IMF and the World Bank structural adjustment programmes (SAPs). The SAP reforms "included removal of credit ceilings, liberalization of interest rates, restructuring and privatization of state-owned banks, introduction of a variety of measures to promote the development of private banking systems and financial markets" (Otchere et al., 2017). Figure 7.1 shows that although financial development, financial institutions, and financial markets have improved in SSA from the 1980s, the indices still lag the levels of financial sector development (FSD) in the other regions in the world.

This is partly a reflection of three ongoing weaknesses. First, despite robust economic growth, SSA's average income levels are much lower than in the other regions in the world, which in turn has led to low private sector credit extension (IMF, 2016). Second, SSA continues to suffer from "partial reform syndrome" (van der Walle, 2001, p. 61), which, on the one hand, has driven banking sector-led FSD, but on the other hand has 'crowded out' smaller firms, hampered competition, and worsened financial repression (Rajan & Zingales, 2003a). Third, a sizeable portion of deposits in SSA's banks are held offshore rather than being used to finance domestic investment or credit (Honohan & Beck, 2007).

According to the income-narrowing hypothesis, FSD in SSA should decrease inequality by broadening access to credit (Clarke et al., 2006;

S. Gossel, *The Promise and Peril of FDI in Sub-Saharan Africa*, Palgrave Studies in African and Development Economics,
https://doi.org/10.1007/978-3-032-01320-0_7

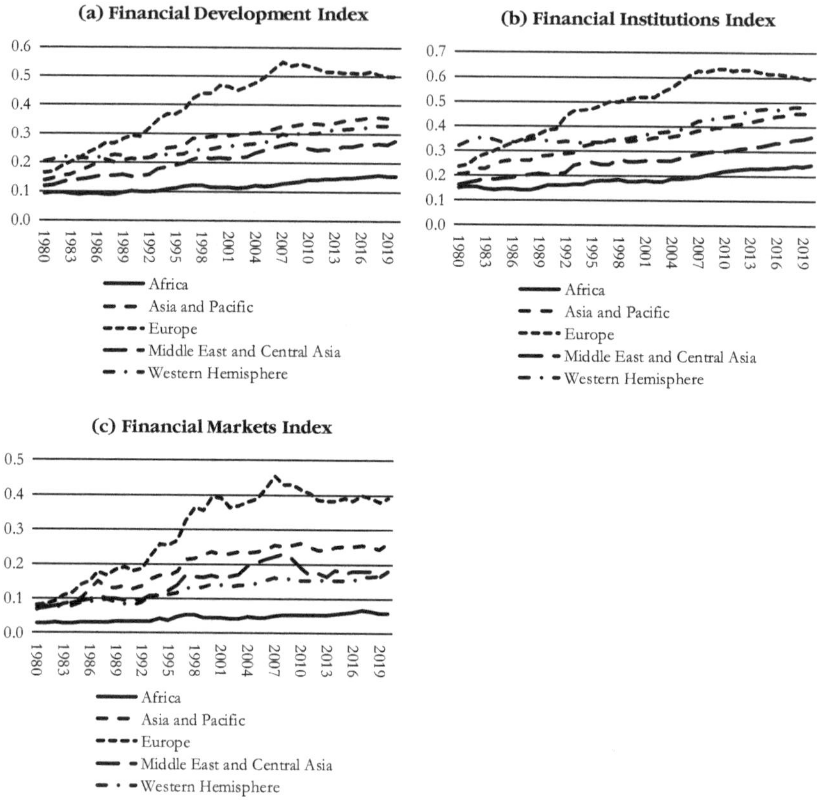

Fig. 7.1 Regional FSD. (Data source: IMF)

Hamori & Hashiguchi, 2012) and economic opportunities for the poor (Beck et al., 2007). The income-widening hypothesis counters however, that FSD can increase inequality if it benefits the wealthy elite at the expense of the poor (Rajan & Zingales, 2003a; Law et al., 2014); or if the lack of collateral stifles credit access, worsens information asymmetries, or disproportionately raises transaction costs (Rajan & Zingales, 2003b). Alternatively, the effects of FSD may be related to a country's stage of development whereby inequality increases in the early stages of FSD as a result of the effects associated with the income-widening hypothesis but then begins to fall in accordance with the income-narrowing hypothesis as consumers gain access to the financial system and costs decline accordingly (Clarke et al., 2006; Kim & Lin, 2011; Roine et al., 2009).

In addition to inequality and financial exclusion, SSA's relatively undeveloped FSD may also contribute to the region's instability because countries with less-developed financial markets tend to have higher economic growth volatility, and lower consumption and investment growth (Ibrahim & Alagidede, 2017a). According to the IMF (2016), FSD affects economic growth through three main channels. First, by mobilising domestic and foreign savings, FSD supports the efficient allocations of investment and capital, fosters improved risk management and risk diversification, facilitates information sharing, reduces information asymmetries, enhances corporate governance, and reduces transaction and oversight costs. Second, FSD increases total factor productivity and lowers the barriers for the exchange of goods and services. Third, FSD strengthens monetary and fiscal policy transmission mechanisms.

Among the most important gatekeepers for FSD are the international credit ratings agencies, which use a range of macroeconomic, fiscal, and political factors to qualitatively determine sovereign credit risk. In theory, a sovereign credit rating (SCR) is believed to be a "good proxy for the degree of transparency and future country risk" (Kim & Wu, 2008). Consequently, SRCs are important determinants of public and private investment returns, cost of capital, borrowing costs (Johnson & Kriz, 2005; Kisgen, 2006), and international capital flows (Reinhart & Rogoff, 2004). Hence, countries with low SCRs will have difficulty accessing international credit markets, have higher capital and borrowing costs, and attract more 'hot money' flows than FDI (Mensah et al., 2017).

However, credit rating agencies have been sharply criticised, even before the 2008 global financial crisis, for issuing SCRs based on subjective biases (Altenkirch, 2005). In SSA, these biases are worsened by the unavailability of the required financial and economic data (Botha & Pretorius, 2020). In addition, SSA's natural resource dependence may exacerbate these weaknesses by acting as a channel between SCR changes and socio-economic and political risk. By their nature, natural resource-dependent states derive most of their revenues from the export taxes and resource extraction royalties of international resource companies rather than from the wealth, savings, and taxation of the citizenry (Mcferson, 2010). Hence, an SCR downgrade in a resource-dependent state will lead to an increase in the cost of doing business for resource companies, which could detrimentally affect domestic economic and

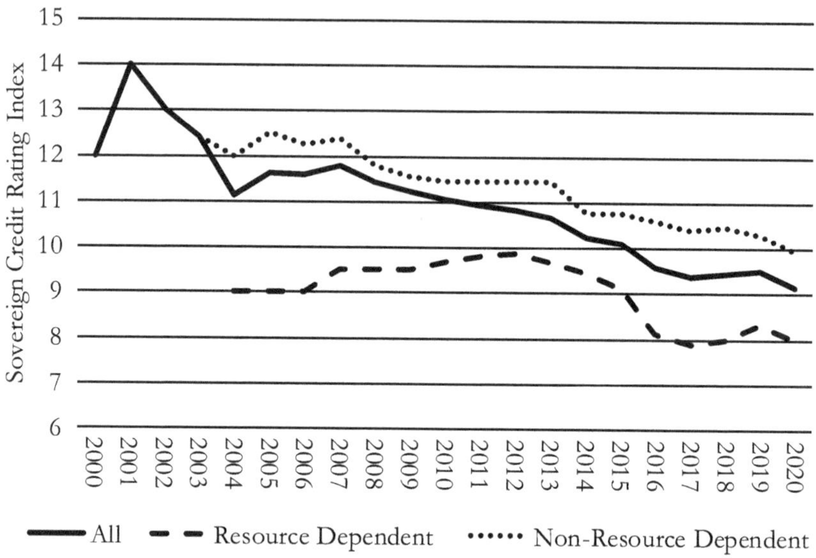

Fig. 7.2 Average SCRs in SSA. (Data sources: S&P, Fitch, Freedom House)

socio-political stability, raising the prospect of further SCR downgrades, thus creating a vicious cycle (Leite & Weidmann, 1999; Isham et al., 2005; Sala-i-Martin & Subramanian, 2008; Zalle, 2019). Consequently, resource-dependent states tend to have lower SCRs than more diversified countries.

This can be seen from Fig. 7.2, which presents the average SCRs of the 22 SSA countries that received a rating from one of the three major credit rating agencies (Moody's, Standard & Poor's, and Fitch) during 2000–2020 (linearly transformed from an ordinal rating scales into numerical values in accordance with Afonso et al., 2012).[1] Overall, SCRs in SSA peaked in 2002 with an average credit score of 14.0 (equivalent to a BBB− rating) before steadily weakening to a score of 9.1 in 2020 (equivalent to a B rating). However, comparing the average SCRs of the nine resource-dependent countries[2] against the average of the remaining

[1] See Appendix for further details.

[2] Comprising Angola, Benin, Burkina Faso, Congo, Democratic Republic of Congo, Gabon, Mozambique, Rwanda, and Zambia.

non-dependent countries[3] shows that the SCRs of diversified countries have remained consistently higher than for resource-dependent SSA countries. Between 2000 and 2020, the SCRs of the resource-dependent countries fell from an average of 9.0 (equivalent to a B rating) to 8.0 (equivalent to a B− rating) in 2020 despite improving from 9.0 in 2006 to 9.9 in 2012 (spanning an equivalent of a B rating) whereas the average SCRs of the non-dependent countries declined from an average of 12.0 (equivalent to a BB rating) to 9.9 (equivalent to a B rating). Overall, the average SCR for the resource-dependent SSA countries is 8.8 (equivalent to a rating of B−) while the average for the diversified SSA countries is 11.2 (equivalent to a rating of BB-). Thus, resource-dependent SSA countries have an average SCR that is three notches lower than diversified SSA countries.

In addition to SCRs, SSA's resource dependence also limits FSD through the two transmission channels associated with commodity price shocks (IMF, 2016). First, declining commodity prices erodes exports incomes and widens fiscal deficits. Second, significant bank withdrawals in the wake of declining commodity prices can weaken bank liquidity and increase the risk of a liquidity crisis while depreciation of the domestic currency can worsen bank losses if banks have significant net open foreign exchange positions or when unhedged creditors cannot service their loans. Beyond SSA's resource dependence, the region also suffers from financial informalisation and fragmentation with non-banked financial assets in excess of 50% in Lesotho, Namibia, Swaziland, and South Africa while foreign banks own over 70% of total bank assets in Angola, Burkina Faso, Gabon, Mozambique, Niger, Rwanda, Senegal, and Uganda; and over 50% in Ghana, Kenya, Mali, Tanzania, and Zambia (ibid.; Iddrisu et al., 2023).

However, FSD in SSA is not static and in recent decades the region has experienced the expansion of pan-African banks, mobile money, online financial services, and microfinance. Since the global financial crisis of 2008, the scale and scope of pan-African banks (PABs) have outpaced the European and American banks on the continent with all six of the PABs in SSA having operations in at least ten and representatives in over 30 SSA countries (IMF, 2016). These include the three PABs based in Morocco—Attijariwafa Bank, Bank of Africa, and Group Banque Centrale Populaire; United Bank for Africa based in Nigeria, Standard Bank in South Africa,

[3] Comprising Botswana, Cameroon, Cape Verde, Ethiopia, Ghana, Ivory Coast, Kenya, Lesotho, Namibia, Nigeria, Senegal, South Africa, and Uganda.

and Ecobank Transnational in Togo (IMF, 2015). According to IMF (2019), during the years from 2000 to 2015, PABs invested USD 376 million per year (a total of USD 6 billion) in cross-border subsidiaries, with the bulk being invested in Nigeria (USD 1.6 billion), Kenya (USD 800 million), Namibia (USD 600 million), and Ghana (USD 450 million).

Beyond traditional bank intermediation, SSA's PABs are actively involved in SSA's capital markets, insurance and pension funds, money markets, microfinance, and leasing, and thus fulfil a greater intermediation role than the domestic banks (Raga & Tyson, 2021). In addition, there is evidence that PABs have a greater risk appetite than foreign banks, possibly because PABs have an information and location advantage (Kanga et al., 2021) and can therefore act as intermediaries for financial services and infrastructure finance in overseas markets (Raga & Tyson, 2021).

SSA has a predominately rural population and thus is a world leader in mobile banking adoption, enabled by the increase in mobile phone subscriptions, expansion of mobile and online network coverage, declining prices of mobile devices, technological adaptation, and the growth in financial services companies (IMF, 2016). In 2023, nearly half of the world's 1.8 billion mobile money accounts were registered in SSA, boosting SSA's GDP by USD 150 billion (GSMA, 2024). The relatively low costs of mobile banking services overcome the financial exclusion and urban concentration of traditional financial institutions and mobile services by making it easier for customers to pay their utility rates, taxes, vehicle, and other asset financing; open savings accounts, and purchase credit and insurance products (IMF, 2016). The top three mobile money platforms in Africa are M-Pesa, which was launched in Kenya in 2007 and now has over 40 million users; Airtel Money with 19 million users; and EcoCash, which was launched in Zimbabwe in 2011 and has 10 million users.[4]

In addition to mobile banking, SSA has also experienced the expansion of microfinance institutions (MFIs) offering financial services such as loans, money transfers, savings accounts, insurance, and other financial services to clients who have no collateral or are too poor to be serviced by traditional financial institutions (Fadikpe et al., 2022). Microfinance has therefore been identified as a significant mechanism for reducing poverty and financial exclusion in SSA (IMF, 2016). Chikalipah and Makina (2019) report that in 2015, there were 4134 MFIs in Africa with

[4] https://www.africa.com/the-growth-of-mobile-money-in-africa/ [accessed April 2024]

combined asset holdings totalling USD 16.5 billion. While the highest number of MFIs are situated in West Africa (2333 MFIs) and MFIs in Southern Africa have the highest asset holdings (USD 5.8 billion), MFIs tend to be concentrated in particular countries with 40.7% (950) of the West African institutions being concentrated in Nigeria (holding USD 1.1 billion), 68.2% (500) of the Central African institutions in Cameroon (holding USD 1 billion), 53.4% (300) of the Southern African institutions in Mozambique (while South Africa dominates in asset holding of USD 1 billion), and 84.9% (281) of the North African institutions in Egypt (holding nearly 1.7 billion) (ibid.).

Having briefly discussed the state of FSD in SSA, this chapter continues with an exploration of SSA's bank- and market-led FSD, the effects of sovereign credit ratings on SSA's FSD, the interaction between FSD and democracy in SSA, and the region's financial resource curse. Thereafter, the chapter focusses more explicitly on the relationship between FDI and FSD.

7.1 Bank-Led versus Market-Led Financial Sector Development

In the modern world of financial globalisation, developed financial markets fulfil the functions of "channelling resources efficiently, mobilizing savings, reducing information problem, facilitating trading, hedging, pooling and diversification of risk, aiding the exchange of goods and services and monitoring managers by exerting corporate control" (Dutta & Roy, 2011). Emerging countries however suffer from small tax bases and a lack of investable domestic savings and are thus reliant on international capital for growth and development (Reisen, 1998; Mody & Murshid, 2005). International companies in turn are attracted to emerging economies by the prospects of higher yields and capital accumulation (Dutta & Roy, 2011). FSD is thus crucial for the beneficial transmission of capital flows because the high transaction costs and liquidity constraints associated with undeveloped financial markets make it difficult for international companies to budget, borrow, and sustainably generate profits in emerging countries (Hermes & Lensink, 2003).

Despite the socio-economic benefits of FSD, it is however empirically unclear whether FSD drives economic growth (supply-side FSD) or whether the reverse applies (demand-side FSD) (McKinnon, 1988,

p. 390). Schumpeter's (1911) pioneering supply-side hypothesis posits that "a well-developed financial system spurs growth in technological innovations by redistributing resources from less productive to more productive sectors" (Ibrahim & Alagidede, 2018). Thus, according to the supply-side hypothesis, FSD stimulates economic growth—typically referred to as the finance-led growth hypothesis (Adeyeye et al., 2015). In contrast, the demand-side hypothesis argues that economic growth and development in emerging economies will naturally lead to higher demand for capital (Robinson, 1952). Since a portion of this capital cannot be provided by domestic banks, a market-based financial system emerges to fill the gap (Bhattacharyya, 2013). The demand-side hypothesis thus argues that economic growth drives financial sector development—commonly referred to as the growth-led finance hypothesis (Adeyeye et al., 2015). Patrick (1966) however argues that the supply-side hypothesis applies in the early stage of economic development, but as the economy grows and develops, the demand-side hypothesis becomes more prevalent. Consequently, it is possible that SSA countries in the early stages of development will be more prone to supply-side FSD whereas more sophisticated SSA countries (such as South Africa) benefit from demand-side FSD.

Although it has been argued that the market-led (demand-side) success of the UK and USA should be emulated by emerging countries, the bank-led (supply-side) industrialisation of Germany and Japan also provides compelling counter arguments (Bhattacharyya, 2013). As noted by Bats and Houben (2017), before the 2008 global financial crisis, most studies argued that bank and market financing are equally important for economic growth (Levine & Zervos, 1998; World Bank, 2001; Beck & Levine, 2004) whereas the degree of financial development and openness are more important for the real economy (Demirgüç-Kunt & Levine, 2001; Levine, 2002; Beck & Levine, 2002; Demirgüç-Kunt & Maksimovic, 2002). After the 2008 financial crisis however, studies have increasingly favoured market-led FSD, mainly because the economic effects of the banking crisis were significantly more damaging than the ensuing market effects (Gambacorta et al., 2014).

Historically, FSD in SSA has tended to be bank-led rather than market-led. This is because banks "mobilize savings, allocate capital, supervise the investment decisions of the firm directors and present different tools for risk management" whereas financial markets are integrated into the banking system (Moradi et al., 2016). However, despite being complimentary, banks and markets "mobilize savings, price risks, allocate capital, and absorb shocks in different ways" (Bats & Houben, 2017). Banks either bear the risks on their balance sheets or systemically via financial intermediation whereas financial markets merely reflect the risk-reward outcome of equity and debt securities (ibid.).

The pertinence of market-led FSD in SSA is debatable because the optimal mix of banks and markets depends on an economy's labour, capital, and natural resource endowment. Capital-intensive developed economies are dominated by large production companies and are thus more likely to have market-based financial systems and big banks whereas less developed labour-intensive economies will comprise small companies and the financial sector will therefore be served by small banks (Lin et al., 2009). Bank size however can hamper FSD because small businesses typically rely on credit from small banks rather than from large banks, and when companies grow, they can no longer be optimally serviced by small banks, and must instead rely on the impersonal, bureaucratic, and standardised decisions of large banks (Kurronen, 2015). Consequently, companies may 'fall between the gap' when they become too large to be serviced by small banks but not large enough to be attractive to large banks (EIB, 2013). This creates a negative feedback loop that hinders company and FSD development.

In addition, the financial systems in most SSA countries are still underdeveloped compared to the rest of the world (Allen et al., 2011, 2014). Until the 1980s, SSA's financial systems were highly regulated and dominated by state-owned banks, which stifled financial liberalisation and institutional and regulatory development (World Bank, 2023). In the early years of post-independence, many African governments adopted import substitution, trade restrictions, and capital controls to protect domestic companies and preserve scarce foreign reserves (Ibrahim & Acquah, 2021). This had the effect of crowding out FDI, disincentivised investment, and hampered economic growth (Rodriguez & Rodrik, 2000). When African governments subsequently undertook trade and investment reforms in the 1990s, FDI was deemed to be the best channel to enhance economic growth, supplement SSA's low savings rates, and provide the financial foundation for development (Ibrahim & Acquah, 2021) but due to the region's weak institutional quality, poor governance, and political and economic instability (Honohan & Beck, 2007, p. 6; Ibrahim & Alagidede, 2018), SSA is still deemed to be a high-risk frontier market. Furthermore, due to low income and savings rates, financial institutions in SSA suffer from a lack of creditworthy borrowers even while households and companies suffer from a lack of credit (Andrianova et al., 2015), negating capital for start-ups and innovation (Ayyagari et al., 2011; Gorodnichenko & Schnitzer, 2013). Instead, unlike most other regions in the world, most bank credit in SSA is to the public sector rather than to the private sector (Honohan & Beck, 2007) and the relatively high level of ethno-linguistic fractionalisation in SSA (Easterly & Levine, 1997) drives financial market segmentation (Aker et al., 2010) and raises transaction costs and sectoral complexities accordingly.

The outcome of these weaknesses is that SSA's financial sector suffers from low investment rates, high levels of information asymmetry, opaque informal markets (Andrianova et al., 2015), and a high rate of loan defaults (Daumont et al., 2004; Andrianova et al., 2011). Consequently, SSA is dominated by commercial banks and, except for the African Development Bank and the Development Bank of South Africa, suffers from a dearth of investment banks (Soumaré et al., 2021), mainly as a result of SSA's weak accounting standards, poor credit information collection and sharing, a lack of credit bureaus; and undeveloped regulatory and judicial institutions for the protection of property rights (Sacerdoti, 2005).

Following the banking sector reforms undertaken by many SSA countries after the 1990s, SSA's banking sector has become increasingly sophisticated, efficient, and resilient (Andrianaivo & Yartey, 2009), yet compared to other emerging regions, the banking systems in SSA are still evolving (EIB, 2013). The weakness of SSA's banking sector can be seen from Table 7.1(a). Averaged over the period of 2010–2020, domestic credit to the private sector has been on par with the averages in other developing regions of the world whereas domestic credit to the private sector by banks and the monetary sector is around half that of other emerging regions. The health of the banking sector in Table 7.1(b) further shows that although the bank liquidity ratio of SSA is relatively consistent with the other regions, commercial bank branches, credit bureau coverage, and credit information depth are significantly below the averages for the other regions.

Although "stock markets are expected to increase economic growth by increasing the liquidity of financial assets, making global and domestic risk diversification possible, promoting better investment decisions, and influencing corporate governance-solving institutional problems by increasing shareholders interest or value" (Adjasi et al., 2012), this is not the case for SSA, mainly because SSA's stock markets are still embryonic (Otchere et al., 2016) and compared to other emerging regions, SSA's stock market capitalisation is low, the number of listed companies is small, and the

Table 7.1 Regional domestic credit

Region	*Measurement*	*Central Europe and the Baltics*	*East Asia & Pacific*	*Latin America & Caribbean*	*Middle East & North Africa*	*North America*	*Sub-Saharan Africa*
(a) Credit provision:							
Domestic credit to private sector	% of GDP	48.7	143.3	49.1	48.0	185.7	43.2
Domestic credit to private sector by banks	% of GDP	48.7	127.5	45.4	48.7	51.5	27.1
Monetary sector credit to private sector	% of GDP	48.7	127.9	45.5	48.8	51.5	27.3
(b) Banking system:							
Bank liquid reserves to bank assets ratio	%	19.8	19.5	20.6	14.4	–	18.3
Commercial bank branches	per 100,000 adults	27.4	10.0	13.4	13.1	27.4	4.1
Private credit bureau coverage	% of adults	57.7	31.2	38.2	15.2	100.0	7.3
Depth of credit information index	0 = low to 8 = high	6.5	4.6	4.9	4.6	8.0	2.7

Data source: World Development Indicators

exchanges tend to be dominated by a few large companies that represent a high proportion of total market capitalisation (Andrianaivo & Yartey, 2009).

This is not too surprising given SSA's relatively nascent stock market development. Before the 1990s, SSA only had five stock markets (Yartey & Adjasi, 2007), subsequently growing to 11, only South Africa's Johannesburg Stock Exchange (JSE) has a market capitalisation of over USD 100 billion. Consequently, SSA's stock markets suffer from illiquidity and narrow trading, which hinders the development of domestic trading systems, market analysis, and brokerage; and in turn slows the pace of trading, clearing, and settlement (Klagge & Zademach, 2018). SSA's relatively underdeveloped financial markets are a reflection of the region's enduring weaknesses, small domestic economies, unstable macroeconomic and business environments, weak institutions, uneven financial infrastructures, high capital and bureaucratic requirements, and a lack of transparency (Soumaré et al., 2021).

7.2 Sovereign Credit Ratings

Although SCR downgrades negatively affect domestic financial market performance and capital flows (Ammer & Clinton, 2004; Kim & Wu, 2008; Mateev, 2012), there is evidence that financial market performance affects SCRs (Hooper et al., 2008). This creates the risk of a vicious cycle, which is especially pertinent to SSA because, as mentioned, the region's capital markets suffer from thin trading, illiquidity, and domination by a few companies (Mlambo & Biekpe, 2005) while the secondary bond markets are dominated by short-maturity government rather than corporate debt markets (except for South Africa, Côte d'Ivoire, Ghana, Gabon, Senegal and Nigeria) (Andrianaivo & Yartey, 2009). Consequently, an SCR downgrade could lead to lower financial market performance because international investors may consider the downgrade as a signal of lower future performance, and the resultant economic slowdown may then drive further downgrades (Mutize & Gossel, 2019).

In addition to the effects on financial markets, SCRs may also share a bidirectional relationship with economic growth. On the one hand, deteriorating economic growth could lead to an SCR downgrade because of the associated negative effects on credit risk (Dudian & Popa, 2012) but on the other hand, an SCR downgrade could negatively affect economic growth via the affected channels of interest rates, sovereign bond yield spreads, and capital flows (Chen et al., 2016). In the case of SSA, it has been empirically shown that SCRs unidirectionally affect economic growth, which suggests that credit rating agencies proactively set SCRs as a determinant of future economic growth prospects (Mutize & Mugobo, 2020).

Unfortunately, beyond the effects of SCR changes on the rated country, there are also spillover and contagion risks for regional economies (He & Schiereck, 2019). These can be as a result of geographic, cultural, or trade commonalities (Gande & Parsley, 2005; Ferreira & Gama, 2007; Arezki et al., 2011; Afonso et al., 2012; Mutize & Gossel, 2018b), trade and financial linkages, credit and intermediation channels (Ismailescu & Kazemi, 2010; He & Schiereck, 2019), or changes in asset prices, risk premiums, and portfolio reallocations (Christopher et al., 2012; Chen et al., 2016; Mutize & Gossel, 2018a, 2020). Beyond these direct channels, SCR changes in one country may also highlight the credit risks in neighbouring countries (Fleming et al., 1998; Kaminsky & Schmukler, 2001; Kaminsky & Reinhart, 2000; Kaminsky et al., 2003) or because procyclical SCR changes propagate contagion and crises (Ferri et al., 1999; Kiff et al., 2010; Broto & Molina, 2016).

Table 7.2 presents the SCR changes among 22 SSA countries that were rated by the 'big three' rating agencies (Standard & Poor's, Moody's, and Fitch). Over the whole period of 2000–2020, the number of SCR downgrades is more than double the number of upgrades (41 versus 18 respectively). However, during the period of 2000–2009, the frequency of SCR upgrades was double than that of downgrades (6 to 3 respectively) whereas during the subsequent decade of 2010–2020, the number of downgrades was over three times greater than upgrades (38 against 12 respectively). Thus, the credit rating agencies tend to positively rate SSA countries when they are first granted an SCR but then subsequently downgrade the SCR over time.

After the 2008 global financial crisis, credit rating agencies have been sharply criticised for relying on overly subjective rating methodologies, having insufficient staff and resources to realistically rate developing countries, lacking competition, suffering from perverse incentive structures, are biased towards developed countries, and unaccountability for the consequences of their ratings ("opinions") (Prieg, 2011; UNCTAD, 2024). In the case of SSA, the region's SCRs tend to be procyclical (Pretorius & Botha, 2017) and downwardly biased for two reasons. First, the rating agencies over-emphasise political factors and demonstrate political prejudices (Barta & Johnston, 2017; Mutize, 2019), thus undermining the economic and political sovereignty of SSA's governments (Mutize & Nkhalamba, 2021). Second, the methodologies used by the credit rating agencies are ill-suited to developing countries, do not adequately take account of the different macroeconomic dynamics underlying developing countries, continue to make errors in their ratings, and are too retrospectively orientated to account for fast-changing economies (APRM, 2023). Consequently, over the period of 2004–2021, countries in SSA had to pay

Table 7.2 SCR changes in SSA

	2000–2020 [22]		*2000–2009 [13]*		*2010–2020 [9]*	
	Upgrades	*Downgrades*	*Upgrades*	*Downgrades*	*Upgrades*	*Downgrades*
Angola	2	4	NR		2	4
Benin	1	–	NR		1	–
Botswana	–	2	UC		–	2
Burkina Faso	1	1	UC		1	1
Cameroon	2	2	2	1	–	1
Cape Verde	–	1	UC		–	1
Congo	–	1	NR		–	1
DRC	1	4	NR		1	4
Ethiopia	UC		NR		UC	
Gabon	–	1	NR		–	1
Ghana	1	3	UC		1	3
Ivory Coast	1	–	NR		1	–
Kenya	1	1	–	1	1	–
Lesotho	1	2	1	–	–	2
Mozambique	2	3	1	–	1	3
Namibia	–	2	UC		–	2
Nigeria	1	4	–	1	1	3
Rwanda	2	1	NR		2	1
Senegal	UC		UC		UC	
South Africa	2	4	2	–	–	4
Uganda	–	1	UC		–	1
Zambia	–	4	NR		–	4
Total	18	41	6	3	12	38

NR indicates that the country was not rated during the period. UC indicates that the rating was unchanged during the period. *[#]* indicates the number of SSA countries that received a SCR over the period. Note that the number of upgrades and downgrades does not take account of the rating level of the upgrade or downgrade. For example, a SCR downgrade from 12 (equivalent to BB) to 9 (equivalent to B) is reflected as one occurrence.

Source: Gossel and Mutize (2025)

coupon rates that were on average 2.1% higher than the rest of the world and 1.3% higher than other emerging and developing countries (Gbohoui et al., 2023).

A recent example is the contentious rerating of Ghana (AU, 2022). Moody's downgraded Ghana's SCR from B3 to Caa1 in February 2022. Ghana raised concerns about the accuracy of the credit rating agency's SCRs downgrade and an African Peer Review Mechanism (APRM) review then found that Moody's rating was based merely on a desk review by one analyst who only had a few days to derive the rating and who had never visited Ghana, that some important data was excluded, and that inaccurate balance of payments data were used to derive the rerating.[5] Kenya and Nigeria have similarly expressed unhappiness with the quality of their SCRs (APRM, 2023).

According to a recent UNDP report (UNDP, 2023), if African countries were rated according to economic fundamentals rather than on subjective opinions, SSA could access an additional USD 31 billion in finance and save USD 14.2 billion in interest costs. In addition, if all 13 SSA countries included in the report were realistically rated, they would be able to access an additional USD 45 billion in capital, equivalent to all the net ODA SSA received in 2021 (Lopes, 2024). Consequently, credit rating agencies have been accused of enforcing neoliberal economic policies in line with Washington Consensus ideology (Williamson, 2004) and of being imperialist enforcers for economic exploitation (Barta & Johnston, 2017; Mutize & Nkhalamba, 2021).

In addition to the association between SCRs and financial and economic systems, SCRs also affect, and are affected by, democratisation. According to the "democratic advantage" hypothesis (North & Weingast, 1989; Schultz & Weingast, 1996, 2003), democratic governments are more likely to repay their creditors and maintain fiscal responsibility, and should thus have lower interest rates, higher SCRs, and better credit access and more favourable credit terms (Beaulieu et al., 2012) than undemocratic countries. Hence, the democratic advantage arises from democratic institutions, open and competitive financial and trade markets (Rajan & Zingales, 2003b; Becerra et al., 2012), entrenched rule of law and property rights, and stronger civil liberties (Haber & Perotti, 2008; Biglaiser & Staats, 2012).

Critics counter however that much of the democratic advantage literature focusses too narrowly on bank credit, does not take adequate cognisance of bond market dynamics, exaggerates the effect that democracy has on interest rates (Saiegh, 2005; Biglaiser & DeRouen, 2007), and incorrectly presumes that the effects of political factors outweigh the impact of macroeconomic factors (Archer et al., 2007). In addition, interest rate changes may also negate democratisation if the capital entrenches the

[5] Ghana did default on its debt after the SCR downgrades in December 2022, but it is possible that the downgrades accelerated the financial decline to default rather than prewarned creditors about a possible default.

undemocratic elite and fuels heightened military spending and foreign conflicts (DiGiuseppe, 2015a, 2015b; DiGiuseppe et al., 2012).

It has also been argued that the democratic advantage hypothesis does not sufficiently consider the variable effects of SCRs. On the one hand, an SCR upgrade could deepen democracy by facilitating the financing of socio-economic development (Biglaiser et al., 2011). On the other hand, however, an SCR downgrade may force an undemocratic government to channel limited capital away from socio-economic expenditure to shore up patronage and loyalty (DiGiuseppe & Shea, 2015). A financially constrained undemocratic regime may also adopt populist or redistributive policies to preserve the predatory capitalist system (Comeau, 2003; Ghardallou, 2022; Sandow et al., 2022). In addition, the regime may channel limited finances to the military and other enforcement structures to supress domestic social instability arising from macroeconomic hardship and repress political opposition (DiGiuseppe et al., 2012). In the case of SSA, Gossel and Mutize (2025) find that SCR changes negatively affect long-run democracy in relatively more democratic SSA countries but drive democratic deepening in less democratic SSA countries, and thus SCR changes are "not democratically agnostic" and potentially "spark a negative cycle in SSA countries whereby a downgrade leads to a deterioration in socio-political stability coupled with increased financial economic constraints that in turn drive further downgrades and macroeconomic hardship."

7.3 Financial Sector Development and Democracy

Political choices affect access to capital (Girma & Shortland, 2008; Rajan & Zingales, 2003a), and thus the progress and stability of FSD are determined by events in the political economy (Ghardallou, 2022). Historically, economic theories have debated the extent to which FSD is politically and socially neutral, stabilising, and self-correcting. According to John Maynard Keynes (1936), FSD can be detrimental to the economy if financial speculation outweighs productive capital, upsetting the equilibrium between financial and industrial capital (Walby, 2013). Hyman Minsky (1986) further argues that the profit motive of FSD means that capitalism is inherently destabilising rather than self-correcting (Walby, 2013). However, Karl Polanyi (1957) argues that although the commoditisation of money, assets, and labour fosters self-destructive instability, the lobbying power of civil society for increased welfare and the regulation of 'fictitious commodities' can act as a stabilising force (Walby, 2013). The modern understanding of the relationship between the political economy and FSD is that there is both a direct and indirect social relationship, that FSD is potentially socio-economically destabilising; that FSD is not efficient, neutral, or self-correcting; and that intervention is required to counter disequilibria (Walby, 2007, 2009, 2013).

Recent studies argue that the reason why some countries have more developed financial sectors is because they have more open financial systems, which promotes competition and access to finance while also weakening the power of incumbent companies (Rajan & Zingales, 2003a; Becerra et al., 2012). However, the degree of trade and financial openness is a policy decision, and is therefore a political choice (Baltagi et al., 2009; Aluko et al., 2019). According to the political institutions view, the power of the banking sector in non-democratic states reflects the power of the political elite and thus weak FSD is a function of poor political accountability (Acemoglu & Johnson, 2005; Haber & Perotti, 2008). Similarly, in SSA it has been found that the extent to which foreign banks affect FSD depends on the quality of domestic institutions (Iddrisu et al., 2023).

Thus, in environments of strong political elites and weak institutions, the elite can channel rents to state-owned or -operated banks while also enacting regulations that hinders possible competition and forgives loan defaults (Faccio, 2006; Faccio et al., 2005; Khwaja & Mian, 2005) while in exchange, the politically captured banks share a portion of their rents with the political elite. This cyclical relationship exists only so long as the political elite can control the rents and stave off competition (Khanna & Yafeh, 2007). The effect is that an economy that comprises a large portion of low-wage labour will tend to have bank-led FSD because unions will seek to preserve labour stability and wealth (Perotti & von Thadden, 2006). As the middle-class grows however, incomes and asset holdings rise, switching bank-led FSD to market-led FSD (Haber & Perotti, 2008).

The ability of the political elite to suppress competition, weaken financial regulations and oversight, and engage in distortionary lobbying is dependent on a country's property rights protection and civil liberties (Haber & Perotti, 2008). Thus, the legal origins view argues that political institutions and regulatory quality are interlinked (La Porta et al., 1998; Beck et al., 2003). Systemically, emerging countries, including countries in SSA that adopted British legal traditions "through conquest, colonisation, or imitation" (Ibrahim & Alagidede, 2017b), commonly have better property rights protection and civil liberties than countries that adopted the more codified and statist French justice system (Bhattacharyya, 2013). A possible reason is because English common law provided strong protection of investors' rights whereas French and German civil law focussed on the governments' control of the judiciary, which thereby dissuaded private sector-led FSD in favour of public sector-led FSD (Beck et al., 2001). Consequently, countries with English heritage institutions tend to have more market-based FSD whereas French and German legacy institutions are predominantly bank-based (Demirgüç-Kunt & Levine, 2001).

However, there is evidence that the relationship between FSD and democracy is non-linear and is instead U-shaped or inverted U-shaped. The implication of a U-shaped relationship is that democracy initially undermines FSD because the erosion of the state's autonomy leads to reduced investments and possible financial repression (Huntington, 1968). Above a certain threshold however, democracy promotes FSD, because democratic institutions secure property and investor rights, and improve the enforcement of civil liberties (Olson, 1993), which in turn contributes to FSD (Clague et al., 1996; Acemoglu et al., 2019). In addition, the widening involvement of decision-makers facilitates diversification, lowers risk-taking, and increases stability and certainty (Apergis, 2017). The U-shaped relationship thus implies that emerging countries suffer from instability and high risk, which hinders investment and FSD (Gates et al., 2006), because they cannot yet benefit from strong institutions (Acemoglu & Robinson, 2006).

In contrast, an inverted U-shaped relationship implies that democratisation is associated with improved FSD at lower levels of society but erodes autocratic authority, reduces rents, and weakens the economic and political power of the elite (Barro, 1996). Over time, FSD should benefit from heightened property rights and investor protection (Acemoglu, 2003; Ho et al., 2018; Delis et al., 2020) but in emerging countries, eroding the power of the elites can harm FSD because the economy may become exposed to the distortionary policies of interest groups or the pressure to adopt short-term, populist, or redistributive policies (Comeau, 2003; Ghardallou, 2022).

Regardless of whether the relationship between democracy and FSD is linear or non-linear, it is affected by political instability, and this in turn could have significant ramifications for FDI. This is because political instability can lead to poor macroeconomic policy choices, which in turn will hamper entrepreneurship, lower savings, and heighten financial market volatility (Dutta & Roy, 2011). Political stability in contrast creates the environment conducive for FDI by lowering the risk of expropriation and ensuring the efficient functioning of financial markets, which in turn hastens the integration of new technologies and spillovers, and, in turn, improves investor confidence (ibid.).

In the case of SSA, the scatterplots of financial sector development and democracy (Polity 2) (averaged over the period of 1980–2018) in Fig. 7.3 indicate that there is a positive association between the metrics of FSD (financial development, financial institutions, and financial markets) and democracy. Table 7.3 further shows that the SSA countries with above average Polity 2 democracy index scores have significantly higher levels of FSD compared to FSD in SSA countries that have below-average Polity scores.

7.4 The Financial Resource Curse

Studies that explore the relationship between natural resources and FSD can be grouped into three hypotheses (Kurronen, 2015). The first is the demand hypothesis, which argues that investment by resource companies can overwhelm the domestic banking systems of natural resource-dependent host economies, and thus risk mitigation and portfolio optimisation must be satisfied by international financial markets (Berglof & Lehmann, 2009). This has the effect of stifling development of the domestic banking sector in the host country by distorting the lending-borrowing mechanisms and increasing adverse selection and moral hazard lending (Ahmad & Ali, 2010), as well as by hindering entrepreneurship and small- and medium-sized enterprise development (Mo, 2001; Ndikumana & Baliamoune-Lutz, 2008; Bologna & Ross, 2015). Eventually, these distortions stimulate the host government to adopt tighter regulations of entry and capital requirements (Lin et al., 2009).

The second is the interest group hypothesis (Rajan & Zingales, 2003a), which posits that incumbent companies may form interest groups to frustrate FSD if the entry of foreign competitors endangers their benefits. On the other hand, trade liberalisation may erode incumbent opposition to FSD if the expanded product markets benefit the incumbents financially (Kurronen, 2015). The third is the volatility hypothesis (Van der Ploeg & Poelhekke, 2009), which argues that commodity price volatility feeds into macroeconomic and political volatility, and in turn stifles FSD (Boyd et al., 2001; Roe & Siegel, 2011; Hattendorff, 2014; Mlachila & Ouedraogo, 2020). Although commodity price shocks have been found to negatively

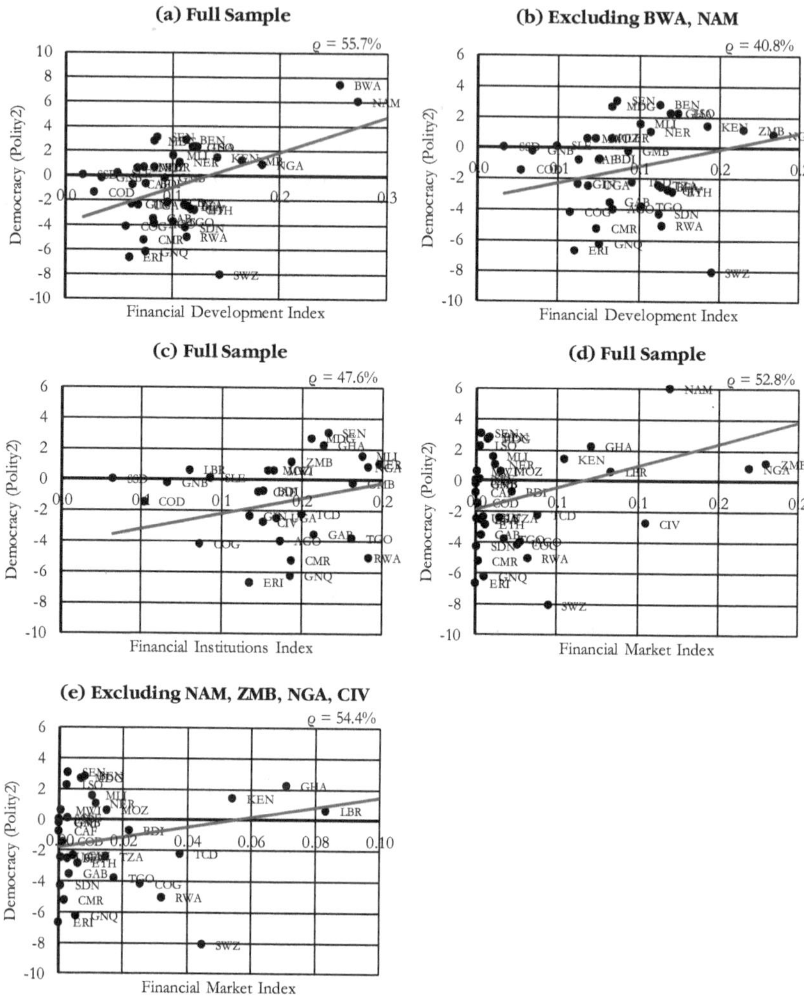

Fig. 7.3 Scatterplot of FSD and democracy. (Data sources: Polity V, IMF)

affect FSD, it has been argued that there are mediating factors that can limit the negative effects (Asif et al., 2020), such as the rule of law, export diversification, FDI inflows (Mlachila & Ouedraogo, 2020), human capital development, and government expenditures (Law & Moradbeigi,

Table 7.3 FSD and democracy

Average	*(a) Above-average polity [20]*	*(b) Below-average polity [20]*	*(a)/(b)*
Polity2	2.09	−3.52	−1.6
Financial development index	0.13	0.09	1.5
Financial institutions index	0.19	0.16	1.2
Financial markets index	0.06	0.02	3.5

[#] indicates the number of SSA countries in the sample

Data sources: Polity V and IMF (1980–2018)

2017). In addition to commodity price shocks, FSD is also shaped by commodity price cyclicality. During resource booms, natural resource rents are channelled into the banking sector and then extended as credit, but this exposes the banks to resource price volatility, drives moral hazard lending, and reduced asset quality. During natural resource price downturns, the banking sector then experiences rising loan defaults and capital instability (Dwumfour & Ntow-Gyamfi, 2018).

Despite the risks associated with these hypotheses, rising natural resource revenues could benefit FSD when the funds facilitate higher banking sector credit to households and companies (Bhattacharyya & Hodler, 2014). In theory, an efficient market improves trade, counteracts negative externalities, and attracts much needed investment and skills (Ali et al., 2022). This ability to channel natural resource wealth and offset negative effects gives rise to the "financial market resource blessing hypothesis". History shows however that natural resources are commonly associated with real exchange rate appreciation and Dutch disease (Babatunde et al., 2013), the erosion of manufacturing and services exports (Gylfason et al., 1999; Mehlum et al., 2006), lower levels of beneficiation (Arvanitis & Weigert, 2017), stock market volatility and disequilibria (Lakshmi et al., 2021), the diversion of skills and investment (Beck, 2002), rent-seeking and corruption (Ahmed, 2020; Sharma, 2021), increased transaction costs (Acemoglu & Verdier, 2000), decreased investor confidence, and capital flight (Yartey, 2010). Hence, this negative association between natural resources and FSD is referred to as the "financial market resource curse hypothesis".

The factor that is commonly cited as the determinant of whether natural resources are an FSD blessing or a curse is institutional quality (Acemoglu et al., 2001; Bhattacharyya & Hodler, 2014; Abdulahi et al., 2019; Islam et al., 2020; Khan et al., 2020). The logic is that high natural resource endowment does not invariably lead to an FSD curse (Robinson et al., 2006) because democratic countries have the institutional ability to enforce the law (Mlachila & Ouedraogo, 2020). Hence, countries with strong institutional quality can turn the FSD resource curse into a blessing because of the heightened oversight and regulatory control of the financial channels, which then lessen the effects of rent-seeking, corruption, and elite power concentration (Mehlum et al., 2006; Marcelin & Mathur, 2014; Mlachila et al., 2016; Henri, 2019), strengthens contract enforcement (Acemoglu & Johnson, 2005), and entrenches the democratic, economic and political institutions (Boschini et al., 2007; Acemoglu & Robinson, 2012). In contrast, countries with low levels of democracy and weak institutions have little FSD because the associated systemic corruption distorts the banking sector via dishonest lending (Sharma & Paramati, 2020), which then stifles development of financial institutions and domestic financial markets (Venard & Hanafi, 2008).

Countries that suffer from the financial market resource curse tend to have a powerful elite that are more focussed on political control and access to resource rents than on socio-economic development (Rajan & Zingales, 2003a; Sandow et al., 2022), and this has three detrimental effects. First, there is little interest in diversifying trade into manufacturing and thus the emphasis on low-skilled, low wage employment hampers future development due to skills mismatches (Kurronen, 2015). Second, an insecure elite use the resource windfalls to entrench their own positions of political power and resist the pressure to deepen democracy, property rights, or the rule of law (Beck, 2011; Bhattacharyya & Hodler, 2014).[6] It is possible however for the elite to be challenged and ousted by new entrants who gain access to the political and economic levers of power as a result of the cyclicality of the resource rents because the domestic market conditions of resource-dependent states are largely determined by international commodity price volatility (Kurronen, 2015). Third, the elite will establish relationships with natural resource multinationals directly and thus they

[6] Africa's diamond wars show that elite access to resource rents can be used to fund conflicts, insurgencies, and instability (Collier & Hoeffler, 1998, 2005; Tornell & Lane, 1998; Khan et al., 2020).

do not need, nor want, regulatory oversight from a sophisticated banking system (Acemoglu & Johnson, 2005; Beck et al., 2003; La Porta et al., 1997, 1998). Consequently, creditors may struggle to enforce contracts, debtors may not feel the need to honour their debt obligations, and investors and banks may be less willing to borrow or lend (Dwumfour & Ntow-Gyamfi, 2018).

While there is a substantial body of international literature on the financial resource curse, studies devoted to SSA are still relatively uncommon. Dwumfour and Ntow-Gyamfi (2018) find that natural resources are detrimental to banking sector stability in both low- and middle-income SSA countries but have a positive effect on credit provision to the private sector. Sandow et al. (2022) report that SSA's legal and political institutions have not yet reached the level where natural resource rents can benefit FSD whereas Nurmakhanova et al. (2023) report that natural resources negatively affect FSD inside SSA countries, it has a significantly positive effect on FSD in neighbouring countries, mainly due to capital flight to less resource-dependent neighbours, and because labour moves from the less resource-endowed countries to resource-rich countries, but the wages are repatriated as capital remittances thus leading to FSD in the home countries.

SSA's resource dependence and weak institutions also exacerbate the socio-economic and political effects of SCRs (Gossel and Mutize, 2024). This is because resource-dependent states tend to be ruled by elite gatekeepers who are overly responsive to the resource rent effects that SCR changes have on international mining companies (Rajan & Zingales, 2003a, 2003b). In addition, this dependence increases the likelihood of SCR downgrades because elitist and predatory capitalist regimes resist reform and regulation of the domestic banking system (Acemoglu & Johnson, 2005; Beck et al., 2003; La Porta et al., 1997, 1998), which in turn increases credit risk and limits credit access (Torvik, 2002; Bhattacharyya & Hodler, 2010, 2014; Dwumfour & Ntow-Gyamfi, 2018).

However, the scatterplot of SSA's financial sector development and institutional quality (averaged over the period of 1996–2020) in Fig. 7.4a–i shows that there are significantly positive associations between the FSD metrics and the composite Institutional Quality Index (IQI).[7] Furthermore,

[7] The composite institutional quality series is calculated as the annual average of the six World Governance Indicators (Control of Corruption, Government Effectiveness, Political Stability and Absence of Violence/Terrorism, Regulatory Quality, Rule of Law, and Voice

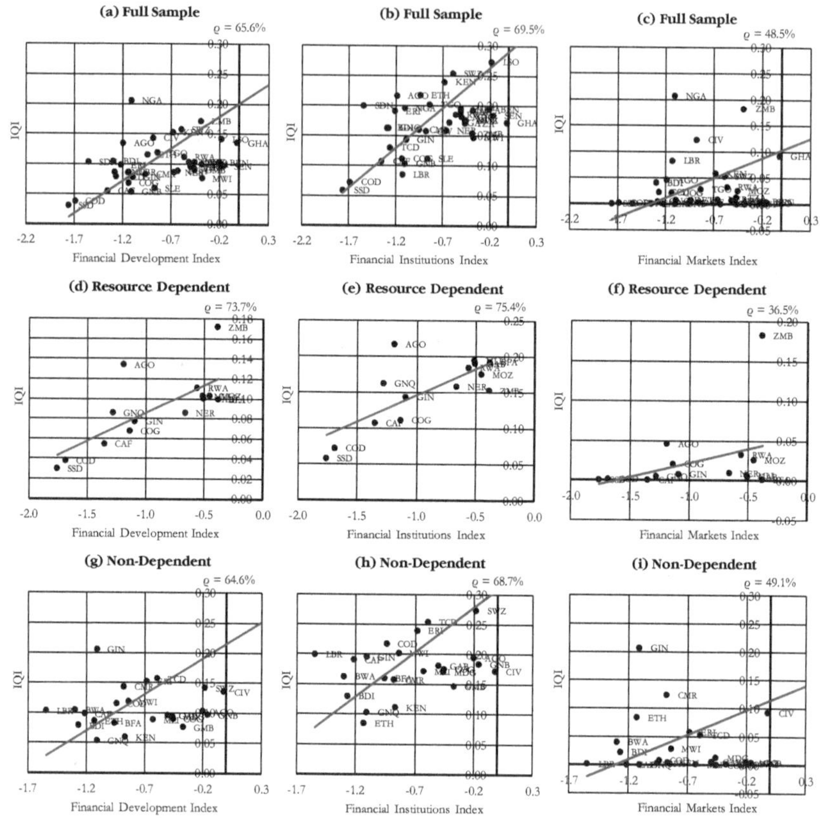

Fig. 7.4 Scatterplots of FSD and institutional quality. (Data sources: World Governance Indicators, IMF)

the correlation coefficients between the Financial Development Index and IQI and the Financial Institutions Index and IQI are higher in the resource-dependent sub-sample than in the non-dependent sub-sample whereas the correlations between the Financial Market Index and IQI are higher for the non-dependent sub-sample.

Table 7.4 further indicates that (similar to the results in Table 7.3), SSA countries with above-average IQI tend to have significantly higher FSD

and Accountability) for each of the 40 countries in the sample. The years of missing data for 1997, 1999, and 2001 have been interpolated.

Table 7.4 FSD and the institutional quality

Average	*(a) Above-average IQI [21]*	*(b) Below-average IQI [19]*	*(a)/(b)*	*(c) Non-dependent [25]*	*(d) Resource dependent [15]*	*(c)/(d)*
Institutional quality index (IQI)	−0.30	−1.17	0.3	−0.63	−0.84	0.8
Financial development index	0.15	0.09	1.7	0.14	0.09	1.6
Financial institutions index	0.24	0.15	1.6	0.22	0.15	1.4
Financial markets index	0.06	0.03	2.0	0.06	0.02	2.7

[#] indicates the number of SSA countries in the sample

Data sources: World Governance Indicators and IMF (1996–2020)

levels, and this is also matched by the SSA countries that are less resource export dependent compared to the SSA countries that are resource dependent. Thus, SSA countries that are more democratic, have deeper institutional quality, and are less resource dependent tend to have higher levels of FSD than SSA countries that are more autocratic, institutionally weak, and resource dependent.

7.5 Financial Sector Development and FDI

While it is to be expected that FDI and FSD will share a bidirectional relationship, an outcome of the financial market resource blessing and curse hypotheses is that the relationship between FDI and FSD can also be positive or negative. More specifically, there are five reasons why FDI should have a positive association with FSD (Otchere et al., 2016; Mbratana et al., 2021). First, FDI inflows will inject additional capital into the financial system for fixed investment, boosting domestic bank and financial market intermediation (Henry, 2000; Claessens et al., 2001; Agarwal & Mohtadi, 2004; Jeffus, 2004; Desai et al., 2006). Second, increased FDI inflows will erode the power of the elites (Henry, 2000; Desai et al., 2006; Kholdy & Sohrabian, 2008) and thus stimulate market-friendly regulatory reforms (Rajan & Zingales, 2003b; Kholdy & Sohrabian, 2005, 2008).

Third, in emerging countries with poor FSD levels and weak institutional quality, FDI can also act as a substitute for immature financial markets (Claessens et al., 2001; Nasser & Gomez, 2009), thus enhancing FSD over time (Agarwal & Mohtadi, 2004; Jeffus, 2004), creating a virtuous cycle of rising FSD and FDI (Henry, 2000; Otchere et al., 2016), and lowering risk premia and the cost of capital (Desai et al., 2006). Fourth, the spill-over effects of FDI will drive stock market development because international affiliates may list on a domestic stock market and the multinational's activities will thus be financed through this domestic stock market (Irandoust, 2021), which similarly leads to a virtuous cycle because additional investment is attracted as the domestic market becomes more liquid, open, and deep. Finally, FSD arising from FDI increases financial sector competition, broadening access to external finance (Harrison et al., 2004; Antràs et al., 2009; Adeniyi et al., 2012; Desbordes & Wei, 2017; Bilir et al., 2019), and improving the efficient allocation of capital (Levine, 1997, 2005). These benefits in turn suggest that over time, FDI nurtured FSD will make the economy less dependent on foreign investment and more reliant on domestic investment (Dutta & Roy, 2011).

Conversely however there are three reasons why FDI may hamper FSD (Mbratana et al., 2021). First, by its nature, FDI inflows exemplify a source of financing that may give international companies an unfair, uncompetitive, or exclusionary advantage over domestic companies and financial markets (Levine, 1997; Claessens et al., 2001; Desbordes & Wei, 2017). Second, borrowing by international companies from domestic banks can worsen the financial constraints of domestic companies (Harrison & McMillan, 2003) and thus erode FSD (Desbordes & Wei, 2017). Third, asymmetric information may render FDI investors overly reliant on SCRs and thus a downgrade could stimulate capital outflows to higher rated countries (Cai et al., 2018) whereas an upgrade has little effect (Brooks et al., 2004; Ferreira & Gama, 2007; Afonso et al., 2012).

In the case of SSA, although empirical studies find that there is a positive bidirectional relationship between FDI and FSD (Agbloyor et al., 2013; Mbratana et al., 2021) and that FDI crowds in private investment (Ndikumana & Verick, 2008); on a more nuanced level however, it is noted that the positive economic effect of FDI is dependent on a country's savings and private sector credit levels (Adjasi et al., 2012), and that FDI has a stronger association with financial market development than with banking sector development (Soumaré & Tchana, 2015; Acquah & Ibrahim, 2020) even though SSA has traditionally had bank-led FSD.

As can be seen from the scatterplots of FSD and net FDI inflows to SSA (averaged over the period of 1980–2020) in Fig. 7.5, there is positive correlation between FDI and FSD in the full sample and non dependent samples (a–c and g–i respectively) but weakly negative correlations between FDI and the financial development index, and FDI and the financial markets index in the resource-dependent sub-sample (d–f). However, once the outliers are removed, the scatterplots in Fig. 7.6 show that there is a deterioration in the correlation coefficients, particularly in the full and non-dependent samples, while the correlations in the resource-dependent sub-sample become more negative. Thus, these scatterplots suggest that

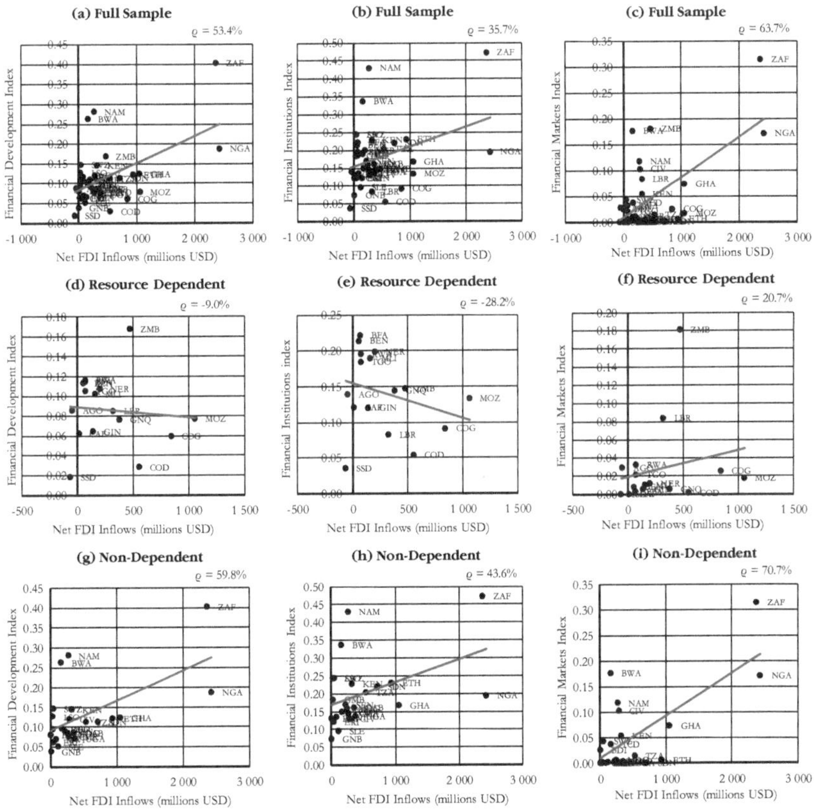

Fig. 7.5 Scatterplot of FSD and FDI inflows. (Data sources: World Development Indicators, IMF)

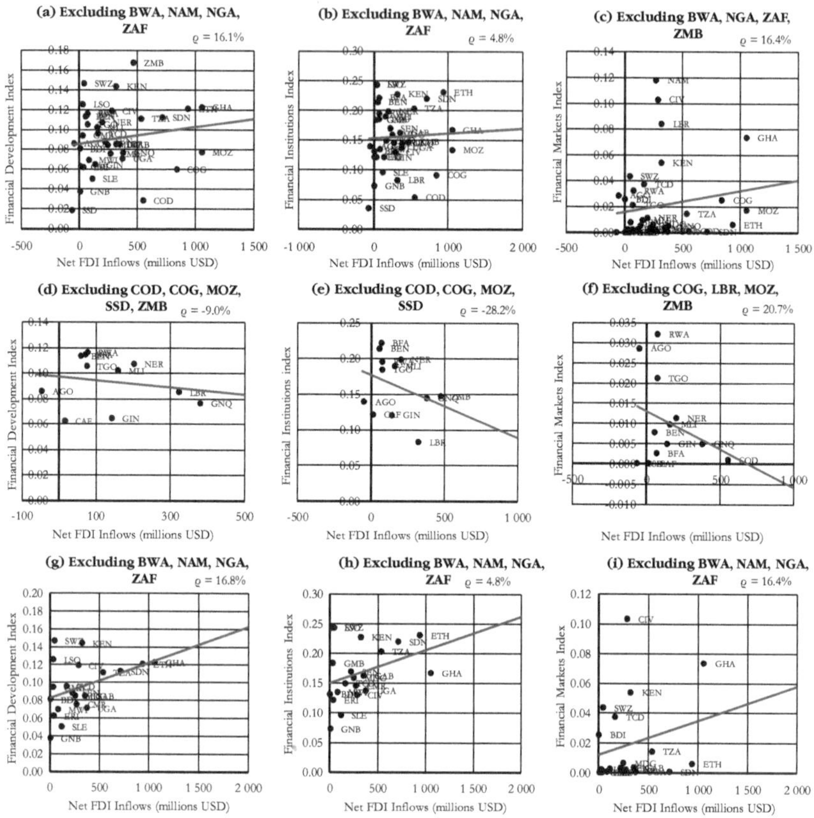

Fig. 7.6 Scatterplot of FSD and FDI inflows excluding outliers. (Data sources: World Development Indicators, IMF)

there is a positive association between FDI and FSD in non-dependent SSA countries but a negative association in resource-dependent countries.

Table 7.5 further shows that SSA countries receive above-average FDI inflows and non-dependent SSA countries have significantly higher levels of FSD compared to countries with below-average FDI inflows and high natural resource dependence.

Table 7.5 FSD and FDI

Average	*Measure*	*(a) Above-average FDI [10]*	*(b) Below-average FDI [30]*	*(a)/(b)*	*(c) Non-dependent [24]*	*(d) Resource dependent [16]*	*(c)/(d)*
Net FDI inflows	Millions USD	1104.35	156.66	7.0	468.13	288.13	1.6
Financial development	Index	0.14	0.10	1.4	0.13	0.09	1.5
Financial institutions	Index	0.19	0.17	1.1	0.20	0.14	1.4
Financial markets	Index	0.08	0.03	3.1	0.05	0.03	1.8

[#] indicates the number of SSA countries in the sample

Data sources: World Development Indicators and IMF (1980–2020)

Appendix

Standard & Poor, Moody's, and Fitch Foreign Currency Rating System

Characterisation of debt and issuer	*Rating*			*Linear transformation*
	S&P	*Moody's*	*Fitch*	
Highest quality	AAA	Aaa	AAA	23
High quality	AA+	Aa1	AA+	22
	AA	Aa2	AA	21
	AA−	Aa3	AA−	20
Strong payment capacity	A+	A1	A+	19
	A	A2	A	18
	A−	A3	A−	17
Adequate payment capacity	BBB+	Baa1	BBB+	16
	BBB	Baa2	BBB	15
	BBB−	Baa3	BBB−	14
Likely to fulfil obligation, ongoing uncertainty	BB+	Ba1	BB+	13
	BB	Ba2	BB	12
	BB−	Ba3	BB−	11
High credit risk	B+	B1	B+	10
	B	B2	B	9

Characterisation of debt and issuer	*Rating*			*Linear transformation*
	S&P	*Moody's*	*Fitch*	
	B−	B3	B−	8
Very high credit risk	CCC+	Caa1	CCC+	7
	CCC	Caa2	CCC	6
	CCC−	Caa3	CCC−	5
Near default with possibility of recovery	CC	Ca	CC	4
			C	3
Default	SD	C	DDD	2
	D		DD	1
			D	0

Source: Mutize and Gossel (2019)

References

Abdulahi, M. E., Shu, Y., & Khan, M. A. (2019). Resource Rents, Economic Growth, and the Role of Institutional Quality: A Panel Threshold Analysis. *Resources Policy, 61*, 293–303.

Acemoglu, D. (2003). The Form of Property Rights: Democratic Versus Oligarchic Societies. *NBER Working Paper Series*. National Bureau of Economic Research Cambridge.

Acemoglu, D., & Johnson, S. (2005). Unbundling Institutions. *Journal of Political Economy, 113*(5), 949–995.

Acemoglu, D., Johnson, S., & Robinson, J. A. (2001). The Colonial Origins of Comparative Development: An Empirical Investigation. *American Economic Review, 91*(5), 1369–1401.

Acemoglu, D., Naidu, S., Restrepo, P., & Robinson, J. (2019). Democracy Does Cause Growth. *Journal of Political Economy, 127*(1), 47–100.

Acemoglu, D., & Robinson, J. A. (2006). *Economic Origins of Dictatorship and Democracy*. Cambridge University Press.

Acemoglu, D., & Robinson, J. A. (2012). *Why Nations Fail*. Crown Publishers.

Acemoglu, D., & Verdier, T. (2000). The Choice Between Market Failures and Corruption. *American Economic Review, 90*(1), 194–211.

Acquah, A. M., & Ibrahim, M. (2020). Foreign Direct Investment, Economic Growth and Financial Sector Development in Africa. *Journal of Sustainable Finance & Investment, 10*(4), 315–334.

Adeniyi, O., Omisakin, O., Egwaikhide, F. O., & Oyinlola, A. (2012). Foreign Direct Investment, Economic Growth and Financial Sector Development in

Small Open Developing Economies. *Economic Analysis and Policy, 42*(1), 105–127.

Adeyeye, P. O., Fapetu, O., Aluko, O. A., & Migiro, S. O. (2015). Does Supply-Leading Hypothesis Hold in a Developing Economy? A Nigerian Focus. *Procedia Economics and Finance, 30*, 30–37.

Adjasi, C. K. D., Abor, J., Osei, K. A., & Nyavor-Foli, E. E. (2012). FDI and Economic Activity in Africa: The Role of Local Financial Markets. *Thunderbird International Business Review, 54*(4), 429–439.

Afonso, A., Furceri, D., & Gomes, P. (2012). Sovereign Credit Ratings and Financial Markets Linkages: Application to European Data. *Journal of International Money and Finance, 31*(3), 606–638.

Agarwal, S., & Mohtadi, H. (2004). Financial Markets and the Financing Choice of Firms: Evidence from Developing Countries. *Global Finance Journal, 15*, 57–70.

Agbloyor, E. K., Abor, J., Adjasi, C. K. D., & Yawson, A. (2013). Exploring the Causality Links between Financial Markets and Foreign Direct Investment in Africa. *Research in International Business and Finance, 28*, 118–134.

Ahmad, N., & Ali, S. (2010). Corruption and Financial Sector Performance: A Cross-Country Analysis. *Economics Bulletin, 30*(1), 303–308.

Ahmed, W. M. A. (2020). Corruption and Equity Market Performance: International Comparative Evidence. *Pacific-Basin Finance Journal, 60*, 101282.

Aker, J., Klein, M., O'Connell, S., & Yang, M. (2010). Are Borders Barriers? The Impact of International and Internal Ethnic Borders on Agricultural Markets in West Africa. *Working Paper 208*. Center for Global Development.

Ali, A., Ramakrishnan, S., & Faisal. (2022). Financial Development and Natural Resources. Is There a Stock Market Resource Curse? *Resources Policy, 75*, 102457.

Allen, F., Carletti, E., Cull, R., Qian, J., Senbet, L., & Valenzuela, P. (2014). The African Financial Development and Financial Inclusion Gaps. *Journal of African Economies, 23*, 614–642.

Allen, F., Otchere, I., & Senbet, L. (2011). African Financial Systems: A Review. *Review of Development Finance, 1*, 79–113.

Altenkirch, C. (2005). The Determinants of Sovereign Credit Ratings: A New Empirical Approach. *South African Journal of Economics, 73*, 462–473.

Aluko, O. A., Fapetu, O., & Ibitoye, J. O. (2019). Do Openness and Democracy Deepen Banking Sector in Sub-Saharan Africa? *Global Business Review, 22*(2), 279–289.

Ammer, J., & Clinton, N. (2004). Good News Is No News? The Impact of Credit Rating Changes on the Pricing of Asset-Backed Securities. *International Finance Discussion Paper No. 809*. Federal Reserve Board.

Andrianaivo, M., & Yartey, C. A. (2009). Understanding the Growth of African Financial Markets. *Working Paper No. WP/09/182*. International Monetary Fund.

Andrianova, S., Baltagi, B., & Demetriades, P. (2011). Loan Defaults in Africa. *Discussion Papers in Economics 11/36*. Division of Economics, School of Business, University of Leicester.

Andrianova, S., Baltagi, B., Demetriades, P., & Fielding, D. (2015). Why Do African Banks Lend So Little? *Oxford Bulletin of Economics and Statistics, 77*(3), 339–359.

Antràs, P., Desai, M. A., & Foley, C. F. (2009). Multinational Firms, FDI Flows, and Imperfect Capital Markets. *The Quarterly Journal of Economics, 124*(3), 1171–1219.

Apergis, N. (2017). Democracy and Market Crashes: Evidence from a Worldwide Panel of Countries. *Finance Research Letters, 22*, 244–248.

APRM. (2023). Africa Sovereign Credit Ratings Review: 2023 – Mid-Year Outlook. *African Peer Review Mechanism Report No. G&SR-CRA05/2023*.

Archer, C. C., Biglaiser, G., & DeRouen, K. (2007). Sovereign Bonds and the 'Democratic Advantage': Does Regime Type Affect Credit Rating Agencies in the Developing World? *International Organization, 61*(2), 341–365.

Arezki, R., Candelon, B., & Sy, A. N. R. (2011). Sovereign Rating News and Financial Markets Spillovers: Evidence from the European Debt Crisis. *IMF Working Paper No. 11*. International Monetary Fund.

Arvanitis, Y., & Weigert, M. (2017). Turning Resource Curse into Development Dividends in Guinea-Bissau. *Resources Policy, 53*, 226–237.

Asif, M., Khan, K. B., Anser, M. K., Nassani, A. A., Abro, M. M. Q., & Zaman, K. (2020). Dynamic Interaction Between Financial Development and Natural Resources: Evaluating the 'Resource Curse' Hypothesis. *Resources Policy, 65*, 101566.

AU. (2022, February 8). APRM Denounces Moody's Inaccuracies in Ghana's Rating Downgrade. *Press Release No. 000003456/2021*.

Ayyagari, M., Demirgüç-Kunt, A., & Maksimovic, V. (2011). Firm Innovation in Emerging Markets: The Role of Finance, Governance, and Competition. *Journal of Financial and Quantitative Analysis, 46*(6), 1545–1580.

Babatunde, M. A., Adenikinju, O., & Adenikinju, A. F. (2013). Oil Price Shocks and Stock Market Behaviour in Nigeria. *Journal of Economic Studies, 40*(2), 180–202.

Baltagi, B. H., Demetriades, P. O., & Law, S. H. (2009). Financial Development and Openness: Evidence from Panel Data. *Journal of Development Economics, 89*(2), 285–296.

Barro, R. (1996). Democracy and Growth. *Journal of Economic Growth, 1*(1), 1–27.

Barta, Z., & Johnston, A. (2017). Rating Politics? Partisan Discrimination in Credit Ratings in Developed Economies. *Comparative Political Studies, 51*(5), 587–620.

Bats, J., & Houben, A. (2017). Bank-Based Versus Market-Based Financing: Implications for Systemic Risk. *Working Paper No. 577*. De Nederlandsche Bank.

Beaulieu, E., Cox, W., & Saiegh, S. (2012). Sovereign Debt and Regime Type: Reconsidering the Democratic Advantage. *International Organization, 66*(4), 709–738.

Becerra, O., Cavallo, E., & Scartascini, C. (2012). The Politics of Financial Development: The Role of Interest Groups and Government Capabilities. *Journal of Banking & Finance, 36*(3), 626–643.

Beck, T. (2002). Financial Development and International Trade: Is there a Link? *Journal of International Economics, 57*(1), 107–131.

Beck, T. (2011). Finance and Oil: Is there a Resource Curse in Financial Development? *European Banking Center Discussion Paper No 2011–004*. Tilburg University.

Beck, T., Demirguc-Kunt, A., & Levine, R. (2001). Legal Theories of Financial Development. *Oxford Review of Economic Policy, 17*(4), 483–501.

Beck, T., Demirguc-Kunt, A., & Levine, R. (2003). Law and Finance: Why Does Legal Origin Matter? *Journal of Comparative Economics, 31*(4), 653–676.

Beck, T., Demirguc-Kunt, A., & Levine, R. (2007). Finance, Inequality and the Poor. *Journal of Economic Growth, 12*(1), 27–49.

Beck, T., & Levine, R. (2002). Industry Growth and Capital Accumulation: Does Having a Market- or Bank-Based System Matter? *Journal of Financial Economics, 64*(2), 147–180.

Beck, T., & Levine, R. (2004). Stock Markets, Banks and Growth: Panel Evidence. *Journal of Banking and Finance, 28*, 423–442.

Berglof, E., & Lehmann, A. (2009). Sustaining Russia's Growth: The Role of Financial Reform. *Journal of Comparative Economics, 37*(2), 198–206.

Bhattacharyya, S. & Hodler, R. (2010). "Natural Resources, Democracy, and Corruption," *European Economic Review*, 54(4), 608–621.

Bhattacharyya, S. (2013). Political Origins of Financial Structure. *Journal of Comparative Economics, 41*, 979–994.

Bhattacharyya, S., & Hodler, R. (2014). Do Natural Resource Revenues Hinder Financial Development? The Role of Political Institutions. *World Development, 57*, 101–113.

Biglaiser, G., & DeRouen, K. (2007). Sovereign Bond Ratings and Neoliberalism in Latin America. *International Studies Quarterly, 51*(1), 121–138.

Biglaiser, G., DeRouen, K., & Archer, C. C. (2011). Politics, Early Warning Systems, and Credit Rating Agencies. *Policy Analysis, 7*(1), 67–87.

Biglaiser, G., & Staats, J. L. (2012). Finding the 'Democratic Advantage' in Sovereign Bond Ratings: The Importance of Strong Courts, Property Rights Protection, and the Rule of Law. *International Organization, 66*(3), 515–535.
Bilir, L. K., Chor, D., & Manova, K. (2019). Host-Country Financial Development and Multinational Activity. *European Economic Review, 115*, 192–220.
Bologna, J., & Ross, A. (2015). Corruption and Entrepreneurship: Evidence from Brazilian Municipalities. *Public Choice, 165*(1), 59–77.
Boschini, A. D., Pettersson, J., & Roine, J. (2007). Resource Curse or Not: A Question of Appropriability. *Scandinavian Journal of Economics, 109*(3), 593–617.
Botha, I., & Pretorius, M. (2020). The Geographical and Income Differences in the Determinants of African Sovereign Credit Ratings. *African Journal of Economic and Management Studies, 11*(4), 609–624.
Boyd, J. H., Levine, R., & Smith, B. D. (2001). The Impact of Inflation on Financial Sector Performance. *Journal of Monetary Economics, 47*(2), 221–248.
Brooks, R., Faff, R. W., Hillier, D., & Hillier, J. (2004). The National Market Impact of Sovereign Rating Changes. *Journal of Banking & Finance, 28*(1), 233–250.
Broto, C., & Molina, L. (2016). Sovereign Ratings and their Asymmetric Response to Fundamentals. *Journal of Economic Behavior & Organization, 130*, 206–224.
Cai, P., Gan, Q., & Kim, S.-J. (2018). Do Sovereign Credit Ratings Matter for Foreign Direct Investments? *Journal of International Financial Markets Institutions and Money, 55*, 50–64.
Chen, S. S., Chen, H. Y., Chang, C. C., & Yang, S. L. (2016). The Relation Between Sovereign Credit Rating Revisions and Economic Growth. *Journal of Banking and Finance, 64*, 90–100.
Chikalipah, S., & Makina, D. (2019). Chapter 6: A Survey of Microfinance Institutions and Informal Finance in Africa. In D. Makina (Ed.), *Extending Financial Inclusion in Africa*. Academic Press.
Christopher, R., Kim, S. J., & Wu, E. (2012). Do Sovereign Credit Ratings Influence Regional Stock and Bond Market Interdependencies in Emerging Countries? *Journal of International Financial Markets Institutions and Money, 22*(4), 1070–1089.
Claessens, S., Klingebiel, D., & Schmukler, S. L. (2001). FDI and Stock Market Development: Complements or Substitutes? *Working Paper*. World Bank.
Clague, C., Keefer, P., Knack, S., & Olson, M. (1996). Property and Contract Rights in Autocracies and Democracies. *Journal of Economic Growth, 1*, 243–276.
Clarke, G. R. G., Colin, X. L., & Zou, H. (2006). Finance and Income Inequality: What do the Data Tell Us? *Southern Economic Journal, 72*, 578–596.
Collier, P., & Hoeffler, A. (1998). On Economic Causes of Civil War. *Oxford Economic Papers, 50*(4), 563–573.

Collier, P., & Hoeffler, A. (2005). Resource Rents, Governance, and Conflict. *Journal of Conflict Resolution, 49*(4), 625–633.
Comeau, L. (2003). Democracy and Growth: A Relationship Revisited. *Eastern Economic Journal, 29*(1), 1–21.
Daumont, R., Le Gall, F., & Leroux, F. (2004). Banking in Sub-Saharan Africa: What Went Wrong? *Working Paper No. 04/55*. International Monetary Fund.
Delis, M. D., Hasan, I., & Ongena, S. (2020). Democracy and Credit. *Journal of Financial Economics, 136*(2), 571–596.
Demirgüç-Kunt, A., & Levine, R. (2001). *Financial Structures and Economic Growth: A Cross-Country Comparison of Banks, Markets, and Development*. MIT Press.
Demirgüç-Kunt, A., & Maksimovic, V. (2002). Funding Growth in Bank-Based and Market Based Financial Systems: Evidence from Firm Level Data. *Journal of Financial Economics, 65*(3), 337–363.
Desai, M. A., Foley, C. F., & Hines, J. R., Jr. (2006). Capital Controls, Liberalizations, and Foreign Direct Investment. *The Review of Financial Studies, 19*(4), 1433–1464.
Desbordes, R., & Wei, S. J. (2017). The Effects of Financial Development on Foreign Direct Investment. *Journal of Development Economics, 127*, 153–168.
DiGiuseppe, M. (2015a). The Fiscal Autonomy of Deciders: Creditworthiness and Conflict Initiation. *Foreign Policy Analysis, 11*(3), 317–338.
DiGiuseppe, M. (2015b). Guns, Butter, and Debt: Sovereign Creditworthiness and Military Expenditure. *Journal of Peace Research, 52*(5), 680–693.
DiGiuseppe, M., & Shea, P. E. (2015). Sovereign Credit and the Fate of Leaders: Reassessing the 'Democratic Advantage'. *International Studies Quarterly, 59*(3), 557–570.
DiGiuseppe, M. R., Barry, C. M., & Frank, R. W. (2012). Good for the Money: International Finance, State Capacity, and Internal Armed Conflict. *Journal of Peace Research, 49*(3), 391–405.
Dudian, M., & Popa, R. A. (2012). Analysis on the Relationship Between Rating and Economic Growth for the European Union Emergent Economies. *International Journal of Economics and Management Engineering, 6*(4), 431–434.
Dutta, N., & Roy, S. (2011). Foreign Direct Investment, Financial Development and Political Risks. *The Journal of Developing Areas, 44*(2), 303–327.
Dwumfour, R. A., & Ntow-Gyamfi, M. (2018). Natural Resources, Financial Development and Institutional Quality in Africa: Is there a Resource Curse? *Resources Policy, 59*, 411–426.
Easterly, W., & Levine, R. (1997). Africa's Growth Tragedy: Policies and Ethnic Divisions. *Quarterly Journal of Economics, 112*, 1203–1250.

EIB. (2013). Banking in Sub-Saharan Africa Challenges and Opportunities. *European Investment Bank*. Retrieved October, 2022, from https://www.eib.org/attachments/efs/economic_report_banking_africa_en.pdf

Faccio, M. (2006). Politically Connected Firms. *American Economic Review, 96*(1), 369–386.

Faccio, M., Masulis, R., & McConnell, J. J. (2005). Political Connections and Corporate Bailouts. *Journal of Finance, 61*(6), 2597–2635.

Fadikpe, A. A. A., Danquah, R., Aidoo, M., Chomen, D. A., Yankey, R., & Dongmei, X. (2022). Linkages Between Social and Financial Performance: Evidence from Sub-Saharan Africa Microfinance Institutions. *PLoS One, 17*(3), e0261326.

Ferreira, M. A., & Gama, P. M. (2007). Does Sovereign Debt Ratings News Spill Over to International Stock Markets? *Journal of Banking and Finance, 31*(10), 3162–3182.

Ferri, G., Liu, L.-G., & Stiglitz, J. E. (1999). The Procyclical Role of Rating Agencies: Evidence from the East Asian Crisis. *Economic Notes, 28*(3), 335–355.

Fleming, J., Kirby, C., & Ostdiek, B. (1998). Information and Volatility Linkages in the Stock, Bond, and Money Markets. *Journal of Financial Economics, 49*, 111–137.

Gambacorta, L., Yang, J., & Tsatsaronis, K. (2014). Financial Structure and Growth. *BIS Quarterly Review*, 21–35.

Gande, A., & Parsley, D. C. (2005). News Spillovers in the Sovereign Debt Market. *Journal of Financial Economics, 75*(3), 691–734.

Gates, S., Havard, H., Jones, M. P., & Strand, H. (2006). Institutional Inconsistency and Political Instability: Polity Duration, 1800–2000. *American Political Science Review, 50*(4), 893–908.

Gbohoui, W., Ouedraogo, R., & Some, Y. M. (2023). Sub-Saharan Africa's Risk Perception Premium: In the Search of Missing Factors. *IMF Working Paper No. WP/23/130*. International Monetary Fund.

Ghardallou, W. (2022). Financial System Development and Democracy: A Panel Smooth Transition Regression Approach for Developing Countries. *Journal of the Knowledge Economy, 13*, 1714–1735.

Girma, S., & Shortland, A. (2008). The Political Economy of Financial Development. *Oxford Economic Papers, 60*(4), 567–596.

Gorodnichenko, Y., & Schnitzer, M. (2013). Financial Constraints and Innovation: Why Poor Countries Don't Catch Up. *Journal of the European Economic Association, 11*(5), 1115–1152.

Gossel, S. J., & Mutize, M. (2025). The Effect of Sovereign Credit Ratings on Democracy in Sub-Saharan Africa. *International Journal of Emerging Markets. 20* (13): 223–243.

GSMA. (2024). The State of the Industry Report on Mobile Money. Retrieved May, 2024, from https://www.gsma.com/sotir/wp-content/uploads/2024/03/GSMA-SOTIR-2024_Report_v7 2.pdf

Gylfason, T., Herbertsson, T. T., & Zoega, G. (1999). A Mixed Blessing: Natural Resources and Economic Growth. *Macroeconomic Dynamics, 3*(2), 204–225.

Haber, S., & Perotti, E. (2008). The Political Economy of Financial Systems. *Tinbergen Institute Discussion Paper No. 08-045/2.* Tinbergen Institute.

Hamori, S., & Hashiguchi, Y. (2012). The Effect of Financial Deepening on Inequality: Some International Evidence. *Journal of Asian Economics, 23*(4), 353–359.

Harrison, A. E., Love, I., & McMillan, M. S. (2004). Global Capital Flows and Financing Constraints. *Journal of Development Economics, 75*(1), 269–301.

Harrison, A. E., & McMillan, M. S. (2003). Does Direct Foreign Investment Affect Domestic Credit Constraints? *Journal of International Economics, 61*(1), 73–100.

Hattendorff, C. (2014). *Natural Resources, Export Concentration and Financial Development.* Freie University Berlin, FBWirtschaftswissenschaft.

He, J., & Schiereck, D. (2019). Sovereign Rating Announcements and the Integration of African Banking Markets. *The Journal of Risk Finance, 20*(5), 484–500.

Henri, P. A. O. (2019). Natural Resources Curse: A Reality in Africa. *Resources Policy, 63*, 101406.

Henry, P. B. (2000). Do Stock Market Liberalizations Cause Investment Booms? *Journal of Financial Economics, 58*(1–2), 301–334.

Hermes, N., & Lensink, R. (2003). Foreign Direct Investment, Financial Development and Economic Growth. *Journal of Development Studies, 40*(1), 142–163.

Ho, C. Y., Huang, S., Shi, H., & Wu, J. (2018). Financial Deepening and Innovation: The Role of Political Institutions. *World Development, 109*, 1–13.

Honohan, P., & Beck, T. (2007). *Making Finance Work for Africa.* The World Bank.

Hooper, V., Hume, T., & Kim, S. (2008). Sovereign Rating Changes – Do They Provide New Information for Stock Markets? *Economic Systems, 32*, 142–166.

Huntington, S. (1968). *Political Order in Changing Societies.* Yale University Press.

Ibrahim, M., & Acquah, A. M. (2021). Re-examining the Causal Relationships Among FDI, Economic Growth and Financial Sector Development in Africa. *International Review of Applied Economics, 35*(1), 45–63.

Ibrahim, M., & Alagidede, P. (2017a). Financial Sector Development, Economic Volatility and Shocks in Sub-Saharan Africa. *Physica A, 484*, 66–81.

Ibrahim, M., & Alagidede, P. (2017b). Financial Development, Growth Volatility and Information Asymmetry in Sub-Saharan Africa: Does Law Matter? *South African Journal of Economics, 85*(4), 570–588.

Ibrahim, M., & Alagidede, P. (2018). Effect of Financial Development on Economic Growth in Sub-Saharan Africa. *Journal of Policy Modeling, 40*, 1104–1125.

Iddrisu, K., Abor, J. Y., & Banyen, K. T. (2023). The Effects of Foreign Bank Presence on Financial Development in Africa: The Role of Institutional Quality. *Review of Financial Economics, 42*, 1–16.

IMF. (2015). *Pan-African Banks: Opportunities and Challenges for Cross-Border Oversight*. International Monetary Fund.

IMF. (2016). *Financial Development in Sub-Saharan Africa: Promoting Inclusive and Sustainable Growth*. International Monetary Fund.

IMF. (2019). Drivers of Cross-Border Banking in Sub-Saharan Africa. *IMF Working Paper No. WP/19/146*. International Monetary Fund.

Irandoust, M. (2021). FDI and Financial Development: Evidence from Eight Post-Communist Countries. *Studies in Economics and Econometrics, 45*(2), 102–116.

Isham, J., Woolcock, M., Pritchett, L., & Busby, G. (2005). The Varieties of Resource Experience: Natural Resource Export Structures and the Political Economy of Economic Growth. *World Bank Economic Review, 19*(2), 141–174.

Islam, M. A., Khan, M. A., Popp, J., Sroka, W., & Oláh, J. (2020). Financial Development and Foreign Direct Investment: The Moderating Role of Quality Institutions. *Sustainability, 12*(9), 35–56.

Ismailescu, I., & Kazemi, H. (2010). The Reaction of Emerging Market Credit Default Swap Spreads to Sovereign Credit Rating Changes. *Journal of Banking and Finance, 34*(12), 2861–2873.

Jeffus, W. (2004). FDI and Stock Market Development in Selected Latin American Countries. *International Finance Review, 5*, 35–44.

Johnson, C. L., & Kriz, K. A. (2005). Fiscal Institutions, Credit Ratings, and Borrowing Costs. *Public Budgeting & Finance, 25*, 84–103.

Kaminsky, G., & Schmukler, S. (2001). Emerging Market Instability: Do Sovereign Ratings Affect Country Risk and Stock Returns? *World Bank Economic Review, 16*, 171–195.

Kaminsky, G. L., & Reinhart, C. M. (2000). On Crises, Contagion, and Confusion. *Journal of International Economics, 51*(1), 145–168.

Kaminsky, G. L., Reinhart, C. M., & Végh, C. A. (2003). The Unholy Trinity of Financial Contagion. *NBER Working Paper Series, 17*(4), 51–74.

Kanga, D., Murinde, V., & Soumaré, I. (2021). How Has the Rise of Pan-African Banks Impacted Bank Stability in WAEMU? *Journal of International Financial Markets Institutions and Money, 73*, 101364.

Keynes, J. M. (1936). *The General Theory of Employment, Interest and Money*. Palgrave Macmillan.

Khan, M. A., Gu, L., Khan, M. A., & Oláh, J. (2020). Natural Resources and Financial Development: The Role of Institutional Quality. *Journal of Multinational Financial Management, 56*, 100641.

Khanna, T., & Yafeh, Y. (2007). Business Groups in Emerging Markets: Paragons or Parasites? *Journal of Economic Literature, 45*, 331–372.

Kholdy, S., & Sohrabian, A. (2005). Financial Markets, FDI, and Economic Growth: Granger Causality Test in Panel Data Models. *Working Paper*. California State Polytechnic University.

Kholdy, S., & Sohrabian, A. (2008). Foreign Direct Investment, Financial Markets and Political Corruption. *Journal of Economic Studies, 35*(6), 486–500.

Khwaja, A. I., & Mian, A. (2005). Do Lenders Favor Politically Connected Firms: Rent Provision in an Emerging Financial Market. *Quarterly Journal of Economics, 120*(4), 1371–1411.

Kiff, J., Holland, A., Kisser, M., Nowak, S., Saab, S., Schumacher, L., & Westin, A.-M. (2010). The Uses and Abuses of Sovereign Credit Ratings. *International Monetary Fund (Quarterly Report)* (pp. 85–122).

Kim, D.-H., & Lin, S.-C. (2011). Nonlinearity in the Financial Development-Income Inequality Nexus. *Journal of Comparative Economics, 39*(3), 310–325.

Kim, S.-J., & Wu, E. (2008). Sovereign Credit Ratings, Capital Flows and Financial Sector Development in Emerging Markets. *Emerging Markets Review, 9*, 17–39.

Kisgen, D. J. (2006). Credit Ratings and Capital Structure. *The Journal of Finance, 61*, 1035–1072.

Klagge, B., & Zademach, H.-M. (2018). International Capital Flows, Stock Markets, and Uneven Development: The Case of Sub-Saharan Africa and the Sustainable Stock Exchanges Initiative (SSEI). *De Gruyter, 62*(2), 92–107.

Kurronen, S. (2015). Financial Sector in Resource-Dependent Economies. *Emerging Markets Review, 23*, 208–229.

La Porta, R., Lopez-De-Silanes, F., Shleifer, A., & Vishny, R. W. (1997). Legal Determinants of External Finance. *Journal of Finance, 52*(3), 1131–1150.

La Porta, R., Lopez-de-Silanes, F., Shleifer, A., & Vishny, R. W. (1998). Law and Finance. *Journal of Political Economy, 106*(6), 1013–1155.

Lakshmi, G., Saha, S., & Bhattarai, K. (2021). Does Corruption Matter for Stock Markets? The Role of Heterogeneous Institutions. *Economic Modelling, 94*, 386–400.

Law, S. H., & Moradbeigi, M. (2017). Financial Development and Oil Resource Abundance–Growth Relations: Evidence from Panel Data. *Environmental Science and Pollution Research, 24*, 22458–22475.

Law, S. H., Tan, H. B., & Azman-Saini, W. N. W. (2014). Financial Development and Income Inequality at Different Levels of Institutional Quality. *Emerging Markets Finance and Trade, 50*(Suppl. 1), 21–33.

Leite, C. A., & Weidmann, J. (1999). Does Mother Nature Corrupt? Natural Resources, Corruption, and Economic Growth. *IMF Working Papers 1999/085.* International Monetary Fund.

Levine, R. (1997). Financial Development and Economic Growth: Views and Agenda. *Journal of Economic Literature, 35*, 688–726.

Levine, R. (2002). Bank-Based or Market-Based Financial Systems: Which Is Better? *Journal of Financial Intermediation, 11*(4), 398–428.

Levine, R. (2005). "Finance and Growth: Theory and Evidence," *Handbook of Economic Growth, 1A*, Chapter 12: 865–934, Elsevier.

Levine, R., & Zervos, S. (1998). Stock Markets, Banks and Economic Growth. *American Economic Review, 88*(3), 537–558.

Lin, J. Y., Sun, X., & Jiang, Y. (2009). Toward a Theory of Optimal Financial Structure. *World Bank Policy Research Working Paper 5038.* World Bank.

Lopes, C. (2024, May 5). African Countries Can't Resolve Their Debt Crisis Under a System Rigged Against Them. *The Conversation.* Retrieved July, 2024, from https://theconversation.com/african-countries-cant-resolve-their-debt-crisis-under-a-system-rigged-against-them-228905

Marcelin, I., & Mathur, I. (2014). Financial Development, Institutions and Banks. *International Review of Financial Analysis, 31*, 25–33.

Mateev, M. (2012). The Effect of Sovereign Credit Rating Announcements on Emerging Bond and Stock Markets: New Evidences. *Oxford Journal, 7*(1), 28–41.

Mbratana, T., Fotié, A. K., & Amba, M. C. O. (2021). Foreign Direct Investment and Financial Development in Africa: A Causality Assessment in the Frequency Domain. *The Journal of International Trade & Economic Development, 30*(5), 685–706.

McFerson, H. M. (2010). Extractive Industries and African Democracy: Can the 'Resource Curse' be Exorcised? *International Studies Perspectives, 11*, 335–353.

McKinnon, R. I. (1988). Financial Liberalisation in Retrospect: Interest Rate Policies in LDCs. In G. Ranis & T. P. Shulz (Eds.), *The State of Development Economics: Progress and Perspectives.* Basil Blackwell.

Mehlum, H., Moene, K., & Torvik, R. (2006). Institutions and the Resource Curse. *Economic Journal, 116*(508), 1–20.

Mensah, M. O., Agbloyor, E. K., Harvey, S. K., & Fiador, V. O. (2017). Sovereign Credit Ratings and Bank Funding Cost: Evidence from Africa. *Research in International Business and Finance, 42*, 887–899.

Minsky, H. (1986). *Stabilizing an Unstable Economy.* McGraw Hill.

Mlachila, M., & Ouedraogo, R. (2020). Financial Development Curse in Resource-Rich Countries: The Role of Commodity Price Shocks. *The Quarterly Review of Economics and Finance, 76*, 84–96.

Mlachila, M. M., Jidoud, A., Newiak, M. M., Radzewicz-Bak, B., & Takebe, M. M. (2016). Financial Development in Sub-Saharan Africa: Promoting

Inclusive and Sustainable Growth. *IMF Paper No. 2016/011*. International Monetary Fund.

Mlambo, C., & Biekpe, N. (2005). Thin Trading on African Stock Markets: Implications for Market Efficiency Testing. *Investment Analysts Journal, 34*(61), 29–40.

Mo, P. H. (2001). Corruption and Economic Growth. *Journal of Comparative Economics, 29*(1), 66–79.

Mody, A., & Murshid, A. P. (2005). Growing Up with Capital Flows. *Journal of International Economics, 65*, 249–266.

Moradi, Z. S., Mirzaeenejad, M., & Geraeenejad, G. (2016). Effect of Bank-Based or Market-Based Financial Systems on Income Distribution in Selected Countries. *Procedia Economics and Finance, 36*, 510–521.

Mutize, M. (2019). Why Credit-Rating Agencies Are Still Getting Away with Bad Behaviour. *New Agenda: South African Journal of Social and Economic Policy, 74*(1), 41–44.

Mutize, M., & Gossel, S. J. (2018a). Do Sovereign Rating Change Announcements Influence Excess Bond and Equity Returns in Africa? *International Journal of Emerging Markets, 13*(6), 1522–1537.

Mutize, M., & Gossel, S. J. (2018b). The Effects of Sovereign Credit Rating Spillovers on Neighboring Countries' Financial Markets. *The Journal of International Trade & Economic Development, 27*(8), 857–900.

Mutize, M., & Gossel, S. J. (2019). Sovereign Credit Rating Announcement Effects on Foreign Currency Denominated Bond and Equity Markets in Africa. *Journal of African Business, 20*(1), 135–152.

Mutize, M., & Gossel, S. J. (2020). Do Long-Term Foreign Currency Sovereign Credit Ratings Positively Affect Bond and Equity Market Efficiency in Africa? *International Journal of Sustainable Economy, 12*(4), 364–382.

Mutize, M., & Mugobo, V. V. (2020). An Analysis of Granger Causality Between Sovereign Credit Rating and Economic Growth in Sub-Saharan Africa. *Investment Management and Financial Innovations, 17*(4), 85–93.

Mutize, M., & Nkhalamba, M. P. (2021). International Credit Rating Agencies in Africa: Perceptions, Trends and Challenges. *International Journal of Sustainable Economy, 13*(1), 55–71.

Nasser, O. M., & Gomez, X. G. (2009). Do Well Functioning Financial Markets Promote FDI Flows to Latin America? *International Research Journal of Finance and Economics, 29*, 60–75.

Ndikumana, L., & Baliamoune-Lutz, M. (2008). Corruption and Growth: Exploring the Investment Channel. *UMASS Amherst Economics Working Paper No. 2008-08*. University of Massachusetts Amherst, Department of Economics.

Ndikumana, L., & Verick, S. (2008). The Linkages Between FDI and Domestic Investment: Unravelling the Developmental Impact of Foreign Investment in Sub-Saharan Africa. *Development and Policy Review, 26*(6), 713–726.

North, D. C., & Weingast, B. R. (1989). Constitutions and Commitment: The Evolution of Institutions Governing Public Choice in Seventeenth-Century England. *Journal of Economic History, 49*(4), 803–832.

Nurmakhanova, M., Elheddad, M., Alfar, A. J. K., Egbulonu, A., & Abedin, M. Z. (2023). Does Natural Resource Curse in Finance Exist in Africa? Evidence from Spatial Techniques. *Resources Policy, 80*, 103151.

Olson, M. (1993). Dictatorship, Democracy and Development. *American Political Science Review, 87*(3), 567–676.

Otchere, I., Senbet, L., & Simbanegavi, W. (2017). Editorial: Financial Sector Development in Africa – An Overview. *Review of Development Finance, 7*, 1–5.

Otchere, I., Soumare, I., & Yourougou, P. (2016). FDI and Financial Market Development in Africa. *The World Economy, 39*(5), 651–678.

Patrick, H. (1966). Financial Development and Economic Growth in Underdeveloped Countries. *Economic Development and Cultural Change, 14*(2), 174–189.

Perotti, E., & von Thadden, E.-L. (2006). The Political Economy of Corporate Control and Labor Rents. *Journal of Political Economy, 114*(1), 145–174.

Polanyi, K. (1957). *The Great Transformation*. Beacon.

Pretorius, M., & Botha, I. (2017). Chapter 35: The Procyclicality of African Sovereign Credit Ratings. In N. Tsounis & A. Vlachvei (Eds.), *Advanced in Applied Economic Research* (pp. 537–546).

Prieg, L. (2011, January 25). Credit Rating Firms Are Controlling the Flow of Capital into the Developing World. *The Guardian*. Retrieved August, 2023, from https://www.theguardian.com/global-development/poverty-matters/2011/jan/25/credit-rating-agencies-poor-countries

Raga, S., & Tyson, J. (2021). Impact of Pan-African Banks on Financial Development in Sub-Saharan Africa. *DEGRP Synthesis Report*. The Development and Economic Growth Research Programme.

Rajan, R. G., & Zingales, L. (2003a). The Great Reversals: The Politics of Financial Development in the Twentieth Century. *Journal of Financial Economics, 69*(1), 5–50.

Rajan, R. G., & Zingales, L. (2003b). *Saving Capitalism from the Capitalists: Unleashing the Power of Financial Markets to Create Wealth and Spread Opportunity*. Princeton University Press.

Reinhart, C. M., & Rogoff, K. S. (2004). Serial Default and the 'Paradox' of Rich-to-Poor Capital Flows. *American Economic Review, 94*(2), 53–58.

Reisen, H. (1998). Sustainable and Excessive Current Account Deficits. *Empirica, 25*(2), 111–131.

Robinson, J. A., Torvik, R., & Verdier, T. (2006). Political Foundations of the Resource Curse. *Journal of Development Economics, 79*(2), 447–468.

Robinson, J. C. (1952). *The Generalisation of the General Theory in the Rate of Interest and Other Essays*. Palgrave Macmillan.

Rodriguez, F., & Rodrik, D. (2000). Trade Policy and Economic Growth: A Sceptic's Guide to the Cross-National Evidence. *NBER Macroeconomics Annual, 15*, 261–325.

Roe, M. J., & Siegel, J. I. (2011). Political Instability: Effects on Financial Development, Roots in the Severity of Economic Inequality. *Journal of Comparative Economics, 39*(3), 279–309.

Roine, J., Vlachos, J., & Waldenström, D. (2009). The Long-Run Determinants of Inequality: What Can We Learn from Top Income Data? *Journal of Public Economics, 93*(7–8), 974–988.

Sacerdoti, E. (2005). Access to Bank Credit in Sub-Saharan Africa: Key Issues and Reform Strategies. *IMF Working Paper No. WP/05/166*. International Monetary Fund.

Saiegh, S. M. (2005). Do Countries Have a 'Democratic Advantage'? Political Institutions, Multi-lateral Agencies and Sovereign Borrowing. *Comparative Political Studies, 38*(4), 366–387.

Sala-i-Martin, X., & Subramanian, A. (2008). Addressing the Natural Resource Curse: An Illustration from Nigeria. In D. P. Collier, C. C. Soludo, & C. Pattillo (Eds.), *Economic Policy Options for a Prosperous Nigeria* (pp. 61–92). Palgrave Macmillan.

Sandow, J. N., Oteng-Abayie, E. F., Sakyi, D., & Obuobi, B. (2022). Financial Sector Development and Natural Resource Rents: The Role of Institutions in Sub-Saharan Africa. *Environmental Science and Pollution Research, 29*(59), 89340–89357.

Schultz, K. A., & Weingast, B. R. (1996). The Democratic Advantage: The Institutional Sources of State Power in International Competition. *Essays in Public Policy, 67*, Hoover Institution Press.

Schultz, K. A., & Weingast, B. R. (2003). The Democratic Advantage: Institutional Foundations of Financial Power in International Competition. *International Organization, 57*(1), 3–42.

Schumpeter, J. A. (1911). *Theory of Economic Development*. Harvard University Press.

Sharma, C. (2021). Does Corruption Sand the Wheels of Financial Sector Development? Evidence from Global Panel Data. *Journal of Financial Management, Markets and Institutions, 9*(2), 2150008.

Sharma, C., & Paramati, S. R. (2020). Does Financial Development Reduce the Level of Corruption? Evidence from a Global Sample of 140 Countries. *International Journal of Finance and Economics, 26*(4), 5093–5109.

Soumaré, I., Kanga, D., Tyson, J., & Raga, S. (2021). Capital Market Development in Sub-Saharan Africa: Progress, Challenges and Innovations. *Working Paper No. 2*. A Joint FSD Africa–ODI Research Programme for Financial Sector Development in Africa.

Soumaré, I., & Tchana, F. T. (2015). Causality Between FDI and Financial Market Development. *The World Bank Economic Review, 29*, S205–S216.

Tornell, A., & Lane, P. R. (1998). Are Windfalls a Curse? A Non-Representative Agent Model of the Current Account. *Journal of International Economics, 44*(1), 83–112.

Torvik, R. (2002). Natural Resources, Rent Seeking and Welfare. *Journal of Development Economics, 67*(2), 455–470.

UNCTAD. (2024). Credit Rating Agencies, Developing Countries and Bias. *UNCTAD/GDS/2024/3*. United Nations Conference on Trade and Development.

UNDP. (2023). *Lowering the Cost of Borrowing in Africa – The Role of Sovereign Credit Ratings*. United Nations Development Programme. Retrieved May, 2024, from https://www.undp.org/africa/publications/lowering-cost-borrowing-africa-role-sovereign-credit-ratings

Van der Ploeg, F., & Poelhekke, S. (2009). The Volatility Curse: Revisiting the Paradox of Plenty. *CESifo Working Paper No. 2616*. Center for Economic Studies and ifo Institute (CESifo).

Van der Walle. (2001). *African Economies and the Politics of Permanent Crisis, 1979–1999*. Cambridge University Press.

Venard, B., & Hanafi, M. (2008). Organizational Isomorphism and Corruption in Financial Institutions: Empirical Research in Emerging Countries. *Journal of Business Ethics, 81*(2), 481–498.

Walby, S. (2007). Complexity Theory, Systems Theory and Multiple Intersecting Social Inequalities. *Philosophy of the Social Sciences, 37*(4), 449–470.

Walby, S. (2009). *Globalization and Inequalities*. Sage.

Walby, S. (2013). Finance versus Democracy? Theorizing Finance in Society. *Work, Employment and Society, 27*(3), 489–507.

Williamson, J. (2004). The Washington Consensus as Policy Prescription for Development. *Practitioners of Development*. Retrieved May, 2024, from https://www.piie.com/sites/default/files/publications/papers/williamson0204.pdf

World Bank. (2001). Finance for Growth: Policy Choices in a Volatile World. *World Bank Policy Research Report*. World Bank.

World Bank. (2023). Banking in Africa: Opportunities and Challenges in Volatile Times. *Policy Research Working Paper No. 10632*. World Bank.

Yartey, C. A. (2010). The Institutional and Macroeconomic Determinants of Stock Market Development in Emerging Economies. *Applied Financial Economics, 20*(21), 1615–1625.

Yartey, C. A., & Adjasi, C. K. (2007). Stock Market Development in Sub-Saharan Africa: Critical Issues and Challenges. *IMF Working Paper 07/209*. International Monetary Fund.

Zalle, O. (2019). Natural Resources and Economic Growth in Africa: The Role of Institutional Quality and Human Capital. *Resources Policy, 62*, 616–624.

CHAPTER 8

FDI and Sub-Saharan Africa's Economic Growth Cycle

Since the end of the Second World War, there has been a range of theories that sought to explain SSA's sub-optimal economic growth and development levels (Vokes, 2018, p. 10). Dependency theory argues that the lack of development arises from the Global South's disadvantageous integration into the global economy (Singer, 1949; Prebisch, 1950; Baran, 1957; Frank, 1966; Cardoso, 1977), mainly because these countries (especially in SSA) are reliant on natural resource exports to the wealthy Global North, which in turn transmute the raw materials into manufactured goods. In time, the wealth gap between the Global North and South invariably widens as the productivity gains from resource extraction remain relatively level while the gain from manufactured goods increases. This widening wealth gap traps developing countries in a cycle of poverty and sub-optimal development because an increasing share of resource exports are needed to purchase the manufactured goods (Vokes, 2018, p. 12). Dependency theory therefore argues that protective measures, such as capital controls and import taxes, are required to limit the inflows of capital and technology so that localisation, beneficiation, and import substitution can create the economic space for trade diversification and thus reduce natural resource export dependence (Ogujiuba et al., 2011).

Post-colonial theory (Fanon, 1963, 1967; Rodney, 1981) argues however that colonisation not only disadvantaged SSA economically, but also affected SSA politically, socially, demographically, culturally, and

S. Gossel, *The Promise and Peril of FDI in Sub-Saharan Africa*, Palgrave Studies in African and Development Economics,
https://doi.org/10.1007/978-3-032-01320-0_8

psychologically (Vokes, 2018, p. 13). To grow and develop, post-colonialism thus posits that SSA needs to separate from the extractive neo-colonialism of the Global North and return to its pre-colonial economic, social, and cultural traditions (ibid., p. 14). According to Dependency and Post-colonial theories, SSA currently sits in the uncomfortable zone between impatient domestic socio-economic developmental pressure on the one side and the demands of a mercantilist neo-colonial global economy on the other.

In recent decades, it has been argued that the emergence of the "Asian Tigers" shows that emerging countries can increase their economic growth rates via heightened trade (the export-led and import-led growth hypotheses), FDI inflows (the FDI-led growth hypothesis), and financial sector development (FSD-led growth). Evidence suggests that countries that successfully transition from reliance on comparative advantage to exports of increasingly complex manufactured goods tend to attract the FDI required to support the diversification of trade (Romer, 1992; Cui & Xu, 2019). Eventually countries that have transitioned along this cycle from the initial stages of competitive advantage exports of commodities and basic goods to sophisticated manufactured exports, coupled with diversified FDI, should be able to link their domestic economies into the global economy via stock and bond market activities (UNCTAD, 2022). Thus, the final stage of developmental sophistication is the economic growth enhancing effects associated with heightened liquidity, depth, and mobilisation of financial sector development (FSD) (Schumpeter, 1911; Goldsmith, 1969; McKinnon, 1973; Shaw, 1973).

Hence, developing countries commonly start at the export-led growth (ELG) stage by focussing on comparative advantage exports. This phase may be funded by official development assistance (ODA) and debt since the country typically will not have sufficient internal capital available. Countries, such as most of those in SSA, that rely on natural resource extraction for early-stage export-led development may then attract extractive FDI. While this has developmental benefits and generates capital to potentially pay off debt, there is the risk that ensuing gatekeeping, Dutch disease, predatory capitalism, and political dysfunction will lock the country into a neo-colonial extraction-based development path.

If the country escapes these risks and progresses beyond competitive advantage-based ELG into beneficiation, industrialisation, and diversification, then it could attract FDI related to these activities, and thus FDI will increasingly become more sophisticated and diversified accordingly. This stage should then lead to increasing manufacturing and service-based ELG, as the country uses backward and forward linkages to expand, grow, and progress up the manufacturing value chain, from unsophisticated to sophisticated manufactured goods, and eventually to integrated supply chains and domestically originated brands and products. Over time, reliance on competitive advantage extraction should thus decline and the associated risks of predatory capitalism and extractive FDI should diminish accordingly.

Once the country reaches the stage of sophisticated ELG and is attracting diversified FDI, the domestic population will reap the benefits, and this will stimulate heightened imports of consumer goods in addition to the inputs needed for ELG and diversified FDI. Greater economic sophistication, globalisation, and social mobility will in turn stimulate demand for financial services, thus driving financial sector development (FSD) and financial globalisation. Hence, these causal associations can be stylistically summarised by Fig. 8.1.

Based on the preceding discussion, this chapter commences with an exploration of the trade-led growth hypotheses, comprising the export-led and import-led growth hypotheses, followed by the FDI-led growth

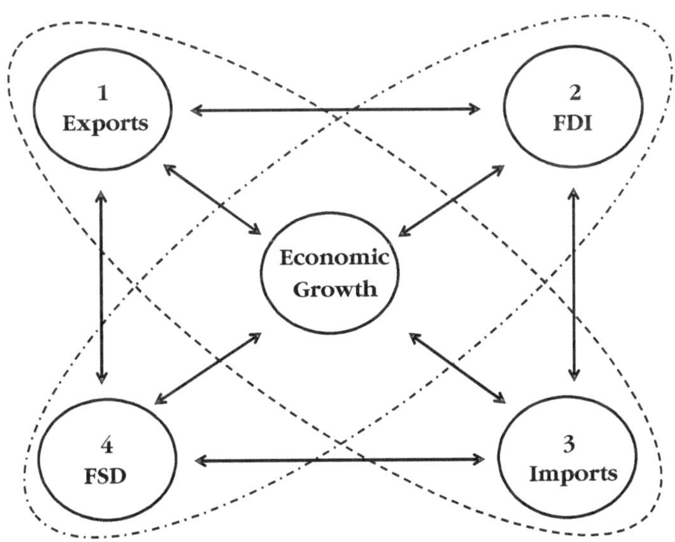

Fig. 8.1 Economic growth cycle

hypothesis, and the financial sector development-led growth hypothesis. The chapter then concludes with a discussion of the interlinkages between these factors, and how these interactions drive economic growth in SSA.

8.1 Trade-Led Growth

According to the neoclassical growth model, economic growth is driven by the exogenous factors of capital accumulation, including FDI, and technological progress (Solow, 1956). Endogenous Growth or New Growth theory however argues that technological progress is endogenous and thus capital formation includes investment in human capital (Lucas, 1988; Wang, 1990), research and development (Romer, 1986), and fixed capital (Arrow, 1962; Findlay, 1978). According to the export-led growth hypothesis (ELG), exports stimulate higher economic growth rates by liberalising foreign exchange regimes (McKinnon, 1964), increasing capital accumulation (Chenery & Strout, 1966; Balassa, 1978; Buffie, 1992; Riezman et al., 1996; Baharumshah & Rashid, 1999), improving economies of scale (Helpman & Krugman, 1985), relieving import shortages (Esfahani, 1991), and promoting the dispersion of technological innovations (Feder, 1983; Lucas, 1988; Romer, 1986; Grossman & Helpman, 1991; Edwards, 1992).

Despite the theoretical elegance of the ELG, the evidence from empirical studies is inconclusive. One strand reports evidence in favour of the ELG hypothesis (Arnade & Vasavada, 1995; Fosu, 1990; Giles & Williams, 2000a, 2000b; Bahmani-Oskooee & Oyolola, 2007; Mutreja et al., 2018) whereas a second strand instead finds significant evidence that economic growth drives the absorption of knowledge and technological developments, which in turn stimulates heightened export capacity, thus pointing to growth-led exports (GLE) (Krugman, 1984; Henriques & Sadorsky, 1996; Bahmani-Oskooee et al., 2005; Reppas & Christopoulos, 2005; Dreger & Herzer, 2013). A third strand further reports that exports and economic growth share a bidirectional rather than unidirectional association whereby increased economic growth drives higher export volumes, which in turn stimulates more economic growth (Helpman & Krugman, 1985; Dutt & Ghosh, 1996; Anwar & Sampath, 2000; Abu-Qarn & Abu-Bader, 2004; Dawson & Sanjuán-López, 2013).

With regards to SSA, studies such as Pazim (2009), Ahmed et al. (2011), and Ee (2016) find that there is general evidence of ELG while Bbaale and Mutenyo (2011) report that ELG applies more specifically to agricultural exports rather than manufactured exports, and Zahonogo (2016) and Odhiambo (2021) find that ELG applies to middle-income SSA countries not to low-income SSA countries. Babatunde (2012) argues that SSA countries cannot take advantage of ELG because the three common growth strategies (import substitution, structural adjustment programs, and neoliberal reforms) are inappropriate for the region; and instead, SSA will need to enhance trade integration and productivity, invest in technology and education, and undertake labour market reforms.

In addition, much of the ELG literature focusses on manufactured exports but it is possible that the association between exports and growth may differ between natural resources and manufactured exports (Wörz, 2005; Bbaale & Mutenyo, 2011). Natural resource endowment could potentially drive sustainable economic growth and development by providing the windfall revenues needed to rectify human capital and infrastructure deficits (Lundgren et al., 2013), development of the tradeable sector (Ross, 2005), and access to international demand, which in turn will stimulate domestic production and thus economic growth (Bbaale & Mutenyo, 2011). However, the extraction of these natural resource assets requires 'well-intentioned, far-sighted, and highly capable governments' but unfortunately many resource-rich states suffer from short-sighted and weak political leadership that undermine rather than maximise the resource wealth (Venables, 2016). This has the effect of entrenching fiscal and export dependence on natural resource extraction, which, because of poor savings, exposes the state to low and volatile growth (Palley, 2012).

Resource-dependent economies are vulnerable to real exchange rate appreciation coupled with a decline in manufacturing sector competitiveness (Sachs & Warner, 1995; Collier, 2008), as well as to commodity price shocks, volatility, and boom-bust cyclicality (Cavalcanti et al., 2015; UNCTAD, 2019). In addition, exploration, identification, and extraction of natural resources require significant investment from foreign companies, and thus any tax, regulatory, or licensing difficulties can deter investment and limit economic growth (Huynh, 2022). Even if the state overcomes these hurdles and resists the short-run temptation to amend the contractual terms of investment, many governments cannot resist the urge to invest the resource revenues in spurious projects (Dabla-Norris et al., 2012) or use the revenues to maintain corrupt patron-client networks (Ades & Di Tella, 1999; Leite & Weidmann, 1999).

Since the late 1990s, SSA has experienced the benefits of global resource booms, which have driven higher levels of economic growth and the emergence of a middle class. Increasingly, the narrative for the region has changed from "the hopeless continent" (The Economist, May 2000) to 'Africa rising' (Schubert et al., 2018, p. 2). However, most countries in the region are still struggling to diversify their trade and economic development away from natural resource competitive advantage to more complex beneficiation and manufactured exports (OECD/UN, 2011; Bahar & Santos, 2018). Collier (2005) thus argues that low-income resource-rich SSA countries should exploit non-agricultural extractive resources whereas resource-scarce and coastal SSA countries should focus on labour-intensive manufacturing exports. Bbaale and Mutenyo (2011) posit that SSA should focus on agricultural exports in the medium term and manufacturing exports in the long term. While agricultural exports have benefited economic development in Asia and Latin America, they have not yet had similar effects in SSA, but in the long-run they could potentially stimulate development by improving nutrition, stabilising food production and food security, increasing employment and wages, damping food price inflation, and reducing poverty levels (especially in rural areas) (Diao et al., 2007).

More broadly however, it has been argued by Palley (2012) that reliance on ELG as a long-run developmental strategy is problematic for five reasons. First, consumers in Western countries are over-indebted and thus their ability to finance consumption expenditure is declining. Second, as emerging economies use ELG to develop, they attract capital, investment, and employment away from industrialised countries, which erodes the long-run economic prospects of the developed economies and thus weakens the long-run demand for the goods and services produced in the emerging countries. Third, declining relative prices of manufactured goods means that countries need to find other means of gaining a trade advantage. This in turn gives rise to the fourth problem, the global 'race to the bottom' as emerging countries compete for capital "through a combination of wage suppression; suppression of labour, environmental and social standards; suppression of business regulation; shifting of tax burdens onto labour income and away from capital income; creating of extra-judicial export processing zones; and competitive devaluations that create financial instability." Finally, the rise of China negates the opportunity for other emerging countries to significantly benefit from ELG and instead locks resource endowed countries (such as much of SSA) into undiversified resource extraction.

In addition to ELG, there has been increasing interest in the growth-enhancing effects associated with heightened imports. According to the import-led growth hypothesis (ILG), economic growth can benefit from the imports of intermediating factors, capital goods, and technologies (Coe & Helpman, 1995), the transfer of foreign R&D (Lawrence & Weinstein, 1999; Mazumdar, 2000), by increasing the total factor production (Mutreja et al., 2018) needed for higher export sophistication, volumes, and efficiency (Ghirmay et al., 2001), and the development of industrial infrastructure (Palley, 2012). Hence, imports can contribute to higher economic growth directly by supplying the inputs needed for ELG (Zhu & Fu, 2013), and indirectly via higher domestic consumption expenditure on capital goods (Mutreja et al., 2018).

While empirical studies devoted to the economic growth effects of imports are less common than studies that explore the impact of exports, it has been argued that imports are more important than exports for economic growth, mainly because imports are a crucial input in the export-led growth cycle (Shan & Sun, 1998; Awokuse, 2007). Thus, it is possible that SSA will have to first focus on ILG and then on ELG as it diversifies away from primary commodities. In common with the literature on ELG however, studies of ILG also report mixed results with some studies finding in favour of ILG (Islam et al., 2012) while others find bidirectionality (Sharma & Smyth, 2009; Çetintaş & Barişik, 2009). In the case of SSA, Bbaale and Mutenyo (2011) report that imports of capital goods, especially from advanced countries, improve economic growth via knowledge and technology effects in accordance with endogenous growth theory (Romer, 1986; Lucas, 1988). Iscan and Yıldırım (2012) similarly find that imports of capital and intermediate goods have a positive effect on economic growth whereas imports of consumption goods have a negative effect. On a country-specific basis, Aluko and Adeyeye (2020) report that there is evidence of short-run ILG in the seven countries of Guinea, Namibia, Nigeria, Senegal, Sierra Leone, Sudan, and Tunisia; and growth-led imports in the four countries of Central African Republic, Morocco, Rwanda, and Seychelles, while there is long-run ILG in the five countries of Chad, Kenya, Malawi, Sierra Leone, and Sudan; and growth-led imports in the ten countries of Algeria, Cote d'Ivoire, Gabon, Guinea, Guinea-Bissau, Morocco, Mozambique, Rwanda, Seychelles, and Togo.

The scatterplots of economic growth and trade presented in Fig. 8.2 show that, averaged over the period of 1990–2020, trade and economic growth only share a weakly positive correlation. Furthermore, once

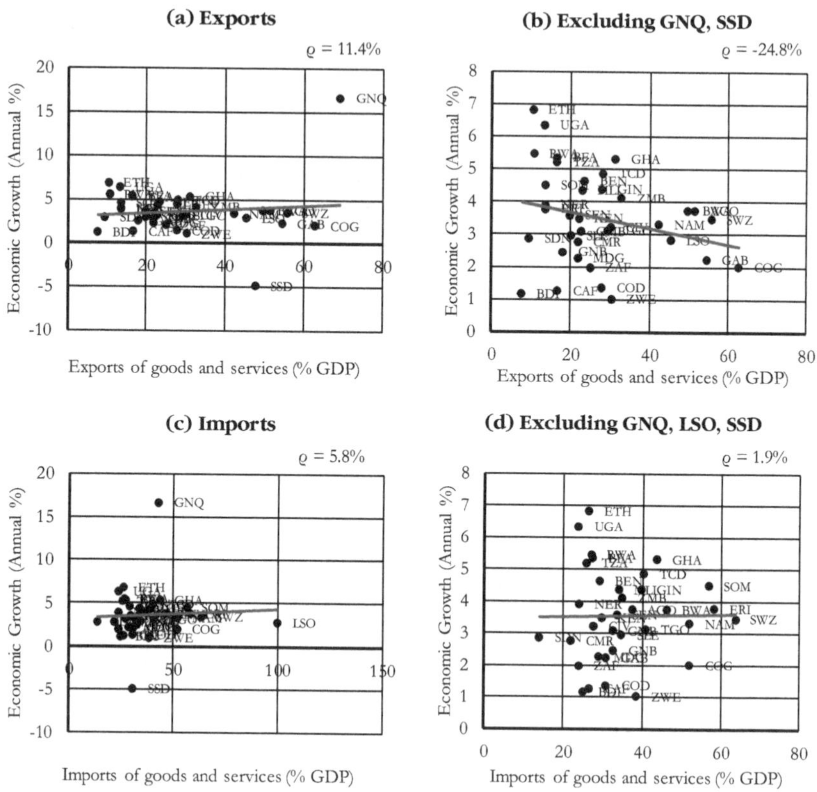

Fig. 8.2 Economic growth and trade. (Data source: World Development Indicators)

Equatorial Guinea (GNQ) and South Sudan (SSD) are excluded from the export scatterplots (Fig. 8.2b), the correlation coefficient becomes negative. In contrast, once the outliers of Equatorial Guinea (GNQ), Lesotho (LSO), and South Sudan (SSD) are excluded from the imports scatterplots, the coefficients remain insignificant but positive.

Table 8.1 further indicates that natural resource-dependent SSA countries experience higher average levels of economic growth, exports, and gross fixed capital formation while non-dependent countries have higher average total labour force and imports. Thus, indications are that resource-dependent SSA countries are prone to ELG while non-dependent countries are prone to ILG.

Table 8.1 Trade and economic growth

Average	*Measure*	*(a) Non-dependent [28]*	*(b) Resource dependent [14]*	*(a)/(b)*
Economic growth	Annual %	3.57	4.47	0.8
Gross fixed capital formation	% GDP	18.81	21.42	0.9
Labour force	Total, thousands	8190.34	5354.70	1.5
Exports of goods and services	% GDP	24.70	33.28	0.7
Imports of goods and services	% GDP	35.78	33.51	1.1

[#] indicates the number of SSA countries in the sample

Data sources: World Governance Indicators (1990–2020)

8.2 FDI-Led Growth

In a post-neoliberal financially globalised world, it has been argued that focussing on trade-led growth without considering the complimentary effects of FDI can be misleading (Goldberg & Klein, 1999) because trade capacity is intricately linked to fixed investment and the technological, production, knowledge, and organisational spillover effects of FDI (de Mello, 1997, 1999; Borensztein et al., 1998). According to the Endogenous Growth or New Growth theory, FDI enhances economic growth by improving capital accumulation, technological transfers (Khan et al., 2015), and the spillover effects then benefit total factor productivity. Hence, Endogenous Growth theory argues that FDI can act "as a catalyst or 'jump starter' for economic growth and development" (Seyoum et al., 2015). Dependency theorists however reject the long-run growth-enhancing effects of FDI, arguing that the benefits tend to be skewed in favour of multinational corporations rather than host countries; and instead of creating beneficial spillover effects, FDI crowds out domestic companies, distorts domestic markets, raises unemployment, widens wealth gaps, drives environmental degradation, and undermines local culture and political processes (Seyoum et al., 2015).

It has however been argued that the benefits of FDI will depend on the host country's stage of development. In the early stages, fixed capital accumulation is most important whereas in later stages, human capital accumulation becomes more important (Galor & Moav, 2004). Hence, in the early stages, FDI benefits domestic production and entrepreneurship (Mthanti & Ojah, 2017) whereas more developed countries will have sufficient absorptive capacity to take advantage of the FDI-induced human capital, trade, institutional, and infrastructure benefits (Glass & Saggi, 1998). The FDI-led growth hypothesis therefore posits that FDI positively affects economic growth directly via higher domestic capital accumulation (Azman-Saini et al., 2010; Mallick & Moore, 2008) and demand for high-skilled labour (Almfraji & Almsafir, 2014; Makiela & Ouattara, 2018); and indirectly via technological, managerial, and human capital spillovers (Azman-Saini et al., 2010). Before FDI can affect economic growth however, the host country needs to have sufficient vertical and horizontal linkages between domestic and foreign companies (Nowbusting, 2009), and adequate absorptive capacity arising from human capital (Borensztein et al., 1998; Li & Liu, 2005). In addition, a range of structural foundations must be in place, including trade openness (Balasubramanyam et al., 1996) and export diversification (Cui & Xu, 2019), macroeconomic stability (Alguacil et al., 2011) and economic sophistication (Antonietti & Franco, 2021), infrastructure development (Gui-Diby & Renard, 2015), financial sector development (Hermes & Lensink, 2003; Alfaro et al., 2004; Durham, 2004; Adjasi et al., 2012; Agbloyor et al., 2013), and institutional quality (Alfaro et al., 2008; Papaioannou, 2009; Buchanan et al., 2012; Matima & Gossel, 2023). Hence, it is unlikely that FDI-led growth can occur in the early stages of economic development.

In the case of SSA, while studies such as Gui-Diby (2014), Malikane and Chitambara (2017), Zekarias (2016), Onuoha et al. (2018), and Adem and Güvercin (2020) find that FDI leads to economic growth, the evidence is not incontrovertible. Buchanan et al. (2012), Agbloyor et al. (2014), and Michael (2018) report that FDI negatively affects growth while Esso (2010) and Seyoum et al. (2015) show that growth unidirectionally leads to FDI (growth-led FDI). According to Sukar et al. (2006), Adams (2009), Abu and Karim (2016), Wako (2021), and Ofori and Asongu (2022), FDI is not growth enhancing, mainly because SSA's education, fixed investment, macroeconomic policy, and institutional quality have not yet reached a level where the region can benefit from the spillover effects.[1]

[1] Asafo-Agyei and Kodongo (2022) find that countries in SSA must cross an annual FDI per capita threshold of USD 44.67 before FDI has a positive effect on economic growth.

Furthermore, recent studies by Opoku et al. (2019b), Asamoah et al. (2022), Idun et al. (2024), and Chukwu and Adewuyi (2023) show that FDI to SSA does not affect economic growth in all sectors evenly. This is largely because of the sectoral variations in the absorptive capacity (Cohen & Levinthal, 1990) associated with the ability to assimilate and integrate knowledge and skills and adopt new technologies (Idun et al., 2024). Hence, absorptive capacity is directly dependent on human capital and education; and indirectly macroeconomic fundamentals, institutional quality, and infrastructure (ibid.). It is thus unsurprising that empirical research has found that the effect of FDI on sectoral economic growth in SSA is ambiguous, mainly because regional economies are still dependent on the natural resource sectors, which tend to have poor industrial linkages and weak absorptive capacity (Chukwu & Adewuyi, 2023).

More specifically, Opoku et al. (2019b) and Idun et al. (2024) find that the interaction between FDI and agriculture positively affects economic growth whereas Asamoah et al. (2022) report a negative effect and Chukwu and Adewuyi (2023) find no significant effect. These varied results may be ascribed to SSA's geography (Diao et al., 2007), unsophisticated small-scale farming methods (Bbaale & Mutenyo, 2011), and because the farmland is often sold for natural resource extraction instead and farmers commonly do not own the farms (Asamoah et al., 2022). While FDI is generally found to boost the economic growth enhancing effects of manufacturing (ibid.; Idun et al., 2024), Opoku et al. (2019b) find that the interaction effect is insignificant once transmission channels are controlled for while Chukwu and Adewuyi (2023) report that the impact is only significant in the short run; which may all be a reflection of SSA's underdeveloped manufacturing sectors, dependence on the mining sector, and deindustrialisation (Taylor, 2018, p. 320; Moyo & Jeke, 2019). Lastly, in the case of services, Opoku et al. (2019b) and Asamoah et al. (2022) find that FDI channelled through the services sector has a beneficial effect on economic growth whereas Idun et al. (2024) report that the effect is insignificant and Chukwu and Adewuyi (2023) find that the positive effect only occurs in the short run.

Even where there is evidence of FDI-led growth, studies find that this only applies to the more developed and less resource export-dependent SSA countries (Agbloyor et al., 2016), to the industrial and services sectors (Asamoah & Alagidede, 2020), over the long-run not the short-run (Ayenew, 2022), only once SSA countries have passed a threshold of inflation, population growth, and financial sector development (Ibhagui,

2020), and only to low-growth SSA countries (Asafo-Adjei et al., 2023). On a country-specific basis, Seyoum et al. (2015) find evidence of FDI-led growth in Egypt, Gabon, and Mauritania but growth-led FDI in Cote d'Ivoire, Kenya, South Africa, and Zambia.

Beyond affecting ELG, reliance on natural resource exports can shape FDI inflows by attracting natural resource extractive FDI rather than diversified export-related FDI (Onyeiwu & Shrestha, 2004; Anyanwu, 2012; de Mauro, 2013; Bokpin et al., 2014; Akhtaruzzaman et al., 2018), which locks SSA into resource export dependence, and increases the risk of the Resource Curse (Hlavac, 2010, p. 3). FDI inflows to SSA thus mirror the colonial experience of natural resource exploitation (de Mauro, 2013) and as a result, instead of stimulating the development of a vibrant and diversified manufacturing export sector, FDI to SSA undermines institutional quality and has "contributed to the region's premature deindustrialization both directly and indirectly through enhancing resource-based extensive growth" (Wako, 2021).

In addition, unlike diversified FDI (such as trade-based greenfield and brownfield FDI), natural resource FDI is subject to international commodity price volatility (Carril-Caccia et al., 2019) and thus tends to be more akin to the 'hot flows' of portfolio investment and bank flows than the more stable long-run manufactured export-orientated FDI. Furthermore, natural resource FDI is reliant on foreign multinational corporations for capital and skills (Schubert et al., 2018, pp. 2–3) but tends to have lower spillover effects than the other forms of FDI (Poelhekke & van der Ploeg, 2013) and crowds out non-resource FDI, further entrenching natural resource dependence (Poelhekke & Van der Ploeg, 2010; Asiedu, 2006, 2013; Aleksynska & Havrylchyk, 2013). Hence, SSA's reliance on natural resources hinders the regions' ability to attract diversified FDI (Morisset, 2000; Onyeiwu & Shrestha, 2004; Anyanwu, 2011; de Mauro, 2013; Bokpin et al., 2014; Akhtaruzzaman et al., 2018) and entrenches a vicious cycle of instability, insufficient foreign investment, and resource dependence (Hlavac, 2010, p. 3). This relationship is borne out by Fig. 8.3, which shows that over the period of 1990–2020, the correlation coefficients between natural resource prices and FDI inflows have exceeded 87%.

The scatterplots of FDI and economic growth (averaged over 1990–2020) presented in Fig. 8.4 indicate that once the outlier of Liberia (LBR) is excluded from the non-dependent sample, the correlation coefficient is positive whereas when the outliers of Equatorial Guinea (GNQ),

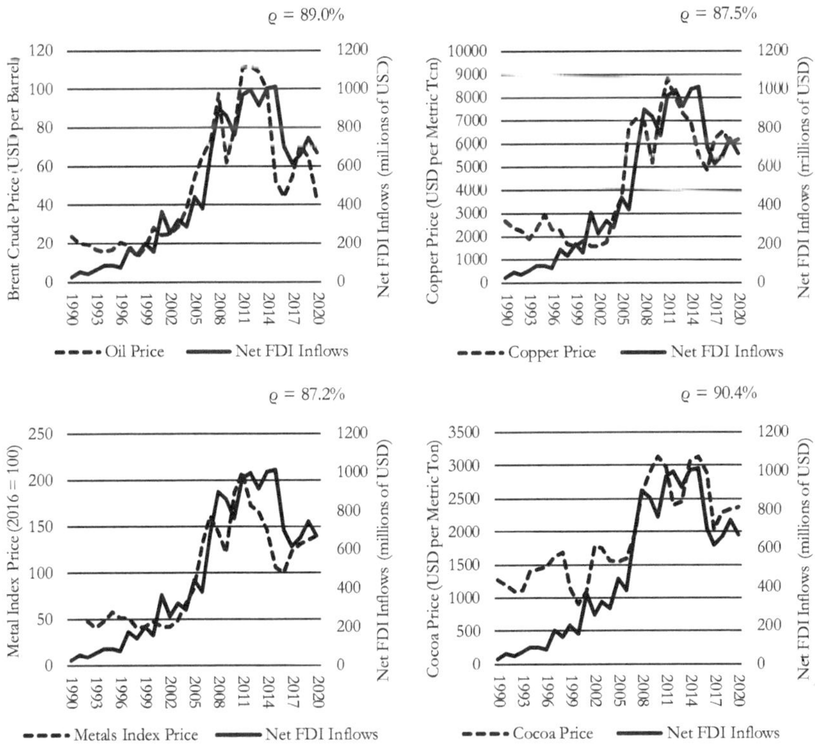

Fig. 8.3 Selected commodity prices and FDI inflows to SSA. (Data sources: Federal Reserve Economic Data and World Development Indicators)

Mozambique (MOZ), and South Sudan (SSD) are removed from the natural resource-dependent sample, the correlations between FDI and economic growth become negative. Thus, FDI and economic growth are generally positively associated in non-dependent SSA countries but negatively associated in the resource-dependent countries.

Despite these associations, Table 8.2 shows that resource-dependent countries receive 40% more FDI inflows compared to non-dependent SSA countries. Considered in combination with Fig. 8.4, this suggests that even though resource-dependent SSA countries receive greater FDI than non-dependent countries, FDI to the non-dependent countries is possibly more growth enhancing than FDI to the dependent countries.

Table 8.2 FDI and economic growth

Average	*Measure*	*(a) Non-dependent [28]*	*(b) Resource dependent [14]*	*(a)/ (b)*
Economic growth	Annual %	3.57	4.47	0.8
Gross fixed capital formation	% GDP	18.81	21.42	0.9
Labour force	Total, thousands	8190.34	5354.70	1.5
Net FDI inflows	% GDP	2.93	4.87	0.6

[#] indicates the number of SSA countries in the sample

Data sources: World Governance Indicators (1990–2020)

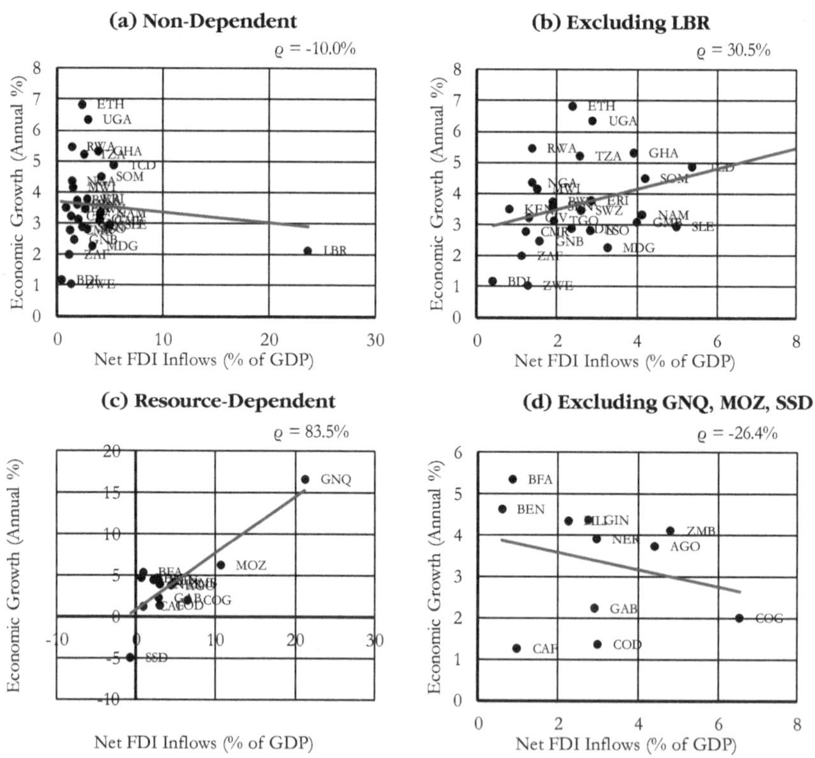

Fig. 8.4 Economic growth and FDI. (Data source: World Development Indicators)

8.3 Financial Sector Development and Economic Growth

In addition to trade and FDI, it has also been posited that financial sector development (FSD) spurs economic growth by channelling resources from less productive to more productive sectors of an economy (Schumpeter, 1911). However, Dependency Theory argues that similar to FDI-led growth, FSD will only boost economic growth once an economy has reached an intermediate stage of development (Kuznets, 1955; Lucas, 1988; Krugman, 1993). This is because demand for financial services in the real sectors stimulates FSD (Fuinhas et al., 2019) and thus international financial integration cannot drive economic development in the early stages of FSD (Bekele & Degu, 2021). Studies that explore the relationship between FSD and economic growth are however inconclusive with some reporting that FSD drives economic growth (supply-leading hypothesis) while others find that growth stimulates FSD (demand-following hypothesis). According to the supply-leading hypothesis (Patrick, 1966), financial institutions facilitate the expansion of productive capacity in the real economy and thereby expand productivity (Roseline, 2012) whereas the demand-following hypothesis counters that as an economy grows and develops, there will be a rising demand for financial services, and this in turn will deepen FSD (Calderón & Liu, 2002).

In addition to the supply-leading and demand-following hypotheses, it is also possible that FSD and economic growth share a bidirectional association or no association. According to the feedback hypothesis (Balcilar et al., 2018; Fuinhas et al., 2019), FSD may arise from economic growth in accordance with the demand-following hypothesis but will then stimulate economic growth in accordance with the supply-leading hypothesis, and thus the supply-leading and demand-following hypotheses will share bidirectional causality (Demetriades & Hussein, 1996; Greenwood & Smith, 1997). In contrast, the neutrality hypothesis argues that FSD and economic growth will have no causal association if financial development is too weak to have any effect on economic growth (Al-Yousif, 2002; Pradhan et al., 2014; Fantessi & Kiprop, 2015).

Empirical studies however are inconclusive, finding varied evidence in favour of all these hypotheses[2] and thus it is unsurprising that empirical studies devoted to SSA are similarly inconclusive. Although studies such as

[2] See Odhiambo et al. (2019) and Ibrahim and Acquah (2021) for a review of the literature.

Ahmed and Wahid (2011), Ghirmay (2004), Akinlo and Egbetunde (2010), Osei and Kim (2020), and Bekele and Degu (2021) find that most SSA countries adhere to the supply-leading hypothesis, it has also been reported that this only holds for upper-middle (Adjasi & Biekpe, 2006) and upper-income SSA countries (An et al., 2019), French-speaking countries (Odhiambo et al., 2019), or the banking sector alone (Kagochi et al., 2013). In contrast, Agbetsiafa (2004) and Ahmed and Wahid (2011) find evidence in support of the demand-following hypothesis while Roseline (2012), Akadiri et al. (2019), and Ibrahim and Acquah (2021) find evidence in favour of the feedback hypothesis, and Adjasi and Yartey (2007), Gries et al. (2009), Demetriades and James (2011), Onuoha et al. (2018), and Opoku et al. (2019a) find no causal associations thus confirming the neutrality hypothesis. On a country-specific basis, Enisan and Olufisayo (2009) find evidence of the supply-leading hypothesis for Egypt and South Africa, the feedback hypothesis for Cote D'Ivoire, Kenya, Morocco, and Zimbabwe; and the demand-following hypothesis for Nigeria.

It is possible that the unclear growth-enhancing effects of FSD in SSA could be because SSA's financial systems are still underdeveloped compared to the rest of the world (Allen et al., 2011, 2014; Kagochi et al., 2013), mainly due to historical policy effects associated with import substitution, trade restrictions, and capital controls (Ibrahim & Acquah, 2021) as well as weak institutional quality, governance, and socio-economic instability (Honohan & Beck, 2007, p. 6; Ibrahim & Alagidede, 2018). Consequently, SSA's financial institutions suffer from high transaction costs, a lack of creditworthy borrowers (Andrianova et al., 2015), and financial market over-segmentation (Aker et al., 2010), thus stifling FSD and limiting the opportunity for the supply-leading hypothesis.

Figure 8.5 shows the scatterplots between three measures of FSD and economic growth (averaged over the period of 1990–2020). Excluding the outliers of Equatorial Guinea (GNQ), Namibia (NAM), Mozambique (MOZ), and South Sudan (SSD), there is a weakly positive correlation between economic growth and the two FSD metrics of bank liquid reserves to bank asset ratio, and domestic credit to the private sector, but a weakly negative correlation between economic growth and the number of commercial bank branches.

Table 8.3 shows that resource-dependent countries have higher average economic growth and average ratios of bank liquid reserves to bank assets whereas non-dependent countries have higher numbers of bank branches

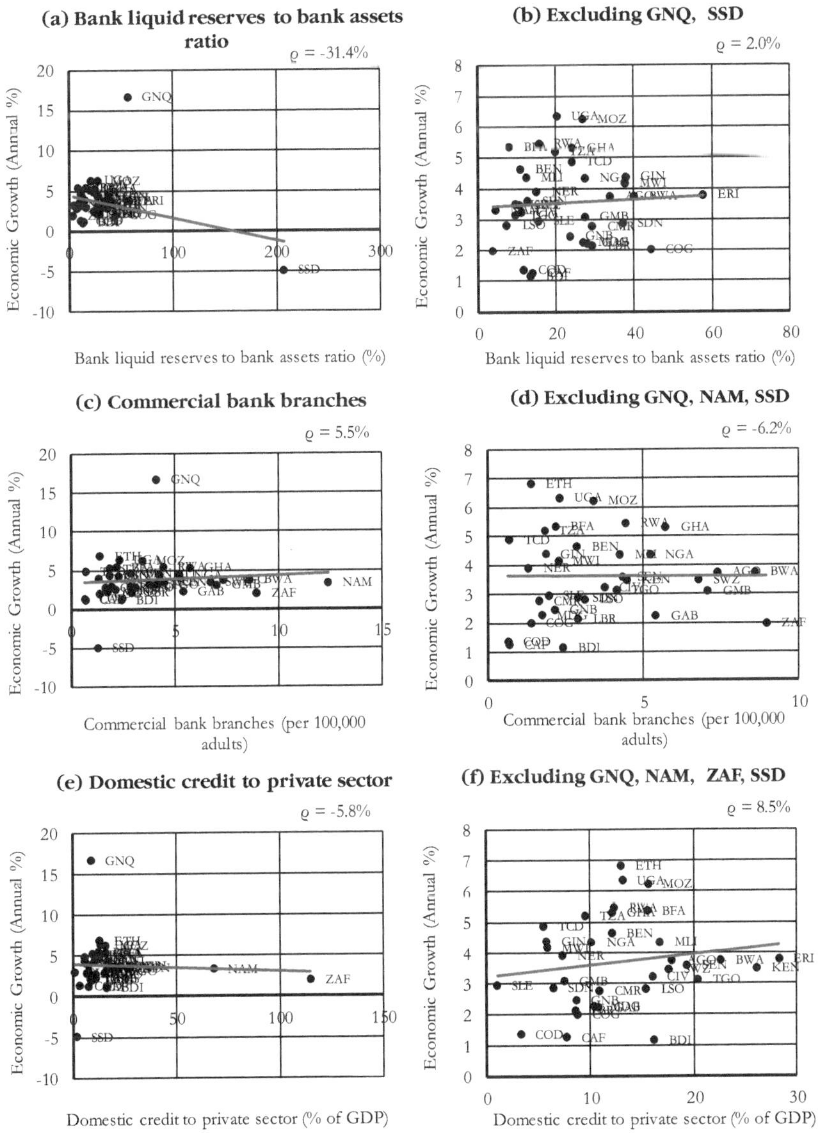

Fig. 8.5 FSD and economic growth. (Data source: World Development Indicators)

Table 8.3 FSD and economic growth

Average	*Measure*	*(a) Non-dependent [28]*	*(b) Resource dependent [14]*	*(a)/(b)*
Economic growth	Annual %	3.57	4.47	0.8
Bank liquid reserves to bank assets ratio	%	20.72	31.72	0.7
Commercial bank branches	Per 100,000 adults	4.37	2.89	1.5
Domestic credit to private sector	% of GDP	17.89	10.37	1.7

[#] indicates the number of SSA countries in the sample

Data sources: World Governance Indicators (1990–2020)

and domestic credit to the private sector. Dwumfour and Ntow-Gyamfi (2018) find that FSD negatively affects the mining, construction, and utilities sectors but positively affects manufacturing and services production, and thus the statistics in Table 8.3 possibly reflects the greater financial volatility and risks in resource-dependent SSA countries compared to the higher levels of financial transactions, customers, and sophistication in non-dependent SSA countries.

8.4 Interlinkages

While much of the literature has focused on the relationships between economic growth and the individual factors of exports, imports, FDI, and FSD, it is possible that these factors interact to benefit economic growth as well (Makki & Somwaru, 2004). According to Mundell (1957), trade restrictions will stimulate capital flows while capital controls will stimulate trade. Purvis (1972) contends however that rather than substituting for trade, FDI can expand trade if it facilitates trade diversification. Kojima (1975) further contends that FDI can improve both productivity and trade via technological spillovers whereby FDI in unskilled labour-intensive industries stimulates exports while FDI in physical capital-intensive industries stimulates imports. Markusen (1984) and Helpman (1984) however posit that horizontal FDI will substitute for trade while vertical FDI will compliment trade but Markusen and Venables (1998) argue that these differing effects of horizontal and vertical FDI arise from skills and trade costs because countries with similar incomes, capital, and moderate to high trade costs will tend to attract horizontal FDI whereas countries that have divergent income levels, capital, and moderate to low trade costs will instead attract vertical FDI.

These theories suggest that FDI improves export performance by increasing domestic competition among production companies, stimulating the search for new markets, and improving the efficiency and capacity of domestic companies because of spillover effects (Asghari et al., 2014). Although empirical studies commonly report that FDI-led growth has benefited South American countries while export-led growth is more applicable to Asian and African countries, the channels interlinking FDI and exports are still unclear (Duttaray et al., 2008). A possible reason is because shifting from comparative advantage to the export of manufactured goods only benefits middle-income and resource-rich countries whereas the positive effects of FDI are limited to the processing industries in middle-income countries (Lectard & Rougier, 2018).

In the case of SSA, Hailu (2010) and Asongu et al. (2021) find that FDI increases exports and imports, which Hailu notes reflects the export orientation and import dependence of MNCs in SSA. Mijiyawa (2017) however finds that the effect of FDI on exports is affected by the level of gross fixed capital formation, mainly because it shapes FDI spillover effects. On a country-specific basis, studies report substantial causal variation between the factors of economic growth, trade, and FDI. Duttaray et al. (2008) report that FDI affects economic growth through exports in Cote d'Ivoire, Mauritania, and South Africa, whereas FDI affects growth through labour productivity and exports in Zambia. Ahmed et al. (2011) find that there is bidirectional Granger causality between FDI and exports in Ghana, Kenya, and Nigeria, unidirectional causality from FDI to exports in South Africa, and from exports to FDI in Zambia. It is also found that exports lead to imports, which then drives economic growth, in all five countries. Thus, FDI and imports benefit economic growth directly or via exports. Using a broader sample of countries, Tekin (2012) reports that FDI unidirectionally drives exports in Benin, Chad, and Togo while exports drive FDI in Madagascar, Malawi, Rwanda, Senegal, and Zambia; FDI and economic growth jointly drive exports in Angola, Benin, Burkina Faso, Chad, Niger, and Zambia, whereas FDI and exports jointly drive economic growth in Sierra Leone, and exports and economic growth jointly drive FDI in Gambia. Tekin posits that the main reasons for these disparities are the countries varied levels of resource dependence and merchandise exports. Finally, Keho (2015) finds evidence of short-run bidirectional causality between FDI and exports in Benin whereas FDI unidirectionally drives exports in Cote d'Ivoire and Kenya. In the long run, both economic growth and exports are found to Granger cause FDI in Benin, Burkina Faso, Gabon, and Senegal whereas bidirectional causality exists between FDI, economic growth, and exports for the DRC; and between FDI and exports in Kenya. The two factors that Keho posit shape these varied causal results are a country's export orientation and level of regulatory reforms.

In addition to the potential beneficial effects of trade and FDI on economic growth, it has also been argued that FSD and FDI can jointly improve economic growth because FSD is needed to actualise FDI spillover effects (Hermes & Lensink, 2003) and is thus a pre-requisite for the FDI-led growth hypothesis (Alfaro et al., 2004, 2010; Azman-Saini et al., 2010). Empirical evidence however shows FSD tends to positively affect economic growth in the early stages of FSD, but once FSD exceeds 14% of GDP (Rioja & Valev, 2004), the effect of FSD on economic growth becomes negligible (Beck et al., 2014; Law & Singh, 2014; Arcand et al., 2015; Samargandi et al., 2015). FSD then acts as an intermediary for FDI-led growth (Acquah & Ibrahim, 2020; Kuttu et al., 2022).

In the case of SSA, Yeboua (2019) finds that FDI only enhances economic growth in SSA countries that have crossed a threshold of FSD while Acquah and Ibrahim (2020) however find that the region's undeveloped FSD negatively affects economic growth and dulls the positive effects of FDI, mainly because SSA's financial systems are unable to efficiently allocate resources, promote financial intermediation, or enforce effective corporate governance. Ibrahim and Acquah (2021) report that FSD and FDI have a bidirectional relationship with each other and with economic growth but argue that FDI can drive FSD because international investors will demand reforms of the financial system before investing, or that FSD reforms can attract FDI. More recently, Abusomwan and Izevbigie (2022) find that FDI stimulates FSD deepening in SSA, and that real per capita GDP, trade openness, and government effectiveness drive FSD financial deepening directly and as mediators of the FDI-FSD deepening nexus. Kuttu et al. (2022) however report that while there is significant evidence of bidirectional causality between FDI, stock market development, and economic growth; in the short run, economic growth and FSD drive FDI whereas in the long run, there is a reduction in the causal relationships between these factors. Kutta et al. explain that this is possibly because, "as people are lifted out of poverty through employment, education, and expansion of economic opportunities, their purchasing power increases, which creates stability in business growth, and this will naturally result in capital inflows increasing." Over time, as profits are repatriated, capital reinvestment and economic growth decline, and the stock market will thus reflect this deterioration.

On a country-specific basis, Adeniyi et al. (2012) find that FSD plays an intermediating role between FDI and economic growth in Gambia, Ghana, and Sierra Leone but does not facilitate the relationship between FDI and economic growth in Nigeria, possibly because of the resource-seeking nature of the FDI. Gossel and Biekpe (2013) report that in South Africa, economic growth is unidirectionally driven by exports but has a bidirectional relationship with imports, and that growth drives FDI rather than the reverse.

To determine the extent to which SSA adheres to the development cycle presented in Fig. 8.1, TYDL Wald causality tests were conducted on a panel of 42 SSA countries covering the period of 1990–2020. The results are graphically summarised in Fig. 8.6.[3] With regards to trade, the full sample results indicate that imports have a unidirectional effect on economic growth while economic growth weakly drives exports, suggesting evidence of ILG and growth-led exports. In addition, while imports and exports share a bidirectional relationship, the significance of imports to exports is higher than the reverse, thus suggesting that imports are the crucial driver of SSA's trade-growth nexus. This is not unexpected considering that most SSA countries are in the early stages of development and thus will be reliant on imports for domestic consumption and to support nascent ELG. In the case of FDI, the results suggest that FDI shares bidirectional causality with exports but unidirectionally, and more significantly, drives imports and economic growth. Hence, there is evidence of FDI-led growth and that FDI is tied into the trade-led growth nexus. Finally, FSD does not have significant causal associations with any of the trade factors nor with FDI (it is possible however that FDI leads to FSD via economic growth) but is significantly driven by economic growth. Hence, the full sample results indicate that FDI and imports are the crucial drivers of SSA's economic growth dynamics.

However, these relationships do not retain significance to the same extent in the sub-samples. Among the 14 resource-dependent countries,

[3]The TYDL methodology, data and tabulated results are included in Appendices 1, 2, and 3.

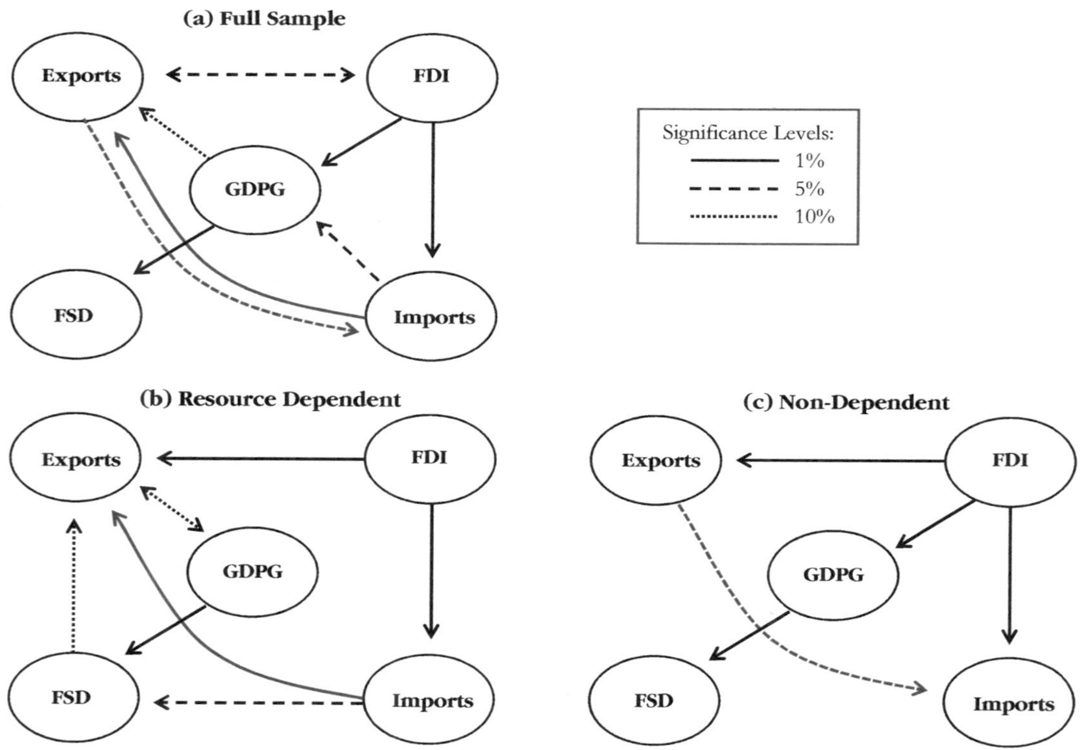

Fig. 8.6 Economic growth cycle in Sub-Saharan Africa. (Data sources: World Development Indicators. Exports are exports of goods and services (% of GDP), FDI is net FDI inflows (% of GDP), Imports are imports of goods and services (% of GDP), FSD is domestic credit to private sector (% of GDP), and GDPG is GDP growth (annual %))

exports and growth share a bidirectional relationship whereas imports drive exports and FSD instead of economic growth. FDI still unidirectionally leads to imports but the bidirectional causality between FDI and exports becomes unidirectional, leading from FDI to exports, and the directionality from FDI to economic growth becomes insignificant. Thus, FDI significantly drives trade whereas imports drive exports. In contrast, FSD is driven by economic growth and imports, and in turn weakly leads to exports, which suggests that there is potential for a trade-FSD-growth nexus if resource-dependent SSA countries can achieve a prerequisite level of FSD.

In the 28 non-dependent countries, there is no significant evidence of trade-led growth but in common with the full sample results, exports unidirectionally drive imports. In contrast, FDI significantly drives trade and economic growth, and growth leads to FSD in turn. Thus, among diversified SSA countries, FDI is tied into the growth-FSD nexus and export-import nexus. Finally, FSD is driven by economic growth but has no significant causal association with any of the other factors.

Thus, among all three of the samples, the only consistent causality is the unidirectionality from FDI to imports, and growth-led FSD. Among the resource-dependent and non-dependent countries, the only additional commonality is the unidirectional causality running from FDI to exports. Hence, despite the implied associations summarised in Fig. 8.6, the interlinkages of the economic growth factors in SSA are still nascent and not significantly causally linked to economic growth. While FDI is consistently integrated into the region's trade-led and FSD-led growth dynamics, suggesting that heightened FDI holds great promise for regional development, the beneficiation, industrialisation, and manufacturing benefits of diversified FDI are only likely to be realised once SSA has progressed away from natural resource dependence to inter-African trade.

Appendices: TYDL Summary

Appendix 1: Methodology

The analysis in Fig. 8.6 used Toda and Yamamoto (1995) and Dolado and Lutkepohl (1996) (TYDL) non-causality tests for a full sample of 42 sub-Saharan African (SSA) countries and two sub-samples comprising 14 resource export-dependent and 28 non-dependent SSA countries over the period of 1990–2020.[4] The empirical specification is based on an aggregate production function (Balassa, 1978):

$$y = F\left[\left(L,K\right);\alpha\right] \tag{8.1}$$

where y is economic growth, measured as the annual percentage change in GDP (*GDP_G*); L is the logarithm of total labour force (*Labour*), K is gross fixed capital formation as a percentage of GDP (*GFCF*), and α represents the additional factors of interest comprising real exports of goods and services as a percentage of GDP (*Exports*), net FDI inflows as a percentage of GDP (*FDI*), real imports of goods and services as a percentage of GDP (*Imports*), and domestic credit to the private sector as a percentage of GDP as a proxy for financial sector development (*FSD*). All the data used in the empirical analysis was obtained from the World Bank's World Development Indicators database.

The causal relationships between the factors are thus empirically investigated using the following VAR model:

$$\begin{bmatrix} GDP\_G_t \\ Labour_t \\ GFCF_t \\ Exports_t \\ FDI_t \\ Imports_t \\ FSD_t \end{bmatrix} = A_0 + A_1 \begin{bmatrix} GDP\_G_{t-1} \\ Labour_{t-1} \\ GFCF_{t-1} \\ Exports_{t-1} \\ FDI_{t-1} \\ Imports_{t-1} \\ FSD_{t-1} \end{bmatrix} + \ldots + A_k \begin{bmatrix} GDP\_G_{t-k} \\ Labour_{t-k} \\ GFCF_{t-k} \\ Exports_{t-k} \\ FDI_{t-k} \\ Imports_{t-k} \\ FSD_{t-k} \end{bmatrix} + \mu_t \tag{8.2}$$

Granger (1969) posits that unidirectional causality between x and y can be said to exist if lags of x are significant in the equation of $y(t)$, while there is evidence of bidirectional causality if lags of x and y are significant in the equations of $y(t)$ and $x(t)$ respectively. In practise when testing for Granger causality however, it is possible that there are stochastic trends in the data, and this could invalidate the traditional F-test and Wald tests used to determine whether the VAR parameters are stable and jointly zero, while

[4] This start date has been limited by the availability of the World Development Indicators labour force participation data.

the use of differenced factors to evaluate the possible causal relationships only captures short-run causality (Sims et al., 1990; Toda & Phillips, 1993).

Hence, to overcome these limitations, Toda and Yamamoto (1995) and Dolado and Lutkepohl (1996) propose the use of a lag-augmented VAR Wald test for non-causality (TYDL), which consists of five steps. First, unit root tests are used to identify the maximum order of integration ($d(max)$) of the variables. Second, information criteria in a level VAR system are used to determine the optimal number of lags (k). Third, a lag-augmented level VAR is produced with a total of $p = [k + d(max)]$ lags, which ensures that the asymptotic chi-squared distribution of the Wald test statistic is normally distributed. Fourth, the lag-augmented VAR is re-specified as a seemingly unrelated regression (SUR) system in accordance with Rambaldi and Doran (1996). Finally, standard Wald tests are applied to the first k coefficients in the lag-augmented system to identify the causal associations. The results of these steps are tabulated in the Appendix 2 and the TYDL results are then summarised in Appendix 3.

Appendix 2: Unit Root and Lag Summary

	Full sample [k = 4]		*Resource dependent [k = 2]*			*Non-dependent [k = 4]*	
	I(0)	*I(1)*	*I(0)*	*I(1)*	*I(2)*	*I(0)*	*I(1)*
Economic growth (GDP_G):							
Levin, Lin & Chu t*	−18.487***	−34.658***	−11.122***	−19.199***		−14.774***	−29.069***
Im, Pesaran and Shin W-stat	−19.010***	−37.457***	−11.281***	−18.785***		−15.302***	−32.736***
ADF - Fisher Chi-square	518.751***	977.344***	182.262***	277.085***		336.489***	700.258***
PP - Fisher Chi-square	547.116***	1098.860***	209.536***	350.212***		337.580***	748.649***
Labour force (Labour):							
Levin, Lin & Chu t*	−6.816***	−6.001***	−1.193	0.736	−5.895***	−7.820***	−6.901***
Im, Pesaran and Shin W-stat	1.720	−10.031***	1.598	−1.418*	−7.534***	0.969	−11.435***
ADF - Fisher Chi-square	110.353**	322.683***	42.787**	46.989***	142.591***	67.566	275.694***
PP - Fisher Chi-square	122.146***	251.459***	16.104	30.400	158.963***	106.042***	221.059***
Gross fixed capital formation (GFCF):							
Levin, Lin & Chu t*	−2.565***	−24.525***	−1.777**	−14.365***		−1.752**	−19.758***
Im, Pesaran and Shin W-stat	−2.199***	−23.655***	−1.418*	−13.729***		−1.685**	−19.268***
ADF - Fisher Chi-square	109.200***	643.636***	38.593**	218.761***		70.607**	424.876***
PP - Fisher Chi-square	110.960***	758.703***	44.554***	242.200***		66.405*	516.503***
Exports:							
Levin, Lin & Chu t*	−3.553***	−24.335***	0.009	−12.039***		−4.407***	−21.410***
Im, Pesaran and Shin W-stat	−3.196***	−24.027***	0.312	−12.718***		−4.184***	−20.476***
ADF - Fisher Chi-square	128.939***	636.557***	22.598	201.710***		106.340***	434.846***

PP - Fisher Chi-square	131.434***	770.436***	26.130	252.376***		105.305***	518.061***
Imports:							
Levin, Lin & Chu t*	−4.991***	−24.042***	−2.102**	−15.893***		−4.711***	−18.428***
Im, Pesaran and Shin W-stat	−5.000***	−24.690***	−2.251***	−14.893***		−4.558***	−19.698***
ADF - Fisher Chi-square	164.305***	657.927***	45.247***	225.907***		119.059***	432.020***
PP - Fisher Chi-square	154.620***	813.452***	50.738***	285.624***		103.882***	527.828***
FDI:							
Levin, Lin & Chu t*	−6.991***	−31.351***	−2.271***	−18.350***		−6.900***	−25.616***
Im, Pesaran and Shin W-stat	−8.754***	−35.960***	−3.881***	−23.665***		−7.939***	−27.470***
ADF - Fisher Chi-square	266.772***	986.483***	67.359***	376.248***		199.413***	610.235***
PP - Fisher Chi-square	281.275***	996.337***	92.344***	344.068***		188.931***	652.269***
Financial sector development (FSD):							
Levin, Lin & Chu t*	−0.594	−21.924***	0.511	−12.735***		−1.008	−17.698***
Im, Pesaran and Shin W-stat	0.673	−19.781***	0.825	−10.358***		0.217	−16.980***
ADF - Fisher Chi-square	81.795	552.717***	24.034	173.825***		57.761	378.893***
PP - Fisher Chi-square	86.965	604.136***	31.240	180.980***		55.725	423.156***

Sample period: 1990–2020. Exogenous variables: Individual effects. Automatic selection of maximum lags based on the Schwartz information criteria (SIC). Newey-West automatic bandwidth selection and Bartlett kernel. Levin, Lin & Chu t* unit root test assumes common unit root process. Im, Pesaran and Shin W-stat; ADF - Fisher Chi-square; and PP - Fisher Chi-square unit root tests assume individual unit root process. *[#]* indicates the VAR lag selection (*k*) based on the Akaike information criteria (AIC)

Appendix 3: TYDL Results

	Full sample [42]		*Resource dependent [14]*		*Non-dependent [28]*	
	Chi-square	*Prob.*	*Chi-square*	*Prob.*	*Chi-square*	*Prob.*
GDP growth equation:						
Exports	4.932	0.29	4.996	0.08*	0.186	1.00
Imports	9.651	0.05**	1.093	0.58	4.327	0.36
FDI	15.568	0.00***	0.562	0.75	29.348	0.00***
DC_PS	1.292	0.86	1.446	0.49	1.115	0.89
Exports equation:						
GDP_G	8.160	0.09*	4.827	0.09*	3.047	0.55
Imports	15.035	0.00***	10.767	0.00***	4.865	0.30
FDI	11.840	0.02**	20.866	0.00***	16.479	0.00***
DC_PS	0.853	0.93	5.634	0.06*	1.534	0.82
Imports equation:						
GDP_G	0.089	1.00	0.177	0.92	0.585	0.96
Exports	11.392	0.02**	0.084	0.96	12.078	0.02**
FDI	28.941	0.00***	11.633	0.00***	13.485	0.01***
DC_PS	1.741	0.78	3.471	0.18	0.943	0.92
FDI equation:						
GDP_G	5.469	0.24	0.634	0.73	5.124	0.27
Exports	11.031	0.03**	3.549	0.17	0.668	0.96
Imports	1.164	0.88	1.300	0.52	2.625	0.62
DC_PS	0.737	0.95	0.928	0.63	0.680	0.95
Financial sector development equation:						
GDP_G	19.015	0.00***	9.541	0.01***	15.162	0.00***
Exports	5.583	0.23	1.605	0.45	4.254	0.37
Imports	2.829	0.59	5.970	0.05**	1.472	0.83
FDI	3.372	0.50	1.282	0.53	5.251	0.26

The $[k + d(max)]$th order level VAR was estimated with $d(max) = 1$ for the full and non-dependent samples and $d(max) = 2$ for the resource dependent sample. The lag length selection of $k = 4$ for the full samples and non-dependent sample, and $k = 2$ for the resource-dependent sample based on the Akaike Information Criteria (AIC). *[#]* indicates the number of SSA countries in the sample. Reported estimates are asymptotic Wald statistics. ***, **, and * represent significance at the 1%, 5%, and 10% level respectively

References

Abu, N., & Karim, M. Z. A. (2016). The Relationships between Foreign Direct Investment, Domestic Savings, Domestic Investment, and Economic Growth: The Case of Sub-Saharan Africa. *Society and Economy, 38*(2), 193–217.

Abu-Qarn, A. S., & Abu-Bader, S. (2004). The Validity of the ELG Hypothesis in the MENA Region: Cointegration and Error Correction Model Analysis. *Applied Economics, 36*, 1685–1695.

Abusomwan, O. S., & Izevbigie, J. N. (2022). Linking Foreign Direct Investment to Financial Deepening: Evidence from Sub-Saharan Africa. *African Development Review, 36*, 1–14.

Acquah, A. M., & Ibrahim, M. (2020). Foreign Direct Investment, Economic Growth and Financial Sector Development in Africa. *Journal of Sustainable Finance & Investment, 10*(4), 315–334.

Adams, D. (2009). Foreign Direct Investment, Domestic Investment, and Economic Growth in Sub-Saharan Africa. *Journal of Policy Modeling, 31*, 939–949.

Adem, G. Ö. K., & Güvercin, D. (2020). The Interaction Between Foreign Direct Investment, Foreign Portfolio Investment and Economic Growth: The Case of Sub-Saharan African Countries. *Akademik İncelemeler Dergisi, 15*(1), 57–82.

Adeniyi, O., Omisakin, O., Egwaikhide, F. O., & Oyinlola, A. (2012). Foreign Direct Investment, Economic Growth and Financial Sector Development in Small Open Developing Economies. *Economic Analysis & Policy, 42*(1), 105–127.

Ades, A., & Di Tella, R. (1999). Rents, Competition, and Corruption. *American Economic Review, 89*(4), 982–993.

Adjasi, C. K. D., Abor, J., Osei, K. A., & Nyavor-Foli, E. E. (2012). FDI and Economic Activity in Africa: The Role of Local Financial Markets. *Thunderbird International Business Review, 54*, 429–439.

Adjasi, C. K. D., & Biekpe, N. B. (2006). Stock Market Development and Economic Growth: The Case of Selected African Countries. *African Development Review, 18*(1), 144–161.

Adjasi, C. K. D., & Yartey, C. A. (2007). Stock Market Development in Sub-Saharan Africa: Critical Issues and Challenges. *IMF Working Paper No. 2007/209*. International Monetary Fund.

Agbetsiafa, D. (2004). The Finance Growth Nexus: Evidence from Sub-Saharan Africa. *Savings and Development, 28*(3), 271–288.

Agbloyor, E. K., Abor, J., Adjasi, C. K. D., & Yawson, A. (2013). Exploring the Causality Links Between Financial Markets and Foreign Direct Investment in Africa. *Research in International Business and Finance, 28*, 118–134.

Agbloyor, E. K., Abor, J. Y., Adjasi, C. K. D., & Yawson, A. (2014). Private Capital Flows and Economic Growth in Africa: The Role of Domestic Financial

Markets. *Journal of International Financial Markets Institutions and Money, 30*, 137–152.

Agbloyor, E. K., Gyeke-Dako, A., Kuipo, R., & Abor, J. Y. (2016). Foreign Direct Investment and Economic Growth in SSA: The Role of Institutions. *Thunderbird International Business Review, 58*, 479–497.

Ahmed, A. D., Cheng, E., & Messinis, G. (2011). The Role of Exports, FDI, and Imports in Development: Evidence from Sub-Saharan African Countries. *Applied Economics, 43*(26), 3719–3731.

Ahmed, A. D., & Wahid, A. N. M. (2011). Financial Structure and Economic Growth Link in African Countries: A Panel Cointegration Analysis. *Journal of Economics Studies, 38*(3), 331–357.

Akadiri, A. C., Gungor, H., Akadiri, S. S., & Bamidele-Sadiq, M. (2019). Is the Causal Relation Between Foreign Direct Investment, Trade, and Economic Growth Complement or Substitute? The Case of African Countries. *Journal of Public Affairs, 20*(2), e2023.

Aker, J., Klein, M., O'Connell, S., & Yang, M. (2010). Are Borders Barriers? The Impact of International and Internal Ethnic Borders on Agricultural Markets in West Africa. *Working Paper 208*. Center for Global Development.

Akhtaruzzaman, M., Yang, S., & Omar, A. (2018). Are Resource Rich Countries More Attractive than Countries with Good Institutions to Foreign Direct Investors in Sub Saharan Africa? *International Journal of Economics and Finance, 10*(6), 65–74.

Akinlo, A. E., & Egbetunde, T. (2010). Financial Development and Economic Growth: The Experience of 10 Sub-Saharan African Countries Revisited. *The Review of Finance and Banking, 2*(1), 17–28.

Aleksynska, M., & Havrylchyk, O. (2013). FDI from the South: The Role of Institutional Distance and Natural Resources. *European Journal of Political Economy, 29*(1), 38–53.

Alfaro, L., Areendam, C., Kalemli-Ozcan, S., & Sayek, S. (2004). FDI and Economic Growth: The Role of the Financial Markets. *Journal of International Economics, 64*(1), 89–112.

Alfaro, L., Chanda, A., Kalemli-Ozcan, S., & Sayek, S. (2010). Does Foreign Direct Investment Promote Growth? Exploring the Role of Financial Markets on Linkages. *Journal of Development Economics, 91*(2), 242–256.

Alfaro, L., Kalemli-Ozcan, S., & Volosovych, V. (2008). Why Doesn't Capital Flow from Rich to Poor Countries? An Empirical Investigation. *Review of Economics and Statistics, 90*(2), 347–368.

Alguacil, M., Ana, C., & Vicente, O. (2011). Inward FDI and Growth: The Role of Macroeconomic and Institutional Environment. *Journal of Policy Modeling, 33*(3), 481–496.

Allen, F., Carletti, E., Cull, R., Qian, J., Senbet, L., & Valenzuela, P. (2014). The African Financial Development and Financial Inclusion Gaps. *Journal of African Economies, 23*, 614–642.

Allen, F., Otchere, I., & Senbet, L. W. (2011). African Financial Systems: A Review. *Review of Development Finance, 1*(2), 79–113.

Almfraji, M. A., & Almsafir, M. K. (2014). Foreign Direct Investment and Economic Growth Literature Review from 1994 to 2012. *Procedia – Social and Behavioral Sciences, 129*, 206–213.

Aluko, O. A., & Adeyeye, P. O. (2020). Imports and Economic Growth in Africa: Testing for Granger Causality in the Frequency Domain. *The Journal of International Trade & Economic Development, 29*(7), 850–864.

Al-Yousif, Y. K. (2002). Financial Development and Economic Growth: Another Look at the Evidence from Developing Countries. *Review of Financial Economics, 11*(2), 131–150.

An, H., Zou, Q., & Kargbo, M. (2019). Impact of Financial Development on Economic Growth: Evidence from Sub-Saharan Africa. *Australian Economic Papers, 60*, 226–260.

Andrianova, S., Baltagi, B., Demetriades, P., & Fielding, D. (2015). Why Do African Banks Lend So Little? *Oxford Bulletin of Economics and Statistics, 77*(3), 339–359.

Antonietti, R., & Franco, C. (2021). From FDI to Economic Complexity: A Panel Granger Causality Analysis. *Structural Change and Economic Dynamics, 56*(C), 225–239.

Anwar, M. S., & Sampath, R. K. (2000). Exports and Economic Growth. *Indian Economic Journal, 47*(3), 79–88.

Anyanwu, J. C. (2011). Determinants of Foreign Direct Investment Inflows to Africa, 1980–2007. *Working Paper Series No. 136*. African Development Bank.

Anyanwu, J. C. (2012). Why Does Foreign Direct Investment Go Where It Goes? New Evidence from African Countries. *Annals of Economics and Finance, 13*(2), 433–470.

Arcand, J. L., Berkes, E., & Panizza, U. (2015). Too Much Finance? *Journal of Economic Growth, 20*, 105–148.

Arnade, C., & Vasavada, U. (1995). Causality between Productivity and Exports in Agriculture: Evidence from Asia and Latin America. *Journal of Agricultural Economics, 46*, 174–186.

Arrow, K. (1962). Economic Welfare and the Allocation of Resources for Invention. In K. Arrow (Ed.), *The Rate, Direction of Inventive Activity: Economic, Social Factors* (pp. 609–626). National Bureau of Economic Research.

Asafo-Adjei, E., Junior, P. O., Adam, A. M., Arthur, C. L., Boateng, E., & Ankomah, K. (2023). Asymmetric Relationships Among Financial Sector Development, Corruption, Foreign Direct Investment, and Economic Growth in Sub-Saharan Africa. *Cogent Economics & Finance, 11*(1), 2182454.

Asafo-Agyei, G., & Kodongo, O. (2022). Foreign Direct Investment and Economic Growth in Sub-Saharan Africa: A Nonlinear Analysis. *Economic Systems, 46*(4), 101003.

Asamoah, M. E., & Alagidede, I. P. (2020). Foreign Direct Investment, Real Sector Growth and Financial Development. *International Journal of Financial Economics, 28*(1), 626–643.

Asamoah, M. E., Alagidede, I. P., & Adu, F. (2022). On the Allocation Puzzle and Capital Flows: Evidence from Foreign Direct Investment and Real Sector Growth in Africa. *African Development Review, 34*, 370–380.

Asghari, M., Hilmi, N., & Safa, A. (2014). FDI Effects on Economic Growth: The Role of Natural Resource and Environmental Policy. *Topics in Middle Eastern and African Economies, 16*(2), 85–104.

Asiedu, E. (2006). Foreign Direct Investment in Africa: The Role of Natural Resources, Market Size, Government Policy, Institutions and Political Instability. *The World Economy, 29*(1), 63–77.

Asiedu, E. (2013). *Foreign Direct Investment.* Natural Resources and Institutions, Department of Economics, University of Kansas.

Asongu, S. A., Nnanna, J., & Acha-Anyi, P. N. (2021). The Openness Hypothesis in the Context of Economic Development in Sub-Saharan Africa: The Moderating Role of Trade Dynamics on FDI. *The International Trade Journal, 35*(4), 336–359.

Awokuse, T. O. (2007). Causality Between Exports, Imports, and Economic Growth: Evidence from Transition Economies. *Economics Letters, 94*, 389–395.

Ayenew, B. B. (2022). The Effect of Foreign Direct Investment on the Economic Growth of Sub-Saharan African Countries: An Empirical Approach. *Cogent Economics & Finance, 10*(1), 1–12.

Azman-Saini, W. N. W., Law, S. H., & Ahmad, A. H. (2010). FDI and Economic Growth: New Evidence on the Role of Financial Markets. *Economics Letters, 107*(2), 211–213.

Babatunde, M. A. (2012). Africa's Growth and Development Strategies: A Critical Review. *African Development, 37*(4), 141–178.

Bahar, D., & Santos, M. A. (2018). One More Resource Curse: Dutch Disease and Export Concentration. *Journal of Development Economics, 132*, 102–114.

Baharumshah, A. Z., & Rashid, S. (1999). Exports, Imports and Economic Growth in Malaysia: Empirical Evidence Based on Multivariate Time Series. *Asian Economic Journal, 13*(4), 389–406.

Bahmani-Oskooee, M., Economidou, C., & Goswami, G. G. (2005). Export-Led Growth Hypothesis Revisited: A Panel Cointegration Approach. *Scientific Journal of Administrative Development, 3*, 40–55.

Bahmani-Oskooee, M., & Oyolola, M. (2007). Export Growth and Output Growth: An Application of Bounds Testing Approach. *Journal of Economics and Finance, 31*(1), 1–11.

Balassa, B. (1978). Exports and Economic Growth: Further Evidence. *Journal of Development Economics, 5*(2), 181–189.
Balasubramanyam, V. N., Salisu, M., & Sapsford, D. (1996). Foreign Direct Investment and Growth in EP and IS Countries. *The Economic Journal, 106*(434), 92–105.
Balcilar, M., Gupta, R., Lee, C. C., & Olasehinde-Williams, G. (2018). The Synergistic Effect of Insurance and Banking Sector Activities on Economic Growth in Africa. *Economic Systems, 42*(4), 637–648.
Baran, P. (1957). *The Political Economy of Growth*. Monthly Review Press.
Bbaale, E., & Mutenyo, J. (2011). Export Composition and Economic Growth in Sub-Saharan Africa: A Panel Analysis. *Consilience, 6*, 1–19.
Beck, R., Georgiadis, G., & Straub, R. (2014). The Finance and Growth Nexus Revisited. *Economics Letters, 124*(3), 382–385.
Bekele, D. T., & Degu, A. A. (2021). The Effect of Financial Sector Development on Economic Growth of Selected Sub-Saharan Africa Countries. *International Journal of Financial Economics, 28*(3), 2834–2842.
Bokpin, G. A., Mensah, L., & Asamoah, M. E. (2014). Foreign Direct Investment and Natural Resources in Africa. *Journal of Economic Studies, 42*(4), 608–621.
Borensztein, E., De Gregorio, J., & Lee, J. W. (1998). How Does Foreign Direct Investment Affect Economic Growth? *Journal of International Economics, 45*, 115–135.
Buchanan, B. L., Le, Q. V., & Rishi, M. (2012). Foreign Direct Investment and Institutional Quality: Some Empirical Evidence. *International Review of Financial Analysis, 21*(C), 81–89.
Buffie, E. (1992). On the Condition for Export-Led Growth. *Canadian Journal of Economics, 25*, 211–225.
Calderón, C., & Liu, L. (2002). The Direction of Causality Between Financial Development and Economic Growth. *Central Bank of Chile Working Paper No. 184*. Central Bank of Chile.
Cardoso, F. (1977). The Consumption of Dependency Theory in the United States. *Latin American Research Review, 12*(3), 7–24.
Carril-Caccia, F., Milgram-Baleix, J., & Paniagua, J. (2019). Foreign Direct Investment in Oil Abundant Countries: The Role of Institutions. *PLoS One, 14*(4), e0215650.
Cavalcanti, D. V. T. V., Mohaddes, K., & Raissi, M. (2015). Commodity Price Volatility and the Sources of Growth. *Journal of Applied Economics, 30*, 857–873.
Çetintaş, H., & Barişik, S. (2009). Export, Import and Economic Growth: The Case of Transition Economies. *Transition Studies Review, 15*(4), 636–649.
Chenery, H. B., & Strout, A. M. (1966). Foreign Assistance and Economic Development. *The American Economic Review, LVI*(4, Part I), 679–733.
Chukwu, A. B., & Adewuyi, A. O. (2023). Foreign Direct Investment, Sectoral Output Performance and Poverty in Africa: Evidence from Panel Structural

Vector Autoregressive and Threshold Regression Models. *International Journal of Finance and Economics, 29*, 2665–2698.
Coe, T. D., & Helpman, E. (1995). International R&D Spillovers. *European Economic Review, 39*, 859–887.
Cohen, W. M., & Levinthal, D. A. (1990). Absorptive Capacity: A New Perspective on Learning and Innovation. *Administrative Science Quarterly, 35*, 128–152.
Collier, P. (2005). *Is Agriculture Still Relevant to Poverty Reduction in Africa?* Speech given to All Party Parliamentary Group on Overseas Development. House of Commons. Retrieved May, 2024, from http://www.odi.org.uk/speeches/apgood_oct05/apgood_oct17/report.html
Collier, P. (2008). *The Bottom Billion: Why the Poorest Countries Are Failing and What Can Be Done About It*. Oxford University Press.
Cui, L., & Xu, Y. (2019). Outward FDI and Profitability of Emerging Economy Firms: Diversifying from Home Resource Dependence in Early-Stage Internationalization. *Journal of World Business, 54*, 372–386.
Dabla-Norris, E., Brumby, J., Kyobe, A., Mills, Z., & Papageorgiou, C. (2012). Investing in Public Investment: An Index of Public Investment Efficiency. *Journal of Economic Growth, 17*(3), 235–266.
Dawson, P. J., & Sanjuán-López, A. I. (2013). The Export-Income Relationship in Developing Countries: Evidence from Panel Cointegration. *The Journal of Developing Areas, 47*(1), 47–62.
de Mauro, A. (2013). Africa's Burden: Labour Markets, Natural Resources and the FDI 'Reliance-Rejection' Paradox. *MPRA Paper No. 50019*. Munich Personal RePEc Archive.
de Mello, L. R. (1997). Foreign Direct Investment in Developing Countries and Growth: A Selective Survey. *Journal of Development Studies, 34*, 1–24.
de Mello, L. R. (1999). Foreign Direct Investment-Led Growth: Evidence from Time Series and Panel Data. *Oxford Economic Papers, 51*(1), 133–151.
Demetriades, P., & James, G. A. (2011). Finance and Growth in Africa: The Broken Link. *Economics Letters, 113*(3), 263–265.
Demetriades, P. O., & Hussein, K. A. (1996). Does Financial Development Cause Economic Growth? Time Series Evidence from 16 Countries. *Journal of Development Economics, 51*, 387–411.
Diao, X., Hazell, P., Resnick, D., & Thurlow, J. (2007). The Role of Agriculture in Development Implications for Sub-Saharan Africa. *Research Report No. 153*. International Food Policy Research Institute.
Dolado, J. J., & Lutkepohl, H. (1996). Making Wald Tests Work for Cointegrated VAR Systems. *Econometric Reviews, 15*, 369–386.
Dreger, C., & Herzer, D. A. (2013). Further Examination of the Export-Led Growth Hypothesis. *Empirical Economics, 45*, 39–60.

Durham, J. B. (2004). Absorptive Capacity and the Effects of Foreign Direct Investment and Equity Foreign Portfolio Investment on Economic Growth. *European Economic Review, 48*(2), 285–306.

Dutt, S. D., & Ghosh, D. (1996). The Export Growth-Economic Growth Nexus: A Causality Analysis. *The Journal of Developing Areas, 30*, 167–181.

Duttaray, M., Dutt, A. K., & Mukhopadhyay, K. (2008). Foreign Direct Investment and Economic Growth in Less Developed Countries: An Empirical Study of Causality and Mechanisms. *Applied Economics, 40*, 1927–1939.

Dwumfour, R. A., & Ntow-Gyamfi, M. (2018). Natural Resources, Financial Development and Institutional Quality in Africa: Is There a Resource Curse? *Resources Policy, 59*, 411–426.

Edwards, S. (1992). Trade Orientation, Distortions and Growth in Developing Countries. *Journal of Development Economics, 39*(1), 31–57.

Ee, C. Y. (2016). Export-Led Growth Hypothesis: Empirical Evidence from Selected Sub-Saharan African Countries. *Procedia Economics and Finance, 35*, 232–240.

Enisan, A., & Olufisayo, A. (2009). Stock Market Development and Economic Growth: Evidence from Seven Sub-Saharan African Countries. *Journal of Economics and Business, 61*, 162–171.

Esfahani, H. S. (1991). Exports, Imports, and Economic Growth in Semi-Industrialized Countries. *Journal of Development Economics, 35*(1), 93–116.

Esso, L. J. (2010). Long-Run Relationship and Causality between Foreign Direct Investment and Growth: Evidence from Ten African Countries. *International Journal of Economics and Finance, 2*, 168–177.

Fanon, F. (1963). *The Wretched of the Earth*. Grove Press.

Fanon, F. (1967). *Black Skin, White Masks*. Grove Press.

Fantessi, A. A., & Kiprop, S. K. (2015). Financial Development and Economic Growth in the West African Economic and Monetary Union (WAEMU). *African Journal of Business Management, 9*(17), 624–632.

Feder, G. (1983). On Exports and Economic Growth. *Journal of Development Economics, 12*(2), 59–73.

Findlay, R. (1978). Relative Backwardness, Direct Foreign Investment, and the Transfer of Technology: A Simple Dynamic Model. *The Quarterly Journal of Economics, 92*, 1–16.

Fosu, A. K. (1990). Exports and Economic Growth: The African Case. *World Development, 18*, 831–835.

Frank, A. (1966). *The Development of Underdevelopment*. New England Free Press.

Fuinhas, J. A., Filipe, M. D., Belucio, M., & Marque, A. C. (2019). The Nexus between Financial Development and Economic Growth: Evidence from European Countries. *Journal of Economic Studies and Research, 2019*, 1–20.

Galor, O., & Moav, O. (2004). From Physical to Human Capital Accumulation: Inequality and the Process of Development. *The Review of Economic Studies, 71*(4), 1001–1026.

Ghirmay, T. (2004). Financial Development and Economic Growth in Sub-Saharan African Countries: Evidence from Time Series Analysis. *African Development Review, 16*, 415–432.

Ghirmay, T., Grabowski, R., & Sharma, C. (2001). Exports, Investment, Efficiency and Economic Growth in LDC: An Empirical Investigation. *Applied Economics, 33*(6), 689–700.

Giles, J. A., & Williams, C. L. (2000a). Export-Led Growth: A Survey of the Empirical Literature and Some Non-Causality Results. Part 1. *The Journal of International Trade and Economic Development, 9*, 261–337.

Giles, J. A., & Williams, C. L. (2000b). Export-Led Growth: A Survey of the Empirical Literature and Some Non-Causality Results. Part 2. *The Journal of International Trade and Economic Development, 9*, 445–470.

Glass, A. J., & Saggi, K. (1998). International Technology Transfer and the Technology Gap. *Journal of Development Economics, 55*(2), 369–398.

Goldberg, L. S., & Klein, M. W. (1999). International Trade and Factor Mobility: An Empirical Investigation. *NBER Working Paper No. 7196*. National Bureau of Economic Research.

Goldsmith, R. (1969). *Financial Structure and Development*. Yale University Press.

Gossel, S. J., & Biekpe, N. (2013). Economic Growth, Trade and Capital Flows: A Causal Analysis of Post-Liberalized South Africa. *The Journal of International Trade and Economic Development, 23*(6), 815–836.

Granger, C. (1969). Investigating Causal Relations by Econometric Models and Cross-Spectral Methods. *Econometrica, 37*(3), 434–448.

Greenwood, J., & Smith, B. (1997). Financial Markets in Development and the Development of Financial Markets. *Journal of Economic Dynamics and Control, 21*, 145–181.

Gries, T., Kraft, M., & Meierrieks, D. (2009). Linkages Between Financial, Deepening, Trade Openness, and Economic Development: Causality Evidence from Sub-Saharan Africa. *World Development, 37*, 1849–1860.

Grossman, G. M., & Helpman, E. (1991). *Innovation and Growth in the Global Economy*. MIT Press.

Gui-Diby, S. L. (2014). Impact of Foreign Direct Investments on Economic Growth in Africa: Evidence from three Decades of Panel Data Analyses. *Research in Economics, 68*, 248–256.

Gui-Diby, S. L., & Renard, M.-F. (2015). Foreign Direct Investment Inflows and the Industrialization of African Countries. *World Development, 74*, 43–57.

Hailu, Z. A. (2010). Impact of Foreign Direct Investment on Trade of African Countries. *International Journal of Economics and Finance, 2*(3), 122–133.

Helpman, E. (1984). A Simple Theory of International Trade with Multinational Corporations. *Journal of Political Economy, 92*(3), 451–471.

Helpman, E., & Krugman, P. (1985). *Market Structure and Foreign Trade*. MIT Press.

Henriques, I., & Sadorsky, P. (1996). Export-led Growth or Growth-Driven Exports? The Canadian Case. *Canadian Journal of Economics, 29*, 540–555.

Hermes, N., & Lensink, R. (2003). Foreign Direct Investment, Financial Development and Economic Growth. *Journal of Development Studies, 40*(1), 142–153.

Hlavac, M. (2010). Comments on Benjamin Smith: Oil Wealth and Regime Survival in the Developing World, 1960–1999. *MPRA Paper No. 25797*. University Library of Munich.

Honohan, P., & Beck, T. (2007). *Making Finance Work for Africa*. The World Bank.

Huynh, C. M. (2022). How Does the Impact of Foreign Direct Investment on Institutional Quality Depend on the Underground Economy? *Journal of Sustainable Finance & Investment, 12*(2), 554–569.

Ibhagui, O. (2020). How Does Foreign Direct Investment Affect Growth in Sub-Saharan Africa? New Evidence from Threshold Analysis. *Journal of Economic Studies, 47*(1), 149–181.

Ibrahim, M., & Acquah, A. M. (2021). Re-Examining the Causal Relationships Among FDI, Economic Growth and Financial Sector Development in Africa. *International Review of Applied Economics, 35*(1), 45–63.

Ibrahim, M., & Alagidede, P. (2018). Effect of Financial Development on Economic Growth in Sub-Saharan Africa. *Journal of Policy Modeling, 40*, 1104–1125.

Idun, A. A.-A., Efiinu, E. E., Adam, M. A., & Agyenim-Boateng, E. (2024). Sectoral Channels of FDI into Productivity Growth in Africa. *Open Journal of Business and Management, 12*, 2824–2853.

Iscan, I. H., & Yıldırım, S. (2012). The Type of Imported Goods and Economic Growth: Panel Evidence. *International Research Journal of Finance and Economics, 91*, 98–108.

Islam, F., Hye, Q. M. A., & Shahbaz, M. (2012). Import-Economic Growth Nexus: ARDL Approach to Cointegration. *Journal of Chinese Economic and Foreign Trade Studies, 5*(3), 194–214.

Kagochi, J. M., Al Nasser, O. M., & Kebede, E. (2013). Does Financial Development Hold the Key to Economic Growth? The Case of Sub-Saharan Africa. *The Journal of Developing Areas, 47*(2), 61–79.

Keho, Y. (2015). Foreign Direct Investment, Exports and Economic Growth: Some African Evidence. *Journal of Applied Economics and Business Research, 5*(4), 209–219.

Khan, Z., Lew, Y. K., & Sinkovics, R. R. (2015). International Joint Ventures as Boundary Spanners: Technological Knowledge Transfer in an Emerging Economy. *Global Strategy Journal, 5*(1), 48–68.

Kojima, K. (1975). International Trade and Foreign Investment: Substitutes or Complements? *Hitotsubashi Journal of Economics, 16*(1), 1–12.

Krugman, P. R. (1984). Import Protection as Export Promotion. In H. Kierzkowski (Ed.), *Monopolistic Competition in International Trade*. Oxford University Press.

Krugman, P. R. (1993). International Finance and Economic Development. In A. Giovannini (Ed.), *Finance and Development: Issues and Experience* (pp. 11–24). Cambridge University Press.

Kuttu, S., Coffie, W., Chipeta, C., & Afedzie, E. (2022). Chapter 29: Foreign Direct Investment, Stock Market Development, and Inclusive Growth in Selected Sub-Saharan African Countries. In J. Y. Abor & C. K. D. Adjasi (Eds.), *The Economics of Banking and Finance in Africa: Developments in Africa's Financial Systems*. Springer International Publishing.

Kuznets, S. (1955). International Differences in Capital Formation and Financing. In *Capital Formation and Economic Growth* (pp. 19–111). National Bureau of Economic Research.

Law, S. H., & Singh, N. (2014). Does Too Much Finance Harm Economic Growth? *Journal of Banking & Finance, 41*, 36–44.

Lawrence, R. Z., & Weinstein, D. E. (1999). Trade and Growth: Import-Led or Export-Led? Evidence from Japan and Korea. *NBER Working Paper No. 7264*. National Bureau of Economic Research.

Lectard, P., & Rougier, E. (2018). Can Developing Countries Gain from Defying Comparative Advantage? Distance to Comparative Advantage, Export Diversification and Sophistication, and the Dynamics of Specialization. *World Development, 102*(C), 90–110.

Leite, C., & Weidmann, J. (1999). Does Mother Nature Corrupt? Natural Resources, Corruption, and Economic Growth. *Working Paper No. 99*. International Monetary Fund.

Li, X., & Liu, X. (2005). Foreign Direct Investment and Economic Growth: An Increasingly Endogenous Relationship. *World Development, 33*(3), 393–407.

Lucas, R. J. (1988). On the Mechanics of Economic Development. *Journal of Monetary Economics, 22*(3), 3–42.

Lundgren, C. J., Thomas, A. H., & York, R. C. (2013). *Boom, Bust, or Prosperity? Managing Sub-Saharan Africa's Natural Resource Wealth*. International Monetary Fund.

Makiela, K., & Ouattara, B. (2018). Foreign Direct Investment and Economic Growth: Exploring the Transmission Channels. *Economic Modelling, 72*, 296–305.

Makki, S. S., & Somwaru, A. (2004). Impact of Foreign Direct Investment and Trade on Economic Growth: Evidence from Developing Countries. *American Journal of Agricultural Economics, 86*, 795–801.

Malikane, C., & Chitambara, P. (2017). Foreign Direct Investment, Democracy and Economic Growth in Southern Africa. *African Development Review, 29*(1), 92–102.

Mallick, S., & Moore, T. (2008). Foreign Capital in a Growth Model. *Review of Development Economics, 12*, 143–159.

Markusen, J. R. (1984). Multinationals, Multi-Plant Economies and the Gains from Trade. *Journal of International Economics, 16*(3–4), 205–226.

Markusen, J. R., & Venables, A. J. (1998). Multinational Firms and the New Trade Theory. *Journal of International Economics, 46*(2), 183–203.

Matima, Z., & Gossel, S. J. (2023). The Relationship between FDI, Political Risk and Institutional Quality in Sub-Saharan Africa. *The Journal of Trade and Economic Development, 32*(3), 461–474.

Mazumdar, J. (2000). Imported Machinery and Growth in LDCs. *Journal of Development Economics, 65*, 209–224.

McKinnon, R. (1964). Foreign Exchange Constraint in Economic Development and Efficient Aid Allocation. *Economic Journal, 74*, 338–409.

McKinnon, R. (1973). *Money and Capital in Economic Development*. Brookings Institution.

Michael, Y. (2018). The FDI and Economic Growth Controversy in Sub-Saharan Africa. In A. H. Heshmati (Ed.), *Determinants of Economic Growth in Africa*. Palgrave Macmillan.

Mijiyawa, A. G. (2017). Does Foreign Direct Investment Promote Exports? Evidence from African Countries. *The World Economy, 40*(9), 1934–1957.

Morisset, J. (2000). Foreign Direct Investment in Africa: Policy Also Matters. *Transnational Corporations, 9*(2), 107–125.

Moyo, C., & Jeke, L. (2019). Manufacturing Sector and Economic Growth: A Panel Study of Selected African Countries. *Journal of Business and Economics Review, 4*(3), 114–130.

Mthanti, T., & Ojah, K. (2017). Entrepreneurial Orientation (EO): Measurement and Policy Implications of Entrepreneurship at the Macroeconomic Level. *Research Policy, 46*(4), 724–739.

Mundell, R. A. (1957). International Trade and Factor Mobility. *American Economic Review, 47*(3), 321–335.

Mutreja, P., Ravikumar, B., & Sposi, M. (2018). Capital Goods Trade, Relative Prices, and Economic Development. *Review of Economic Dynamics, 27*, 101–122.

Nowbusting, B. (2009). FDI, Domestic Investment and Economic Growth: A Theoretical Framework. *Globelics – 7th International Conference on Inclusive Growth, Innovation and Technological Change*, 6–8 October, Dakar, Senegal.

Odhiambo, N. M. (2021). Is Export-Led Growth Hypothesis Still Valid for Sub-Saharan African Countries? New Evidence from Panel Data Analysis. *European Journal of Management and Business Economics, 31*(1), 77–93.

Odhiambo, N. M., Nyasha, S., Zerihun, M. F., & Tipoy, C. (2019). Financial Development in Africa: Is It Demand-Following or Supply-Leading? In D. Makina (Ed.), *Extending Financial Inclusion in Africa* (pp. 37–60). AP Academic Press.

OECD/UN. (2011). *Economic Diversification in Africa: A Review of Selected Countries.* Organization for Economic Co-operation and Development (OECD) and United Nations Report. Retrieved April, 2025, from https://www.oecd.org/countries/tunisia/46148761.pdf

Ofori, I. K., & Asongu, S. A. (2022). *Repackaging FDI for Inclusive Growth: Nullifying Effects and Policy Relevant Thresholds of Governance.* ZBW – Leibniz Information Centre for Economics.

Ogujiuba, K., Nwogwugwu, U., & Kike, E. (2011). Import Substitution Industrialization as Learning Process: Sub-Saharan African Experience as Distortion of the 'Good. *Business and Management Review, 1*(6), 8–21.

Onuoha, F. C., Okonkwo, I. C., Okoro, P., & Okere, K. (2018). The Causal Relationship between Foreign Direct Investment (FDI) and the Macro-economy of Selected West African Countries: Panel ARDL/Granger Causality Analysis. *African Research Review, 12*(1), 140–163.

Onyeiwu, S., & Shrestha, H. (2004). Determinants of Foreign Direct Investment in Africa. *Journal of Developing Societies, 20*(1–2), 89–106.

Opoku, E. E. O., Ibrahim, M., & Sare, Y. A. (2019a). The Causal Relationship Between Financial Development and Economic Growth in Africa. *International Review of Applied Economics, 33*(6), 789–812.

Opoku, E. E. O., Ibrahim, M., & Sare, Y. A. (2019b). Foreign Direct Investment, Sectoral Effects and Economic Growth in Africa. *International Economic Journal, 33*(3), 473–492.

Osei, M. J., & Kim, J. (2020). Foreign Direct Investment and Economic Growth: Is More Financial Development Better? *Economic Modelling, 93*, 154–161.

Palley, T. I. (2012). The Rise and Fall of Export-led Growth. *Investigación Económica, 71*(280), 141–161.

Papaioannou, E. (2009). What Drives International Financial Flows? Politics, Institutions and Other Determinants. *Journal of Development Economics, 88*(2), 269–281.

Patrick, H. (1966). Financial Development and Economic Growth in Underdeveloped Countries. *Economic Development and Cultural Change, 14*(1), 174–189.

Pazim, K. H. (2009). Panel Data Analysis of Export-Led Growth Hypothesis in BIMP-EAGA Countries. *MPRA Paper No. 13264.* University Library of Munich.

Poelhekke, S., & Van der Ploeg, F. (2010). Do Natural Resources Attract FDI? Evidence from Non-Stationary Sector-Level Data. *CEPR Discussion Paper No. 8079*. CEPR.

Poelhekke, S., & van der Ploeg, F. (2013). Do Natural Resources Attract Non-Resource FDI? *Review of Economics and Statistics, 95*(3), 1047–1065.

Pradhan, R. P., Arvin, M. B., Norman, N. R., & Hall, J. H. (2014). The Dynamics of Banking Sector and Stock Market Maturity and the Performance of Asian Economies. *Journal of Economic and Administrative Sciences, 30*(1), 16–44.

Prebisch, R. (1950). *The Economic Development of Latin America and Its Principal Problems*. United Nations Department of Economic Affairs.

Purvis, D. D. (1972). Technology, Trade and Factor Mobility. *Economic Journal, 82*(327), 991–999.

Rambaldi, A. N., & Doran, H. E. (1996). Testing for Granger Non-Causality in Cointegrated Systems Made Easy. *Working Papers in Econometrics and Statistics, 88*, 1–22.

Reppas, P., & Christopoulos, D. (2005). The Export-Output Growth Nexus: Evidence from African and Asian Countries. *Journal of Policy Modeling, 27*, 929–940.

Riezman, R. G., Summers, P. M., & Whiteman, C. H. (1996). The Engine of Growth or Its Handmaiden? A Time Series Assessment of Export-Led Growth. *Empirical Economics, 21*, 177–113.

Rioja, F., & Valev, N. (2004). Does One Size Fit All? A Reexamination of the Finance and Growth Relationship. *Journal of Development Economics, 74*(2), 429–447.

Rodney, W. (1981). *How Europe Underdeveloped Africa*. Howard University Press.

Romer, P. M. (1986). Increasing Returns and Long-Run Growth. *Journal of Political Economy, 94*, 1002–1037.

Romer, P. M. (1992). Two Strategies for Economic Development: Using Ideas and Producing Ideas. *The World Bank Economic Review, 6*(1), 63–91.

Roseline, O. (2012). Financial Development and Economic Growth in Africa: Lessons and Prospects. *Business and Economic Research, 2*(2), 54–67.

Ross, J. (2005). Divergence and Growth Collapses: Theory and Empirical Evidence. In J. A. Ocampo (Ed.), *Beyond Reforms: Structural Dynamics and Macroeconomic Vulnerability* (pp. 211–232). The World Bank-ECLAC.

Sachs, J. D., & Warner, A. M. (1995). Natural Resource Abundance and Economic Growth. *NBER Working Paper 5398*. National Bureau of Economic Research.

Samargandi, N., Fidrmuc, J., & Ghosh, S. (2015). Is the Relationship Between Financial Development and Economic Growth Monotonic? Evidence from a Sample of Middle-Income Countries. *World Development, 6*, 66–81.

Schubert, J., Engel, U., & Macamo, E. (2018). *Extractive Industries and Changing State Dynamics in Africa Beyond the Resource Curse*. Routledge.

Schumpeter, J. A. (1911). *Theory of Economic Development.* Harvard University Press.

Seyoum, M., Wu, R., & Lin, J. (2015). Foreign Direct Investment and Economic Growth: The Case of Developing African Economies. *Social Indicators Research, 122*, 45–64.

Shan, J., & Sun, F. (1998). On the Export-Led Growth Hypothesis: The Econometric Evidence from China. *Applied Economics, 30*(8), 1055–1065.

Sharma, S. S., & Smyth, R. (2009). Is Economic Growth Export-Led or Import-Led in the Pacific Island Countries? Evidence from Panel Data Models. *Discussion Paper DEVDP 09-15.* Department Research Unit, Monash University.

Shaw, E. (1973). *Financial Deepening in Economic Development.* Oxford University Press.

Sims, C., Stock, J. H., & Watson, M. W. (1990). Inference in Linear Time Series Models with Some Unit Roots. *Econometrica, 58*, 113–144.

Singer, H. (1949). Economic Progress in Under-Developed Countries. *Social Research, 16*(1), 1–11.

Solow, R. M. (1956). A Contribution to the Theory of Economic Growth. *Quarterly Journal of Economics, 70*, 65–94.

Sukar, A., Ahmed, S., & Hassan, S. (2006). The Effects of Foreign Direct Investment on Economic Growth: The Case of Sub-Sahara Africa. *Southwestern Economic Review, 34*, 61–73.

Taylor, I. (2018). Chapter 23: Africa's Resource Corner and BRICS. In T. Binns, K. Lynch, & E. Nel (Eds.), *The Routledge Handbook of African Development.* Routledge.

Tekin, R. B. (2012). Economic Growth, Exports and Foreign Direct Investment in Least Developed Countries: A Panel Granger Causality Analysis. *Economic Modelling, 29*, 868–878.

The Economist. (2000, May 13). The Hopeless Continent. Retrieved December, 2022, from https://www.economist.com/leaders/2000/05/11/hopeless-africa

Toda, H. Y., & Phillips, P. C. B. (1993). Vector Autoregressions and Causality. *Econometrica, 61*, 1367–1393.

Toda, H. Y., & Yamamoto, T. (1995). Statistical Inference in Vector Autoregressions with Possibly Integrated Processes. *Journal of Econometrics, 66*, 225–250.

UNCTAD. (2019). *State of Commodity Dependence 2019.* United Nations Conference on Trade and Development.

UNCTAD. (2022). Rethinking the Foundations of Export Diversification in Africa: The Catalytic Role of Business and Financial Services. *Economic Development in Africa Report No. UNCTAD/ALDC/AFRICA/2022.* United Nations Conference on Trade and Development.

Venables, A. J. (2016). Using Natural Resources for Development: Why Has It Proven So Difficult? *The Journal of Economic Perspectives, 30*(1), 161–183.

Vokes, R. (2018). African Perspectives on Development. In T. Binns, K. Lynch, & E. Nel (Eds.), *The Routledge Handbook of African Development*. Routledge.

Wako, H. A. (2021). Foreign Direct Investment in Sub-Saharan Africa: Beyond its Growth Effect. *Research in Globalization, 3*, 100054.

Wang, J. (1990). Growth Technology Transfer, and the Long-Run Theory of International Capital Movements. *Journal of International Economics, 29*, 255–271.

Wörz, J. (2005). Skill Intensity in Foreign Trade and Economic Growth. *Empirica, 32*(1), 117–144.

Yeboua, K. (2019). Foreign Direct Investment, Financial Development and Economic Growth in Africa: Evidence from Threshold Modeling. *Transnational Corporations Review, 11*(3), 179–189.

Zahonogo, P. (2016). Trade and Economic Growth in Developing Countries: Evidence from Sub-Saharan Africa. *Journal of African Trade, 3*(1-2), 41–56.

Zekarias, S. M. (2016). The Impact of Foreign Direct Investment on Economic Growth in Eastern Africa: Evidence from Panel Data Analysis. *Applied Economics and Finance, 3*(1), 145–160.

Zhu, S., & Fu, X. (2013). Drivers of Export Upgrading. *World Development, 51*, 221–233.

Index[1]

A
Absorptive capacity, 284, 285
Advantage seeking FDI, 11
Africa-India Forum, 204
African Continental Free Trade Agreement (ACFTA), 80, 183
African Peer Review Mechanism (APRM), 78, 242
African Renaissance, 77n6, 78
African Socialism, 13, 64–72, 80–83, 97, 194, 209
African states, 39, 64, 79, 108, 149, 184, 198, 214
African Union (AU), 13, 76
Afro-pessimism, 77
Agenda 2063, 13, 75–81, 183
Agriculture, 34, 36, 66–68, 71, 194, 202, 208, 285
Amundsen, Inge, 151, 153
Anocratic, 100
Asian Tigers, 15, 74, 83, 276
Asymmetric information, 254
Austerity, 71
Authoritarian, 43, 97, 105, 107, 116, 147, 152, 198
Authoritarianism, 108, 120, 150
Autocracy, 13, 29, 115

B
Balance of payments, 5, 163, 243
Banking sector, 229, 238, 245, 247, 249–251, 254, 290
Banks, 15, 143, 147, 158, 229, 233, 234, 236–238, 245, 249, 251, 254
Beijing Consensus, 195, 197
Belt and Road Initiative (BRI), 192
Beneficiation, 47, 64, 249, 275, 276, 280, 297

[1] Note: Page numbers followed by 'n' refer to notes.

S. Gossel, *The Promise and Peril of FDI in Sub-Saharan Africa*, Palgrave Studies in African and Development Economics,
https://doi.org/10.1007/978-3-032-01320-0

Biased, 241
Big Men, 97, 101, 136, 152
Bond markets, 240
Border design, 25–30
Borders, 25, 26, 31
Borrowing costs, 15, 231
Boundaries, 26, 28
Bretton Woods, 71, 198
Bribery, 14, 110n5, 111, 135, 137, 140, 153, 159
Bribes, 14, 111, 135, 137, 145, 152, 157, 159
Brownfield FDI, 8, 286
Brownfield investments, 206

C
Capital flight, 5, 14, 154, 155, 157, 249, 251
Capital flows, 12, 14, 81, 140, 154, 231, 235, 240, 292
Capitalism, 24, 66
Capitalist, 24, 66, 69, 73, 109, 244, 251
Capital markets, 103, 109, 234, 240
Causality, 161, 163, 202, 240, 253, 254, 278, 281, 289, 293–295, 297
Centralised, 14, 28, 35, 43, 44, 48, 49, 136, 137, 158
China, 14, 43, 66, 142, 186, 189–202, 204, 205, 207, 209–211, 216, 280
Chinese companies, 189, 194, 197
Civil liberties, 97, 100, 109, 113–115, 243, 245, 246
Civil wars, 31, 70, 75
Class, 66, 67, 69, 103, 104, 119, 142, 202, 245, 280
Clientelism, 13, 79, 100, 101, 103, 116, 119, 136, 143, 153
Cold War, 13, 64, 65, 69, 70, 77, 80, 103, 104, 116, 190, 209
Colonial, 12, 13, 24–28, 30, 33–36, 39, 40, 42–44, 46, 48–50, 63–66, 63n1, 69, 70, 75–78, 83, 97, 101, 103, 104, 109, 119, 136, 137, 140, 142, 154, 157, 194, 198, 202, 209, 276, 286
Colonialism, 13, 14, 23–26, 33, 42, 43, 46, 48, 63, 63n1, 65–67, 69, 75, 109, 119, 136, 141, 195, 197, 202, 276
Colonial states, 23
Commodity prices, 287
Commodity price shocks, 233, 247, 279
Communism, 66, 70
Comparative advantage, 9, 16, 68, 110, 141, 276, 293
Competitiveness, 28, 81, 106, 200, 279
Comprehensive Development Framework (CDF), 74
Conflicts, 25, 28, 40, 43, 66, 69, 76, 104, 108, 209, 211, 244, 250n6
Consumer goods, 194, 199, 277
Consumer market, 199
Consumer rights, 107
Contagion, 240
Contracts, 14, 137, 142, 146, 198, 211, 251
Cooper, Fred, 140
Corporations, 70, 103, 104, 153, 155, 190, 231, 235, 238, 294
Corruption, 3, 14, 47, 73, 76, 79, 100, 106–108, 110–112, 135–138, 140, 141, 143–150, 152, 154, 155, 158–161, 163, 195, 196, 201, 207, 249, 250
Corruption Perception Index (CPI), 137

Cost of capital, 15, 111, 231, 254
Coups, 63, 69, 75, 76, 108, 214
Covid, 79, 191, 195, 214
Credit, 9, 15, 40, 68, 142, 190, 194, 229, 231, 232, 234, 235, 237, 238, 240–243, 249, 251, 254, 290, 292
  markets, 15, 231
  ratings agencies, 231
Crony capitalism, 141, 142, 153
Crowding out/crowd out, 5, 199, 237
Cultural, 26, 44, 69, 74, 76, 79, 81, 119, 138, 140, 190, 192, 197, 210, 240, 276
Culture, 49, 66, 140, 147, 159, 197, 283
Cyclicality, 80, 249, 250, 279

D

Debt, 64, 67, 71, 78, 82–84, 142, 147, 155, 157, 191, 192, 210, 237, 243n5, 251, 276
Debt trap, 195
Decentralisation/decentralised, 14, 28, 46, 48, 72, 73, 137, 154, 158
Deficits, 3, 25, 67, 68, 77, 83, 233
Demand hypothesis, 247
Demand-following hypothesis, 289, 290
Demand-side FSD, 235, 236
Democracy, 13–15, 29, 38, 40, 77, 79, 81, 97, 98, 101, 103–109, 112–115, 120, 140, 148, 150, 160, 195, 197, 213, 235, 243, 244, 246, 247, 250
Democratic advantage' hypothesis, 243
Democratic capital, 106, 113
Democratic rights, 103, 104
Democratization, 13, 97, 97n2, 98, 100, 101, 103–109, 106n4, 111–116, 120, 142, 147–151, 243
Dependence, 12, 13, 48, 73, 101, 108, 109, 157, 184, 193, 202, 233, 251, 279, 285, 286, 293
Dependency Theory, 81, 109, 275, 289
Development finance, 83, 194
Diamond, Jared, 30
Dictators, 70, 75
Differential Rates of Return Theory, 10
Direct (formal) institutions, 44
Diversification, 9, 16, 28, 47, 81, 106, 107, 109, 184, 231, 235, 238, 246, 248, 275, 276, 284, 292
Diversified, 3, 15, 107, 109, 158, 232, 233, 276, 277, 286, 297
Domestic companies, 9, 196, 237, 254, 283, 293
Dos Santos, Jose Eduardo, 143
Dutch Disease, 3
Dysfunctional capitalism, 140–147

E

Eclectic Paradigm Theory (OLI), 10
Economic growth, 3, 4, 8, 12, 14, 15, 28–30, 38, 40, 46, 47, 64, 65, 68, 71, 74, 79–81, 101, 105–107, 110, 114, 115, 135, 147, 155, 157, 158, 189, 199, 204, 229, 231, 235–238, 240, 275, 276, 278, 279, 281–286, 289, 290, 292–295, 297
Economic growth interlinkages, 292–297
Efficiency seeking, 11, 112
Elections, 14, 98, 101, 106, 116, 119, 119n6, 120, 153, 214
Electorate, 100, 120, 152

Elites, 14, 25, 65, 70, 103, 119, 137, 142, 152, 154, 245, 246, 253
Elitism, 47, 107, 113, 119, 136
Endogenous Growth, 278, 281, 283
Endowment theory, 48
Entrepreneurship, 104, 194, 246, 247, 284
Environmental degradation, 5, 76, 143, 153, 197, 283
Equity based FDI, 8
Ethnic, 14, 25, 26, 28, 30, 40, 43, 43n9, 44, 66, 75, 105, 119, 136, 137, 144
European, 23, 26, 34, 36, 40, 44, 48, 63, 76, 136, 233
Exchange rate, 67, 68, 249, 279
Export dependent states, 13
Export–led growth hypothesis (ELG), 278
Extractive institutions, 46, 70

F
False Paradigm theory, 81
FDI Inflows, 7, 164, 287
FDI-led growth, 276, 277, 284, 285, 289, 293–295
Feedback hypothesis, 289, 290
Financial crises, 67
Financial development, 229, 236, 247, 255, 289
Financial globalization, 80
Financial institutions, 234, 250
Financial markets, 15, 148, 229, 231, 235, 236, 240, 247, 250, 254, 255
Financial resource curse, 247–253
Financial sector development, 4, 8, 15, 142, 229, 236, 247, 251, 276–278, 284, 285, 289
Food, 35, 67, 190–192, 214, 280
Foreign capital, 68, 83
Foreign direct investment (FDI), 4, 6–8, 81–84, 111–122, 159–166, 253–257, 283–289
Forum on China-Africa Cooperation (FOCAC), 194
Free markets, 70, 83, 113
Friedman, Milton, 70
Fukuyama, Francis, 43

G
Gatekeeper State, 140, 141n3, 142
G8 countries, 77
Geography, 25n1, 30, 31, 49, 138, 140, 285
Gertler, Dan, 143, 144
Ghettoization, 24
Gifts, 140
Glencore, 108, 145, 145n4
Global financial crisis, 80, 103, 186, 200, 231, 233, 236, 241
Globalization, 13, 65, 77, 83, 103, 113, 141n3, 142, 194, 197, 205, 235
Gorbachev, Mikhail, 210
Governance, 14, 46, 63, 65, 73, 76–79, 98, 101, 104, 106, 107, 112, 135–137, 147, 149, 154–156, 160, 190, 191, 195, 196, 231, 237, 238, 290, 294
Grabbing hand corruption, 159, 160
Greenfield FDI, 8, 10
Greenfield investment, 8, 205
Growth-led FDI, 284, 286
Gupta family, 146, 147

H
Hard power, 197, 210
Hayek, Fredrich, 70
Health, 33–36, 73, 78, 193, 238
Healthcare, 34, 137, 148

Helping hand corruption, 159, 160
Herbst, Jeffrey, 30
Hot money, 15, 231
Hot wars, 69
Households, 158, 237, 249
Human capital, 3, 9, 11, 23, 25, 34, 42, 109, 153, 196, 248, 278, 279, 283, 285
Human rights, 75, 79, 107, 135, 143, 145, 195, 196, 211

I

Illicit financial flows (*IFF*), 154
IMF, 1, 3n2, 8, 13, 15, 24, 46, 64, 68, 71, 73, 82, 83, 145, 152, 229
Imperialism, 23, 66, 83
Import substitution industrialisation, 67, 68, 237, 275, 279, 290
Import-led growth hypothesis (ILG), 281
Inclusive institutions, 46
Income-narrowing hypothesis, 229
Income-widening hypothesis, 230
India, 14, 163n10, 186, 189–193, 202, 204–207, 208n8, 209, 216
Indian companies, 204, 205, 207
Indirect (informal) institutions, 44
Industrialisation, 12, 199, 276, 297
Industrial Organization Theory, 9, 10
Industrial sector, 109
Inequality, 14, 24, 30, 65, 103, 105, 108, 135, 136, 144, 157, 229, 231
Infrastructure, 3, 8, 28, 31, 34, 65, 68, 72, 83, 112, 135, 142, 144, 148, 155, 158, 160, 189, 192–194, 196, 198, 200, 204, 211, 234, 281, 284, 285
Infrastructure deficits, 279
Institutional quality index (IQI), 202, 202n6, 251
Institutional voids, 13, 30, 44, 63, 101, 119, 160
Institutions, 3, 5, 13, 25, 25n1, 28, 34, 40, 42–44, 43n9, 46–49, 63, 64, 70, 71, 74, 83, 100, 101, 104–108, 110, 112, 113, 119, 135, 140, 146, 147, 149, 151, 153–155, 158–160, 195, 200–202, 229, 234, 237, 238, 240, 243, 245–247, 250, 251, 289, 290
  of exchange, 47, 48
  of production, 47, 48
Inter-African trade, 76, 184, 297
Interest group hypothesis, 247
Intermediation, 234, 237, 241, 253, 294
Internalisation Theory, 9
International companies, 14, 107, 120, 137, 163, 235, 254
Investors, 110, 112, 113, 120, 121, 148, 151, 155, 160, 163, 195, 196, 200, 201, 208, 216, 240, 246, 251, 254, 294

K

Kabila, Joseph, 144
Kabila, Laurent, 145
Kaunda, Kenneth, 66
Keynes, John Maynard, 244
Keynesian, 70
Khrushchev, Nikita, 209
Kleptocratic, 135

L

Labour, 9, 11, 13, 23–25, 34, 36, 68, 71, 83, 97, 104, 107, 112, 141, 189, 194–198, 202, 237, 244, 245, 251, 279, 280, 282, 284, 292, 293

Labour rights, 5
Landlocked, 27–29
Legal origins, 245
Legal System, 48
Leopold II, 26
Liberalisation, 71, 72, 98, 104, 114, 115, 137, 189, 237
Liberation governments, 66, 116
Liberation movements, 63, 69, 70, 75, 190
Lipset, Seymour, 104
Liquidity, 4, 16, 233, 235, 238, 276
Lucas Paradox, 10
Lumumba, Patrice, 66

M
Malaria, 33, 35, 36, 38
Manufactured goods, 16, 23, 68, 196, 198, 275–277, 280, 293
Manufacturing, 9, 12, 14, 23, 64, 68, 101, 189, 196, 198, 200, 202, 205–208, 249, 250, 277, 279, 280, 285, 286, 292, 297
Market seeking, 11
Masculinity, 140
Mbasogo, Teodoro Obiang Nguema, 97n1, 143, 144
Mbeki, Thabo, 77
Mergers and acquisitions (M&A), 8
Mexican crisis, 74
Microfinance, 15, 233, 234
Military, 39, 66, 69, 75, 76, 97, 108, 143, 148, 190, 192, 197, 202, 205, 209–212, 214, 215, 244
Millennium Development Goals, 64, 75, 137
Mining companies, 108, 153, 157, 251
Minsky, Hyman, 244
Mobile banking, 234
Modernization Theory, 104
Moral hazard, 247, 249
Moyo, Dambisa, 81
Multinationals, 49, 103, 112, 144, 147, 153, 250

N
Natural resource dependence, 8, 15, 107, 109, 155, 231, 256, 286, 297
Natural resource extraction, 12, 23, 65, 68, 110, 190, 194, 276, 279, 285
Natural resources, 1, 3, 11, 12, 23, 25, 68, 108, 109, 111, 142, 163, 190–192, 194, 196–202, 204, 205, 210, 212, 215, 247, 249–251, 279, 286
Neoliberalism, 13, 65, 70–75
Neoliberal reforms, 14, 15, 72, 83, 142, 279
Neutrality hypothesis, 289, 290
New Institutionalists, 105, 106
New Partnership for Africa's Development (NEPAD), 13, 77
New Public Management (NPM), 72, 137
Nexus, 294, 295, 297
Nkrumah, Kwame, 66
North, Douglass, 42
Nuclear, 192, 211
Nyerere, Julius, 66

O
Obasanjo, Olusegun, 77
Official development assistance (ODA), 64, 276
Oil booms, 68
Oil crises, 83
One-China policy, 197
Organization of African Unity (OAU), 74, 75

P
Pan-African banks (PABs), 233
Parliamentary, 35, 79, 116, 121, 154
Partial reform syndrome, 13, 84, 101, 229
Patrimonialism, 65, 73, 119
Patron-client, 3, 14, 108, 137, 148, 160, 279
Pirate capitalism, 103
Polanyi, Karl, 244
Political corruption, 151–154
Political geography, 12, 25, 30–38
Political instability, 25, 76, 107, 120, 137, 150, 155, 246
Political opposition, 98, 119, 120, 136, 142, 152, 212, 244
Political Resource Curse, 3
Political rights, 97, 112–115, 214
Portfolio investment, 8, 10, 286
Post-colonial theory, 275
Post-independent Africa, 12–14, 63–65, 76, 136, 140
Poverty, 3, 8, 14, 33, 65, 71, 72, 74, 77, 78, 83, 105, 108, 120, 135–137, 144, 155, 157, 191, 234, 275, 280, 294
Pre-colonial Africa, 27, 28, 43, 44, 276
Predatory capitalism, 144, 146, 276, 277
Predatory corporations, 110
Predatory elite, 3, 113
Presidential, 98, 143, 154, 212
Private sector, 14, 47, 67, 72–74, 136, 142, 147, 152, 158, 229, 238, 246, 251, 254, 290, 292
Privatisation, 14, 71
Procyclical, 241
Production Cycle Theory, 9
Property rights, 34, 46–49, 105, 106, 112, 155, 238, 243, 245, 246, 250
Proxy, 69, 70, 120, 191, 231
Public companies, 152
Public sector, 72, 73, 100, 158, 238, 246
Push-Pull Theory, 12
Putin, Vladimer, 210

R
Race, 24, 33
Racial capitalism, 24
Racism, 24, 65
Ramaphosa, Cyril, 147
Reagan, Ronald, 70
Regional Economic Communities (RECs), 183
Remittances, 80, 251
Rentier capitalism, 153
Rentier states, 13, 101, 108
Rent-seeking, 13, 25, 101, 249, 250
Reserves, 1, 67, 237, 290
Resource companies, 15, 110, 231, 247
Resource Curse, 3, 107–111, 286
Resource dependent, 3n2, 16, 47, 98, 101, 107, 109, 110, 113, 114, 144, 150, 161, 163, 199, 199n4, 201, 232, 247, 251, 253, 255, 282, 287, 290, 295, 297
Resource dependent states, 15, 150, 154, 231, 250, 251
Resource extractive FDI, 101, 109, 110, 286
Resource seeking, 11
Revolving-door hypothesis, 157
Risk appetite, 12, 200, 234
Round tripped, 163n10, 208n8
Rule of law, 3, 5, 28, 44, 46, 47, 79, 100, 101, 106, 109, 110, 112, 113, 119, 135, 139, 140, 147, 149, 155, 157, 243, 248, 250

Rural, 28, 34, 47, 66, 67, 72, 234, 280
Russia, 14, 66, 70, 77, 186, 190–193, 209–212, 214, 215
Russia-Africa Summit, 211, 212, 215
Russian companies, 210, 215
Russian invasion, 190–192, 195, 215

S
Sable Mining Africa, 110
Savings, 4, 15, 49, 64, 81, 112, 157, 231, 234–237, 246, 254, 279
Sectoral FDI, 208
Self-enrichment, 14, 136
Sen, Amartya, 104
Senghor, Leopold, 66
Settlers, 24, 34
Shadow state, 107, 146
Shell companies, 110n5, 158
Slavery, 38–42, 39n8
Sleeping sickness, 33–35
Smart power, 197
Socialism, 65, 66, 69, 209
Socialist, 66, 69, 70, 103, 190
Social mobility, 46, 277
Socio-economic development, 3, 14, 40, 65, 78, 109, 137, 244, 250
Socio-political instability, 15, 119
Soft power, 190, 197, 205, 210, 215
Sovereign credit ratings (SCR), 15, 231, 240–244
Spillover, 196, 240, 286, 294
Spillover effects, 4, 196, 283, 286, 293, 294
Stage of development, 160, 230, 283, 289
Stagflation, 83
Stakeholder capitalism, 103
State capture, 146, 149
State-owned enterprises (SOE), 67
Stock markets, 200, 238, 239
StratCom, 212–214
Strategic asset seeking, 11
Structural adjustment loans, 71
Structural adjustment programs (SAPs), 13, 46, 65, 71, 137
Sub-Saharan Africa, 1, 23
Supply-leading hypothesis, 289, 290
Supply-side FSD, 235, 236

T
Tariffs, 25, 76, 80, 184
Taxation, 5, 11, 13, 15, 30, 31, 35, 46, 67, 68, 72, 101, 107, 108, 112, 135, 137, 142, 143, 145, 148, 149, 154, 157–159, 163, 208, 208n8, 231, 235, 279, 280
Taxation avoidance, 157
Taxation revenue, 137
Tax bases, 47, 235
Tax havens, 143, 145, 157, 158, 214
Thatcher, Margaret, 70–71
Thin capitalisation, 159, 163
Touadéra, Faustin-Archange, 212
Trade, 1, 12, 13, 15, 25, 26, 28, 39, 40, 47, 67, 68, 71, 74, 77, 79–81, 97, 106, 107, 114, 115, 156–158, 163, 183, 184, 186, 189–192, 194, 196, 198, 200, 204, 205, 210, 216, 241, 243, 245, 247, 249, 250, 276, 277, 279–281, 283, 284, 289, 290, 292–295, 297
Trade mis-invoicing, 158, 163
Transfer mispricing, 158, 163
Tropical diseases, 32–34
Trust, 35, 40, 44, 46, 49, 100

Tsetse fly, 32, 34, 35
Tshilombo, Félix Antoine
Tshisekedi, 145
Tuna loans, 152

U
Ukraine, 190–193, 210, 211, 214, 215
Undemocratic government, 244
Union of Soviet Socialist Republics (USSR), 13
Urban, 1, 24, 28, 34, 47, 67, 72, 141, 234

V
Vertical and horizontal, 284
Vicious cycle, 15, 107, 120, 232, 240, 286
Villagization, 66, 67
Violence, 24, 76, 84, 108, 116, 119, 119n6, 120, 137, 153, 155
Volatility, 15, 28, 107, 231, 246, 249, 250, 279, 286, 292
Volatility hypothesis, 247
Von Bismarck, Otto, 25

W
Wade, Abdoulaye, 77
Wagner Group, 190, 192, 211, 215
Washington Consensus, 13, 65, 71–74, 80, 101, 137, 195, 197, 198, 243
Wealth, 3, 14, 15, 25, 39, 46, 63, 103, 104, 109, 119, 137, 142–144, 151, 152, 157, 158, 183, 231, 245, 249, 275, 279, 283
Weaponry, 190, 193, 211, 214
Weapons, 70, 210, 211, 213
Western, 14, 15, 24, 35, 39, 43n9, 66, 69, 73, 75, 77, 81, 109, 119, 144, 184, 186, 189–201, 204, 209–211, 216, 235, 280
World Bank, 3, 4, 13, 15, 28, 44, 46, 64, 68, 71–74, 73n5, 82, 83, 112, 135, 138n2, 229, 236, 237
World Trade Organisation (WTO), 183

Z
Zuma, Jacob, 146

FSC
www.fsc.org
MIX
Papier | Fördert gute Waldnutzung
FSC® C083411

Kolibri 360 GmbH
Ferdinand-Jühlke-Straße 7
99095 Erfurt, Deutschland
produktsicherheit@kolibri360.de